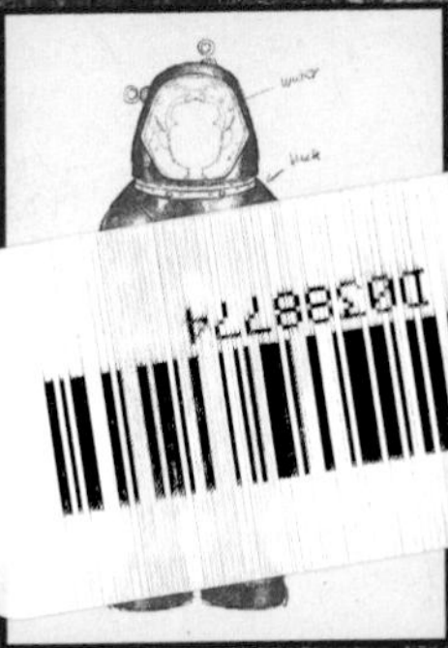

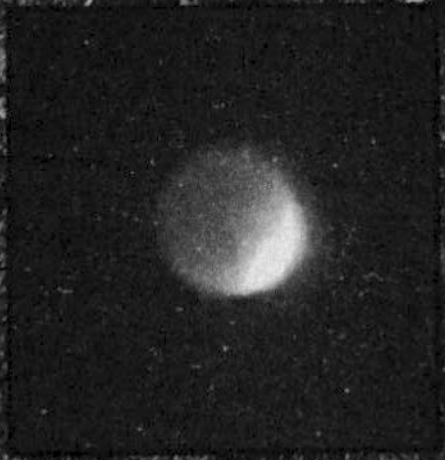

BOICHI

The suits worn during space launches aren't just the well-known EVA ones—they're actually pressurized.

I realized the pressurized suits used by Senku and his fellow astronauts had to serve several purposes. First, they needed to minimize damage in case of an accident while the astronauts were petrified. The suits would potentially need to keep every stone fragment contained to reassemble later. Having them made out of hard metal lets them be filled with water while the astronauts are petrified.

Once the astronauts are revived, it would be a disaster if any broken fragments were to float off in zero gravity inside the ship. To prevent that, the suits are equipped with a vacuum-like feature to suck up fragments and keep everything contained.

After considering all of that, I decided to make the suits an homage to Robby the Robot from 1956's *Forbidden Planet*. I'm sure that Senku or Xeno would appreciate that, right? And so, the design came to be. I love coming up with these sorts of designs, ideas, and homages in the course of working on *Dr. Stone* chapters.

RIICHIRO INAGAKI

I snapped this great pic of the lunar eclipse with my phone! It looked so small in the night sky, though...

If the Earth were a basketball, the moon would be a tennis ball, sizewise. And in this analogy, the moon is as far away as you'd need to throw the basketball Earth to make a three-pointer.

Farther than you might think, right?

That's where Senku and the gang are hoping to get to!

Boichi is a Korean-born artist currently living and working in Japan. His previous works include *Sun-Ken Rock* and *Terra Formars Asimov*.

Riichiro Inagaki is a Japanese manga writer from Tokyo. He is the writer for the sports manga series *Eyeshield 21*, which was serialized in *Weekly Shonen Jump*.

Dr. STONE

25

SHONEN JUMP Edition

Story **RIICHIRO INAGAKI**
Art **BOICHI**

Science Consultant/**KURARE** with Yakuri Classroom of Doom: Aruma Zirou, Cyrano, POKA
Translation/**CALEB COOK**
Touch-Up Art & Lettering/**STEPHEN DUTRO**
Design/**JULIAN [JR] ROBINSON**
Editor/**JOHN BAE**

DR. STONE © 2017 by Riichiro Inagaki, Boichi
All rights reserved.
First published in Japan in 2017 by SHUEISHA Inc., Tokyo.
English translation rights arranged by SHUEISHA Inc.

Printed in the U.S.A.

Published by VIZ Media, LLC
P.O. Box 77010
San Francisco, CA 94107

10 9 8 7 6 5 4 3 2 1
First printing, April 2023

Consulted Works:

• Dartnell, Lewis, *The Knowledge: How to Rebuild Civilization in the Aftermath of a Cataclysm*, Translated by Erika Togo, Kawade Shobo Shinsha, 2015

• Diamond, Jared, *Guns, Germs, and Steel: The Fates of Human Societies*, Translated by Akira Kurahone, Soshisha Publishing Co., 2012

• Harari, Yuval Noah, *Sapiens: A Brief History of Humankind*, Translated by Hiroyuki Shibata, Kawade Shobo Shinsha, 2016

• Weisman, Alan, *The World Without Us*, Translated by Shinobu Onizawa, Hayakawa Publishing, 2009

viz.com

Dr.STONE

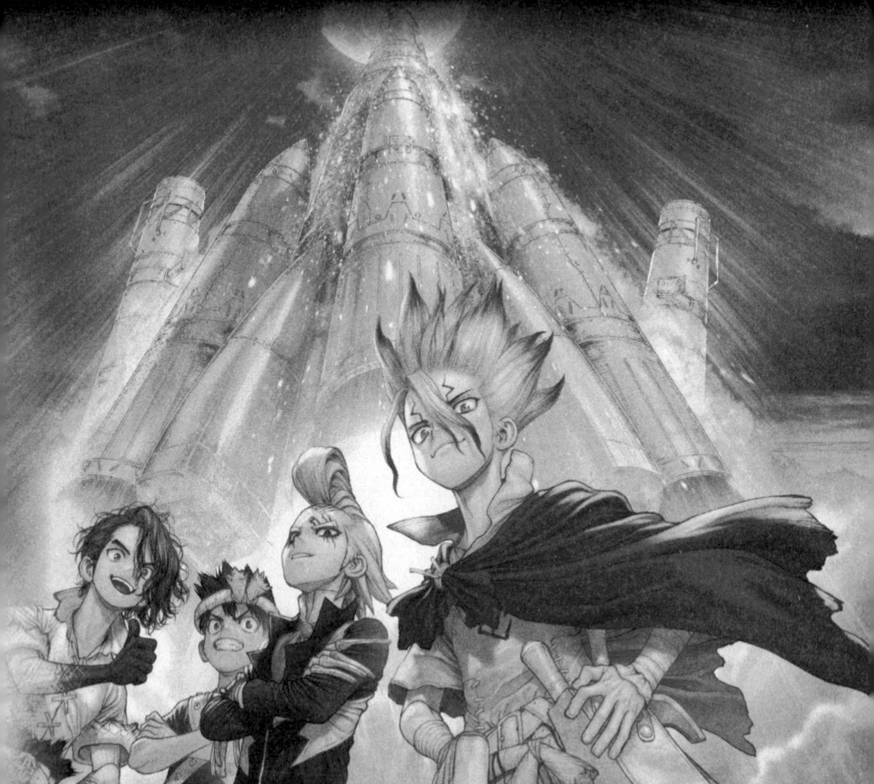

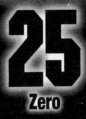

STORY **RIICHIRO INAGAKI**
ART **BOICHI**

25
Zero

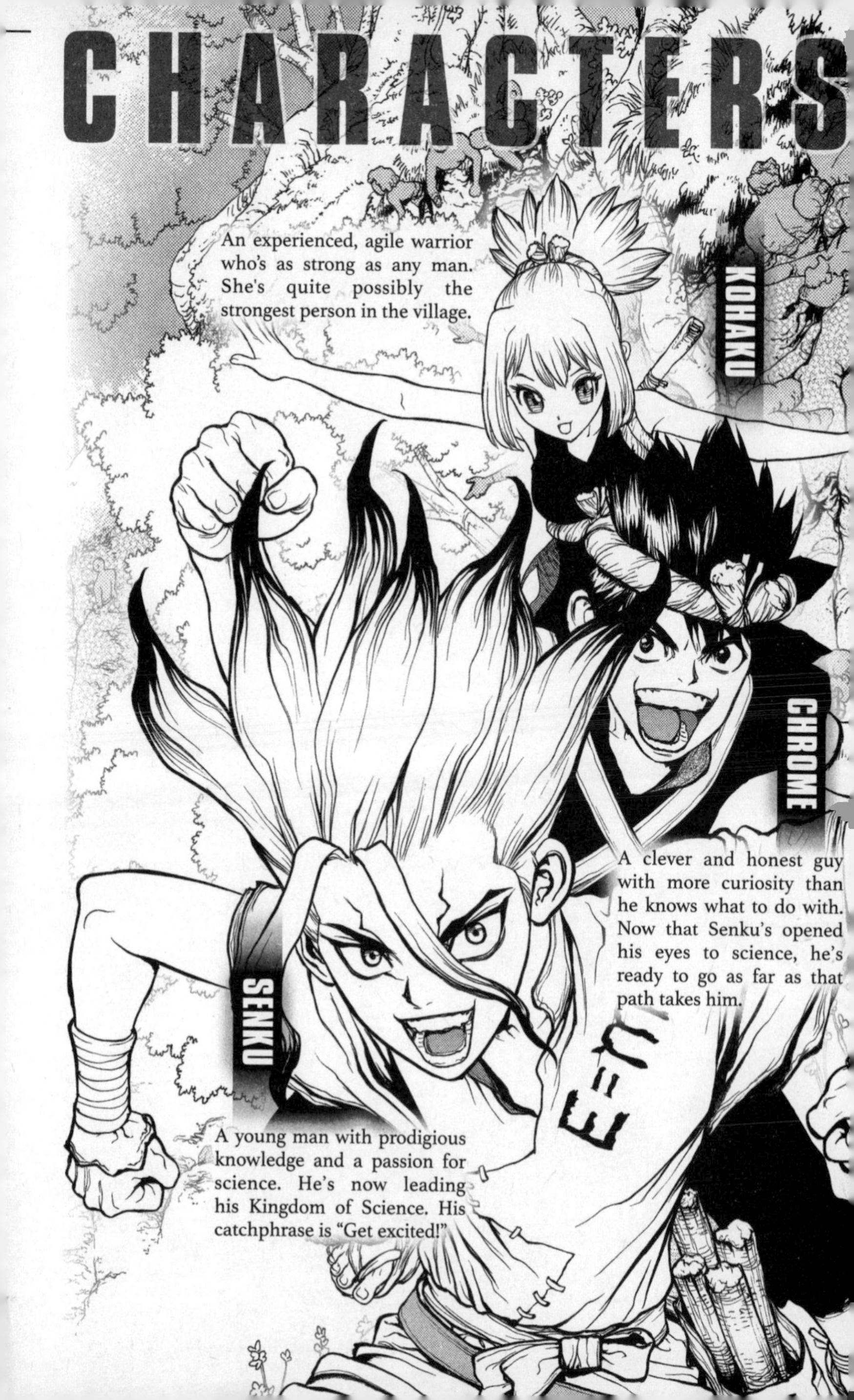
CHARACTERS
KOHAKU
An experienced, agile warrior who's as strong as any man. She's quite possibly the strongest person in the village.
CHROME
A clever and honest guy with more curiosity than he knows what to do with. Now that Senku's opened his eyes to science, he's ready to go as far as that path takes him.
SENKU
A young man with prodigious knowledge and a passion for science. He's now leading his Kingdom of Science. His catchphrase is "Get excited!"

Dr.STONE

STORY

Every human on earth is turned to stone by a mysterious phenomenon, including high school student Taiju. Nearly 3,700 years later, Taiju awakens and finds his friend Senku, who revived a bit earlier. Together, they vow to restore civilization, but Tsukasa, once considered the strongest high schooler alive, nearly kills Senku in order to put a stop to his scientific plans.

When word of Senku's survival gets back to Tsukasa, the war between the two forces begins! Eventually, the factions make peace. After acquiring a petrification device on Treasure Island, Senku and his friends set out for the U.S.A., where they encounter another rival science kingdom, led by the scientist Dr. Xeno. However, their conflict is resolved and both parties agree to work together to restart civilization.

Because of technological and time constraints, the voyage will be a one-way trip. However, Chrome secretly starts working on a way to get the astronauts home. Meanwhile, the crew is also building a satellite—one that will help them pinpoint Why-Man's position on the moon's surface!

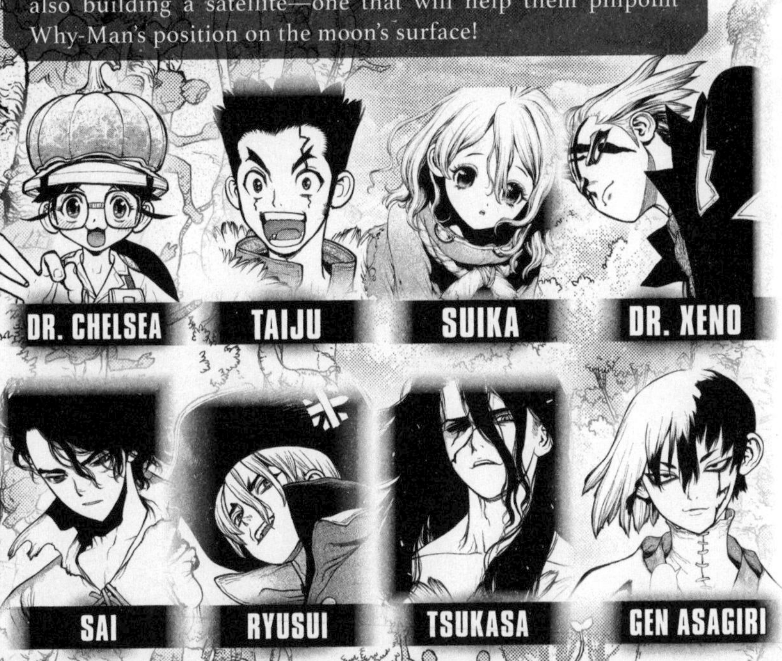
DR. CHELSEA
TAIJU
SUIKA
DR. XENO
SAI
RYUSUI
TSUKASA
GEN ASAGIRI

CONTENTS

25
ZERO

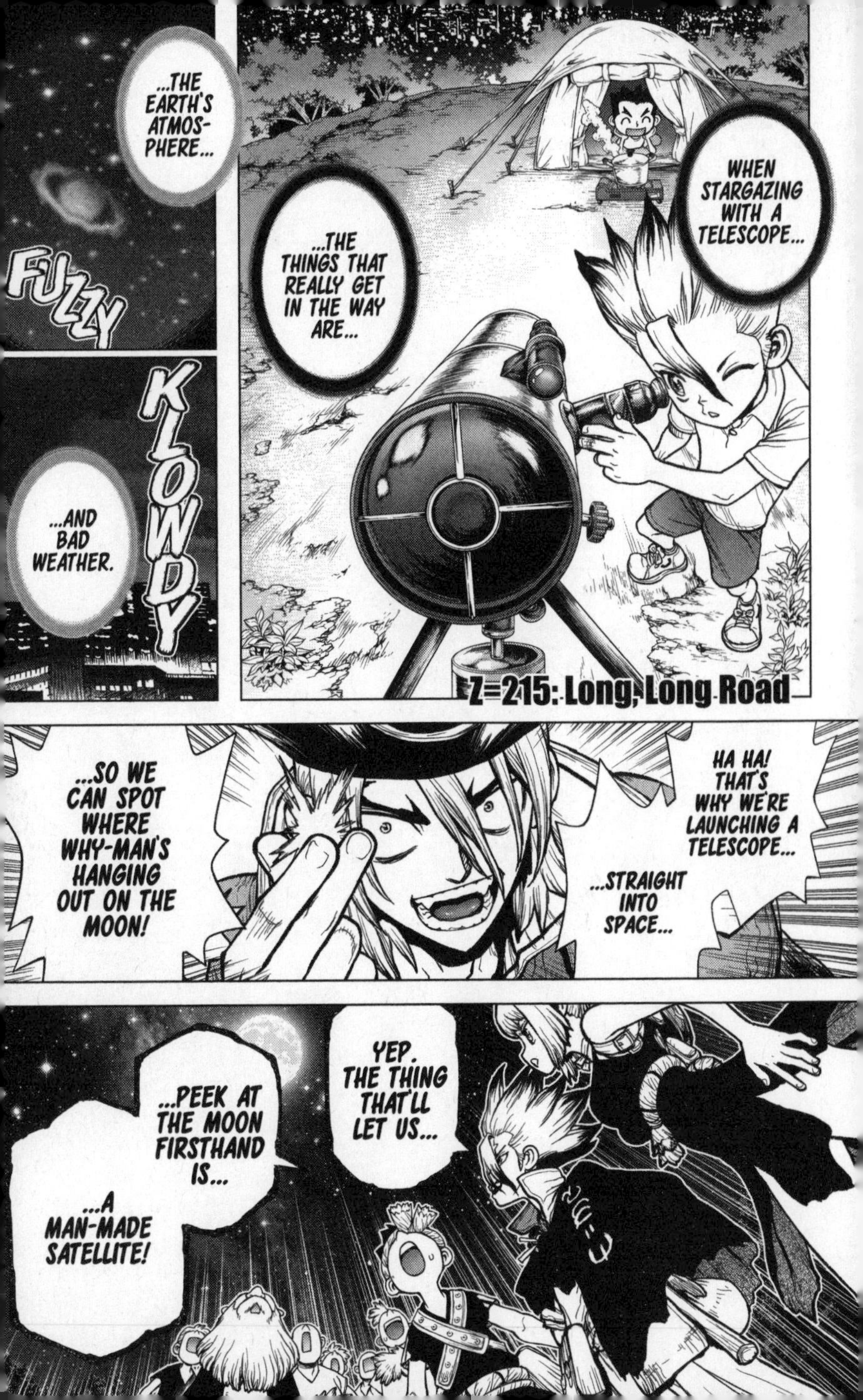
WHEN STARGAZING WITH A TELESCOPE...
...THE THINGS THAT REALLY GET IN THE WAY ARE...
Z=215: Long, Long Road
...THE EARTH'S ATMOSPHERE...
FUZZY
...AND BAD WEATHER.
KLOWDY
HA HA! THAT'S WHY WE'RE LAUNCHING A TELESCOPE...
...STRAIGHT INTO SPACE...
...SO WE CAN SPOT WHERE WHY-MAN'S HANGING OUT ON THE MOON!
YEP. THE THING THAT'LL LET US...
...PEEK AT THE MOON FIRSTHAND IS...
...A MAN-MADE SATELLITE!

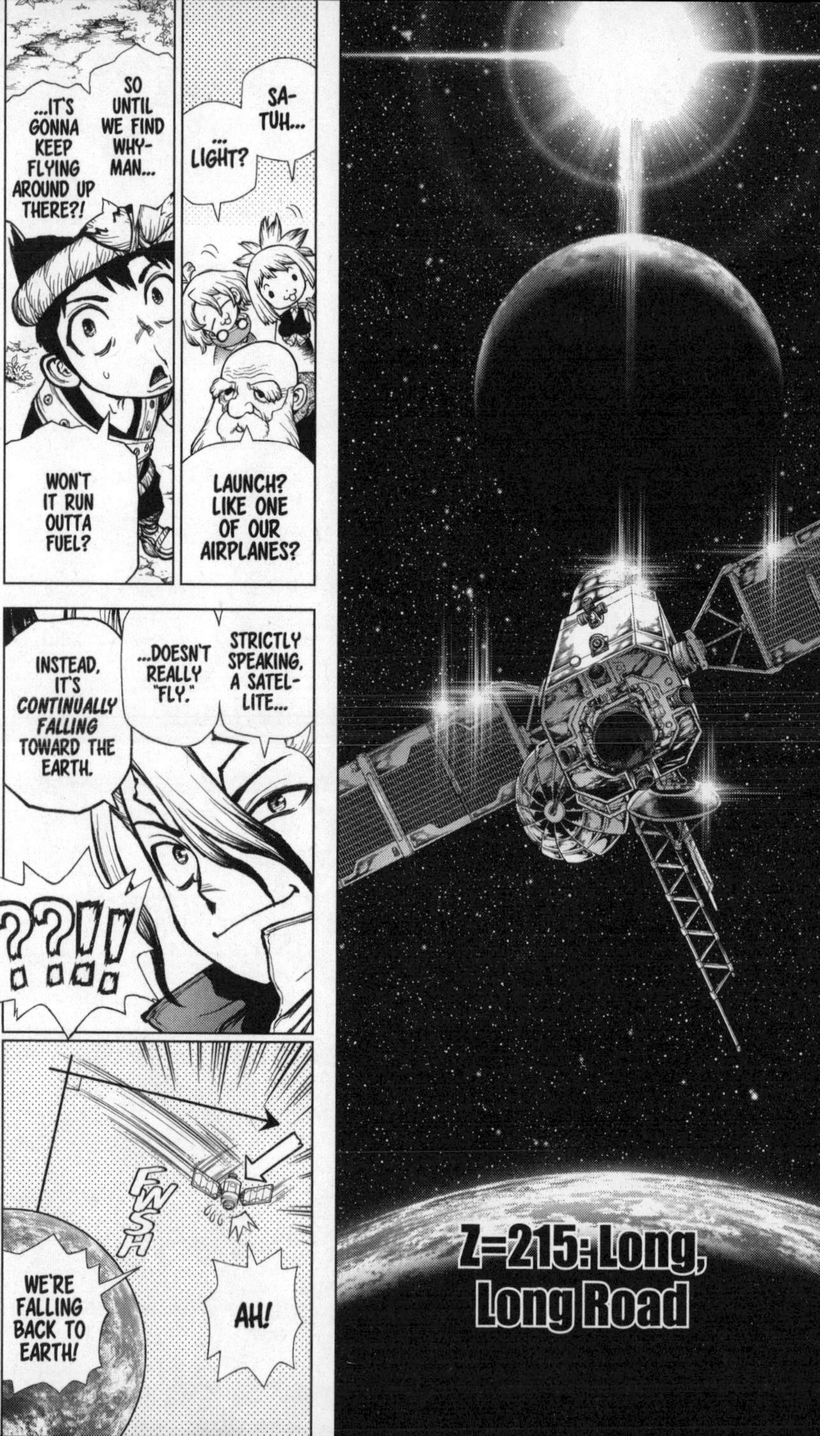
Z=215: Long, Long Road
SA-TUH...
...LIGHT?
LAUNCH? LIKE ONE OF OUR AIRPLANES?
SO UNTIL WE FIND WHY-MAN...
...IT'S GONNA KEEP FLYING AROUND UP THERE?!
WON'T IT RUN OUTTA FUEL?
STRICTLY SPEAKING, A SATEL-LITE...
...DOESN'T REALLY "FLY."
INSTEAD, IT'S CONTINUALLY FALLING TOWARD THE EARTH.
??!!
FWSH
AH!
WE'RE FALLING BACK TO EARTH!

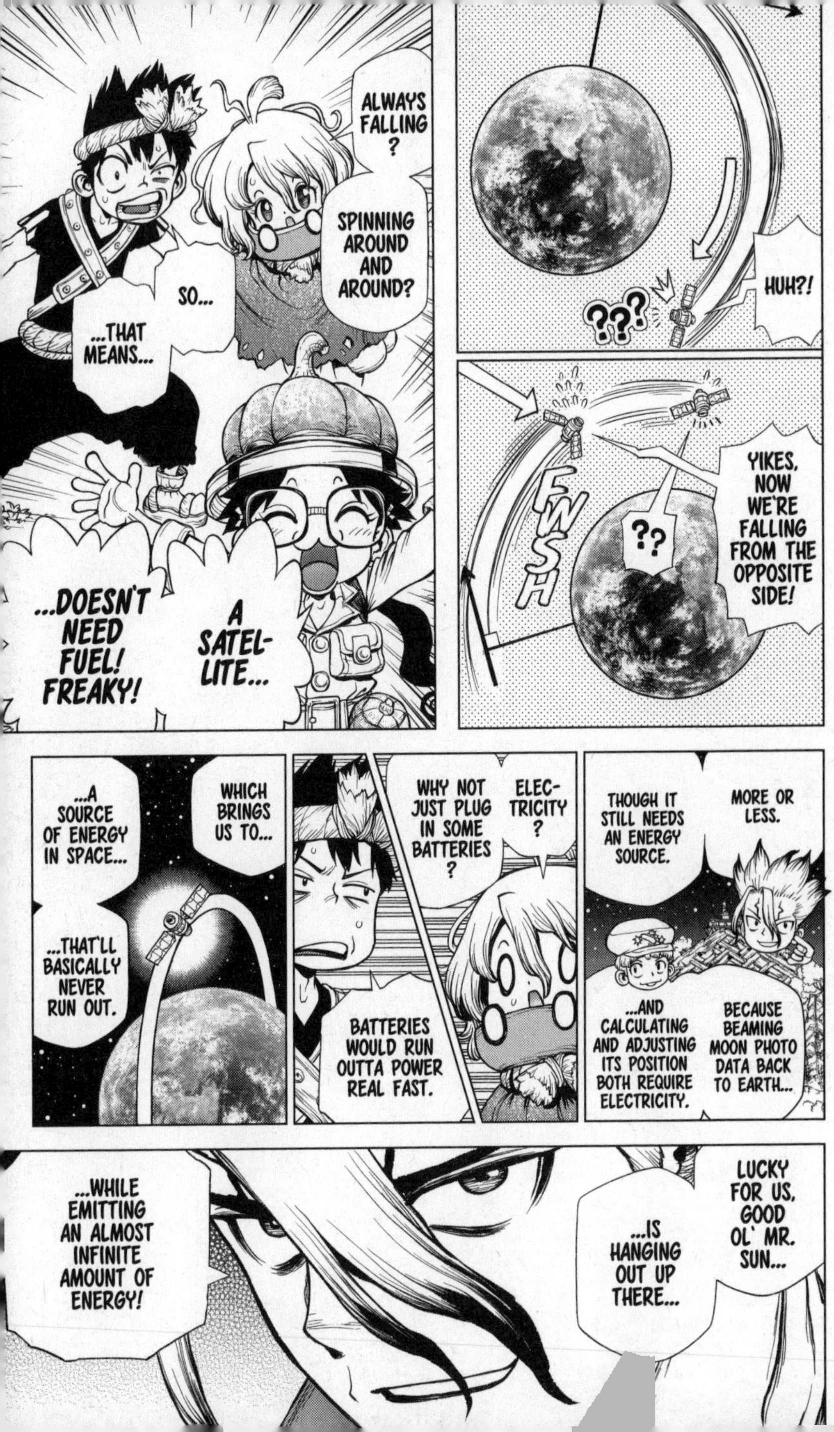
HUH?!
???
YIKES, NOW WE'RE FALLING FROM THE OPPOSITE SIDE!
??
FWSH
ALWAYS FALLING?
SPINNING AROUND AND AROUND?
SO...
...THAT MEANS...
A SATEL-LITE...
...DOESN'T NEED FUEL! FREAKY!
MORE OR LESS.
THOUGH IT STILL NEEDS AN ENERGY SOURCE.
BECAUSE BEAMING MOON PHOTO DATA BACK TO EARTH...
...AND CALCULATING AND ADJUSTING ITS POSITION BOTH REQUIRE ELECTRICITY.
ELEC-TRICITY?
WHY NOT JUST PLUG IN SOME BATTERIES?
BATTERIES WOULD RUN OUTTA POWER REAL FAST.
WHICH BRINGS US TO...
...A SOURCE OF ENERGY IN SPACE...
...THAT'LL BASICALLY NEVER RUN OUT.
LUCKY FOR US, GOOD OL' MR. SUN...
...IS HANGING OUT UP THERE...
...WHILE EMITTING AN ALMOST INFINITE AMOUNT OF ENERGY!

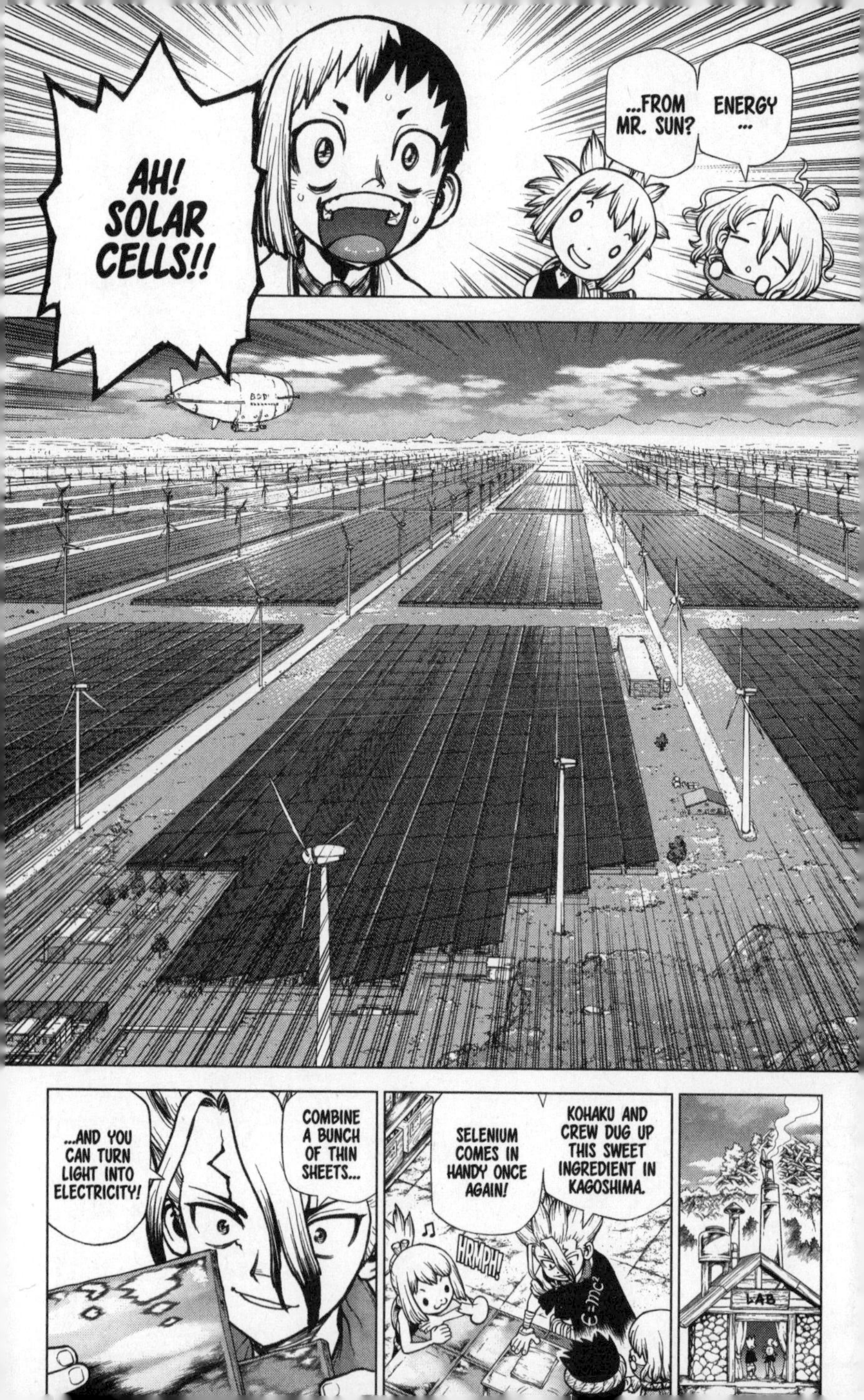
ENERGY ...
...FROM MR. SUN?
AH! SOLAR CELLS!!
LAB
KOHAKU AND CREW DUG UP THIS SWEET INGREDIENT IN KAGOSHIMA.
SELENIUM COMES IN HANDY ONCE AGAIN!
HRMPH!
E=mc²
COMBINE A BUNCH OF THIN SHEETS...
...AND YOU CAN TURN LIGHT INTO ELECTRICITY!

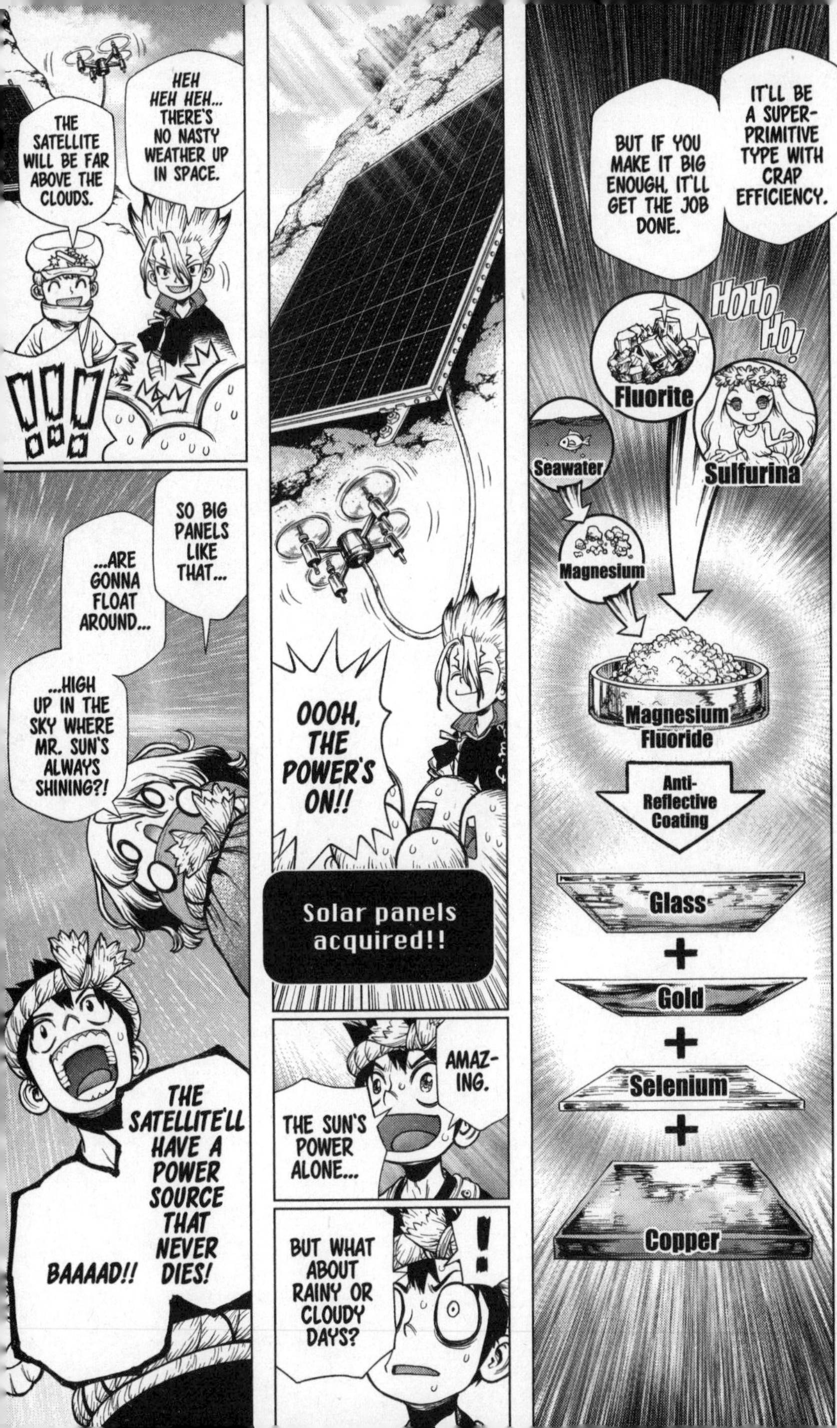
IT'LL BE A SUPER-PRIMITIVE TYPE WITH CRAP EFFICIENCY.
BUT IF YOU MAKE IT BIG ENOUGH, IT'LL GET THE JOB DONE.
HOHOHO!
Fluorite
Sulfurina
Seawater
Magnesium
Magnesium Fluoride
Anti-Reflective Coating
Glass
+
Gold
+
Selenium
+
Copper
OOOH, THE POWER'S ON!!
Solar panels acquired!!
AMAZ-ING.
THE SUN'S POWER ALONE...
!
BUT WHAT ABOUT RAINY OR CLOUDY DAYS?
HEH HEH HEH... THERE'S NO NASTY WEATHER UP IN SPACE.
THE SATELLITE WILL BE FAR ABOVE THE CLOUDS.
!!!
SO BIG PANELS LIKE THAT...
...ARE GONNA FLOAT AROUND...
...HIGH UP IN THE SKY WHERE MR. SUN'S ALWAYS SHINING?!
THE SATELLITE'LL HAVE A POWER SOURCE THAT NEVER DIES!
BAAAAD!!

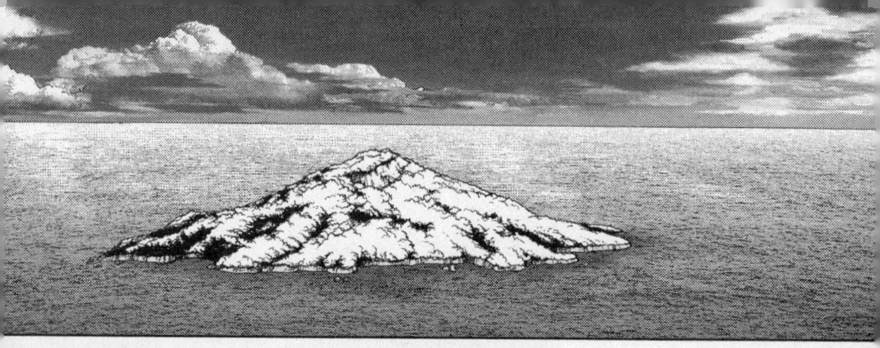

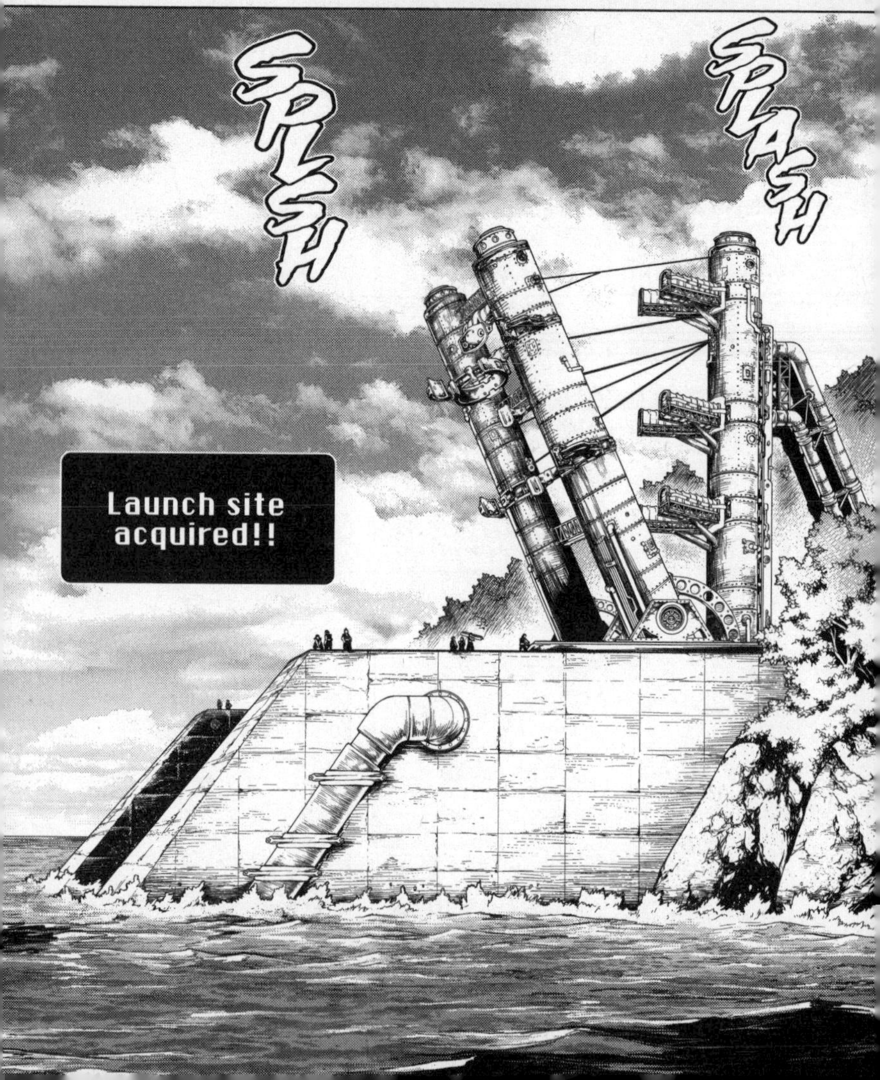
SPLASH
SPLSH
Launch site acquired!!

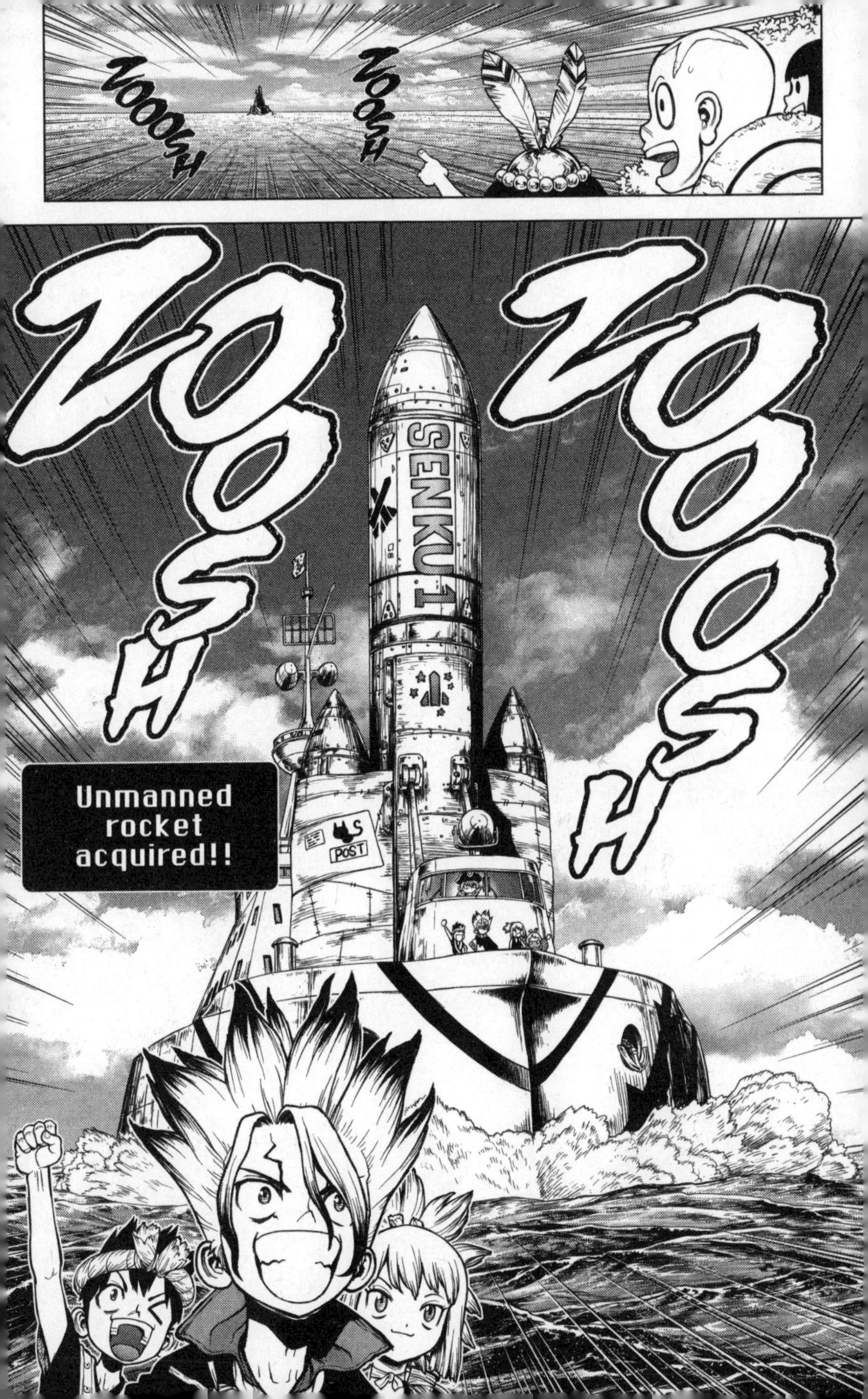
ZOOSH
ZOOOOSH
ZOOOOSH
ZOOSH
Unmanned rocket acquired!!
SENKU 1
POST

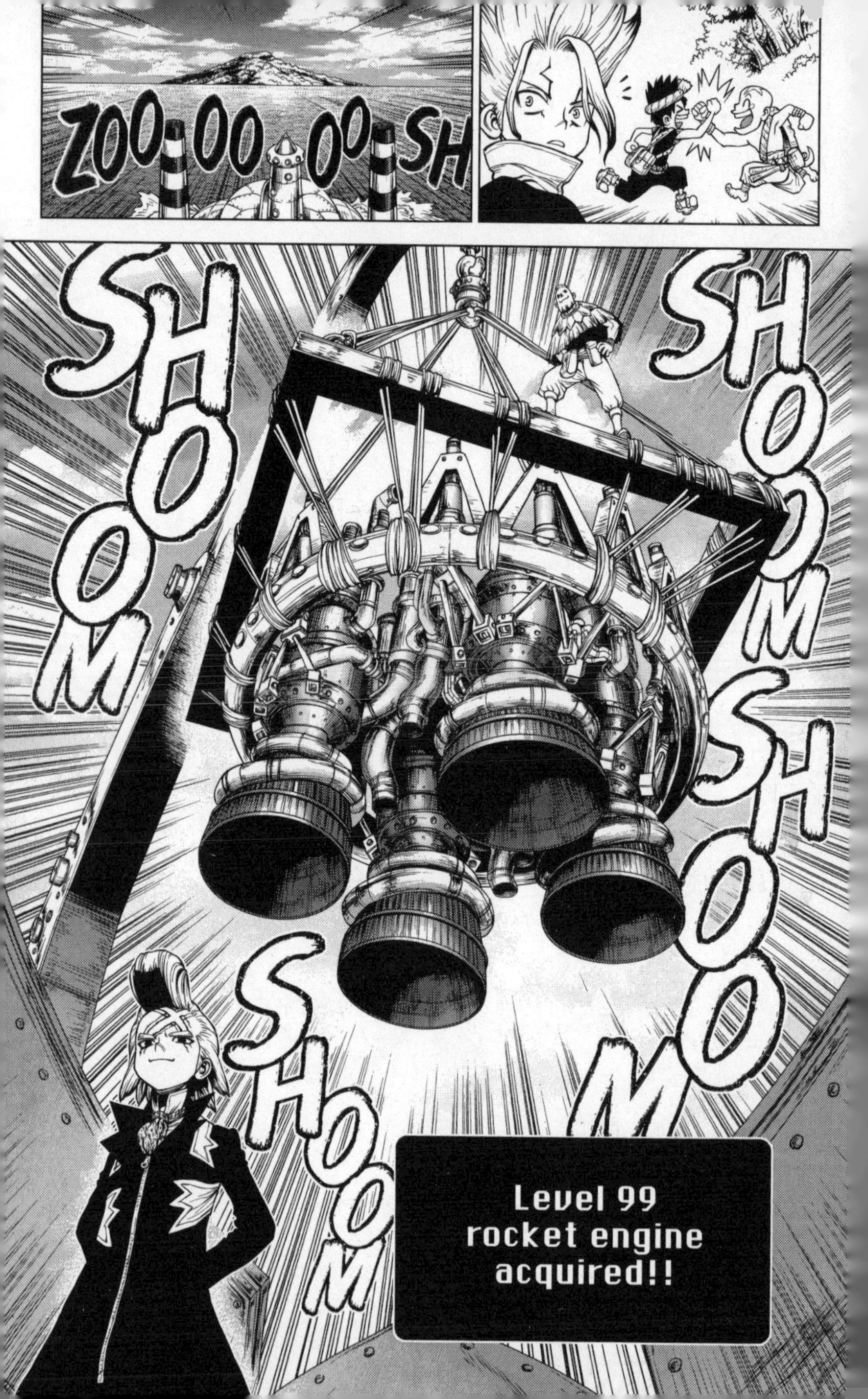
ZOO-OO-OOSH
SHOOM
SHOOM
SHOOOM
SHOOM
Level 99
rocket engine
acquired!!

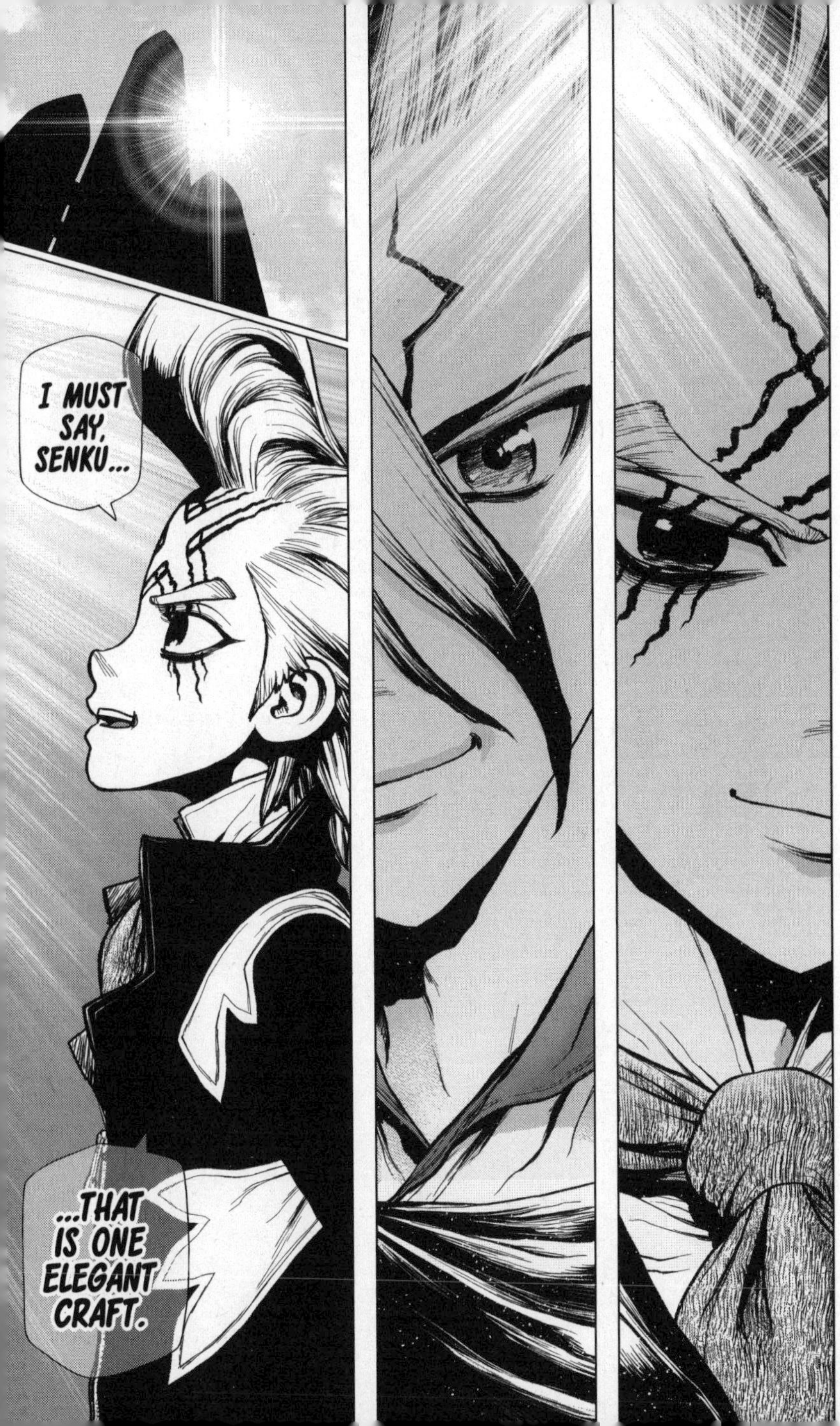
I MUST SAY, SENKU...
...THAT IS ONE ELEGANT CRAFT.

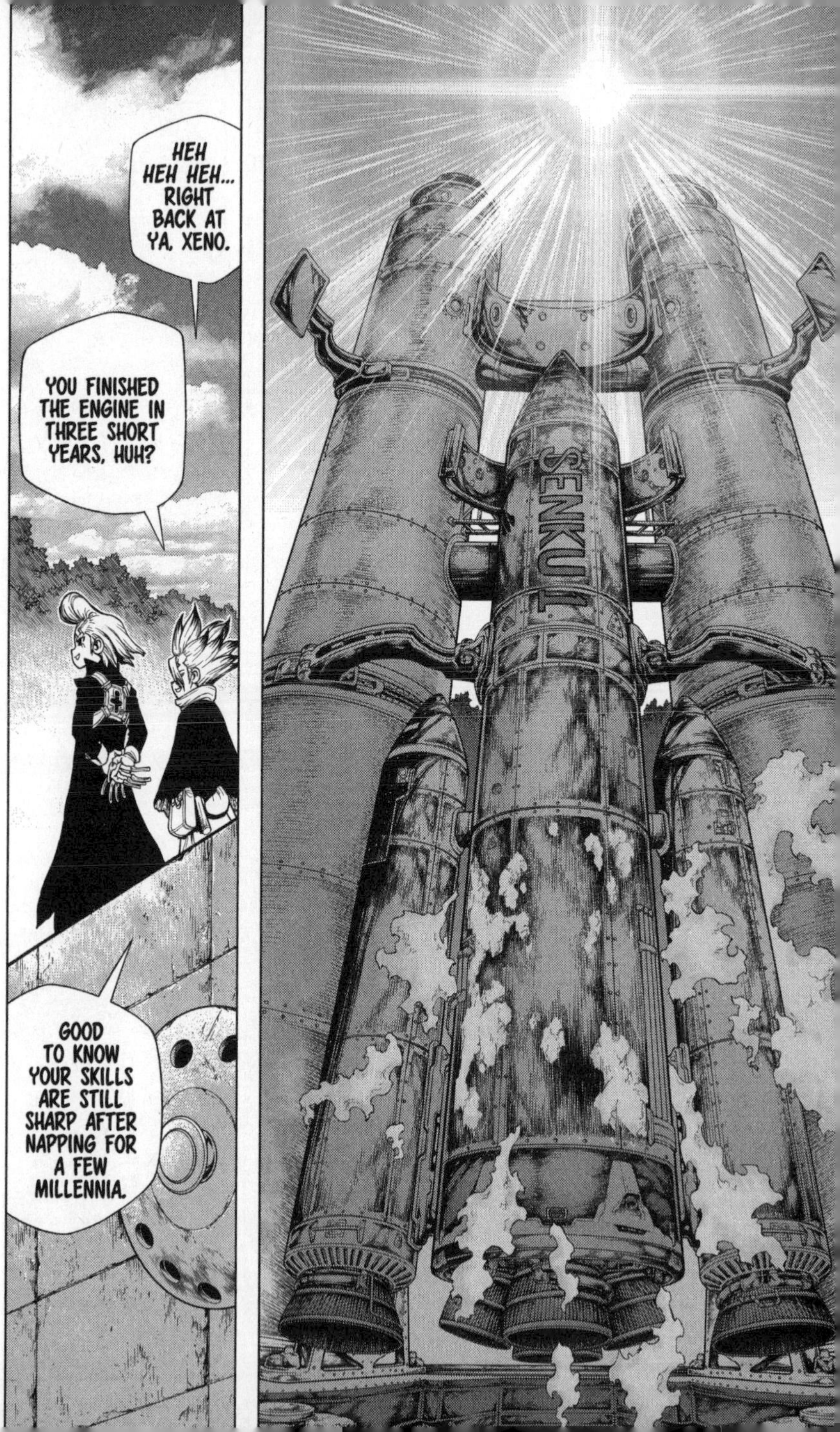
SENKU 1
HEH HEH HEH... RIGHT BACK AT YA, XENO.
YOU FINISHED THE ENGINE IN THREE SHORT YEARS, HUH?
GOOD TO KNOW YOUR SKILLS ARE STILL SHARP AFTER NAPPING FOR A FEW MILLENNIA.

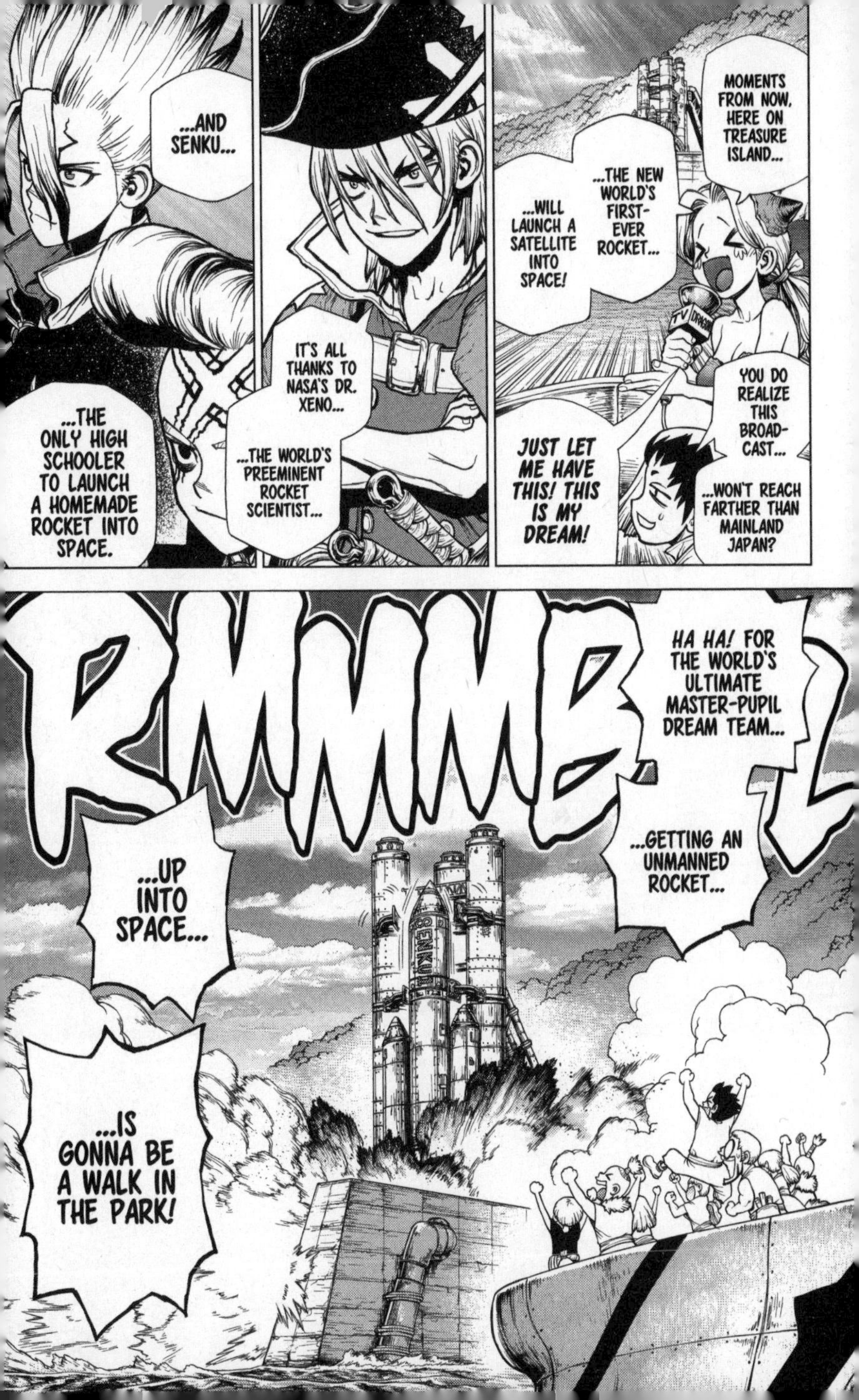
MOMENTS FROM NOW, HERE ON TREASURE ISLAND...
...THE NEW WORLD'S FIRST-EVER ROCKET...
...WILL LAUNCH A SATELLITE INTO SPACE!
TV DRAGON
YOU DO REALIZE THIS BROAD-CAST...
...WON'T REACH FARTHER THAN MAINLAND JAPAN?
JUST LET ME HAVE THIS! THIS IS MY DREAM!
IT'S ALL THANKS TO NASA'S DR. XENO...
...THE WORLD'S PREEMINENT ROCKET SCIENTIST...
...AND SENKU...
...THE ONLY HIGH SCHOOLER TO LAUNCH A HOMEMADE ROCKET INTO SPACE.
RMMMBL
HA HA! FOR THE WORLD'S ULTIMATE MASTER-PUPIL DREAM TEAM...
...GETTING AN UNMANNED ROCKET...
...UP INTO SPACE...
...IS GONNA BE A WALK IN THE PARK!

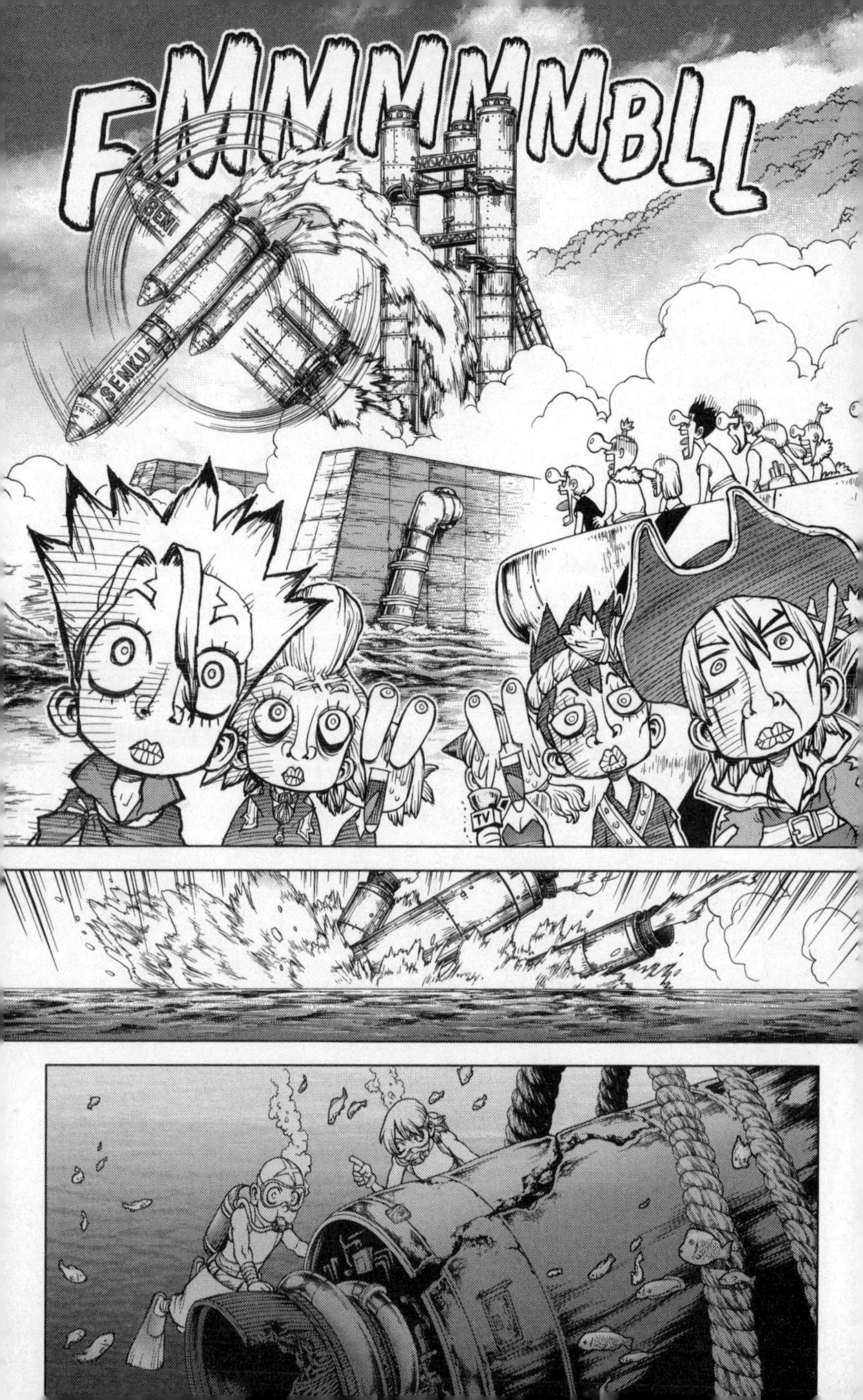
FMMMMMBLL
BENI
SENKU
TV

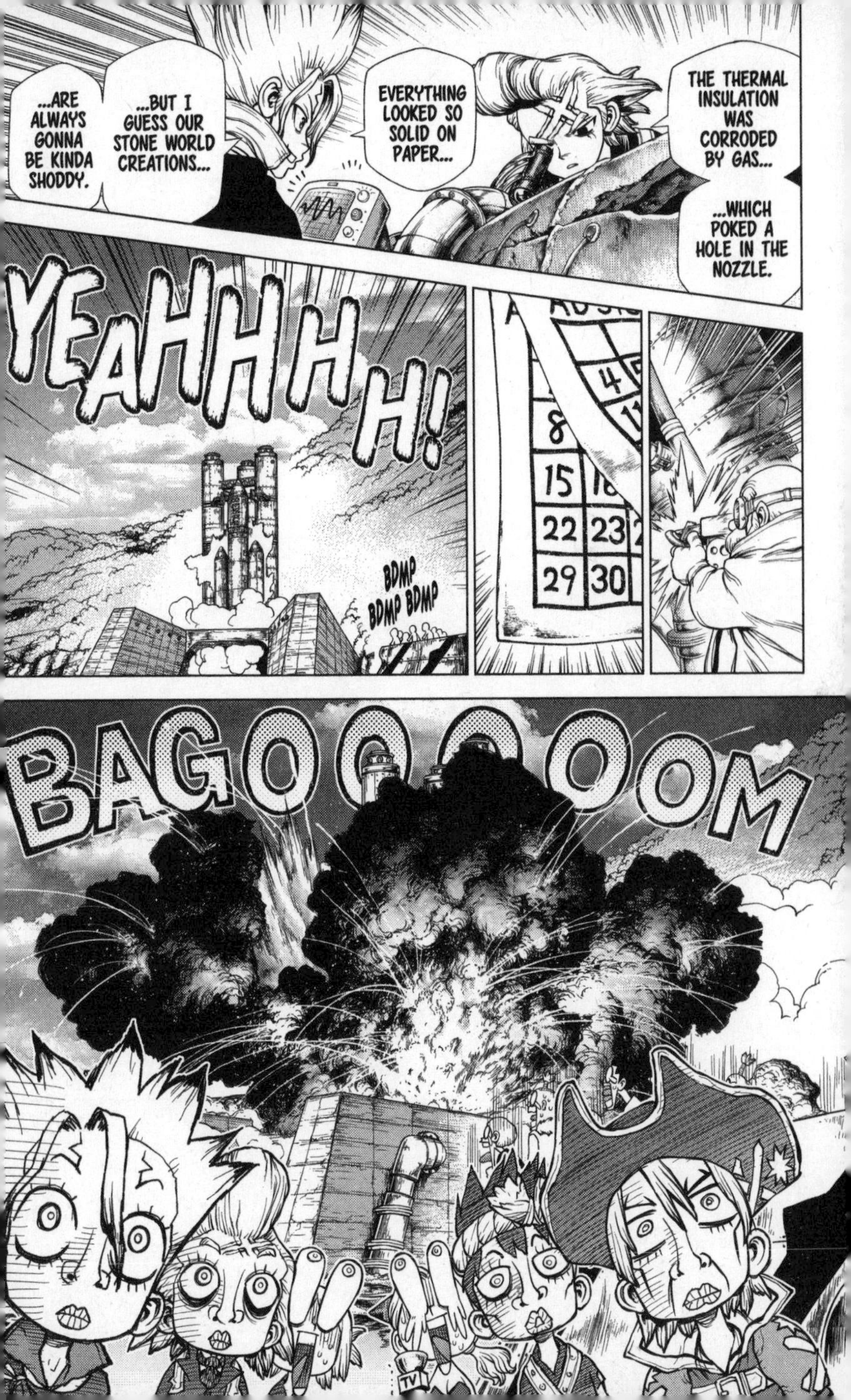
THE THERMAL INSULATION WAS CORRODED BY GAS...
...WHICH POKED A HOLE IN THE NOZZLE.
EVERYTHING LOOKED SO SOLID ON PAPER...
...BUT I GUESS OUR STONE WORLD CREATIONS...
...ARE ALWAYS GONNA BE KINDA SHODDY.
YEAHHHHH!
BDMP BDMP BDMP
BAGOOOOOM

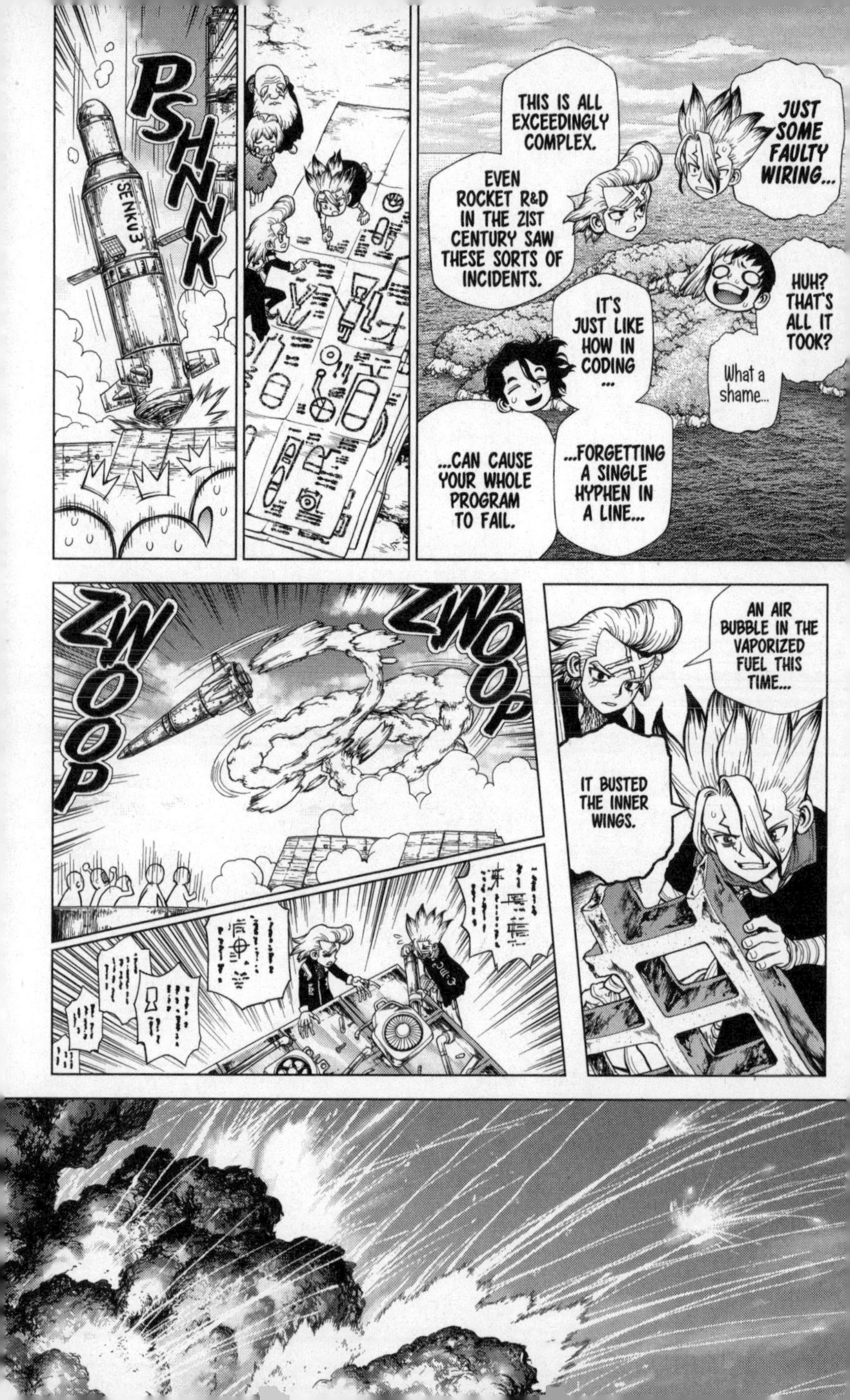
JUST SOME FAULTY WIRING...
HUH? THAT'S ALL IT TOOK?
What a shame...
THIS IS ALL EXCEEDINGLY COMPLEX.
EVEN ROCKET R&D IN THE 21ST CENTURY SAW THESE SORTS OF INCIDENTS.
IT'S JUST LIKE HOW IN CODING...
...FORGETTING A SINGLE HYPHEN IN A LINE...
...CAN CAUSE YOUR WHOLE PROGRAM TO FAIL.
PSHNNK
SENKU 3
AN AIR BUBBLE IN THE VAPORIZED FUEL THIS TIME...
IT BUSTED THE INNER WINGS.
ZWOOOP
ZWOOOP

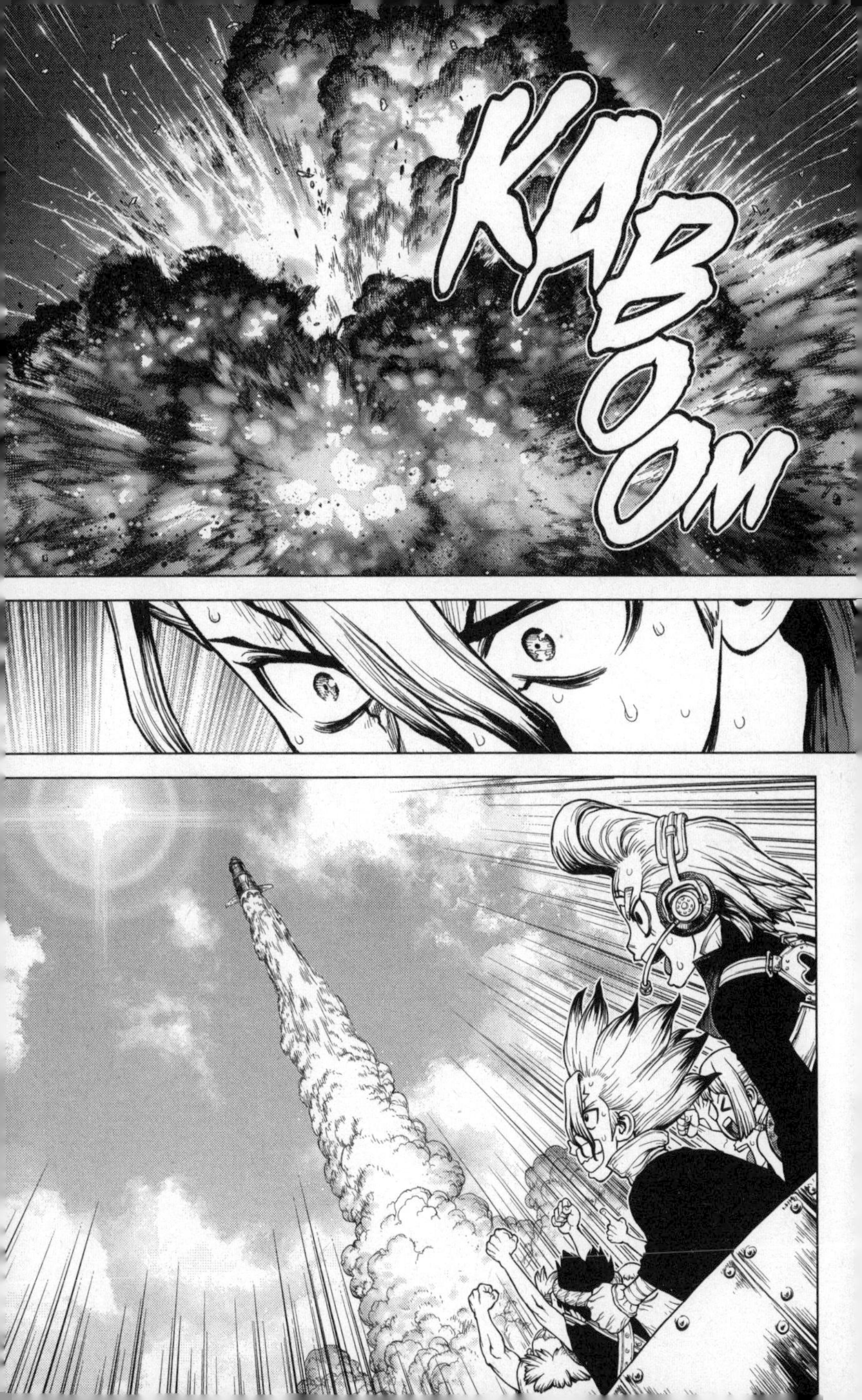
KABOOM

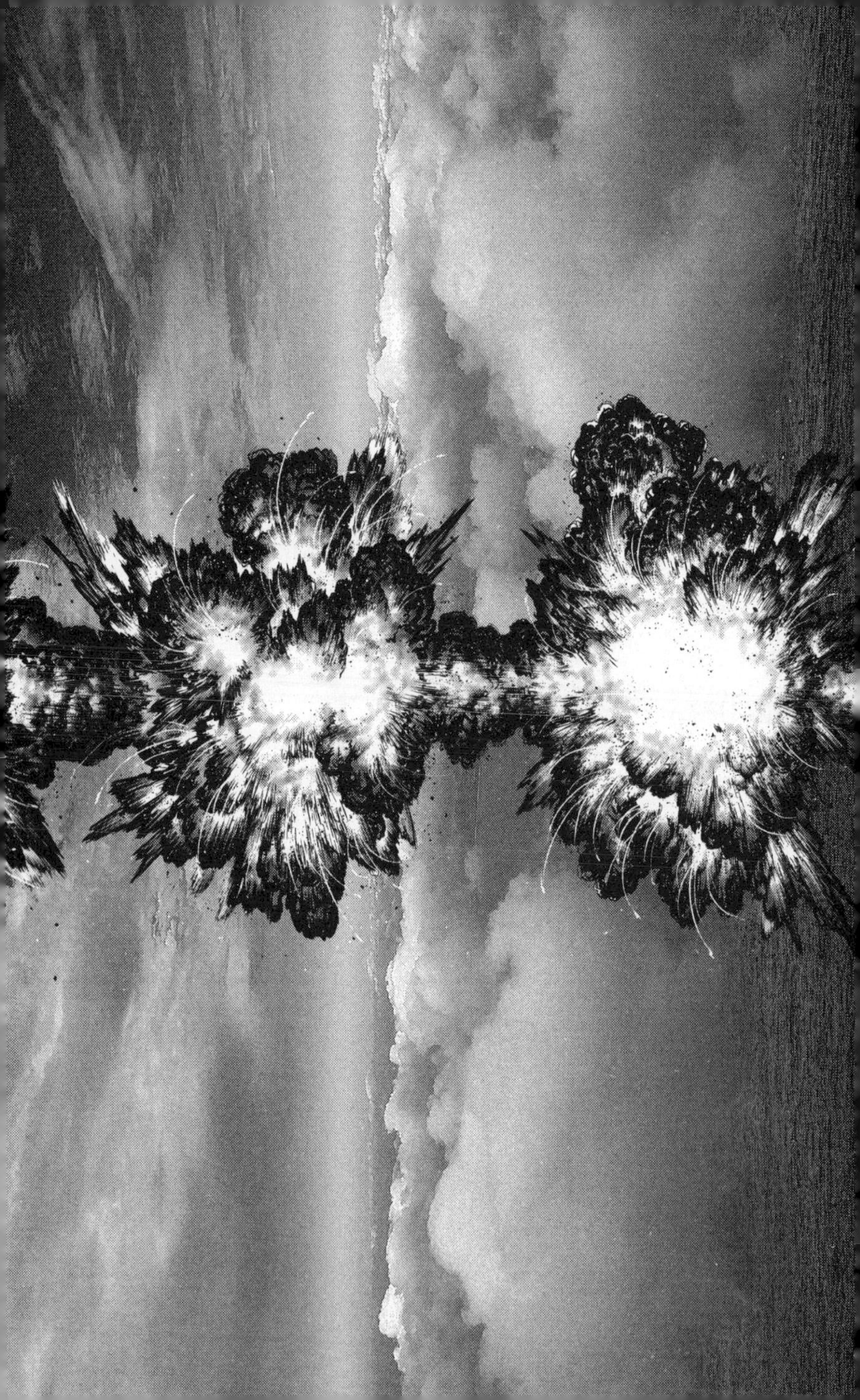

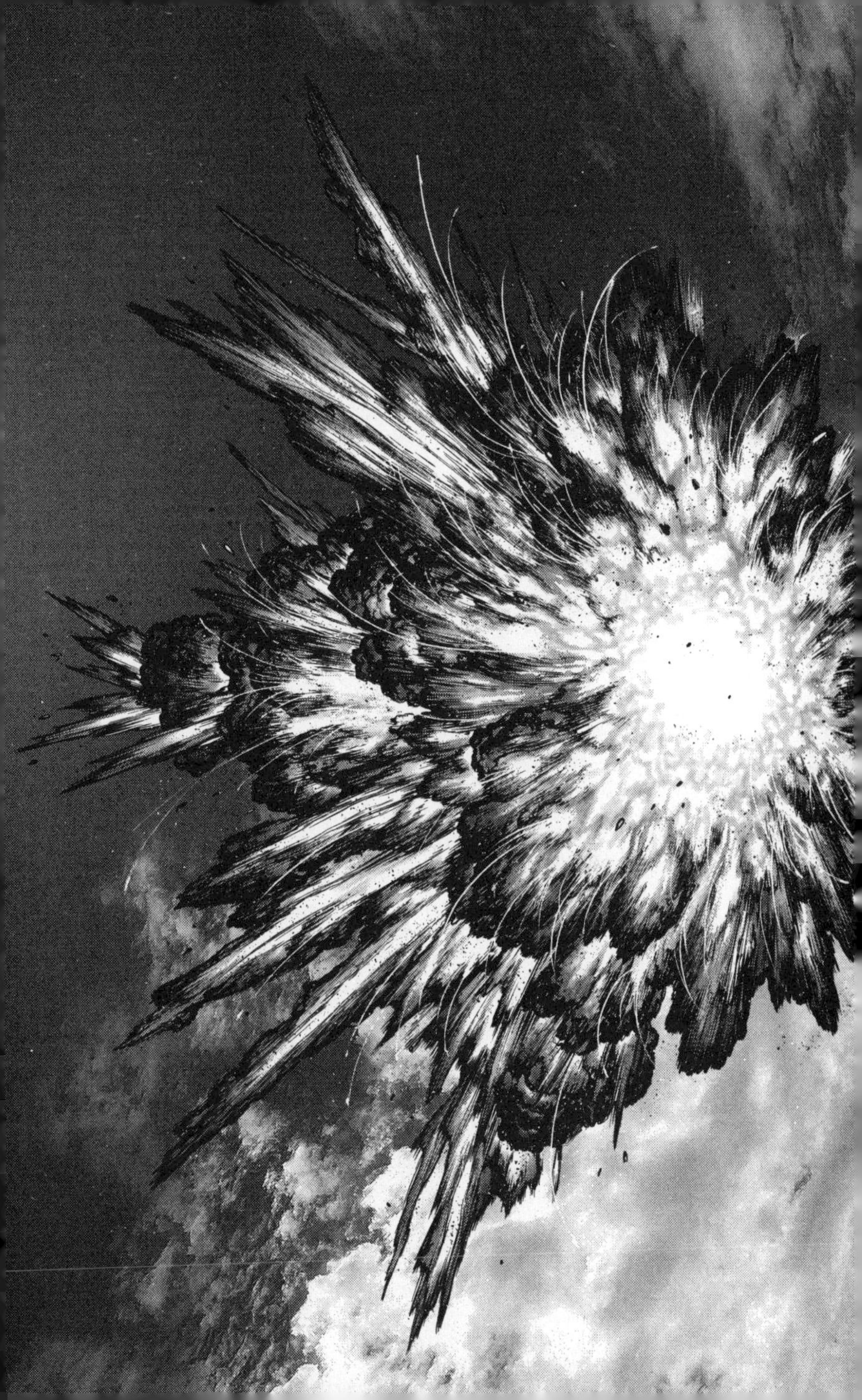

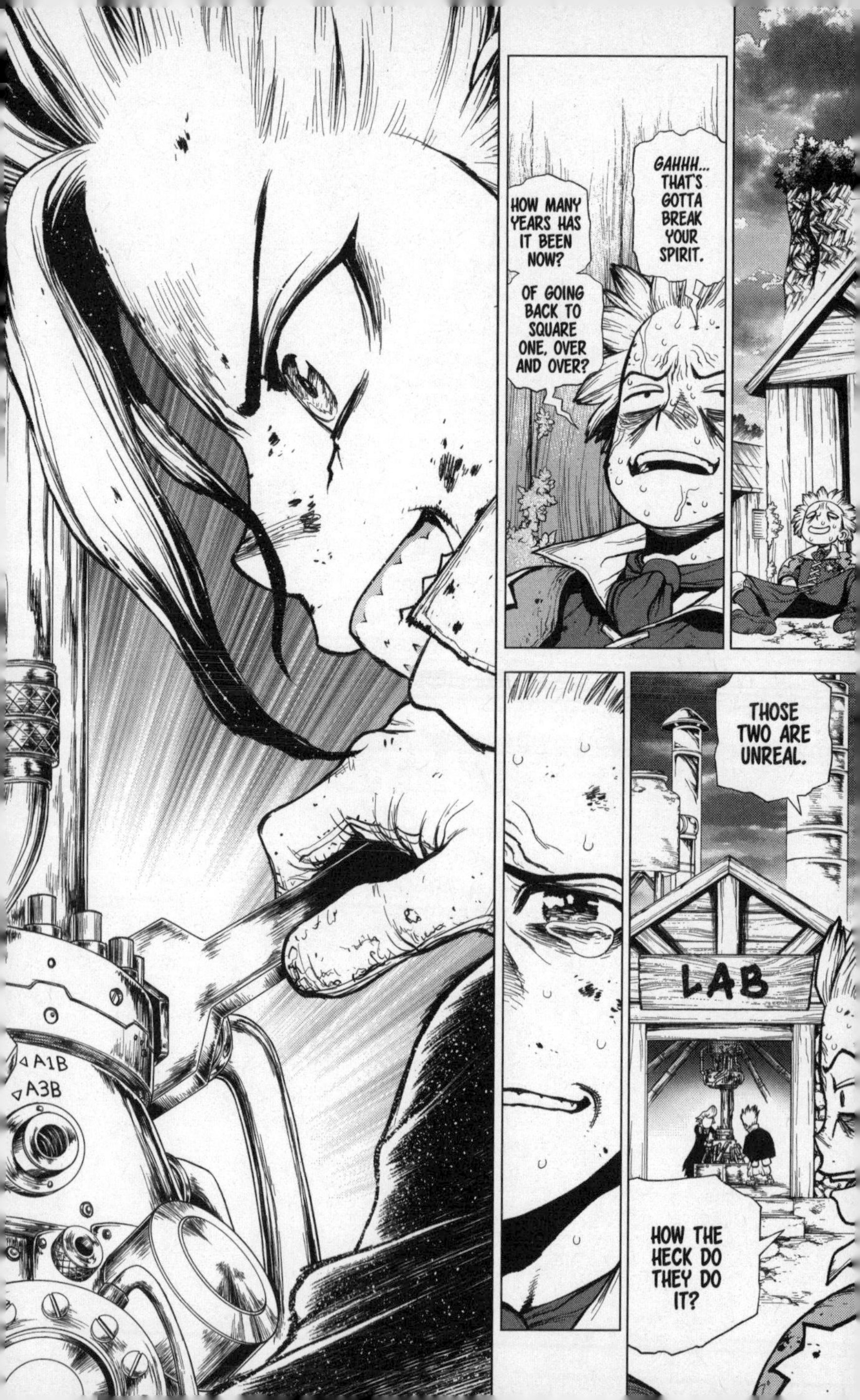
GAHHH... THAT'S GOTTA BREAK YOUR SPIRIT.
HOW MANY YEARS HAS IT BEEN NOW?
OF GOING BACK TO SQUARE ONE, OVER AND OVER?
THOSE TWO ARE UNREAL.
LAB
HOW THE HECK DO THEY DO IT?
A1B
A3B

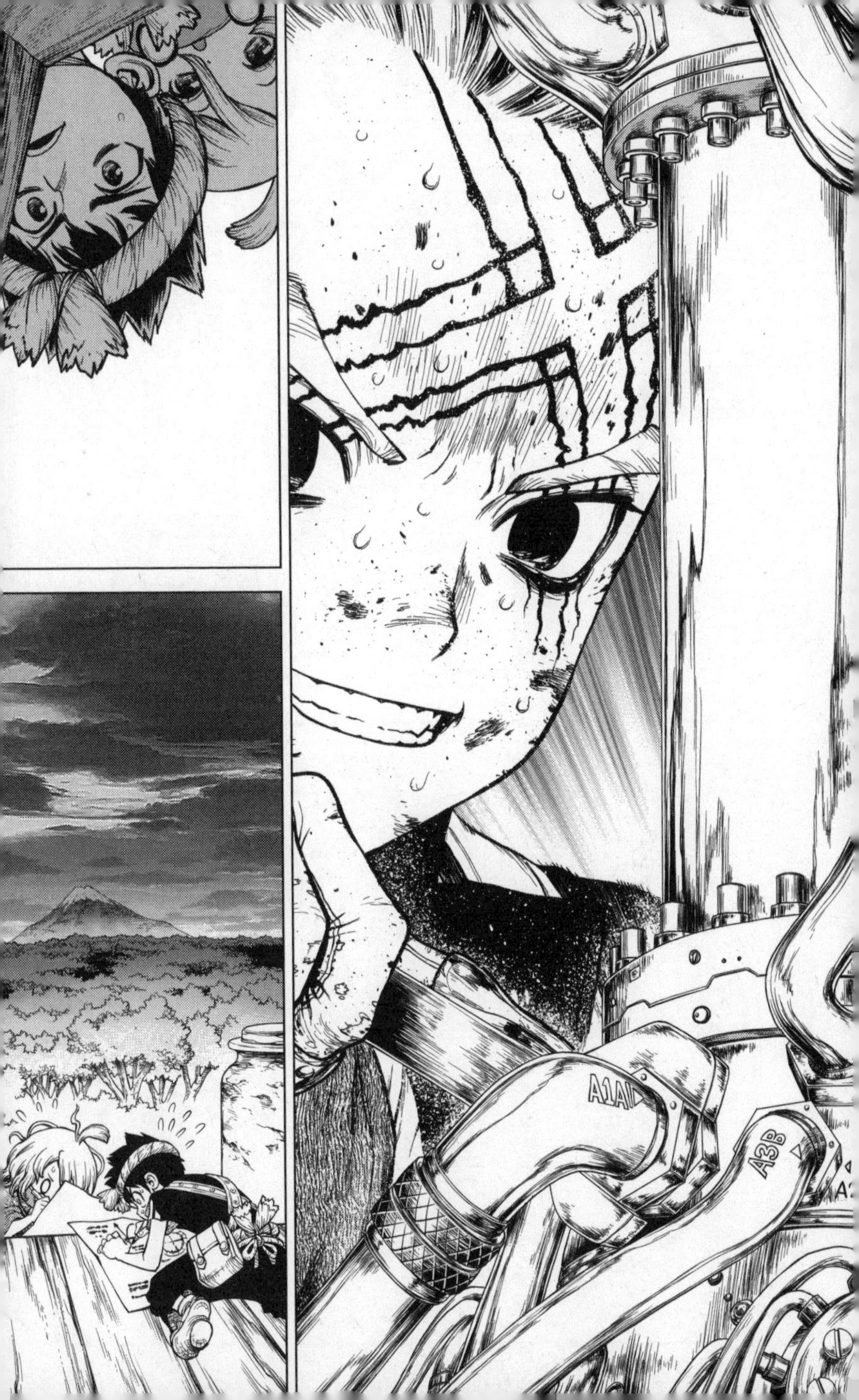

SCHEDULE

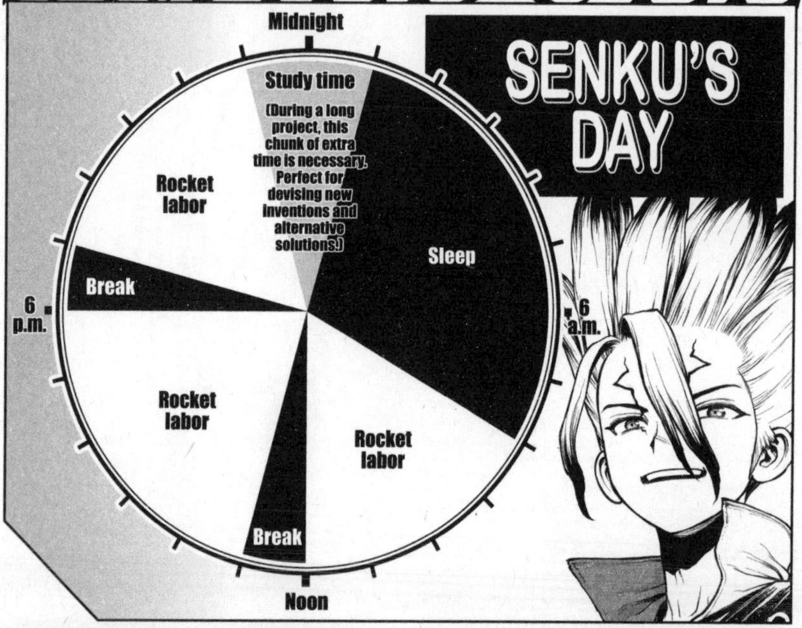

SENKU'S DAY
Midnight
Study time
(During a long project, this chunk of extra time is necessary. Perfect for devising new inventions and alternative solutions.)
Sleep
6 a.m.
Rocket labor
Break
Noon
Rocket labor
6 p.m.
Break
Rocket labor

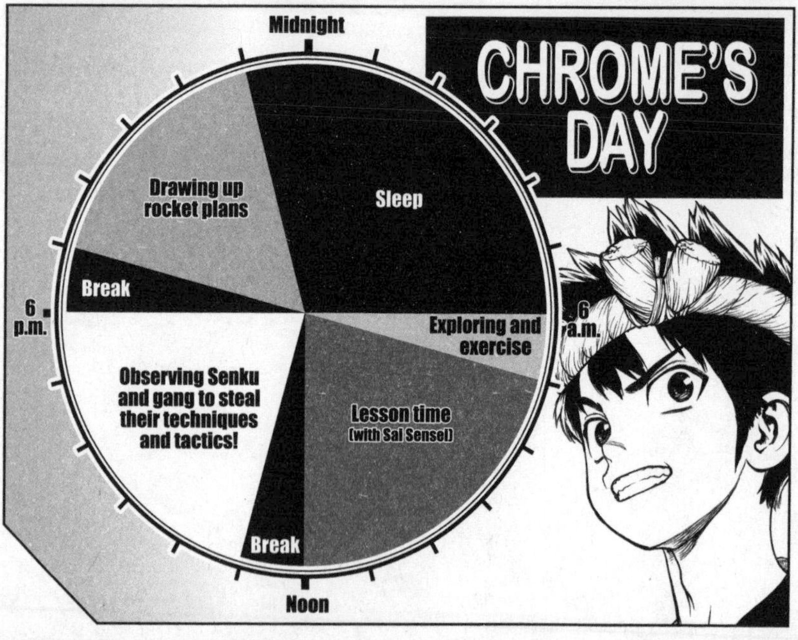

CHROME'S DAY
Midnight
Sleep
6 a.m.
Exploring and exercise
Lesson time
(with Sai Sensei)
Break
Noon
Observing Senku and gang to steal their techniques and tactics!
6 p.m.
Break
Drawing up rocket plans

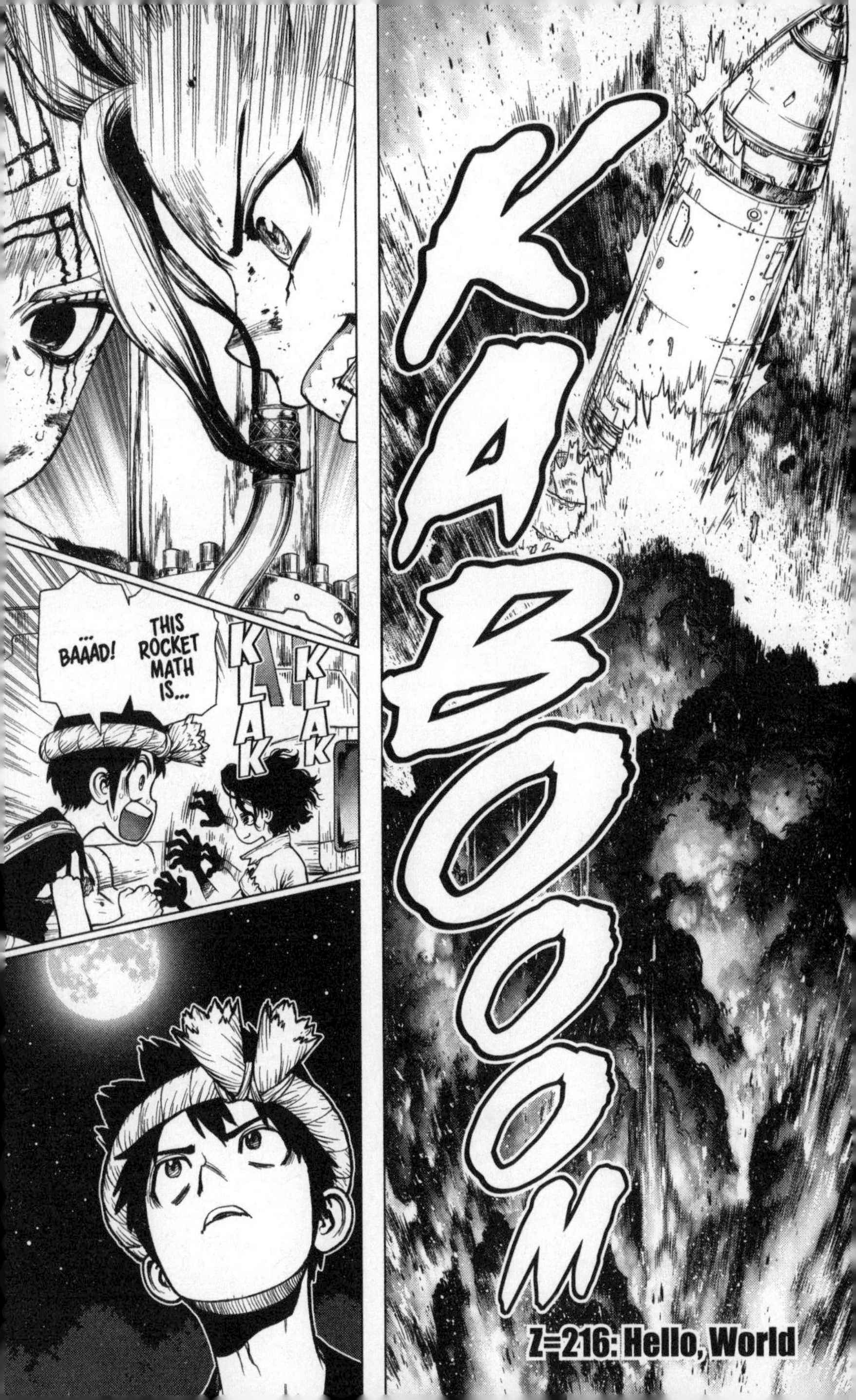
KABOOOOM
Z=216: Hello, World
KLAK KLAK
THIS ROCKET MATH IS... ...BAÄÄD!

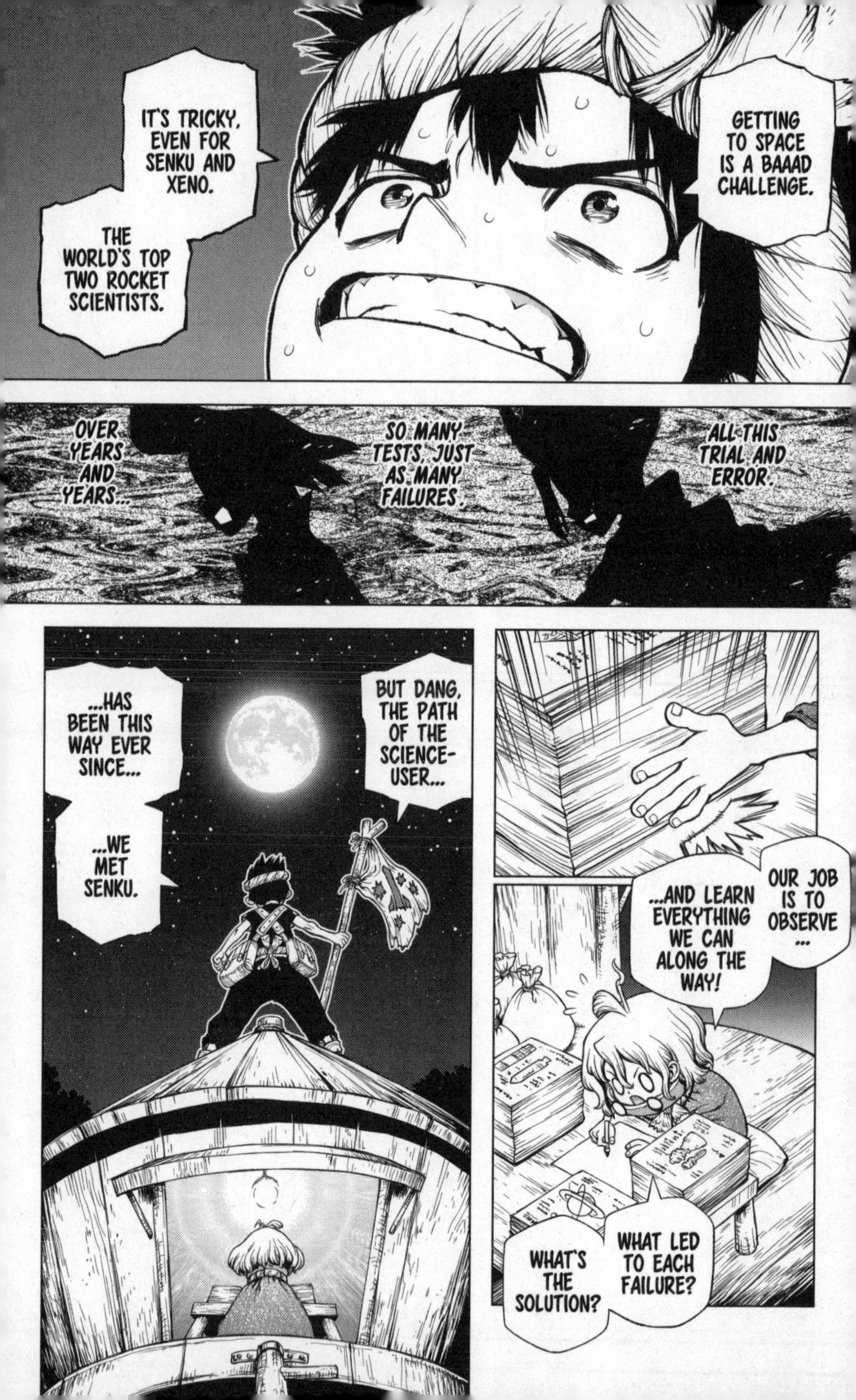
GETTING TO SPACE IS A BAAAD CHALLENGE.
IT'S TRICKY, EVEN FOR SENKU AND XENO.
THE WORLD'S TOP TWO ROCKET SCIENTISTS.
ALL THIS TRIAL AND ERROR.
SO MANY TESTS, JUST AS MANY FAILURES.
OVER YEARS AND YEARS...
OUR JOB IS TO OBSERVE...
...AND LEARN EVERYTHING WE CAN ALONG THE WAY!
WHAT LED TO EACH FAILURE?
WHAT'S THE SOLUTION?
BUT DANG, THE PATH OF THE SCIENCE-USER...
...HAS BEEN THIS WAY EVER SINCE...
...WE MET SENKU.

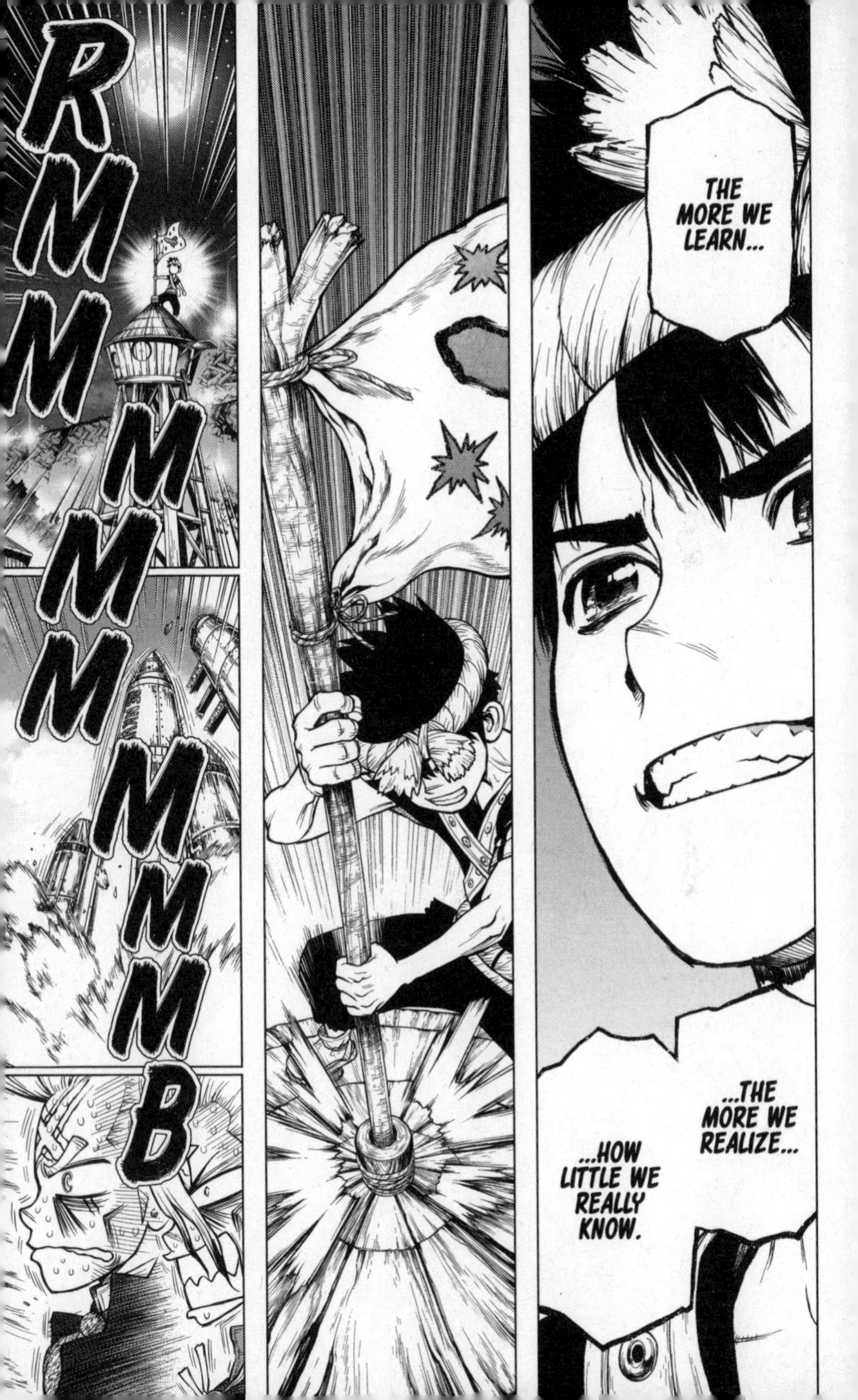
THE MORE WE LEARN...
...THE MORE WE REALIZE...
...HOW LITTLE WE REALLY KNOW.
RMMMMMMMMB

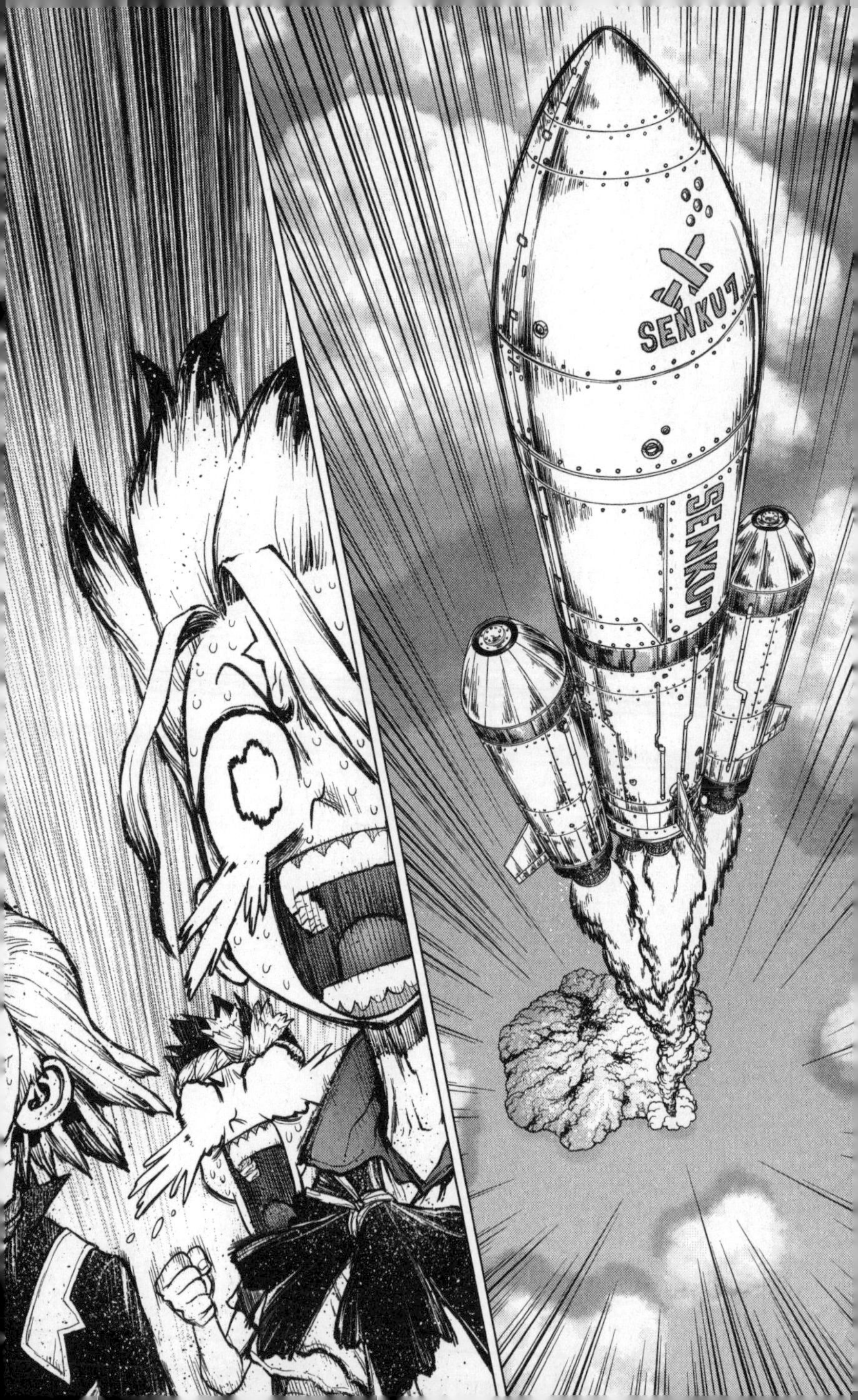
SENKU7
SENKU7

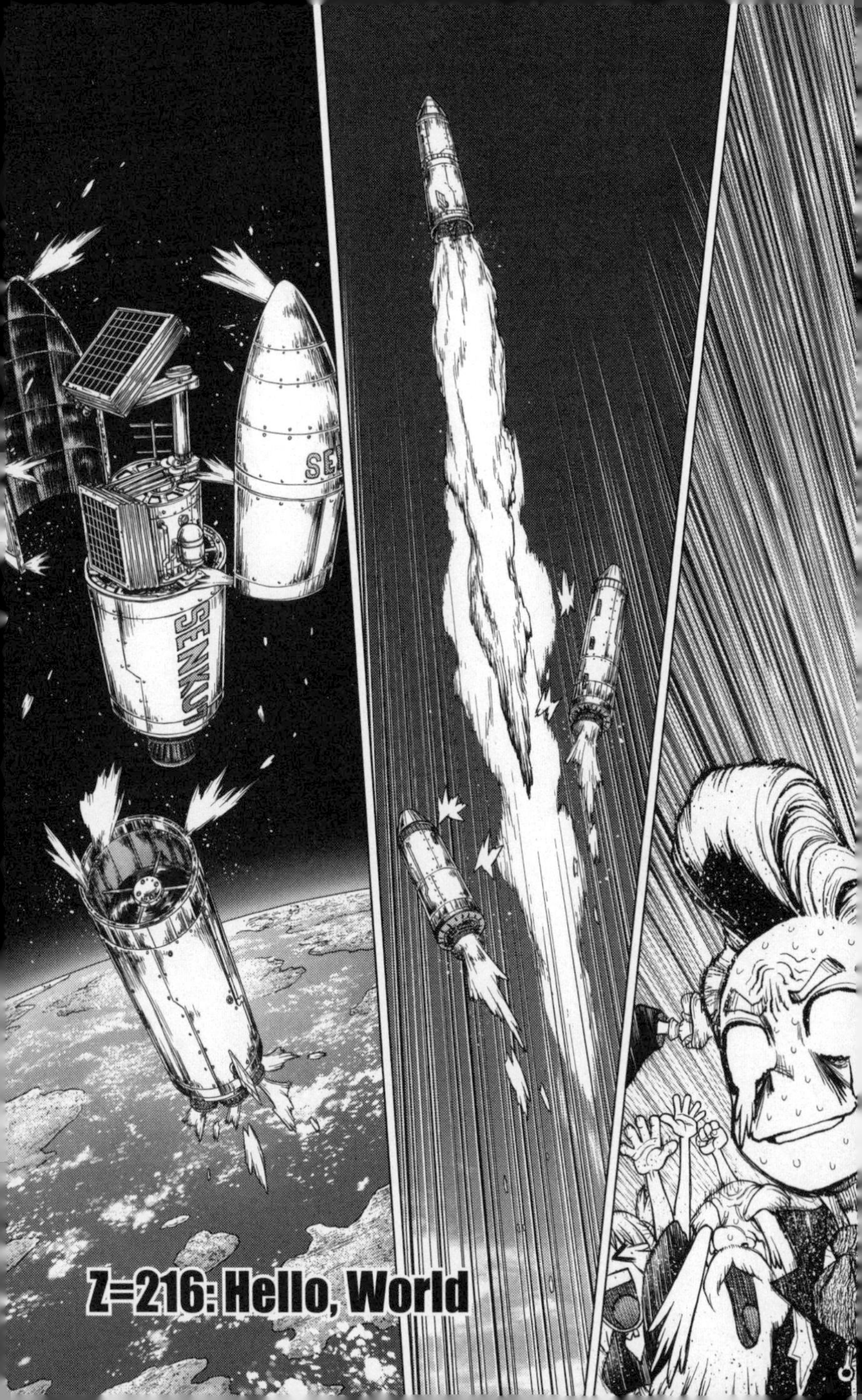
SE
SENKU
Z=216: Hello, World

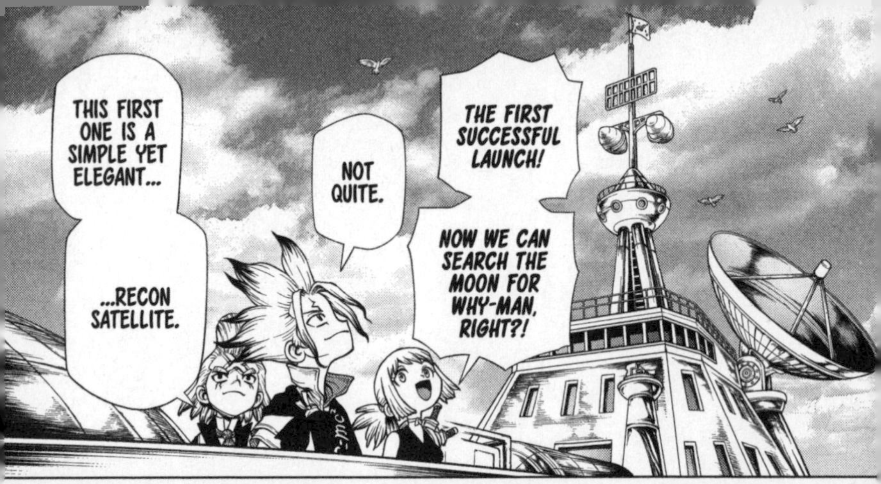
THE FIRST SUCCESSFUL LAUNCH!
NOW WE CAN SEARCH THE MOON FOR WHY-MAN, RIGHT?!
NOT QUITE.
THIS FIRST ONE IS A SIMPLE YET ELEGANT...
...RECON SATELLITE.

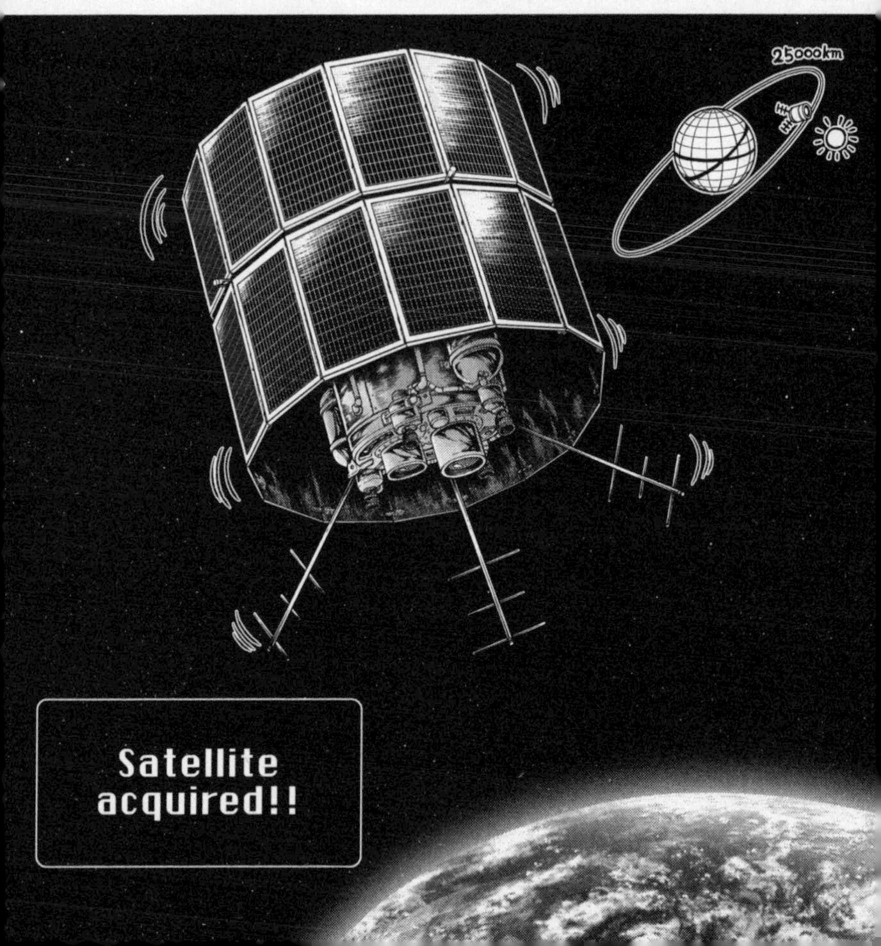
25000km
Satellite acquired!!

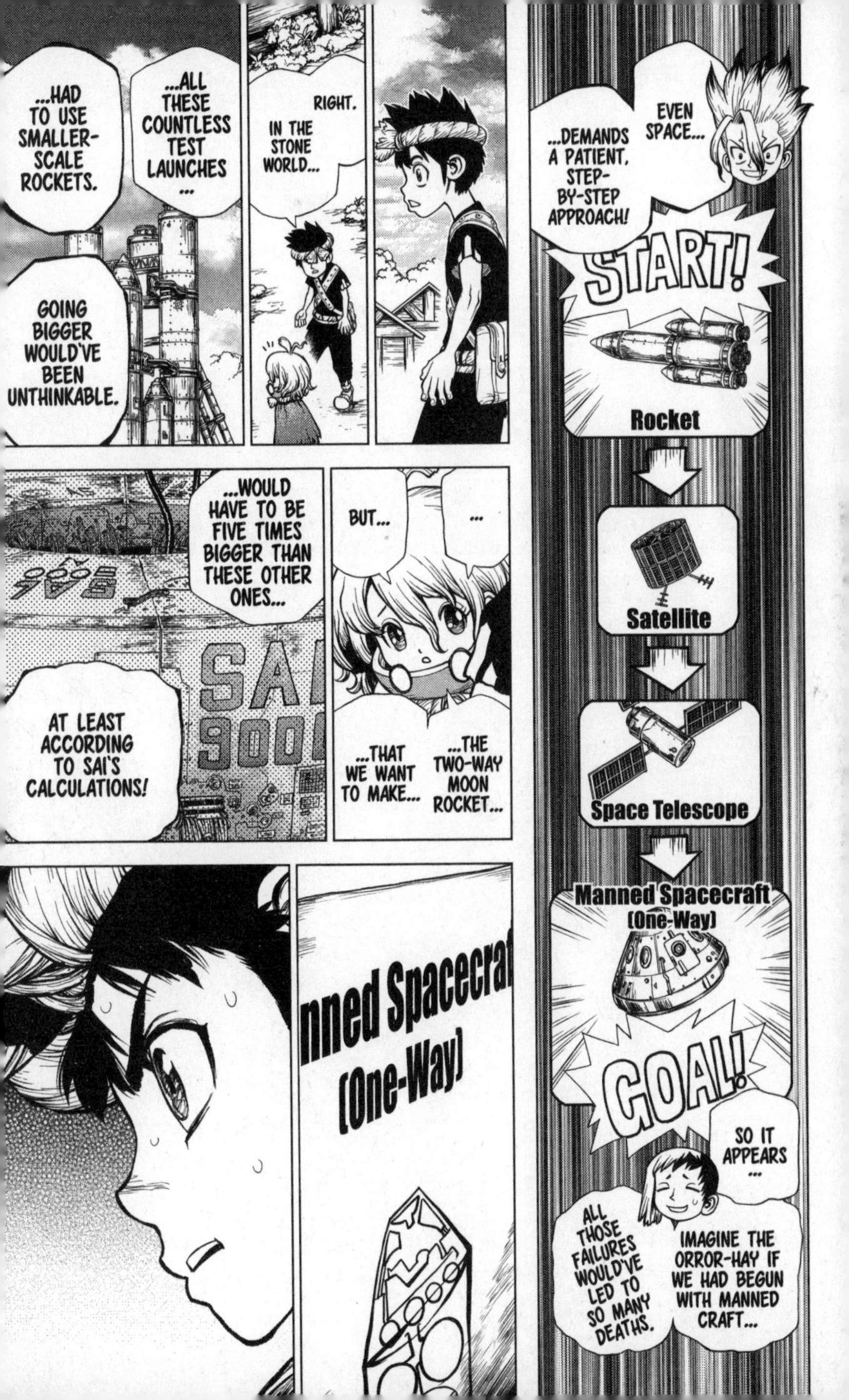
EVEN SPACE...
...DEMANDS A PATIENT, STEP-BY-STEP APPROACH!
START!
Rocket
Satellite
Space Telescope
Manned Spacecraft [One-Way]
GOAL!
SO IT APPEARS...
IMAGINE THE ORROR-HAY IF WE HAD BEGUN WITH MANNED CRAFT...
ALL THOSE FAILURES WOULD'VE LED TO SO MANY DEATHS.
RIGHT.
IN THE STONE WORLD...
...ALL THESE COUNTLESS TEST LAUNCHES...
...HAD TO USE SMALLER-SCALE ROCKETS.
GOING BIGGER WOULD'VE BEEN UNTHINKABLE.
...
BUT...
...THE TWO-WAY MOON ROCKET...
...THAT WE WANT TO MAKE...
...WOULD HAVE TO BE FIVE TIMES BIGGER THAN THESE OTHER ONES...
AT LEAST ACCORDING TO SAI'S CALCULATIONS!
nned Spacecraf
[One-Way]

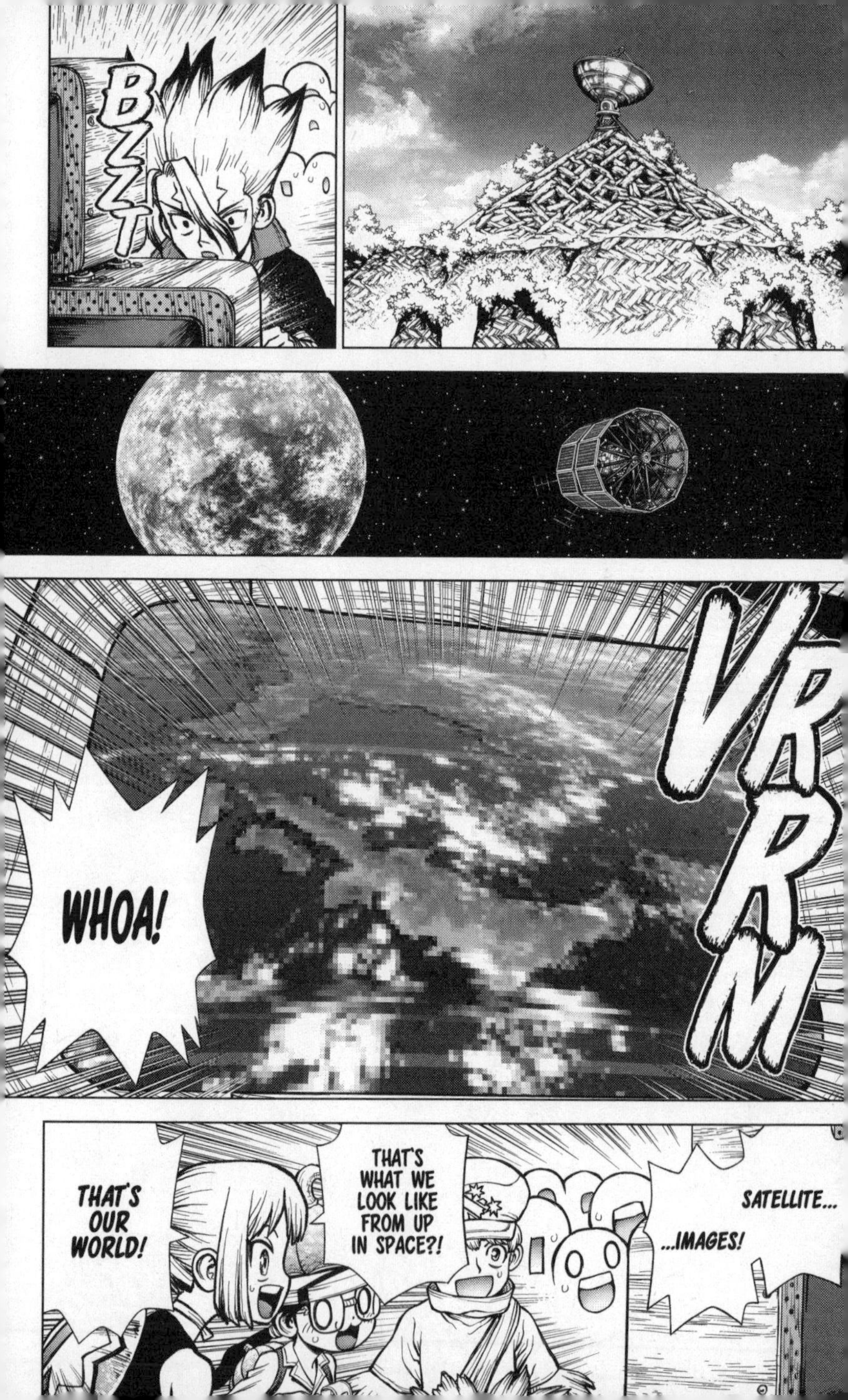
BZZZT
VRRM
WHOA!
SATELLITE...
...IMAGES!
THAT'S WHAT WE LOOK LIKE FROM UP IN SPACE?!
THAT'S OUR WORLD!

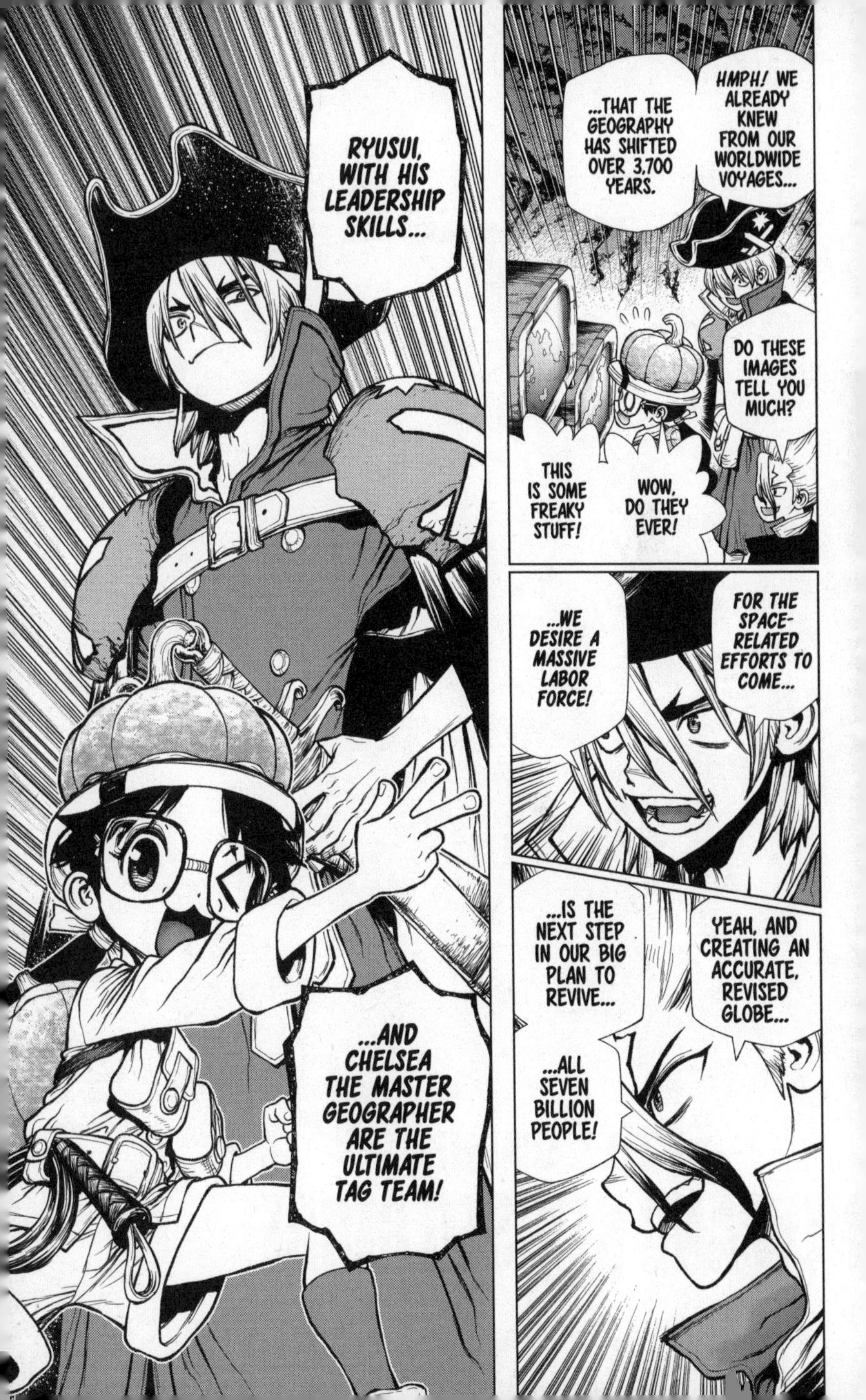
HMPH! WE ALREADY KNEW FROM OUR WORLDWIDE VOYAGES...
...THAT THE GEOGRAPHY HAS SHIFTED OVER 3,700 YEARS.
DO THESE IMAGES TELL YOU MUCH?
WOW, DO THEY EVER!
THIS IS SOME FREAKY STUFF!
FOR THE SPACE-RELATED EFFORTS TO COME...
...WE DESIRE A MASSIVE LABOR FORCE!
YEAH, AND CREATING AN ACCURATE, REVISED GLOBE...
...IS THE NEXT STEP IN OUR BIG PLAN TO REVIVE...
...ALL SEVEN BILLION PEOPLE!
RYUSUI, WITH HIS LEADERSHIP SKILLS...
...AND CHELSEA THE MASTER GEOGRAPHER ARE THE ULTIMATE TAG TEAM!

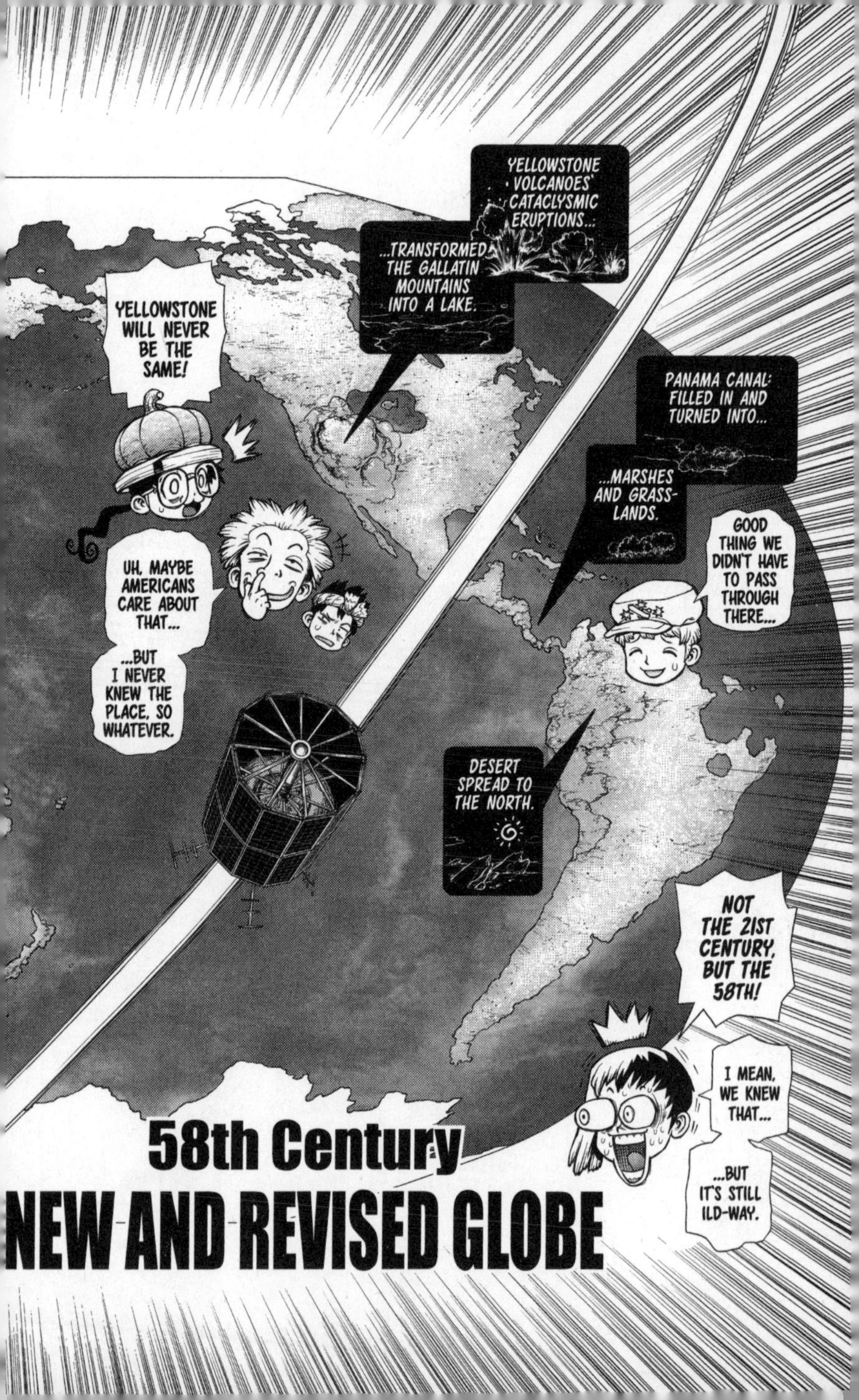
YELLOWSTONE VOLCANOES' CATACLYSMIC ERUPTIONS...
...TRANSFORMED THE GALLATIN MOUNTAINS INTO A LAKE.
YELLOWSTONE WILL NEVER BE THE SAME!
PANAMA CANAL: FILLED IN AND TURNED INTO...
...MARSHES AND GRASS-LANDS.
GOOD THING WE DIDN'T HAVE TO PASS THROUGH THERE...
UH, MAYBE AMERICANS CARE ABOUT THAT...
...BUT I NEVER KNEW THE PLACE, SO WHATEVER.
DESERT SPREAD TO THE NORTH.
NOT THE 21ST CENTURY, BUT THE 58TH!
I MEAN, WE KNEW THAT...
...BUT IT'S STILL ILD-WAY.
58th Century
NEW AND REVISED GLOBE

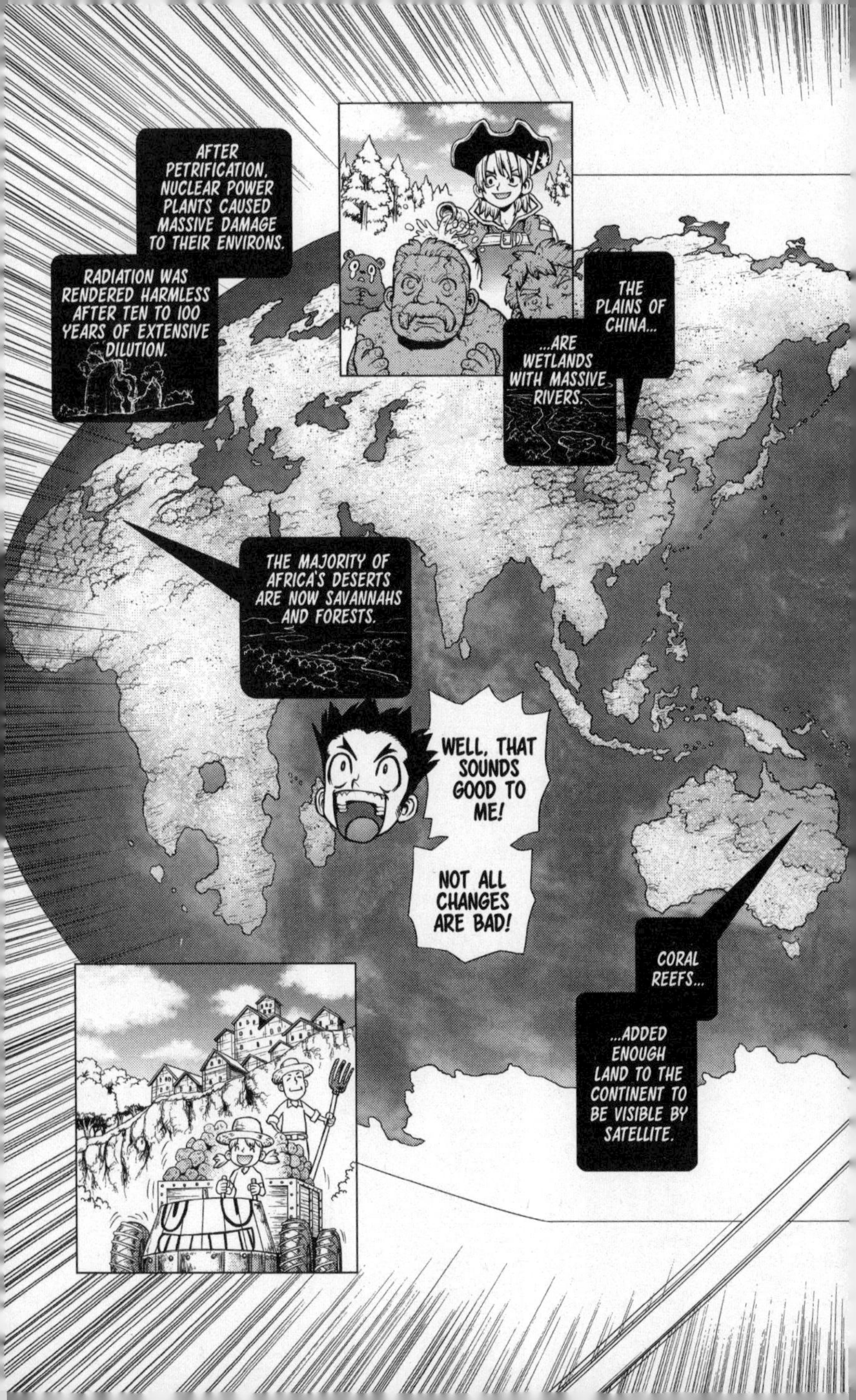
THE PLAINS OF CHINA...
...ARE WETLANDS WITH MASSIVE RIVERS.
AFTER PETRIFICATION, NUCLEAR POWER PLANTS CAUSED MASSIVE DAMAGE TO THEIR ENVIRONS.
RADIATION WAS RENDERED HARMLESS AFTER TEN TO 100 YEARS OF EXTENSIVE DILUTION.
THE MAJORITY OF AFRICA'S DESERTS ARE NOW SAVANNAHS AND FORESTS.
WELL, THAT SOUNDS GOOD TO ME!
NOT ALL CHANGES ARE BAD!
CORAL REEFS...
...ADDED ENOUGH LAND TO THE CONTINENT TO BE VISIBLE BY SATELLITE.

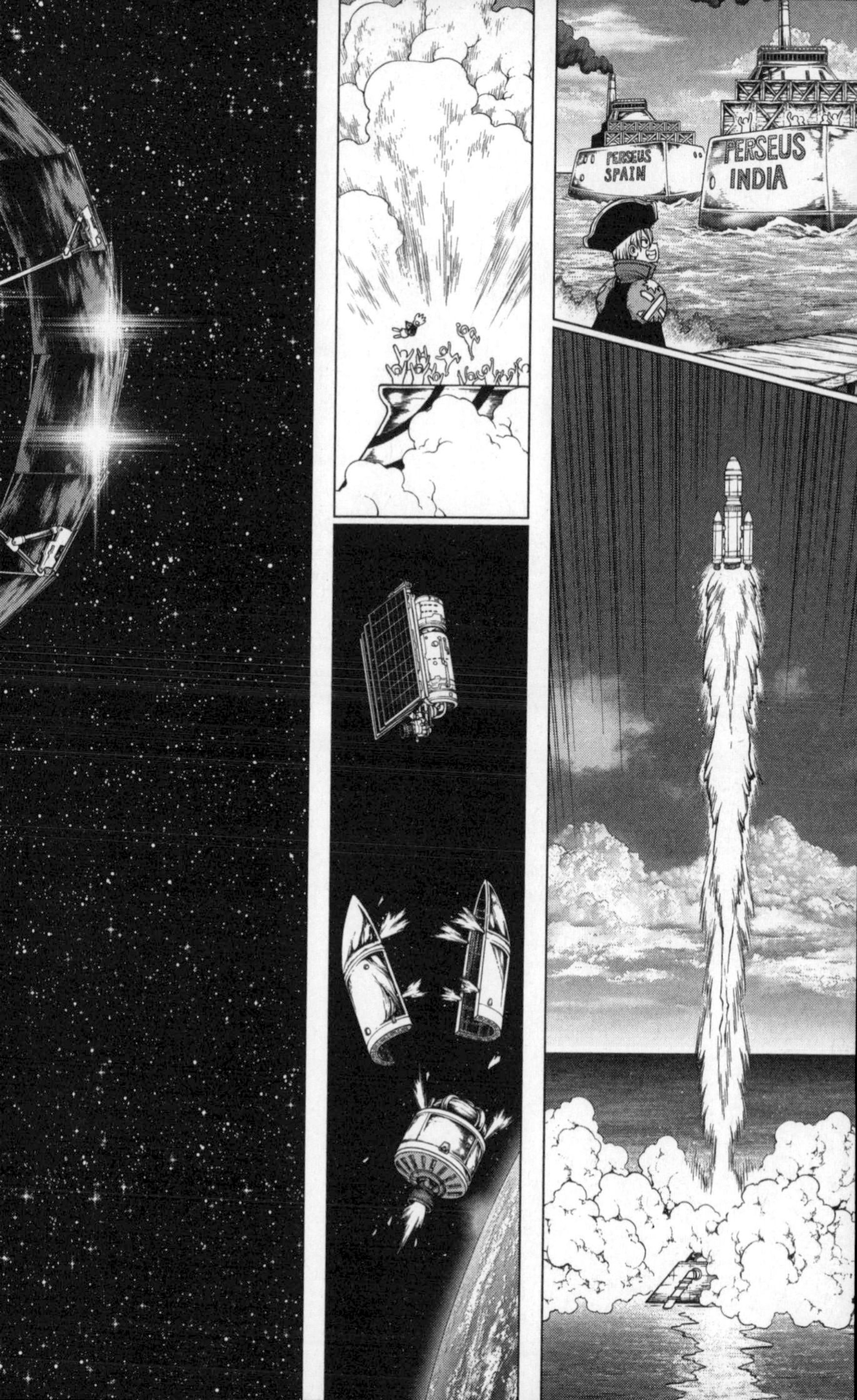
PERSEUS INDIA
PERSEUS SPAIN

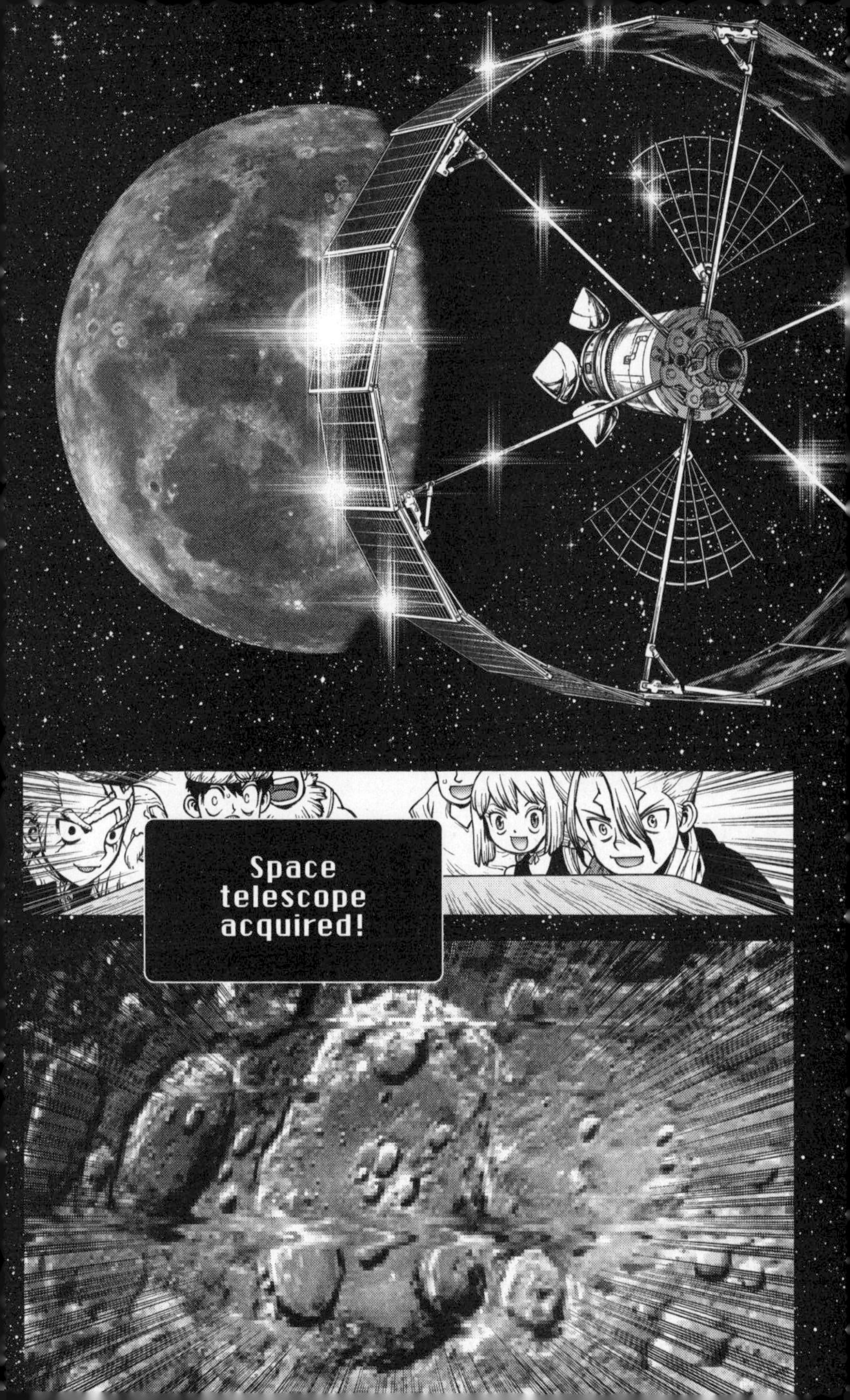
Space telescope acquired!

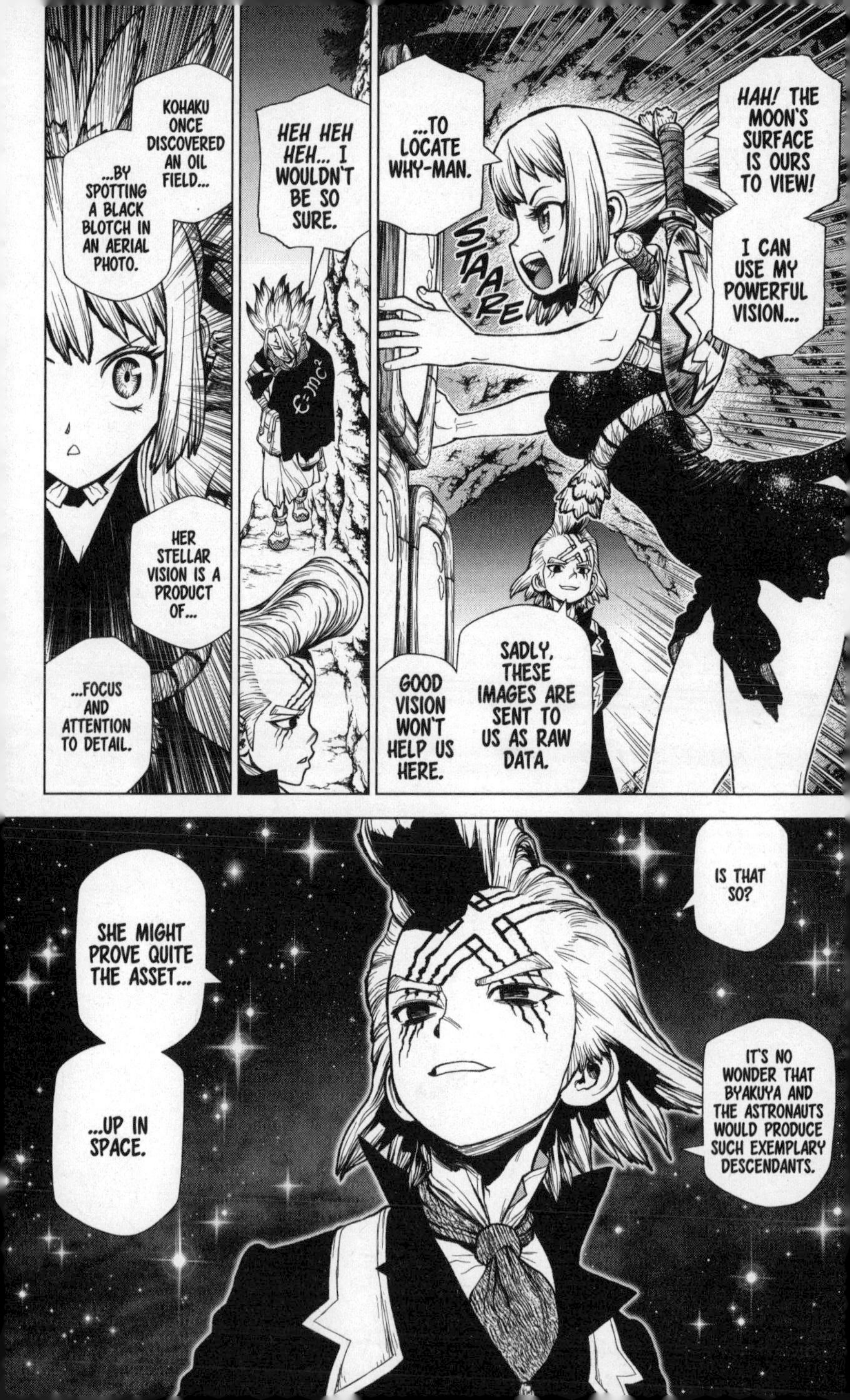
HAH! THE MOON'S SURFACE IS OURS TO VIEW!
I CAN USE MY POWERFUL VISION...
...TO LOCATE WHY-MAN.
STAARE
SADLY, THESE IMAGES ARE SENT TO US AS RAW DATA.
GOOD VISION WON'T HELP US HERE.
HEH HEH HEH... I WOULDN'T BE SO SURE.
KOHAKU ONCE DISCOVERED AN OIL FIELD...
...BY SPOTTING A BLACK BLOTCH IN AN AERIAL PHOTO.
HER STELLAR VISION IS A PRODUCT OF...
...FOCUS AND ATTENTION TO DETAIL.
IS THAT SO?
IT'S NO WONDER THAT BYAKUYA AND THE ASTRONAUTS WOULD PRODUCE SUCH EXEMPLARY DESCENDANTS.
SHE MIGHT PROVE QUITE THE ASSET...
...UP IN SPACE.

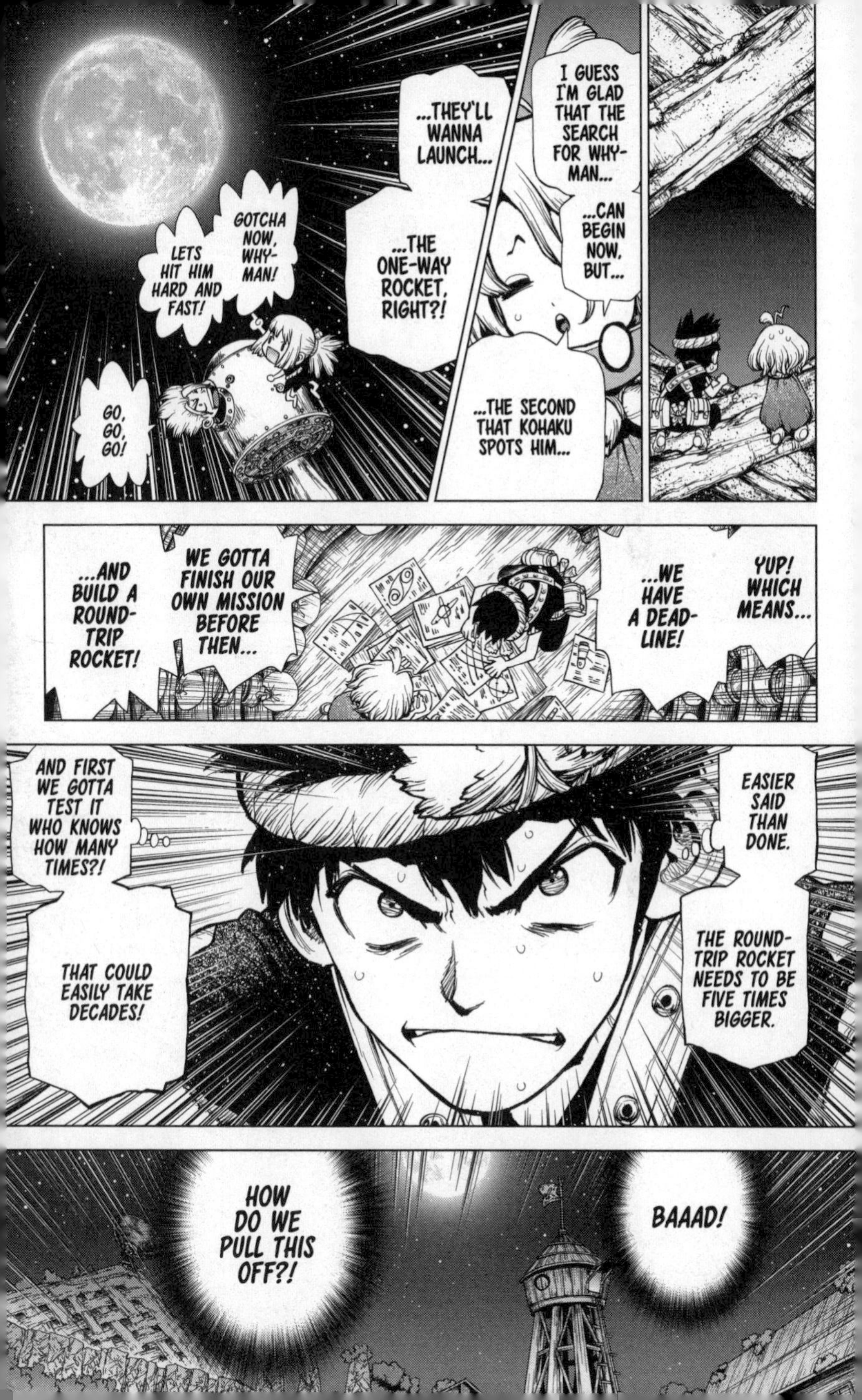

I GUESS I'M GLAD THAT THE SEARCH FOR WHY-MAN...
...CAN BEGIN NOW, BUT...
...THEY'LL WANNA LAUNCH...
...THE ONE-WAY ROCKET, RIGHT?!
...THE SECOND THAT KOHAKU SPOTS HIM...
GOTCHA NOW, WHY-MAN!
LETS HIT HIM HARD AND FAST!
GO, GO, GO!
YUP! WHICH MEANS...
...WE HAVE A DEAD-LINE!
WE GOTTA FINISH OUR OWN MISSION BEFORE THEN...
...AND BUILD A ROUND-TRIP ROCKET!
EASIER SAID THAN DONE.
THE ROUND-TRIP ROCKET NEEDS TO BE FIVE TIMES BIGGER.
AND FIRST WE GOTTA TEST IT WHO KNOWS HOW MANY TIMES?!
THAT COULD EASILY TAKE DECADES!
BAAAD!
HOW DO WE PULL THIS OFF?!

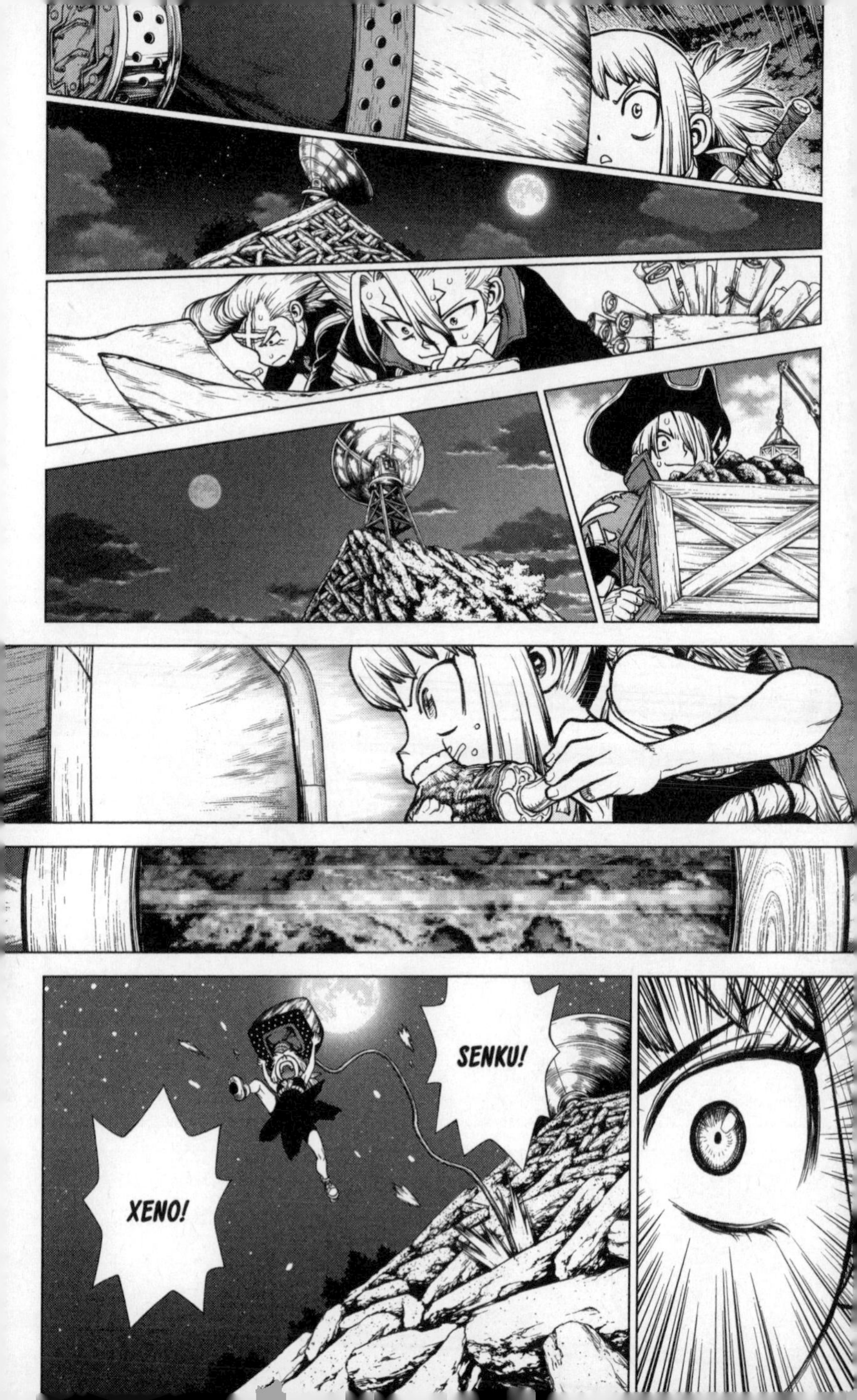
SENKU!
XENO!

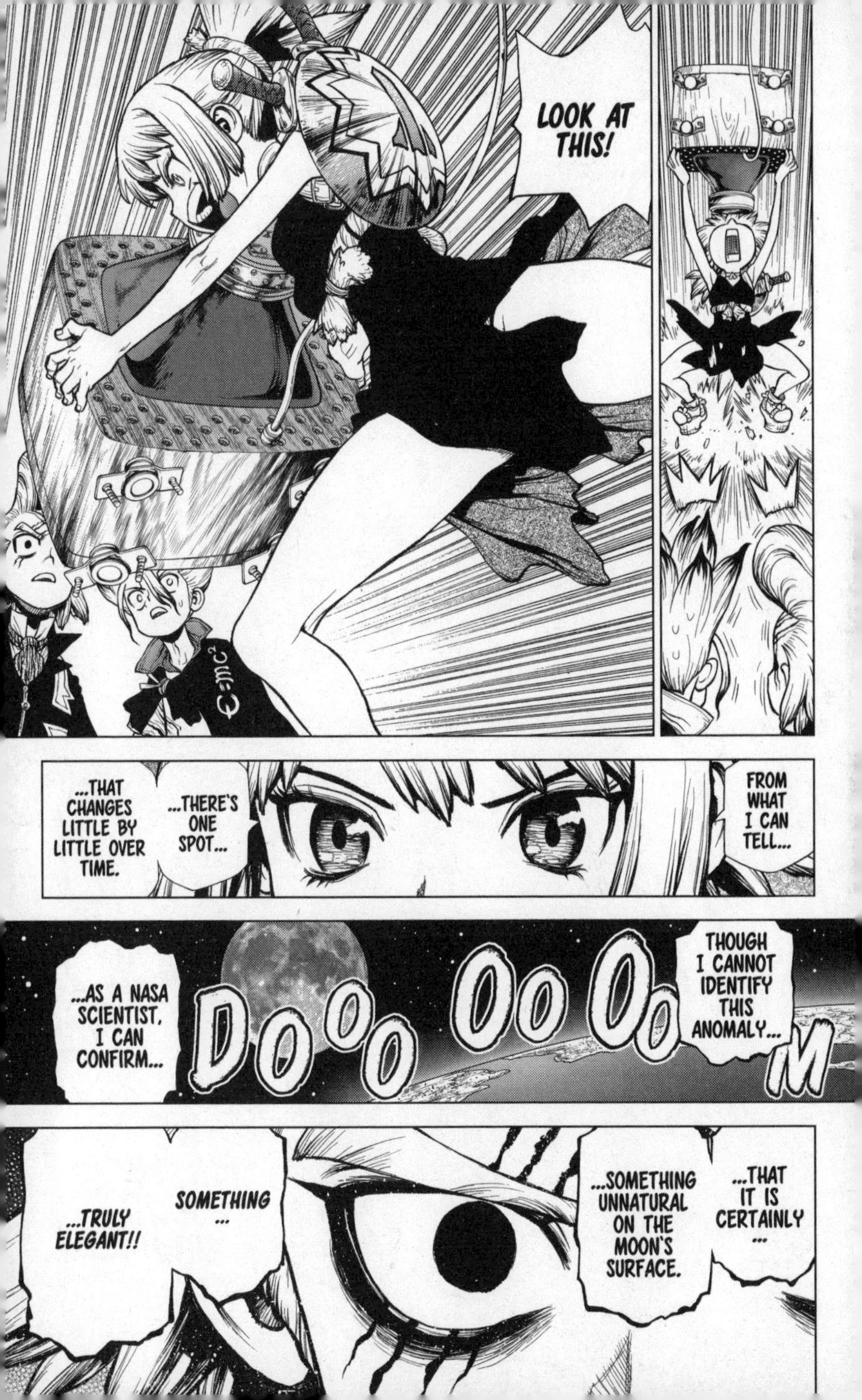
LOOK AT THIS!
$E=mc^2$
FROM WHAT I CAN TELL...
...THERE'S ONE SPOT...
...THAT CHANGES LITTLE BY LITTLE OVER TIME.
THOUGH I CANNOT IDENTIFY THIS ANOMALY...
DOOOOOOOOM
...AS A NASA SCIENTIST, I CAN CONFIRM...
...THAT IT IS CERTAINLY...
...SOMETHING UNNATURAL ON THE MOON'S SURFACE.
SOMETHING...
...TRULY ELEGANT!!

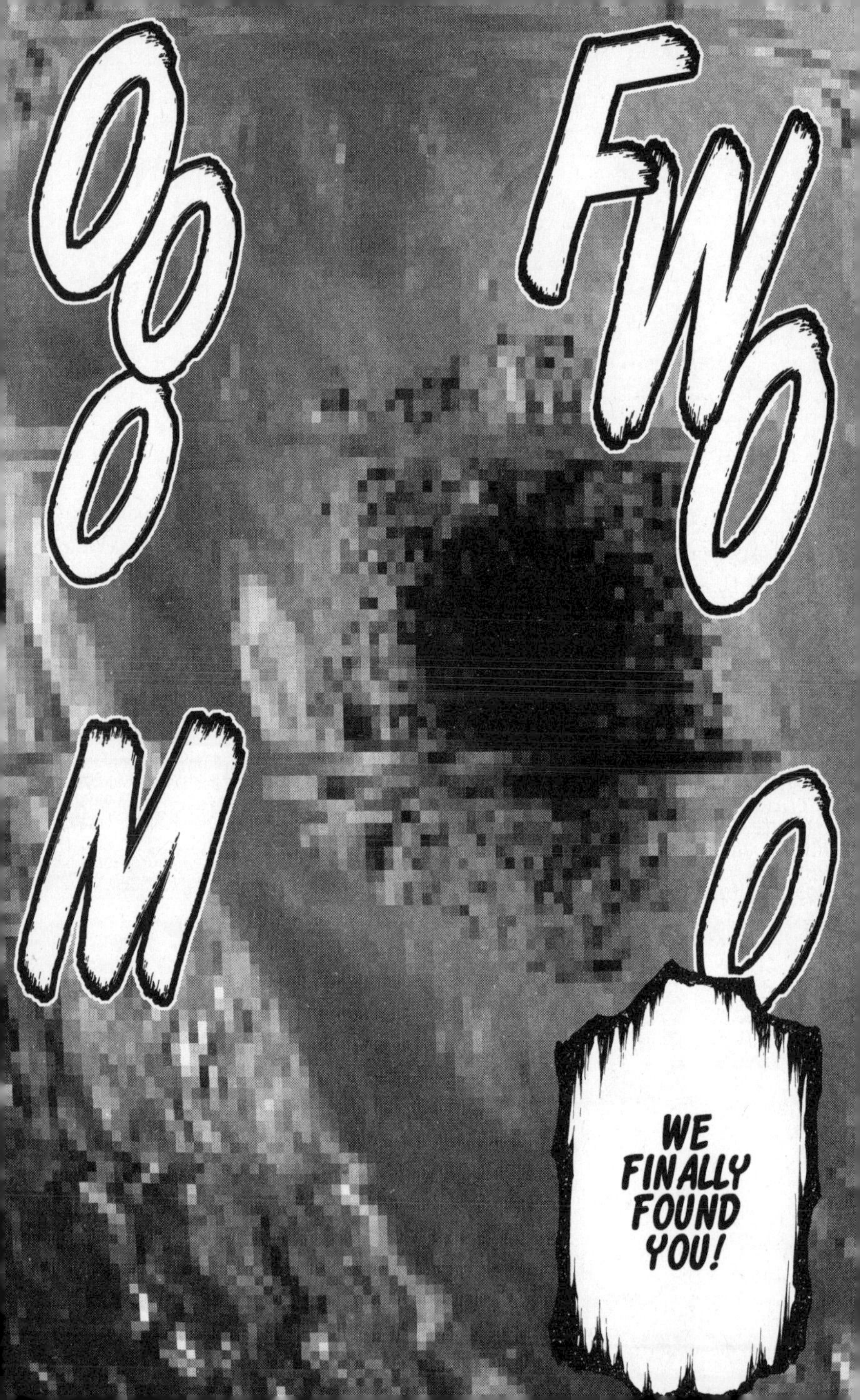
FWOO
WE FINALLY FOUND YOU!
OOOM

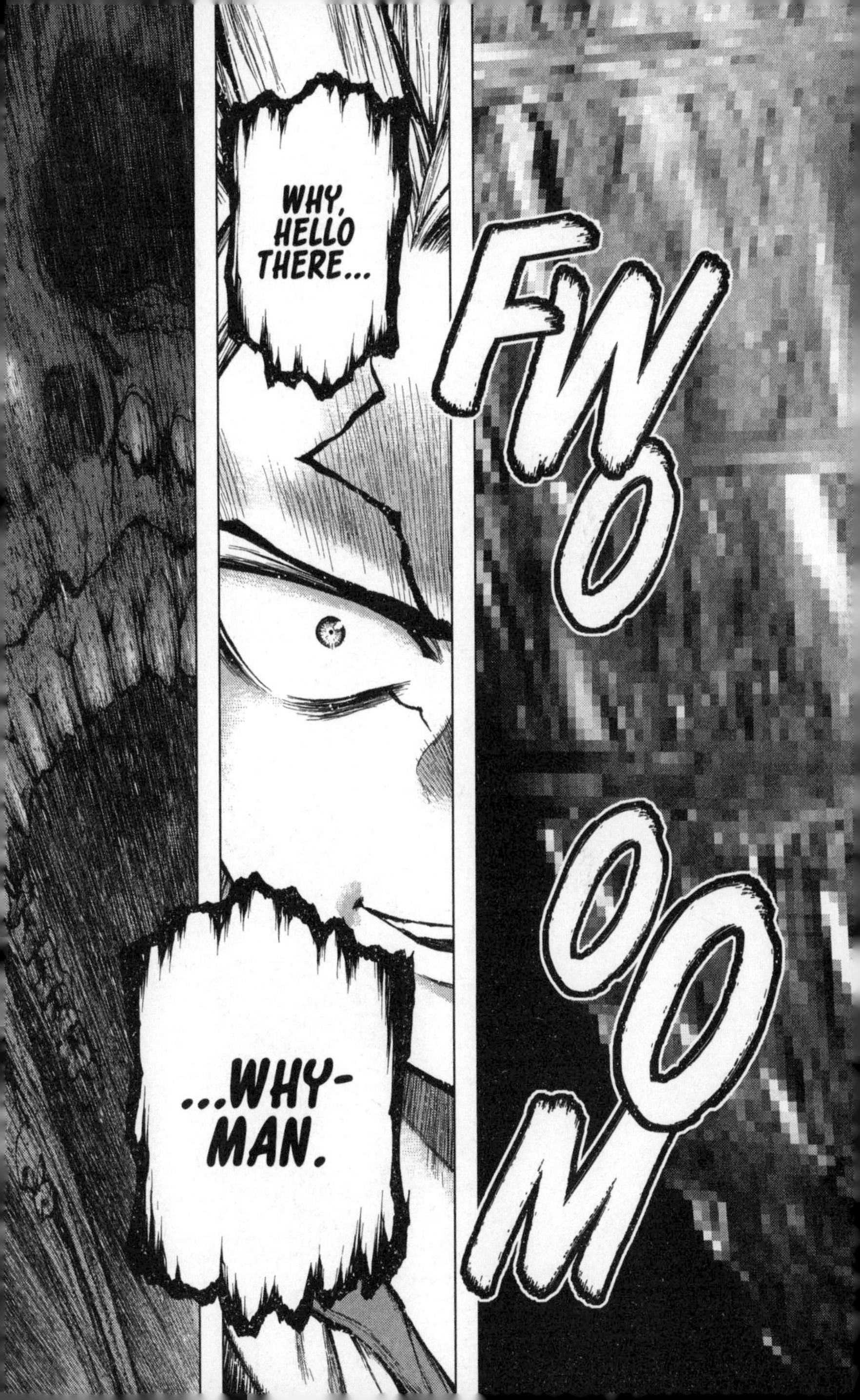
WHY, HELLO THERE...
FWOOOM
...WHY-MAN.

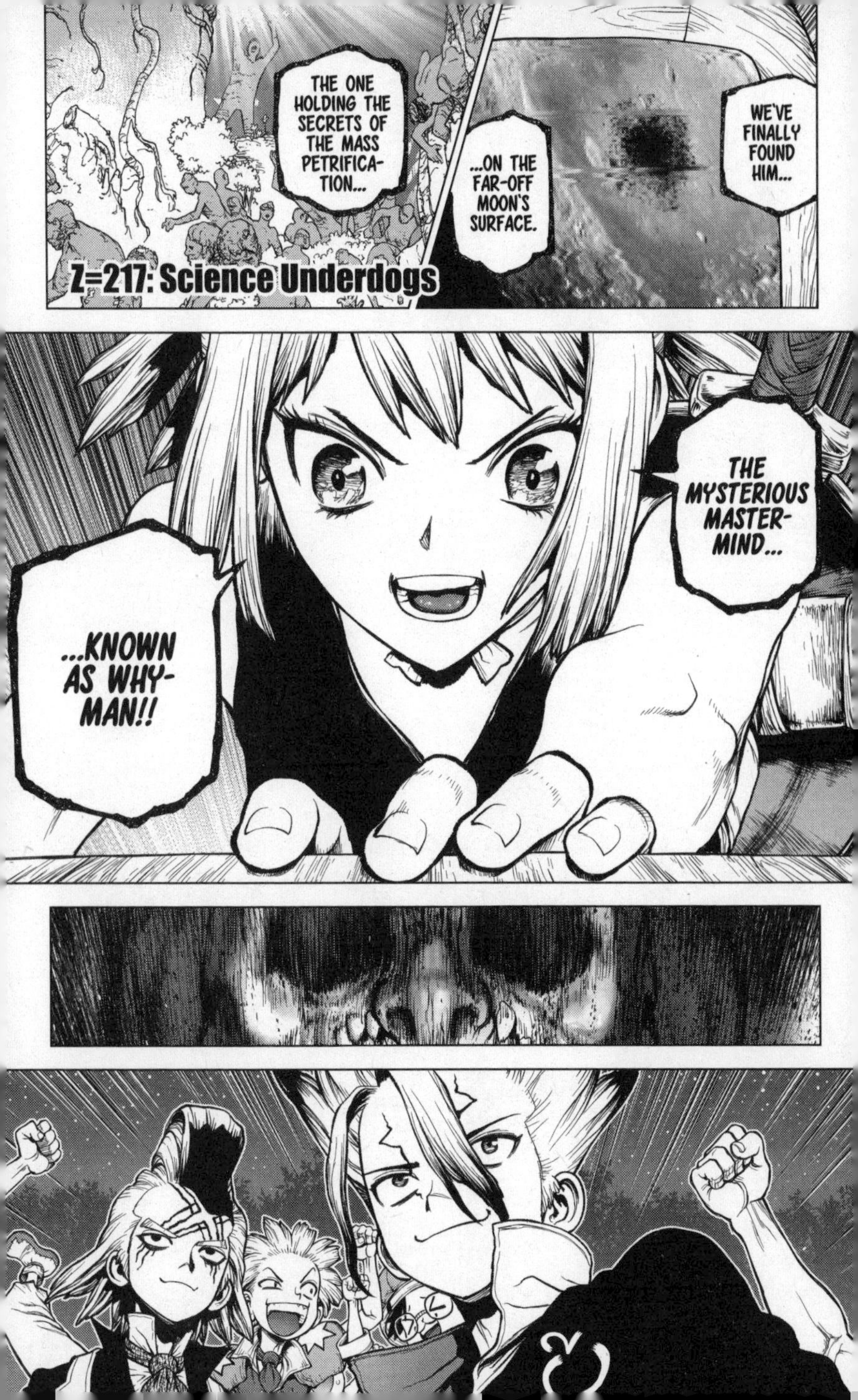
WE'VE FINALLY FOUND HIM...
...ON THE FAR-OFF MOON'S SURFACE.
THE ONE HOLDING THE SECRETS OF THE MASS PETRIFICA-TION...
Z=217: Science Underdogs
THE MYSTERIOUS MASTER-MIND...
...KNOWN AS WHY-MAN!!

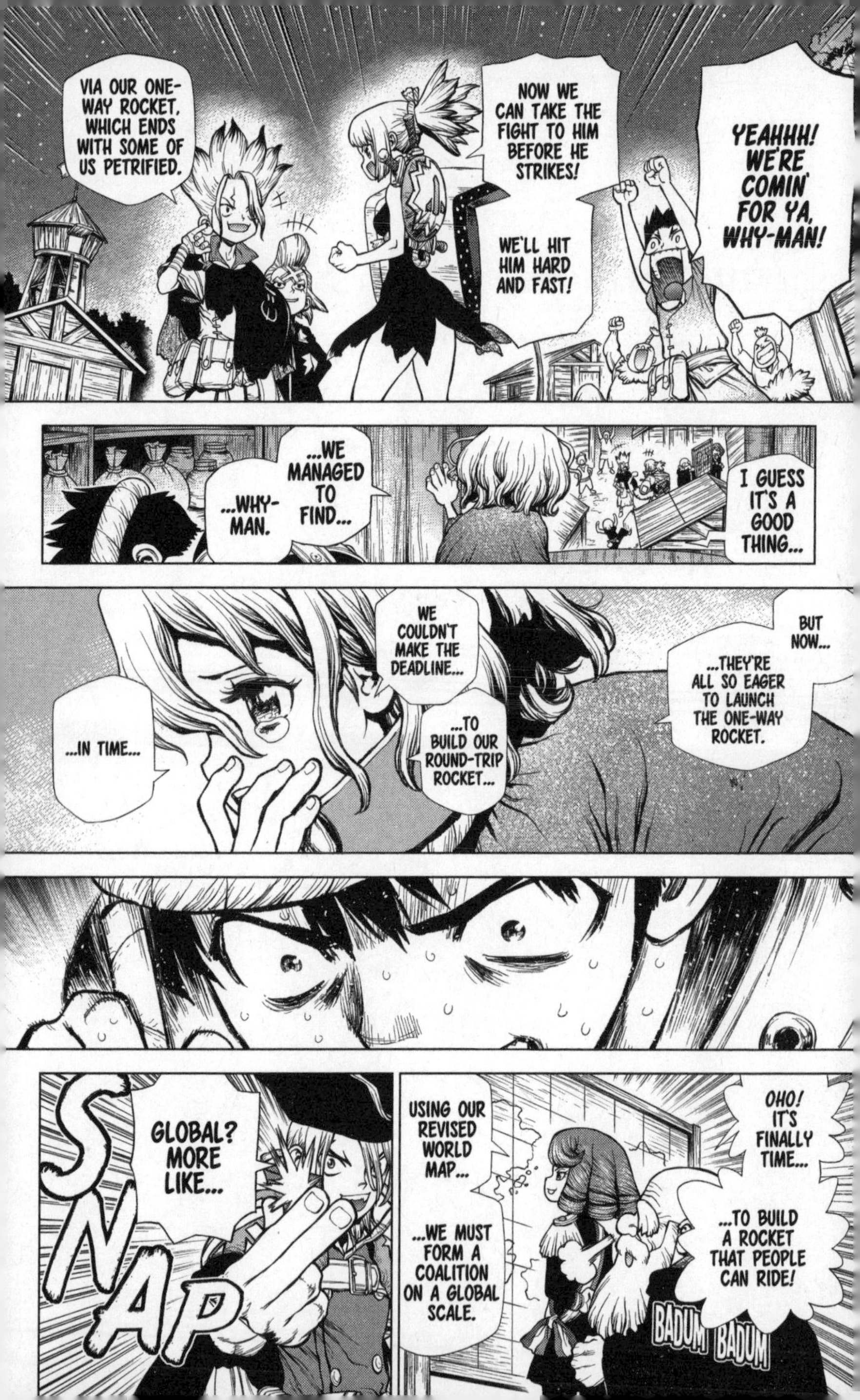
YEAHHH! WE'RE COMIN' FOR YA, WHY-MAN!
NOW WE CAN TAKE THE FIGHT TO HIM BEFORE HE STRIKES!
WE'LL HIT HIM HARD AND FAST!
VIA OUR ONE-WAY ROCKET, WHICH ENDS WITH SOME OF US PETRIFIED.
I GUESS IT'S A GOOD THING...
...WE MANAGED TO FIND...
...WHY-MAN.
BUT NOW...
...THEY'RE ALL SO EAGER TO LAUNCH THE ONE-WAY ROCKET.
WE COULDN'T MAKE THE DEADLINE...
...TO BUILD OUR ROUND-TRIP ROCKET...
...IN TIME...
OHO! IT'S FINALLY TIME...
...TO BUILD A ROCKET THAT PEOPLE CAN RIDE!
BADUM BADUM
USING OUR REVISED WORLD MAP...
...WE MUST FORM A COALITION ON A GLOBAL SCALE.
GLOBAL? MORE LIKE...
SNAP

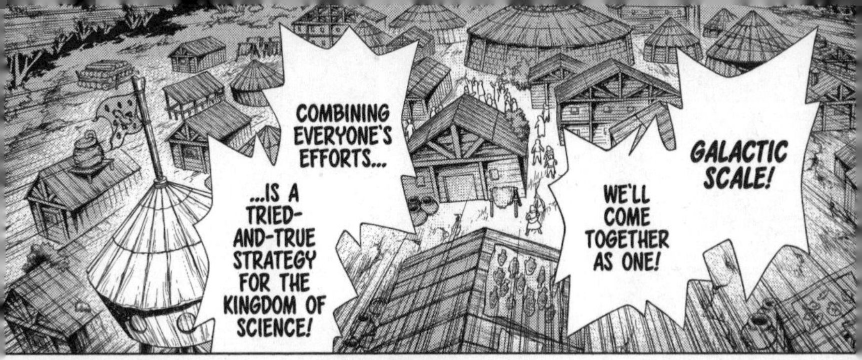
GALACTIC SCALE!
WE'LL COME TOGETHER AS ONE!
COMBINING EVERYONE'S EFFORTS...
...IS A TRIED-AND-TRUE STRATEGY FOR THE KINGDOM OF SCIENCE!
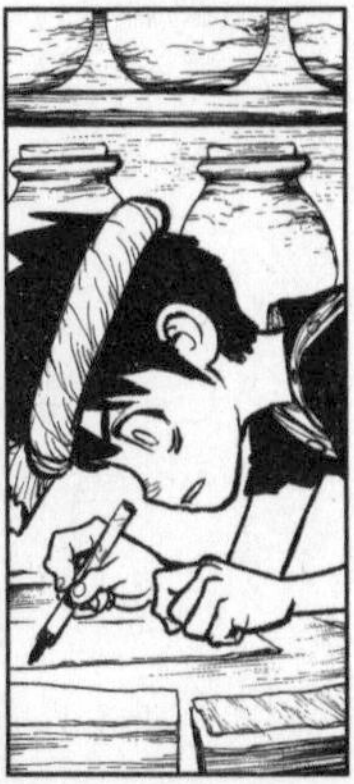
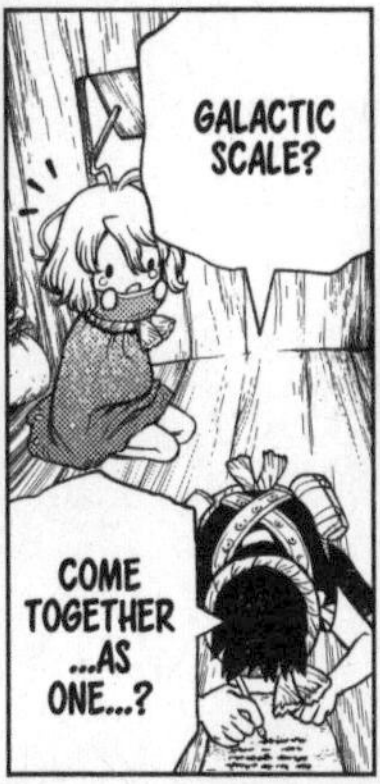
GALACTIC SCALE?
COME TOGETHER ...AS ONE...?
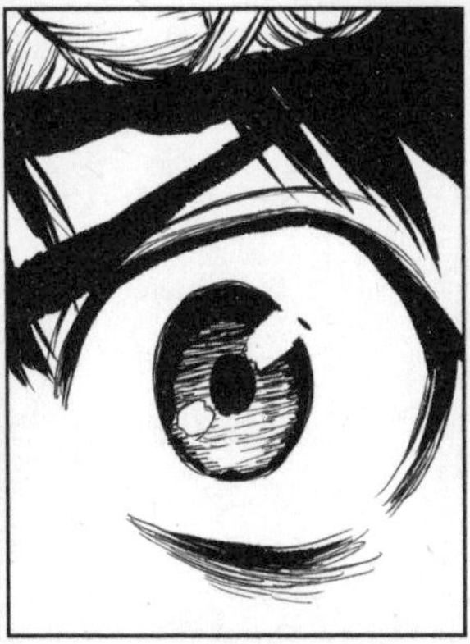
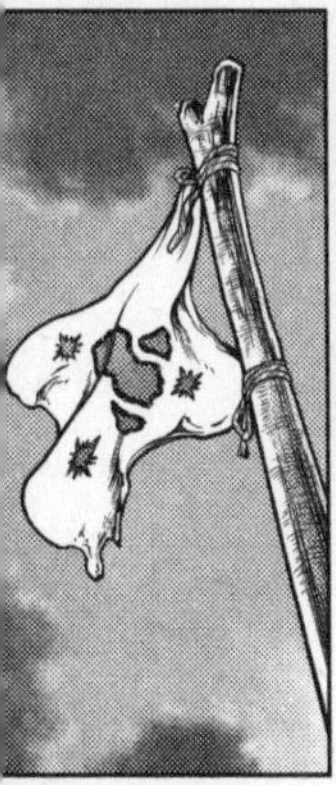
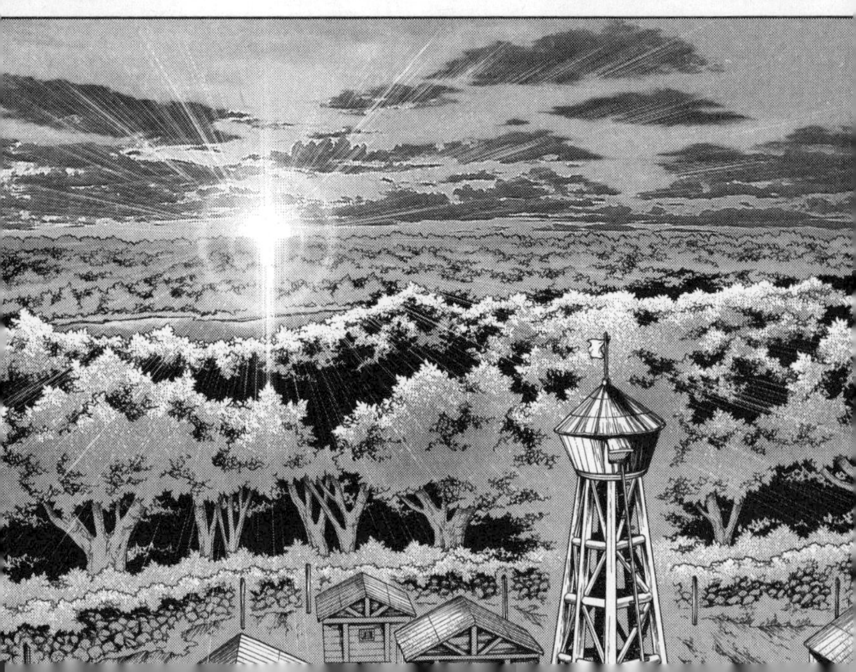

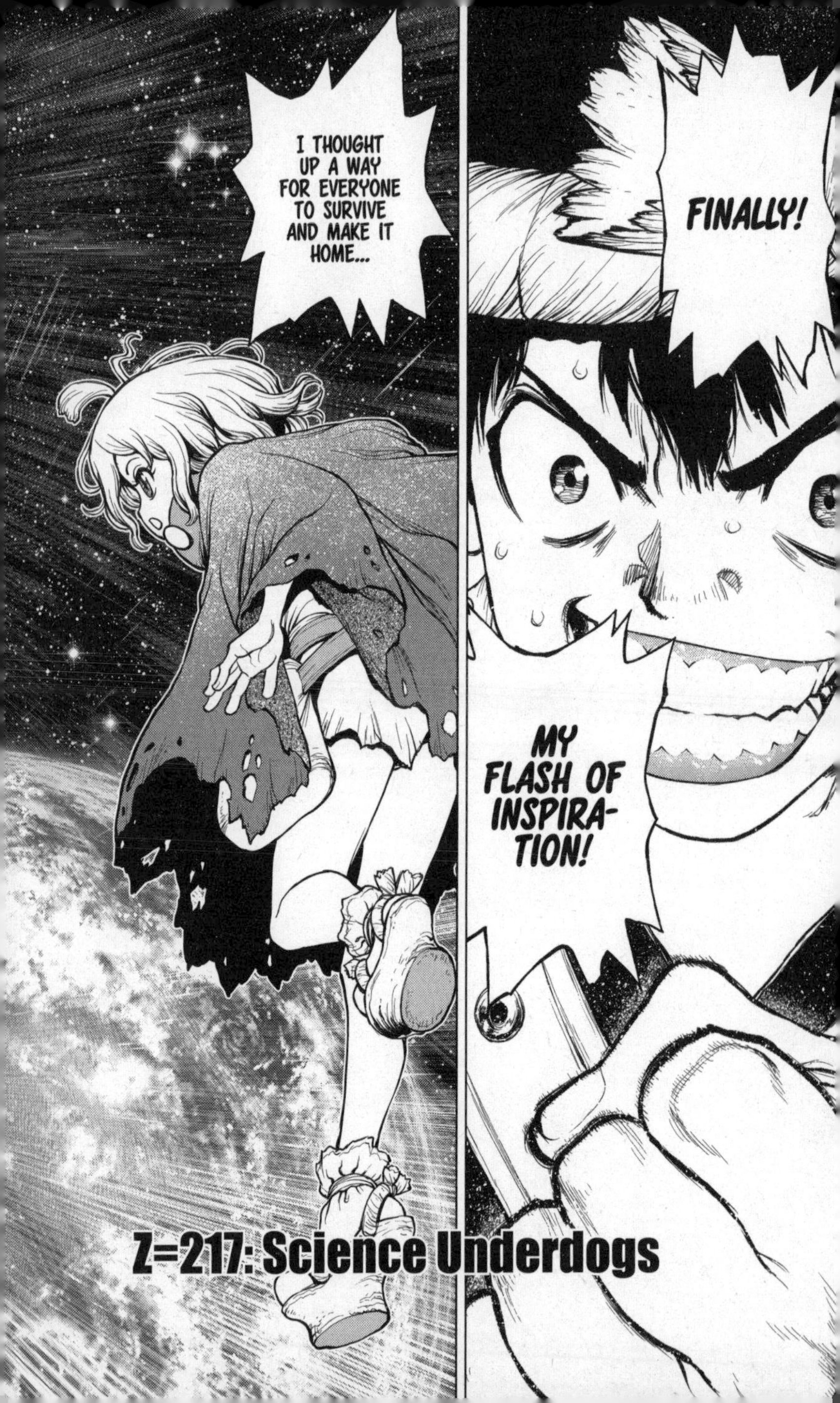
FINALLY!
MY FLASH OF INSPIRATION!
I THOUGHT UP A WAY FOR EVERYONE TO SURVIVE AND MAKE IT HOME...
Z=217: Science Underdogs

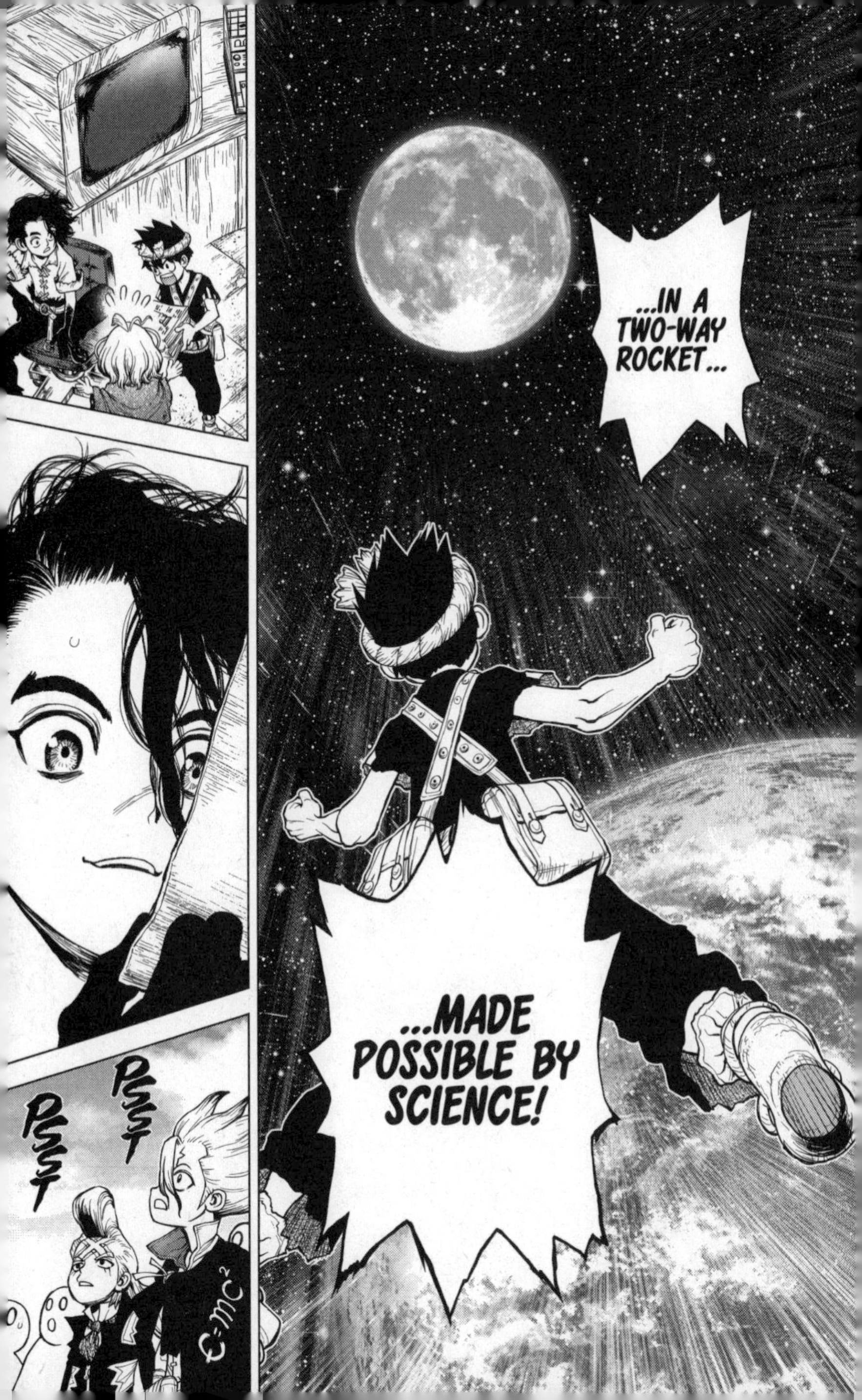
...IN A TWO-WAY ROCKET...
...MADE POSSIBLE BY SCIENCE!
PSST
PSST
E=MC²

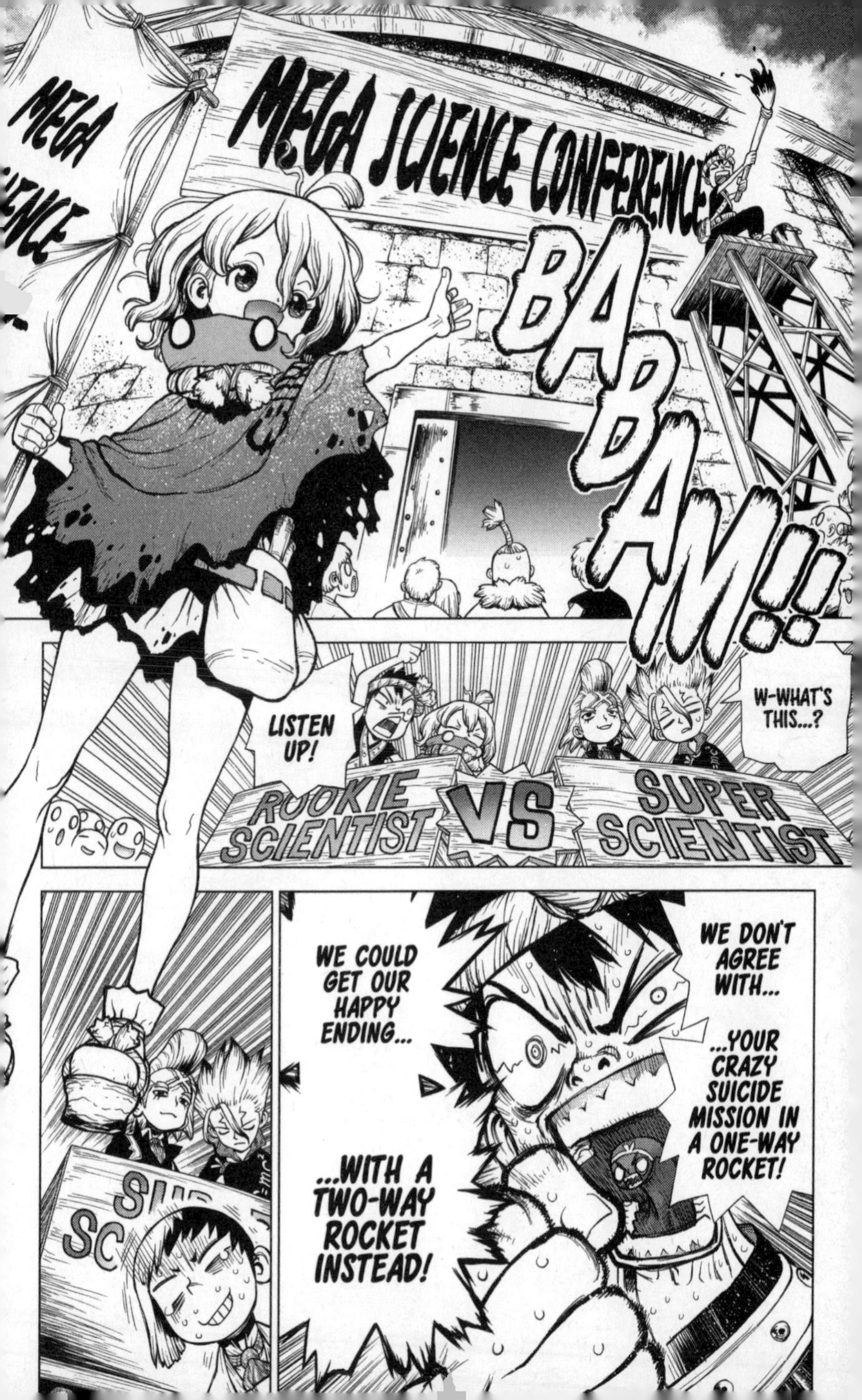
MEGA SCIENCE CONFERENCE
MEGA
BA BAM!!
W-WHAT'S THIS...?
LISTEN UP!
ROOKIE SCIENTIST
VS
SUPER SCIENTIST
WE DON'T AGREE WITH...
...YOUR CRAZY SUICIDE MISSION IN A ONE-WAY ROCKET!
WE COULD GET OUR HAPPY ENDING...
...WITH A TWO-WAY ROCKET INSTEAD!

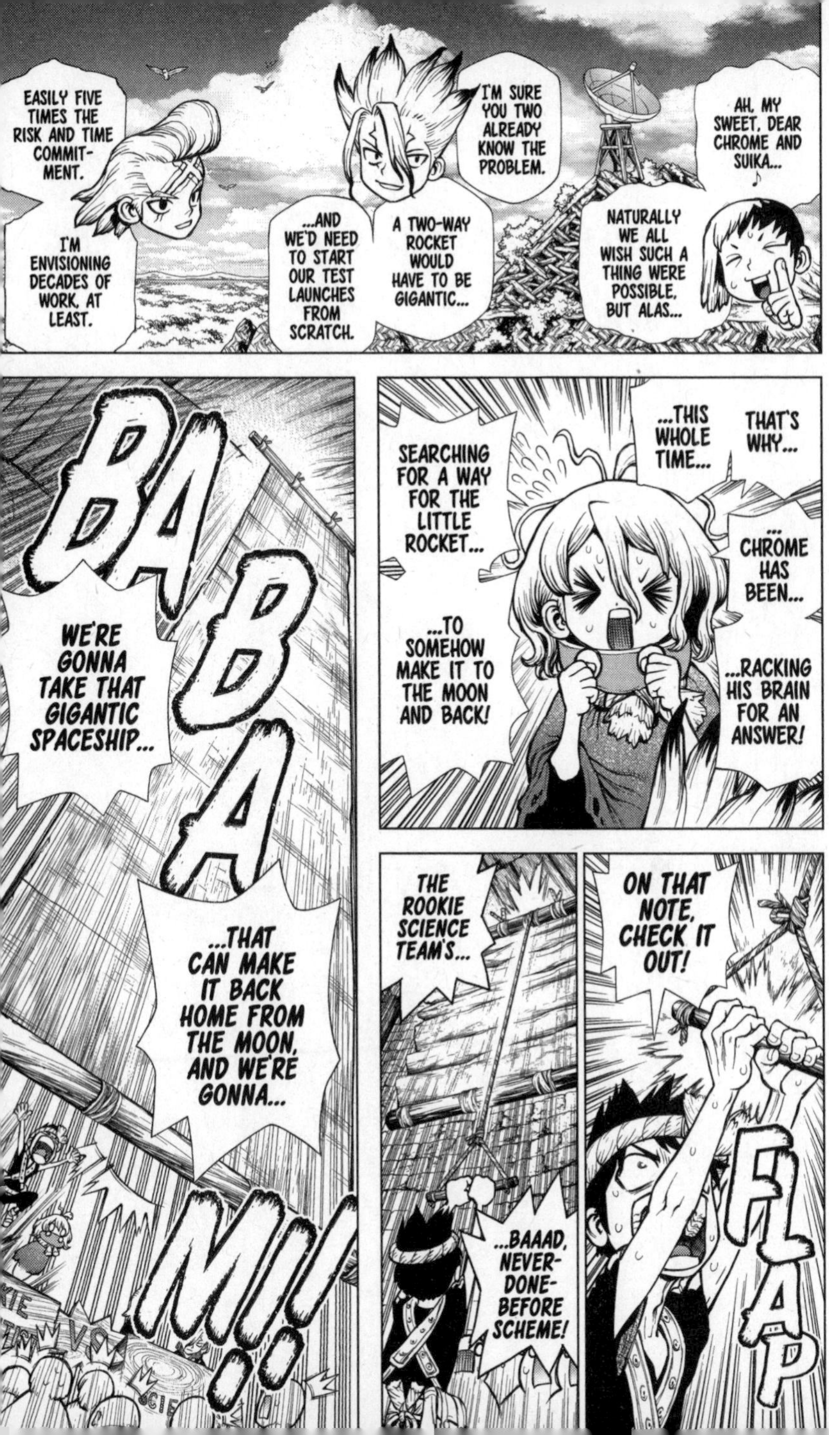
AH, MY SWEET, DEAR CHROME AND SUIKA... ♪
NATURALLY WE ALL WISH SUCH A THING WERE POSSIBLE, BUT ALAS...
I'M SURE YOU TWO ALREADY KNOW THE PROBLEM.
A TWO-WAY ROCKET WOULD HAVE TO BE GIGANTIC...
...AND WE'D NEED TO START OUR TEST LAUNCHES FROM SCRATCH.
EASILY FIVE TIMES THE RISK AND TIME COMMITMENT.
I'M ENVISIONING DECADES OF WORK, AT LEAST.
THAT'S WHY...
...THIS WHOLE TIME...
...CHROME HAS BEEN...
...RACKING HIS BRAIN FOR AN ANSWER!
SEARCHING FOR A WAY FOR THE LITTLE ROCKET...
...TO SOMEHOW MAKE IT TO THE MOON AND BACK!
ON THAT NOTE, CHECK IT OUT!
FLAP
THE ROOKIE SCIENCE TEAM'S...
...BAAAD, NEVER-DONE-BEFORE SCHEME!
WE'RE GONNA TAKE THAT GIGANTIC SPACESHIP...
BABA
...THAT CAN MAKE IT BACK HOME FROM THE MOON, AND WE'RE GONNA...
M!!

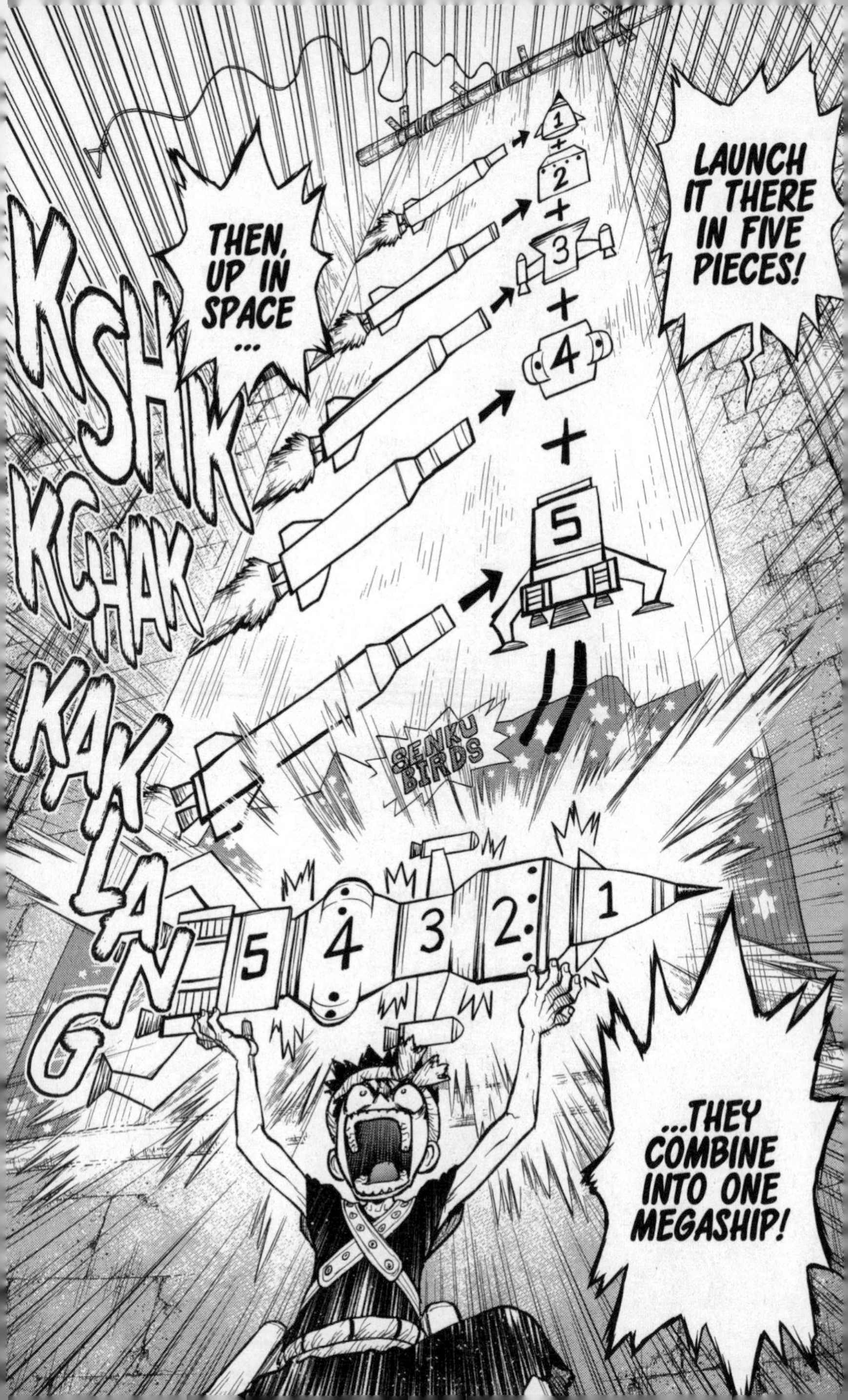
LAUNCH IT THERE IN FIVE PIECES!
THEN, UP IN SPACE...
KSHIK
KCHAK
KAKLANG
1
2
3
4
5
SENKU BIRDS
5 4 3 2 1
...THEY COMBINE INTO ONE MEGASHIP!

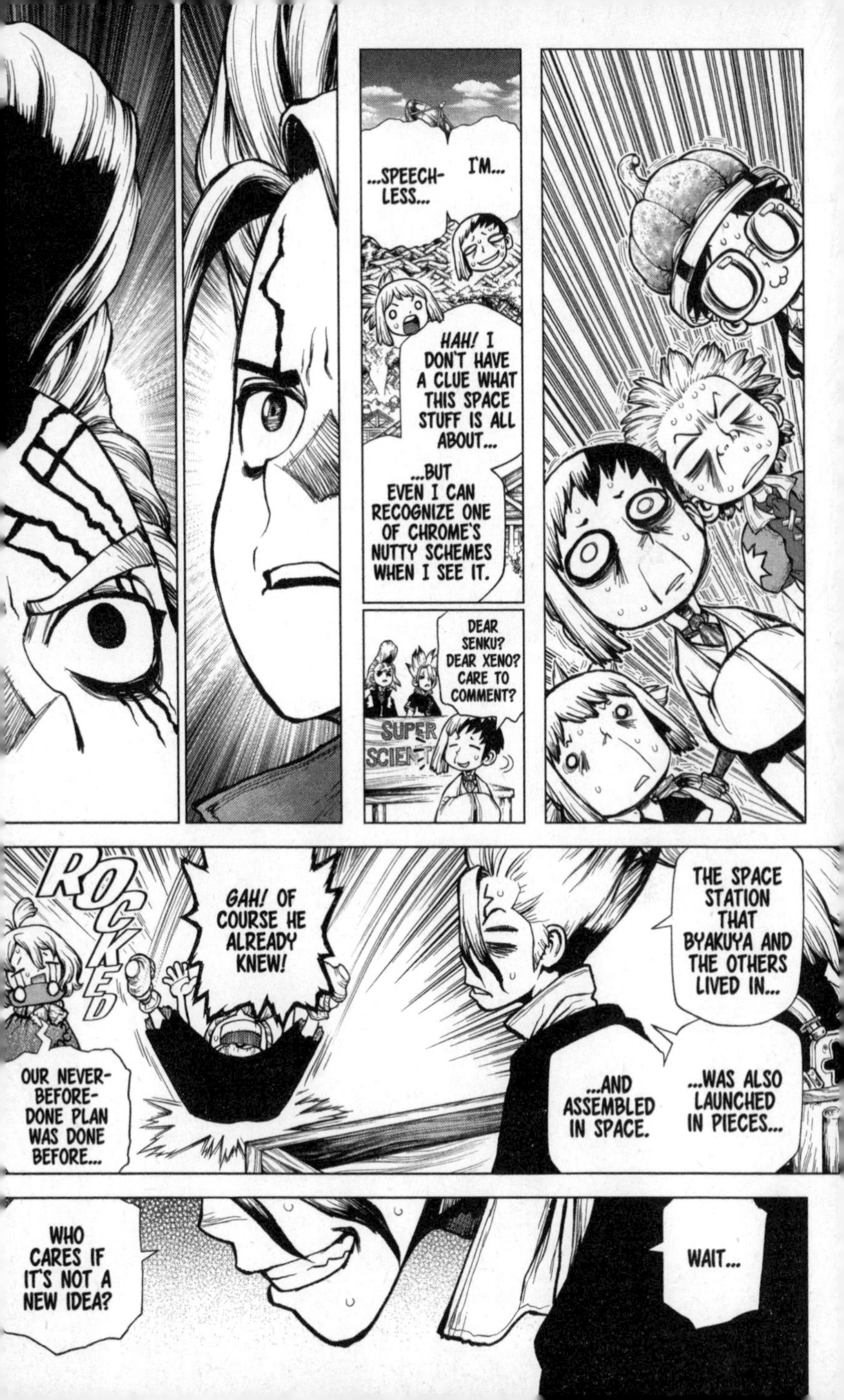
I'M...
...SPEECHLESS...
HAH! I DON'T HAVE A CLUE WHAT THIS SPACE STUFF IS ALL ABOUT...
...BUT EVEN I CAN RECOGNIZE ONE OF CHROME'S NUTTY SCHEMES WHEN I SEE IT.
DEAR SENKU? DEAR XENO? CARE TO COMMENT?
SUPER SCIENT
THE SPACE STATION THAT BYAKUYA AND THE OTHERS LIVED IN...
...WAS ALSO LAUNCHED IN PIECES...
...AND ASSEMBLED IN SPACE.
GAH! OF COURSE HE ALREADY KNEW!
ROCKED
OUR NEVER-BEFORE-DONE PLAN WAS DONE BEFORE...
WAIT...
WHO CARES IF IT'S NOT A NEW IDEA?

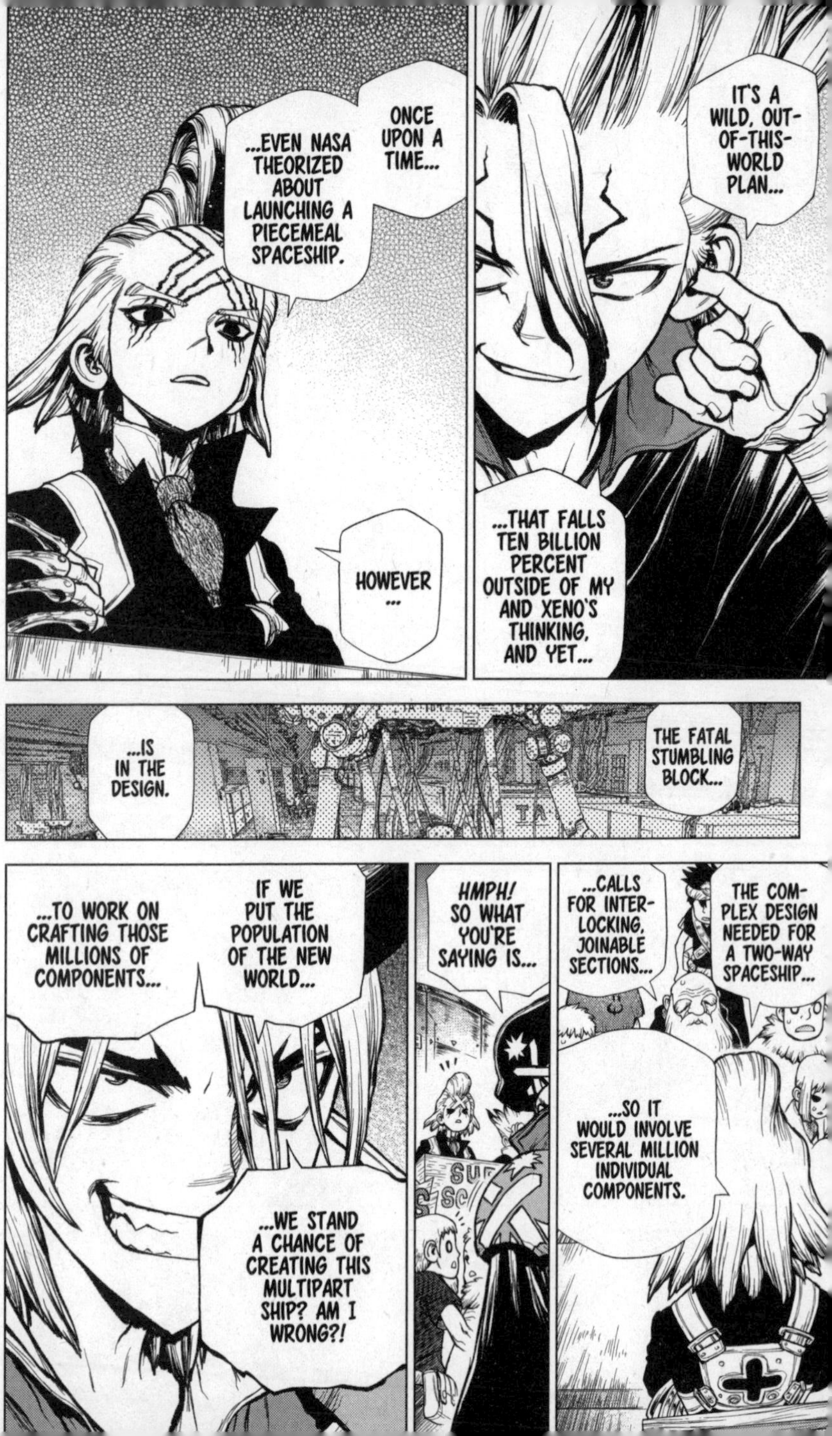
IT'S A WILD, OUT-OF-THIS-WORLD PLAN...
...THAT FALLS TEN BILLION PERCENT OUTSIDE OF MY AND XENO'S THINKING, AND YET...
ONCE UPON A TIME...
...EVEN NASA THEORIZED ABOUT LAUNCHING A PIECEMEAL SPACESHIP.
HOWEVER...
THE FATAL STUMBLING BLOCK...
...IS IN THE DESIGN.
THE COMPLEX DESIGN NEEDED FOR A TWO-WAY SPACESHIP...
...CALLS FOR INTERLOCKING, JOINABLE SECTIONS...
...SO IT WOULD INVOLVE SEVERAL MILLION INDIVIDUAL COMPONENTS.
HMPH! SO WHAT YOU'RE SAYING IS...
IF WE PUT THE POPULATION OF THE NEW WORLD...
...TO WORK ON CRAFTING THOSE MILLIONS OF COMPONENTS...
...WE STAND A CHANCE OF CREATING THIS MULTIPART SHIP? AM I WRONG?!

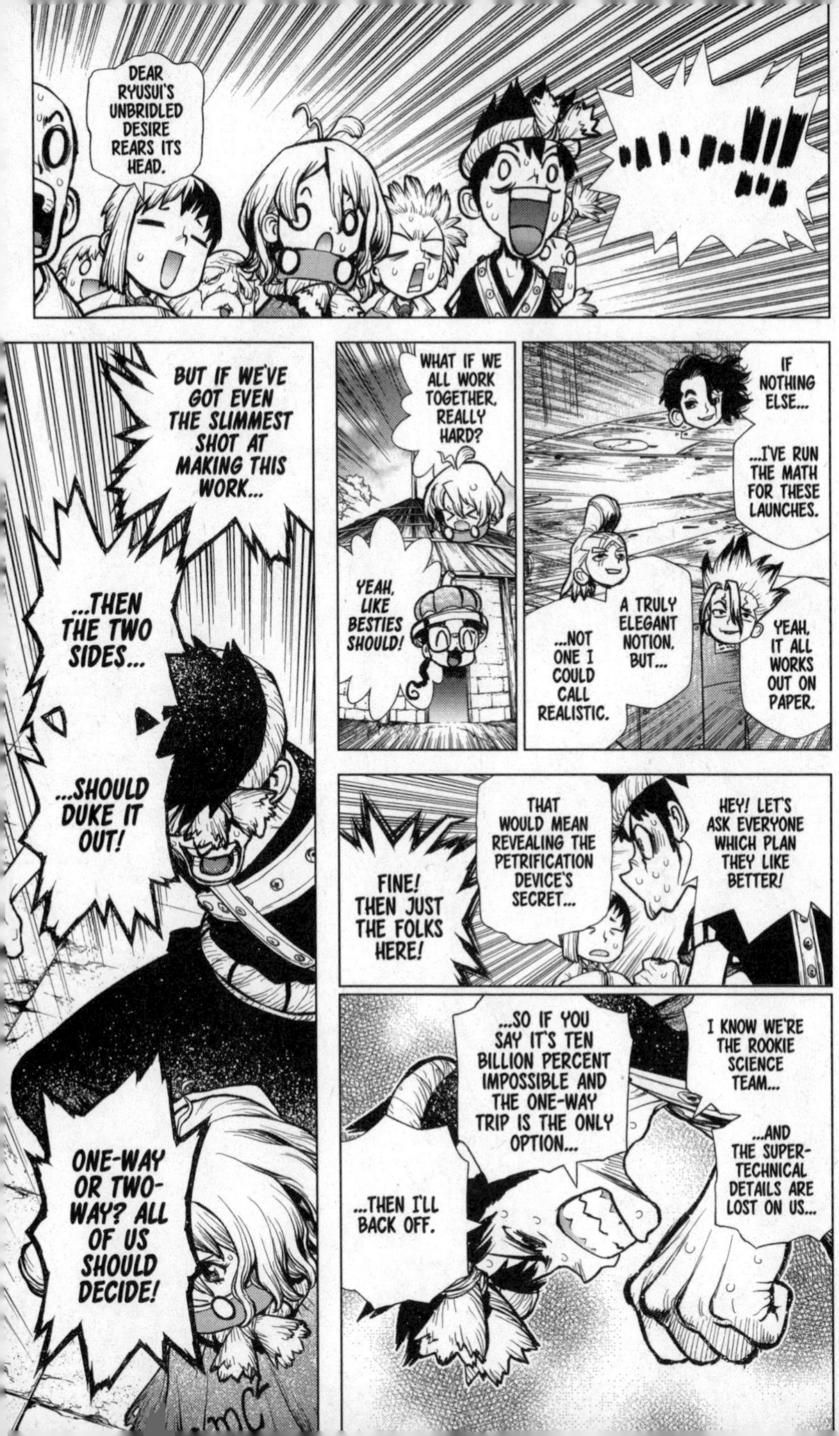
...!!
DEAR RYUSUI'S UNBRIDLED DESIRE REARS ITS HEAD.
IF NOTHING ELSE...
...I'VE RUN THE MATH FOR THESE LAUNCHES.
YEAH, IT ALL WORKS OUT ON PAPER.
A TRULY ELEGANT NOTION, BUT...
...NOT ONE I COULD CALL REALISTIC.
WHAT IF WE ALL WORK TOGETHER, REALLY HARD?
YEAH, LIKE BESTIES SHOULD!
HEY! LET'S ASK EVERYONE WHICH PLAN THEY LIKE BETTER!
THAT WOULD MEAN REVEALING THE PETRIFICATION DEVICE'S SECRET...
FINE! THEN JUST THE FOLKS HERE!
I KNOW WE'RE THE ROOKIE SCIENCE TEAM...
...AND THE SUPER-TECHNICAL DETAILS ARE LOST ON US...
...SO IF YOU SAY IT'S TEN BILLION PERCENT IMPOSSIBLE AND THE ONE-WAY TRIP IS THE ONLY OPTION...
...THEN I'LL BACK OFF.
BUT IF WE'VE GOT EVEN THE SLIMMEST SHOT AT MAKING THIS WORK...
...THEN THE TWO SIDES...
...SHOULD DUKE IT OUT!
ONE-WAY OR TWO-WAY? ALL OF US SHOULD DECIDE!

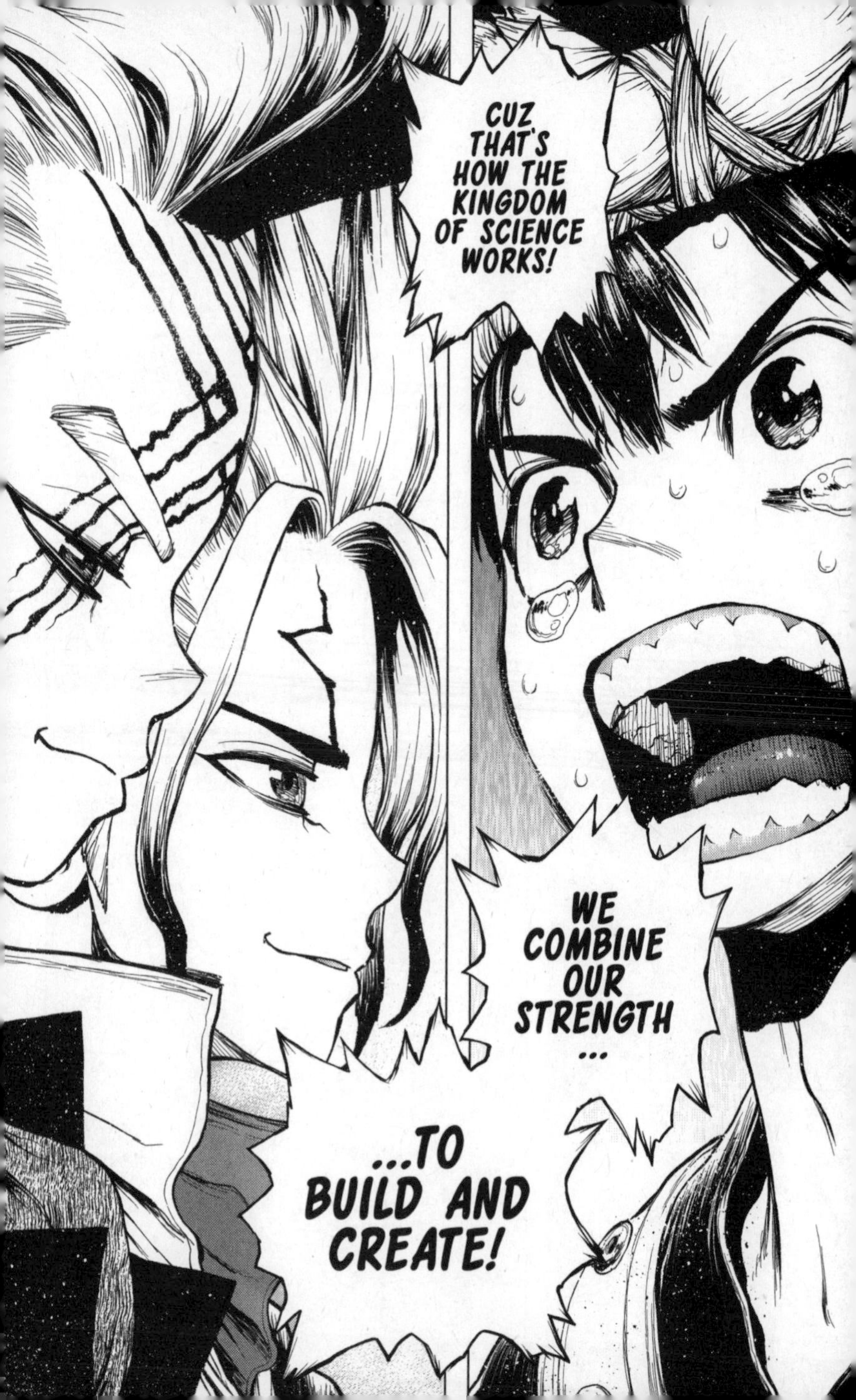
CUZ THAT'S HOW THE KINGDOM OF SCIENCE WORKS!
WE COMBINE OUR STRENGTH...
...TO BUILD AND CREATE!

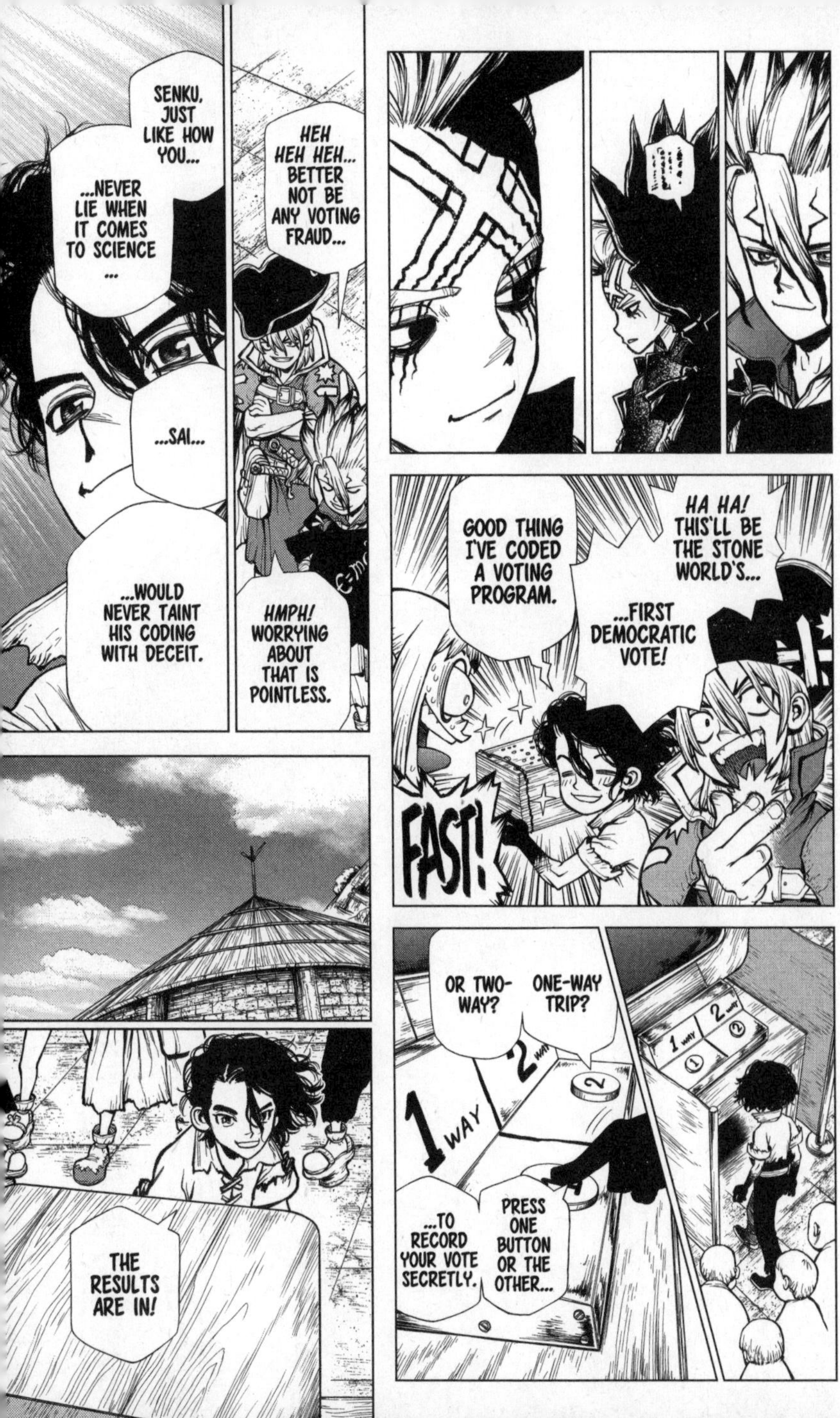
HA HA! THIS'LL BE THE STONE WORLD'S...
...FIRST DEMOCRATIC VOTE!
GOOD THING I'VE CODED A VOTING PROGRAM.
FAST!
ONE-WAY TRIP?
OR TWO-WAY?
2 WAY
1 WAY
PRESS ONE BUTTON OR THE OTHER...
...TO RECORD YOUR VOTE SECRETLY.
HEH HEH HEH... BETTER NOT BE ANY VOTING FRAUD...
HMPH! WORRYING ABOUT THAT IS POINTLESS.
SENKU, JUST LIKE HOW YOU...
...NEVER LIE WHEN IT COMES TO SCIENCE...
...SAI...
...WOULD NEVER TAINT HIS CODING WITH DECEIT.
THE RESULTS ARE IN!

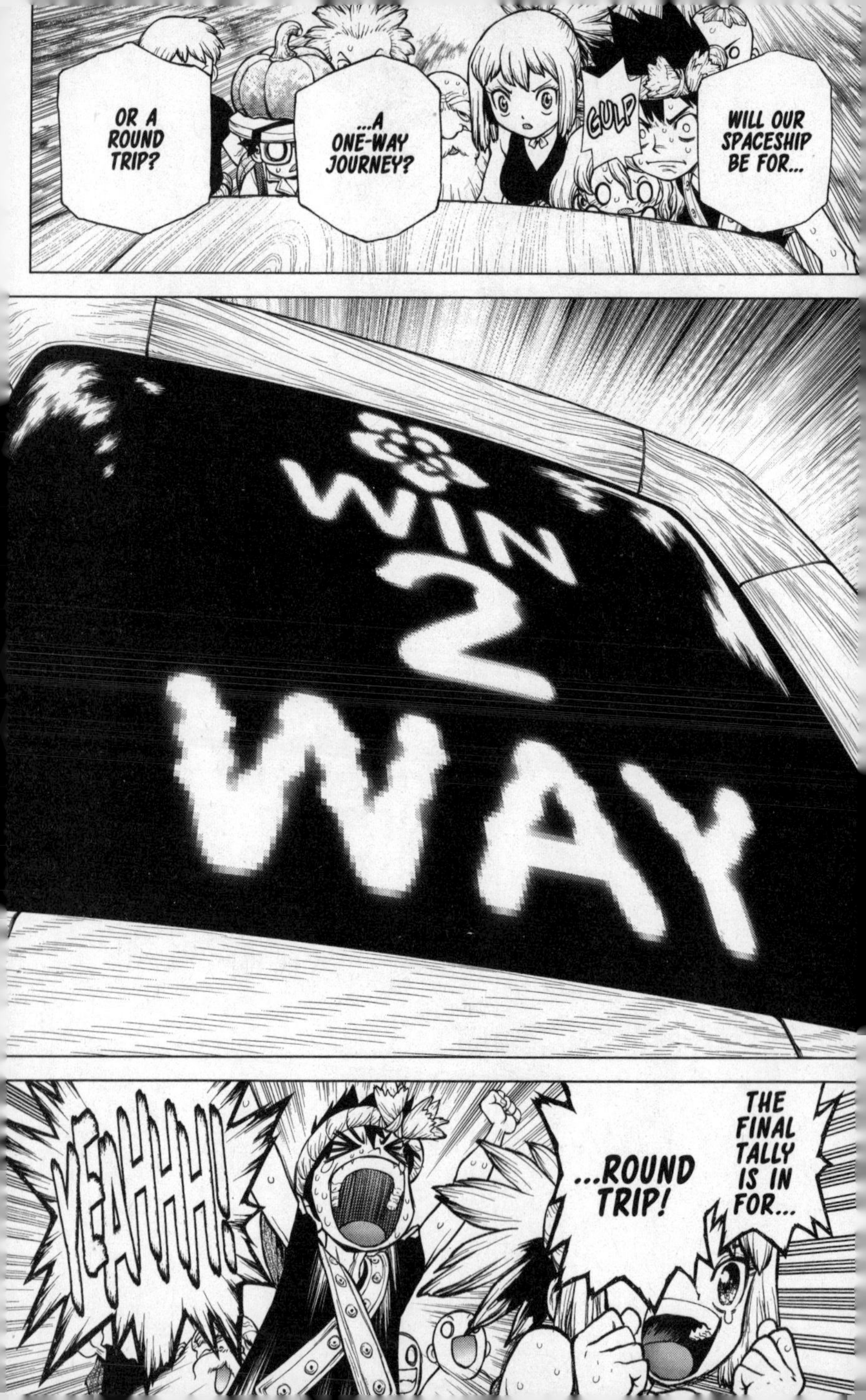
WILL OUR SPACESHIP BE FOR...
GULP
...A ONE-WAY JOURNEY?
OR A ROUND TRIP?
WIN 2 WAY
THE FINAL TALLY IS IN FOR...
...ROUND TRIP!
YEAHHH!

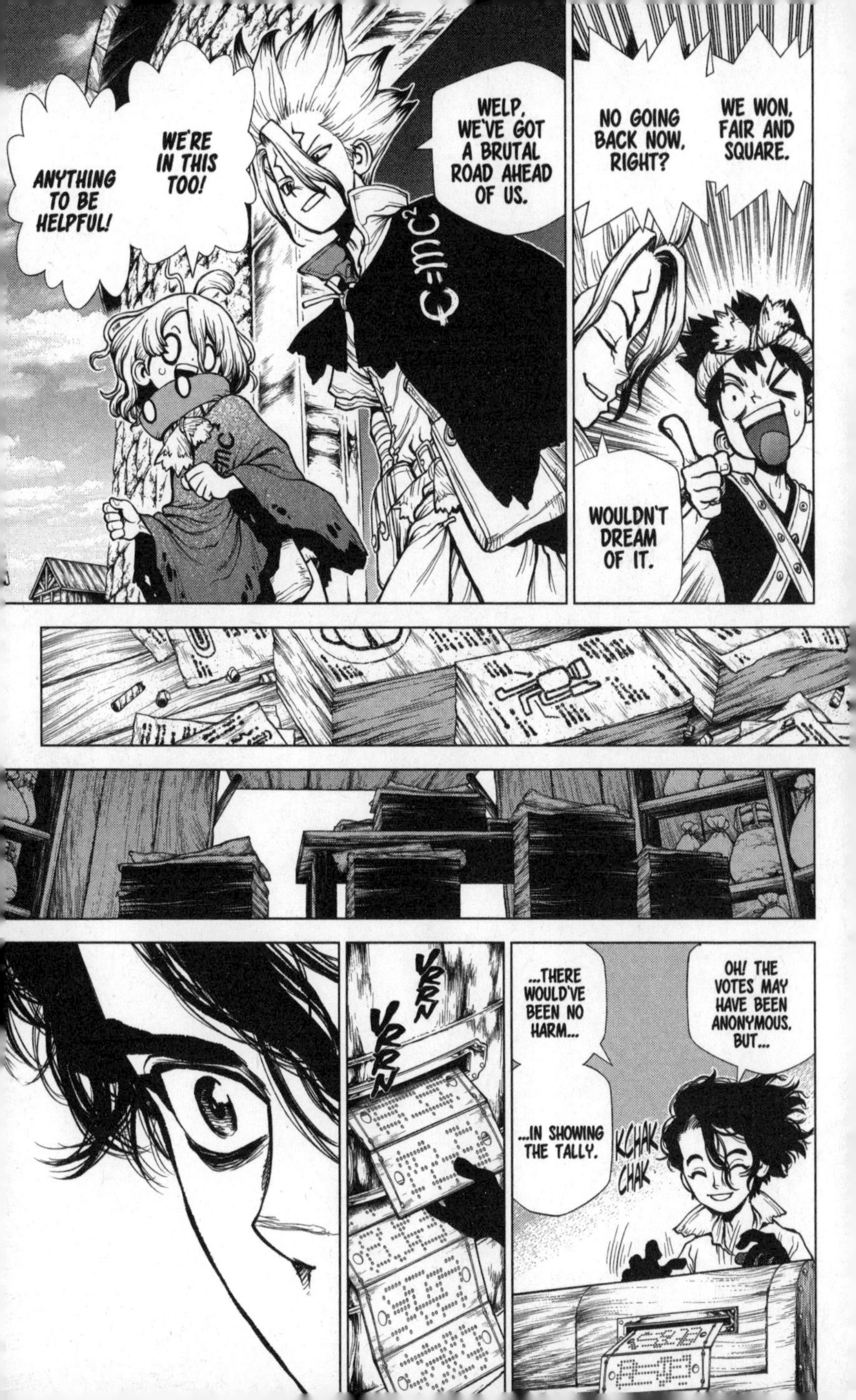
WE WON, FAIR AND SQUARE.
NO GOING BACK NOW, RIGHT?
WOULDN'T DREAM OF IT.
WELP, WE'VE GOT A BRUTAL ROAD AHEAD OF US.
WE'RE IN THIS TOO!
ANYTHING TO BE HELPFUL!
OH! THE VOTES MAY HAVE BEEN ANONYMOUS, BUT...
...THERE WOULD'VE BEEN NO HARM...
...IN SHOWING THE TALLY.
KCHAK CHAK
VRRN
VRRN

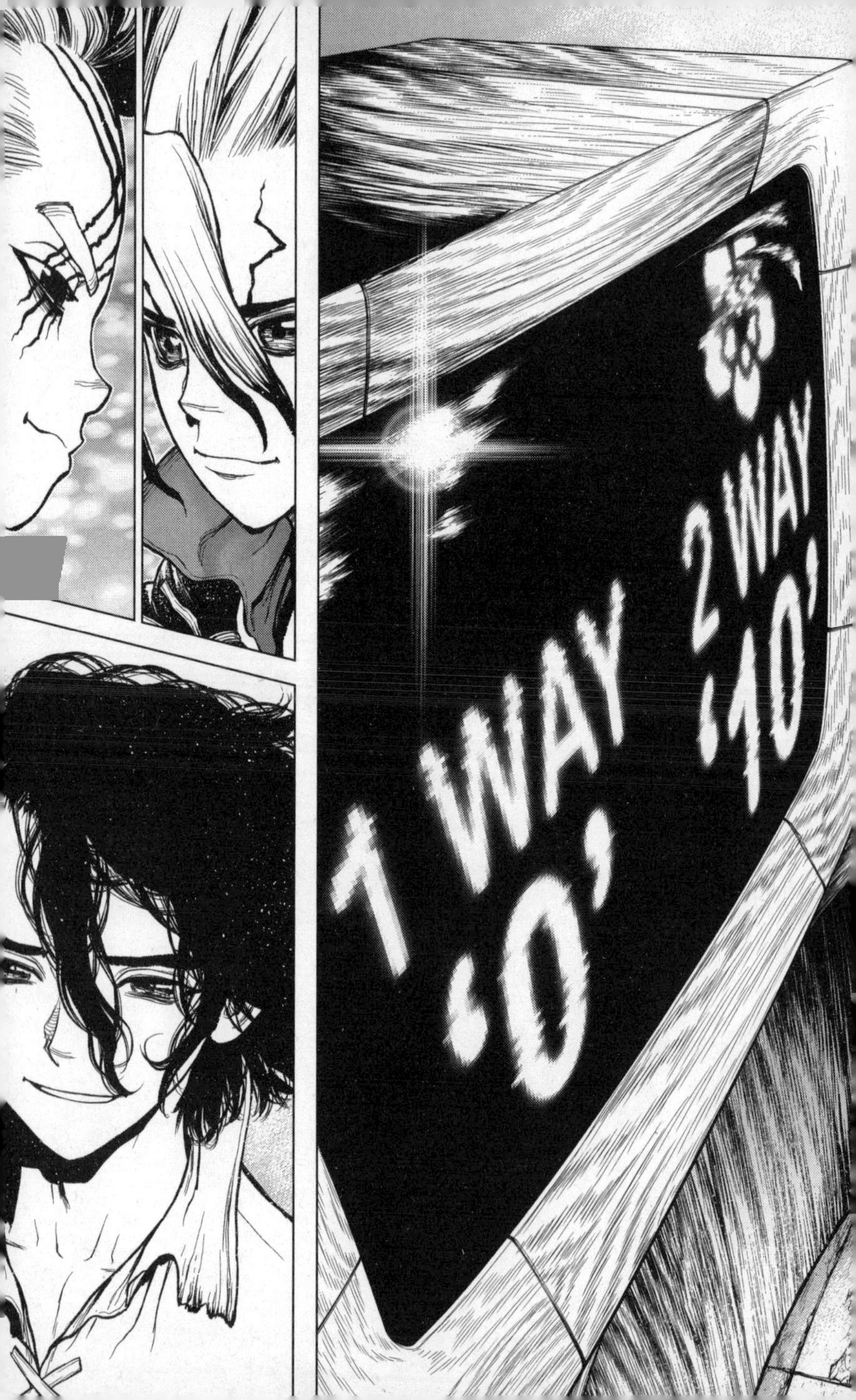
1 WAY :0'
2 WAY :10'

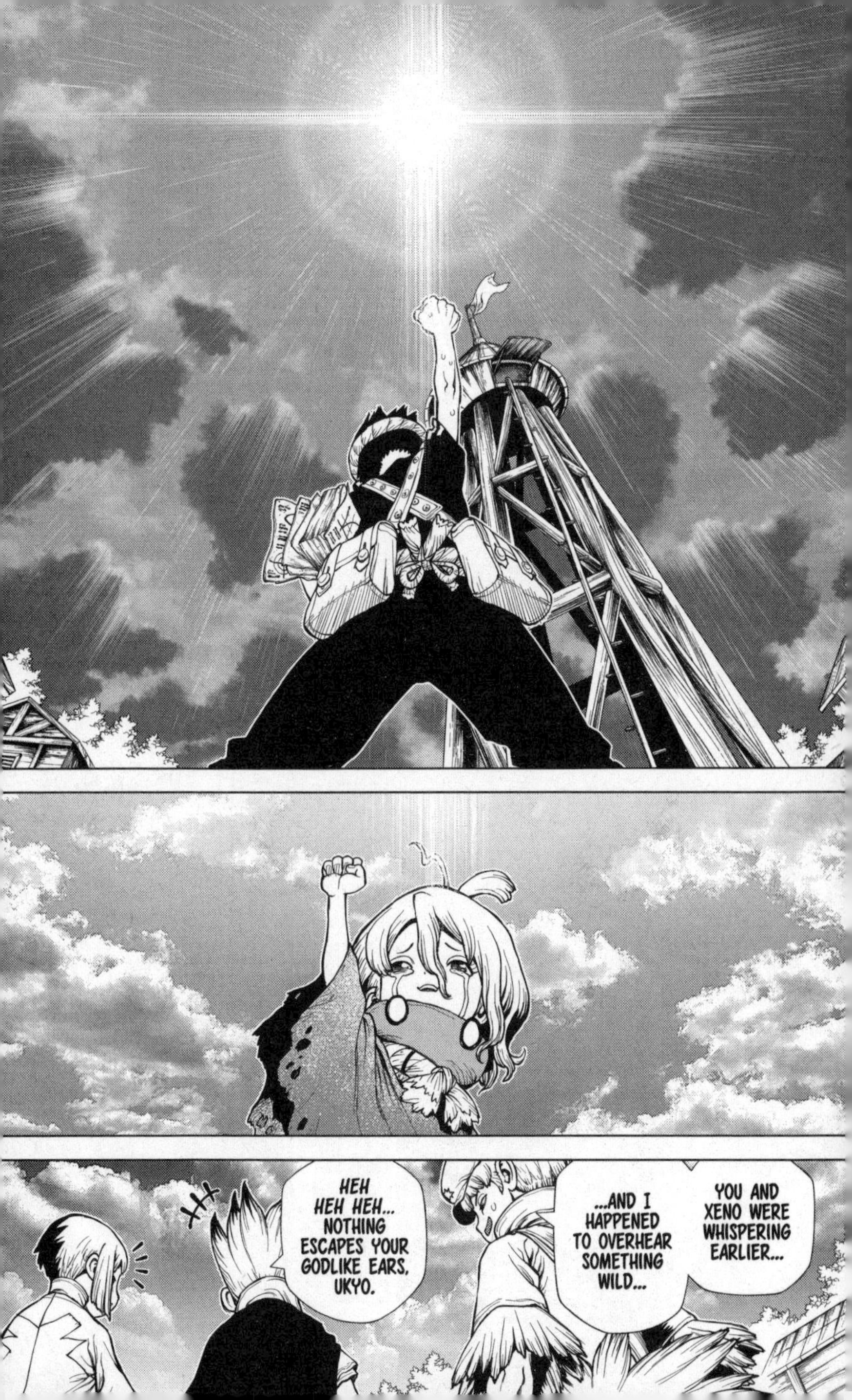
YOU AND XENO WERE WHISPERING EARLIER...
...AND I HAPPENED TO OVERHEAR SOMETHING WILD...
HEH HEH HEH... NOTHING ESCAPES YOUR GODLIKE EARS, UKYO.

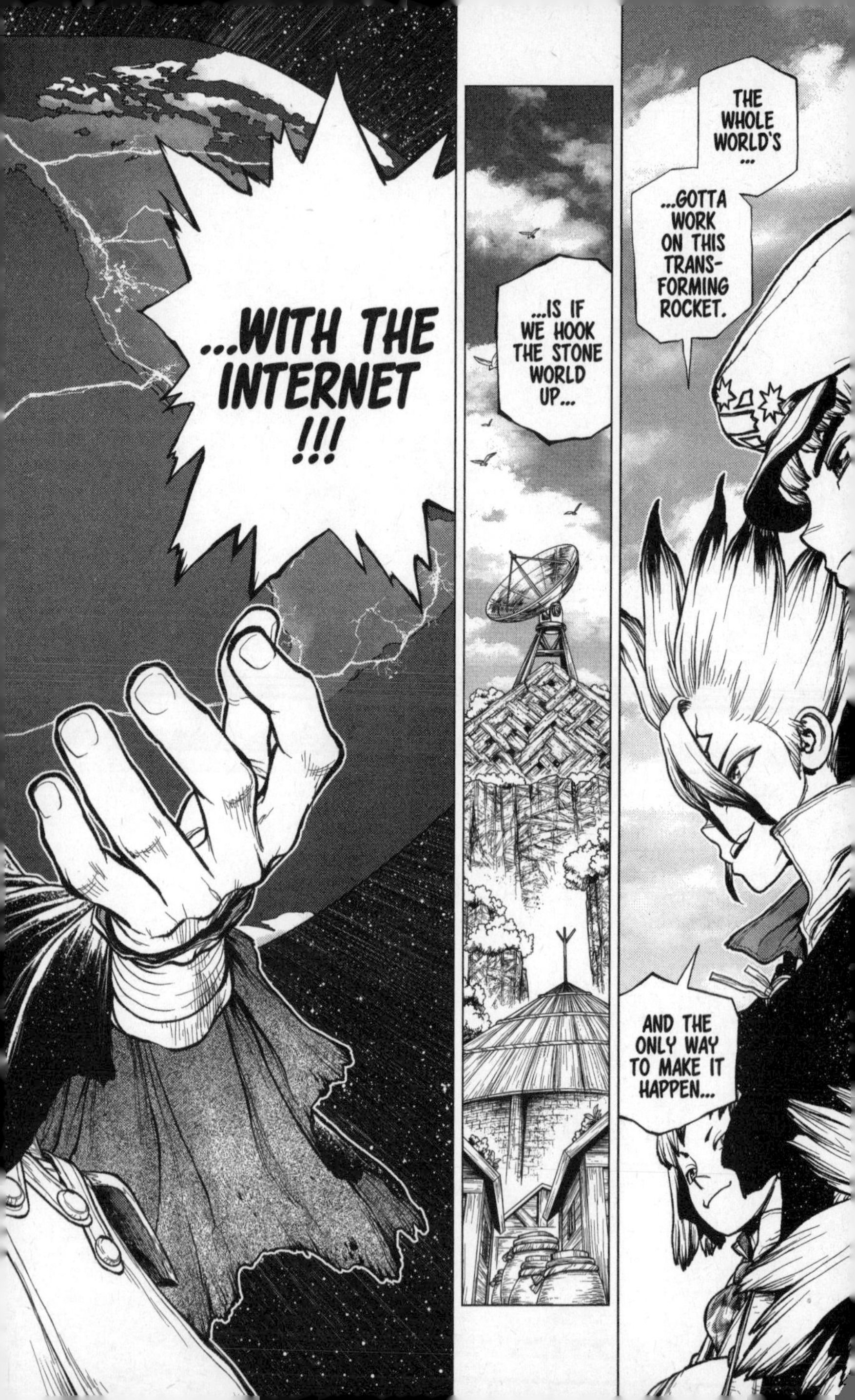
THE WHOLE WORLD'S...
...GOTTA WORK ON THIS TRANS-FORMING ROCKET.
AND THE ONLY WAY TO MAKE IT HAPPEN...
...IS IF WE HOOK THE STONE WORLD UP...
...WITH THE INTERNET!!!

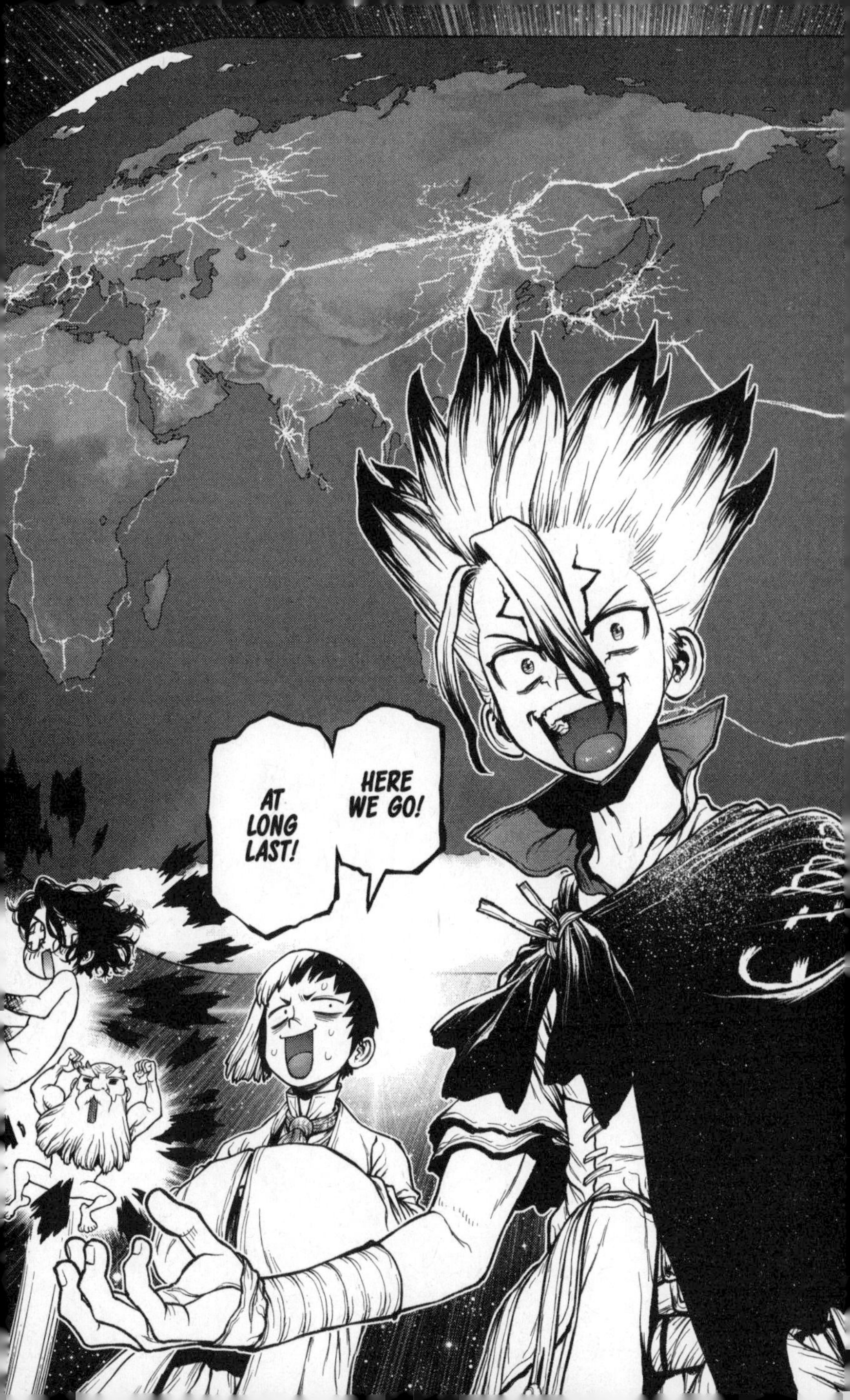
HERE WE GO!
AT LONG LAST!

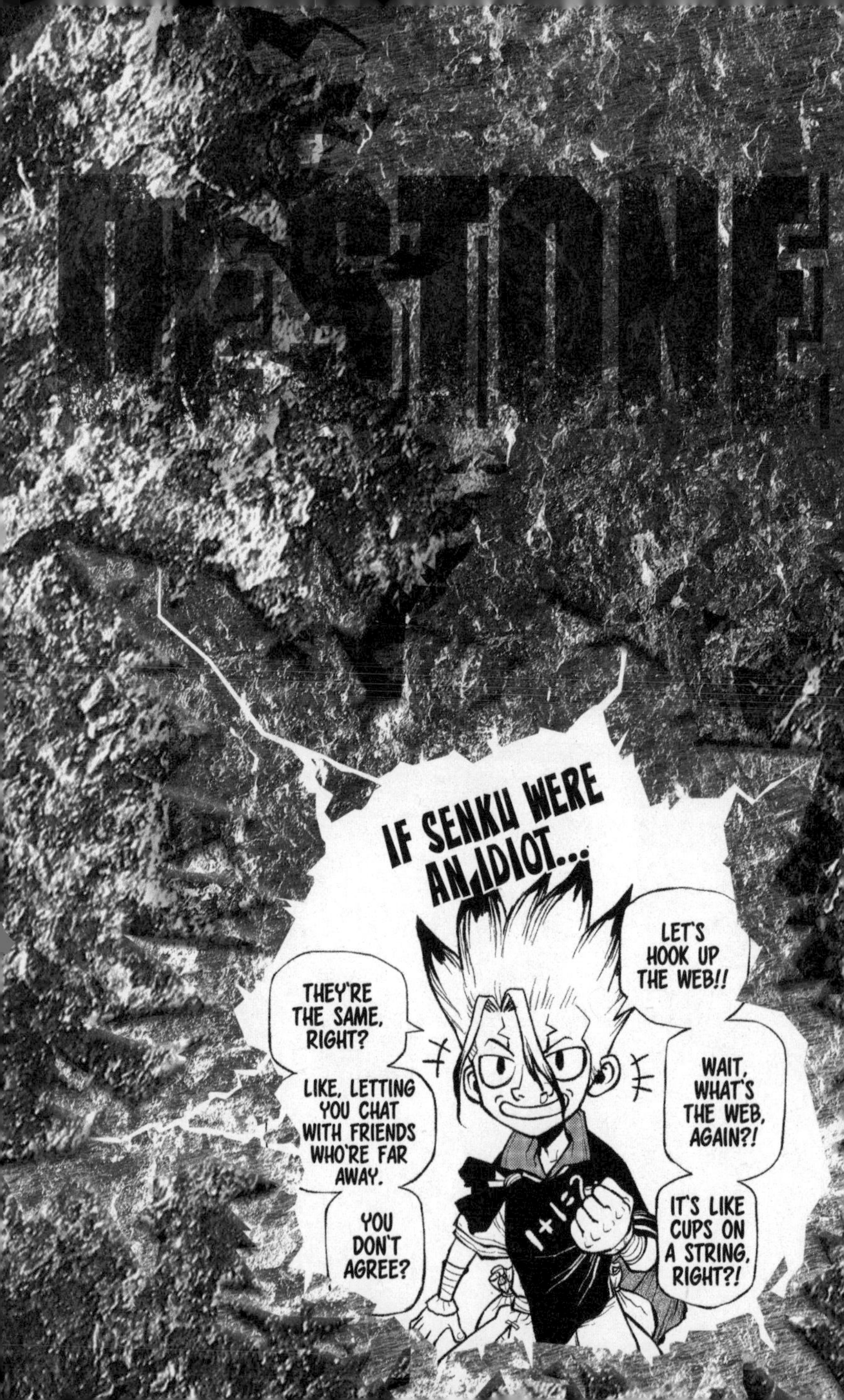
Dr.STONE
IF SENKU WERE AN IDIOT...
LET'S HOOK UP THE WEB!!
WAIT, WHAT'S THE WEB, AGAIN?!
IT'S LIKE CUPS ON A STRING, RIGHT?!
THEY'RE THE SAME, RIGHT?
LIKE, LETTING YOU CHAT WITH FRIENDS WHO'RE FAR AWAY.
YOU DON'T AGREE?
1+1=?

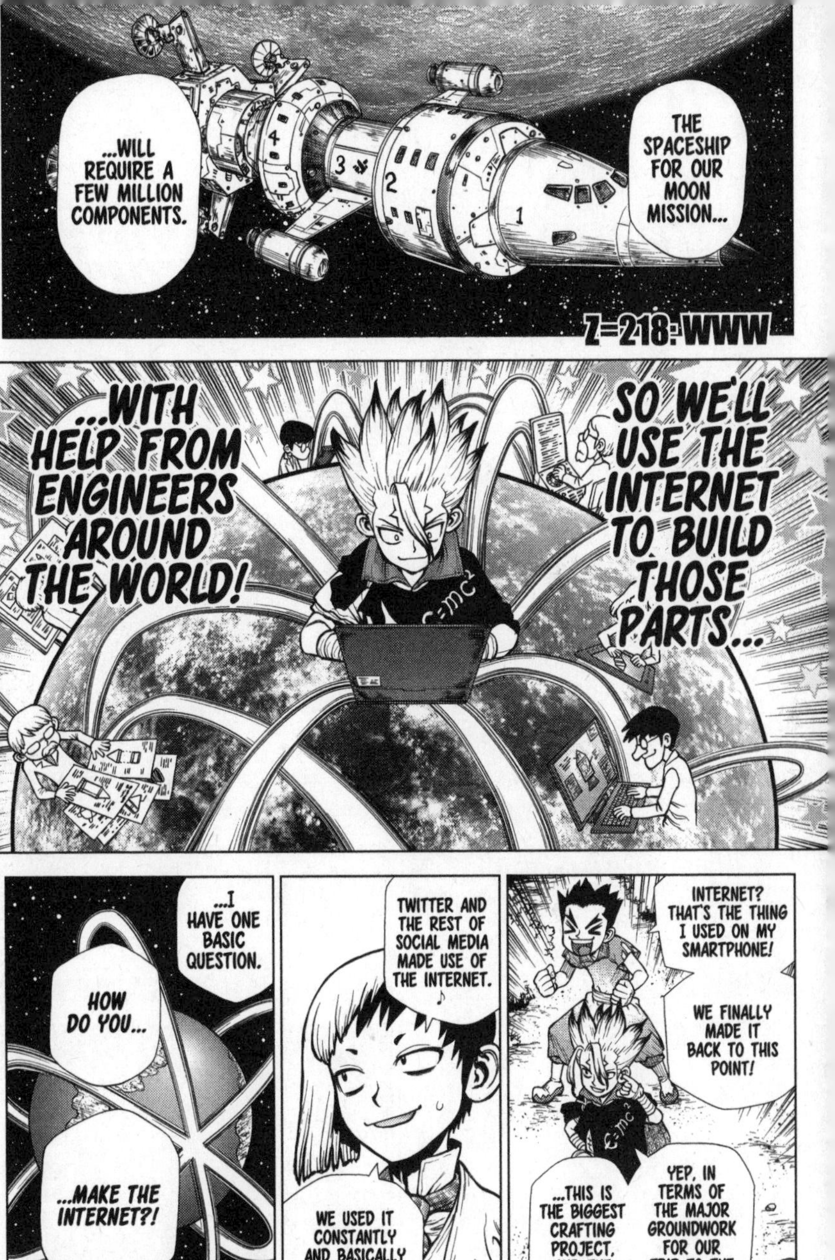
THE SPACESHIP FOR OUR MOON MISSION...
...WILL REQUIRE A FEW MILLION COMPONENTS.
Z=218: WWW
SO WE'LL USE THE INTERNET TO BUILD THOSE PARTS...
...WITH HELP FROM ENGINEERS AROUND THE WORLD!
INTERNET? THAT'S THE THING I USED ON MY SMARTPHONE!
WE FINALLY MADE IT BACK TO THIS POINT!
YEP, IN TERMS OF THE MAJOR GROUNDWORK FOR OUR TRIP TO THE MOON...
...THIS IS THE BIGGEST CRAFTING PROJECT, AND THE FINAL ONE.
TWITTER AND THE REST OF SOCIAL MEDIA MADE USE OF THE INTERNET. ♪
WE USED IT CONSTANTLY AND BASICALLY TOOK IT FOR GRANTED, BUT...
...I HAVE ONE BASIC QUESTION.
HOW DO YOU...
...MAKE THE INTERNET?!

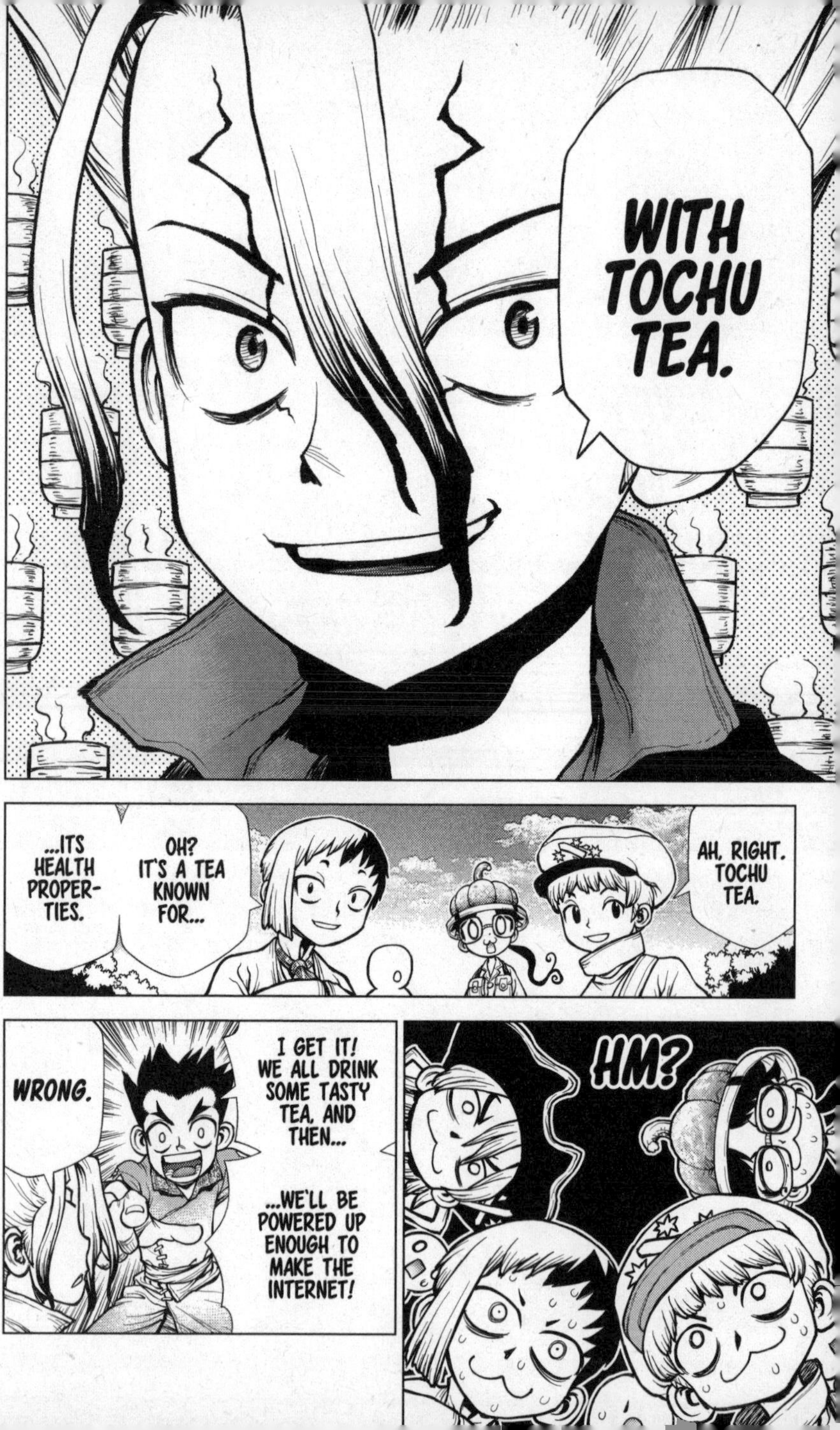
WITH TOCHU TEA.
AH, RIGHT. TOCHU TEA.
OH? IT'S A TEA KNOWN FOR...
...ITS HEALTH PROPERTIES.
HM?
I GET IT! WE ALL DRINK SOME TASTY TEA, AND THEN...
...WE'LL BE POWERED UP ENOUGH TO MAKE THE INTERNET!
WRONG.

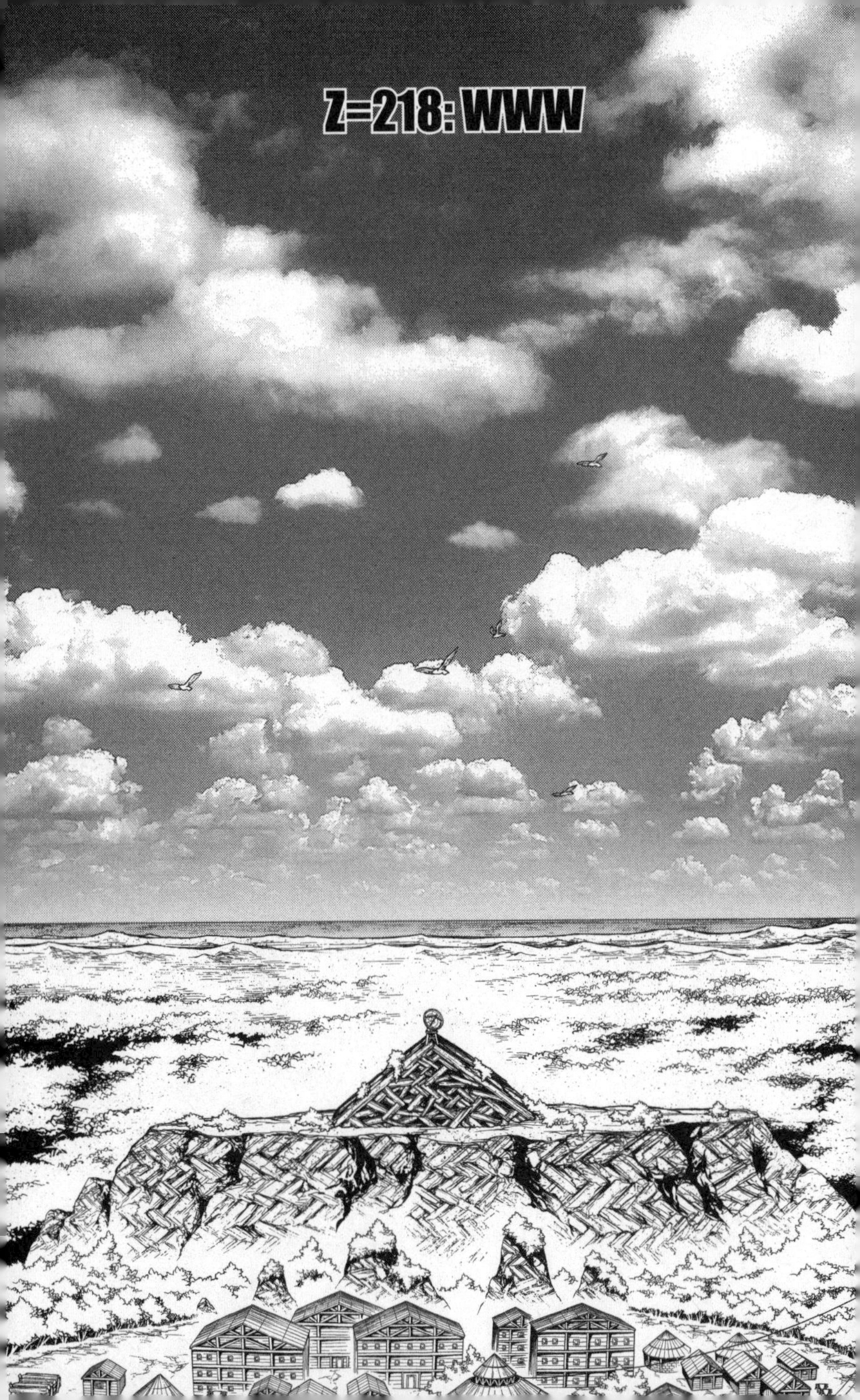
Z=218: WWW

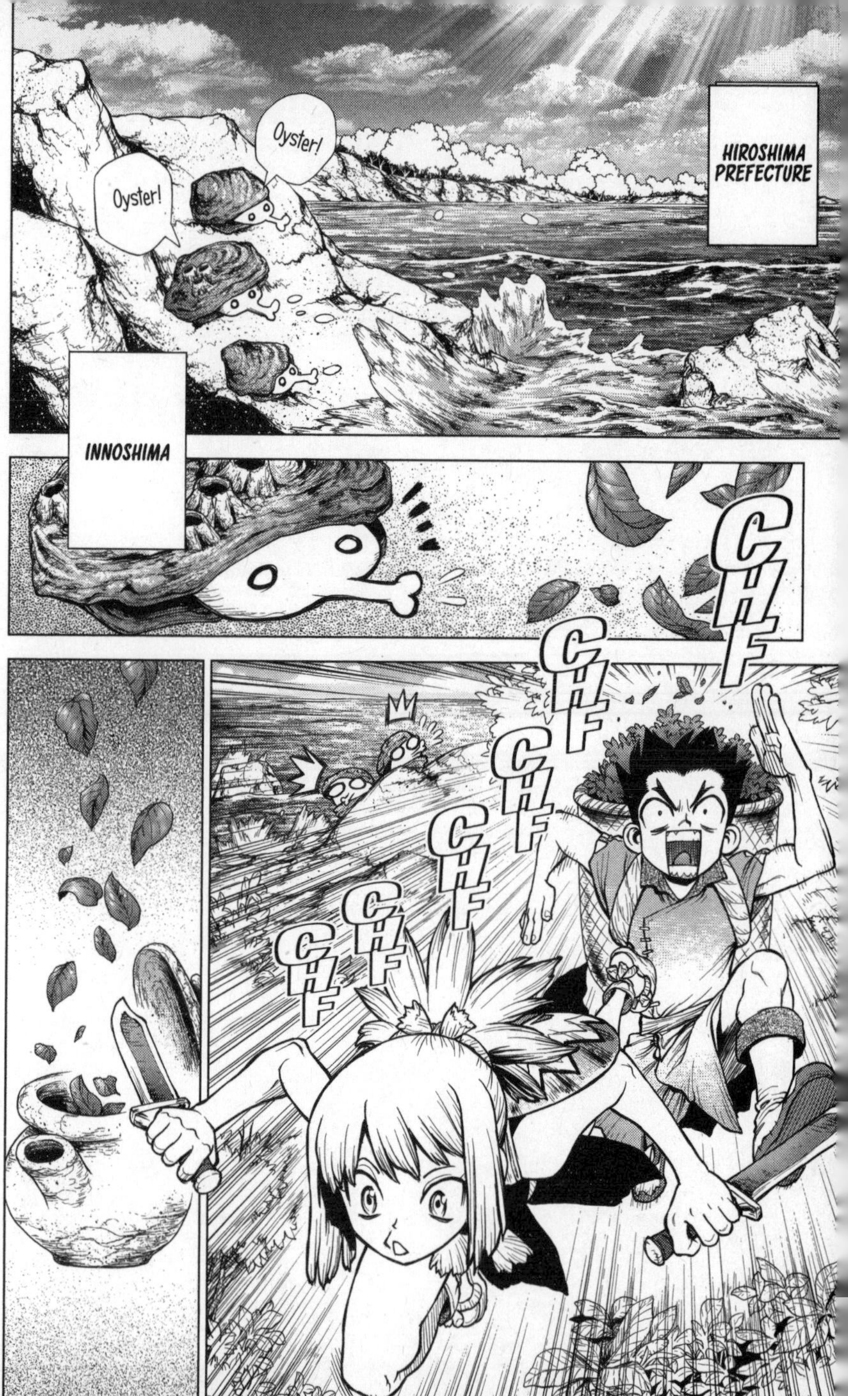
HIROSHIMA PREFECTURE
Oyster!
Oyster!
INNOSHIMA
CHF
CHF
CHF
CHF
CHF
CHF

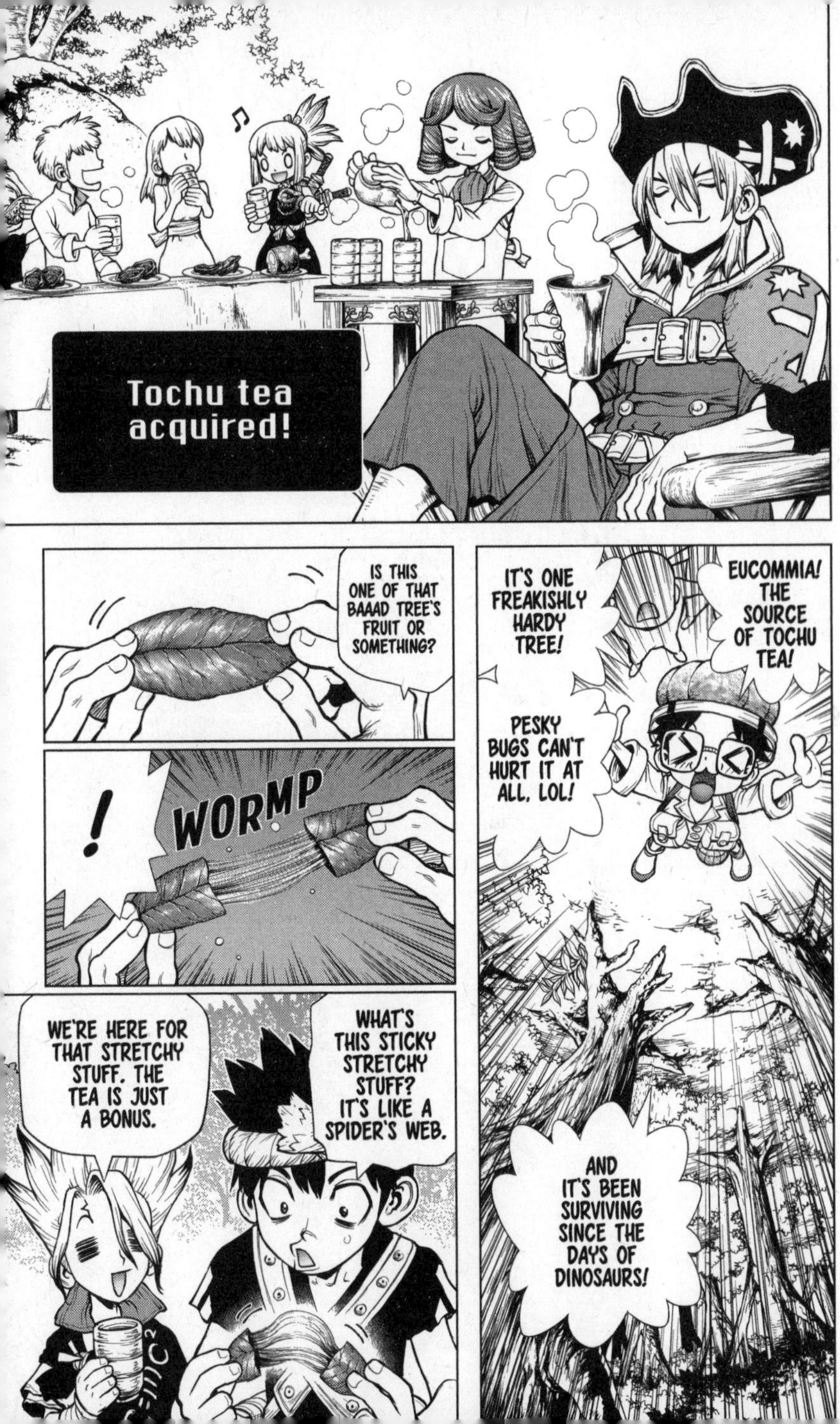
Tochu tea acquired!
EUCOMMIA! THE SOURCE OF TOCHU TEA!
IT'S ONE FREAKISHLY HARDY TREE!
PESKY BUGS CAN'T HURT IT AT ALL, LOL!
AND IT'S BEEN SURVIVING SINCE THE DAYS OF DINOSAURS!
IS THIS ONE OF THAT BAAAD TREE'S FRUIT OR SOMETHING?
!
WORMP
WHAT'S THIS STICKY STRETCHY STUFF? IT'S LIKE A SPIDER'S WEB.
WE'RE HERE FOR THAT STRETCHY STUFF. THE TEA IS JUST A BONUS.

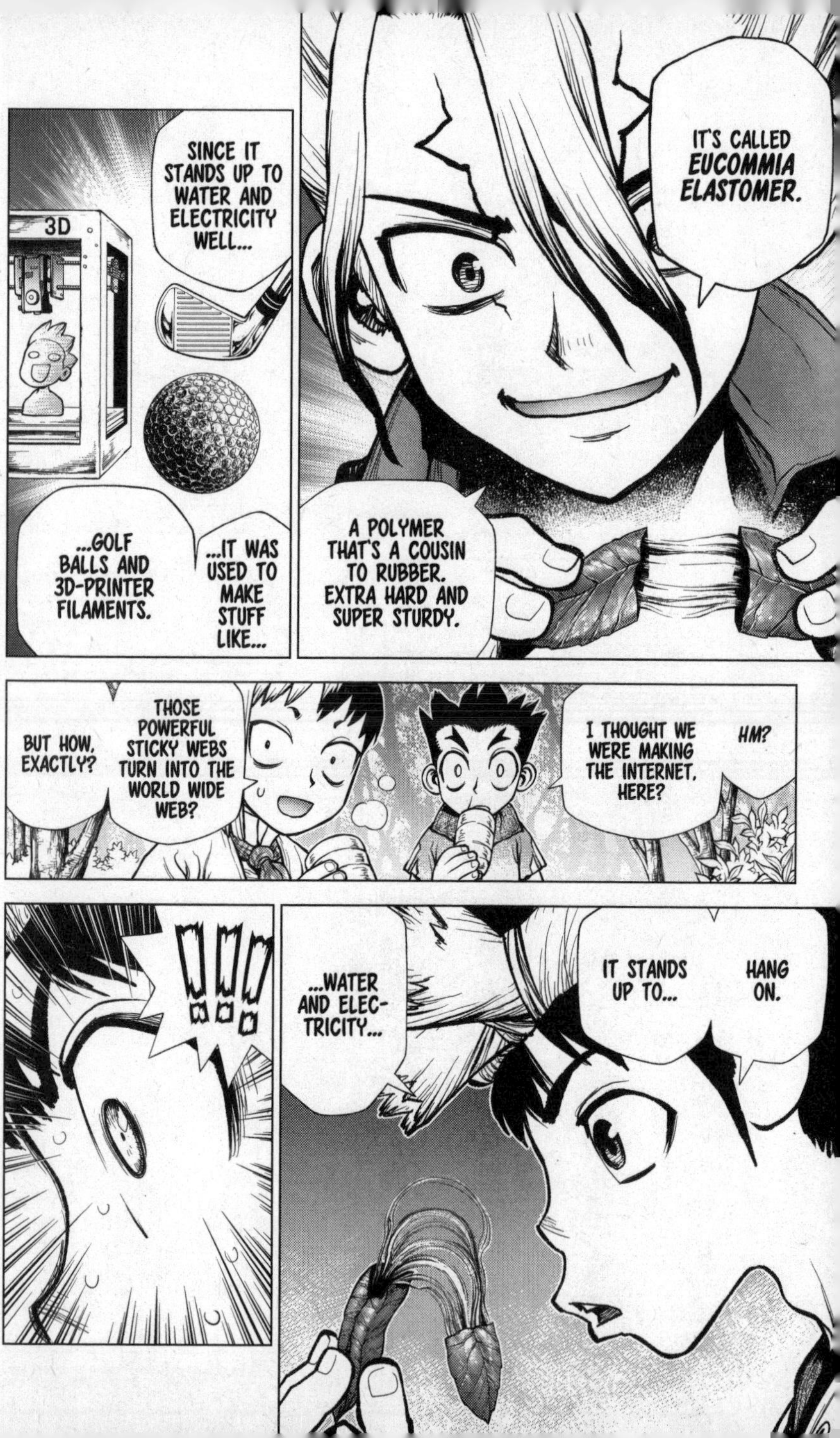
IT'S CALLED EUCOMMIA ELASTOMER.
A POLYMER THAT'S A COUSIN TO RUBBER. EXTRA HARD AND SUPER STURDY.
SINCE IT STANDS UP TO WATER AND ELECTRICITY WELL...
...IT WAS USED TO MAKE STUFF LIKE...
...GOLF BALLS AND 3D-PRINTER FILAMENTS.
3D
HM?
I THOUGHT WE WERE MAKING THE INTERNET, HERE?
THOSE POWERFUL STICKY WEBS TURN INTO THE WORLD WIDE WEB?
BUT HOW, EXACTLY?
HANG ON.
IT STANDS UP TO...
...WATER AND ELEC-TRICITY...
!!!

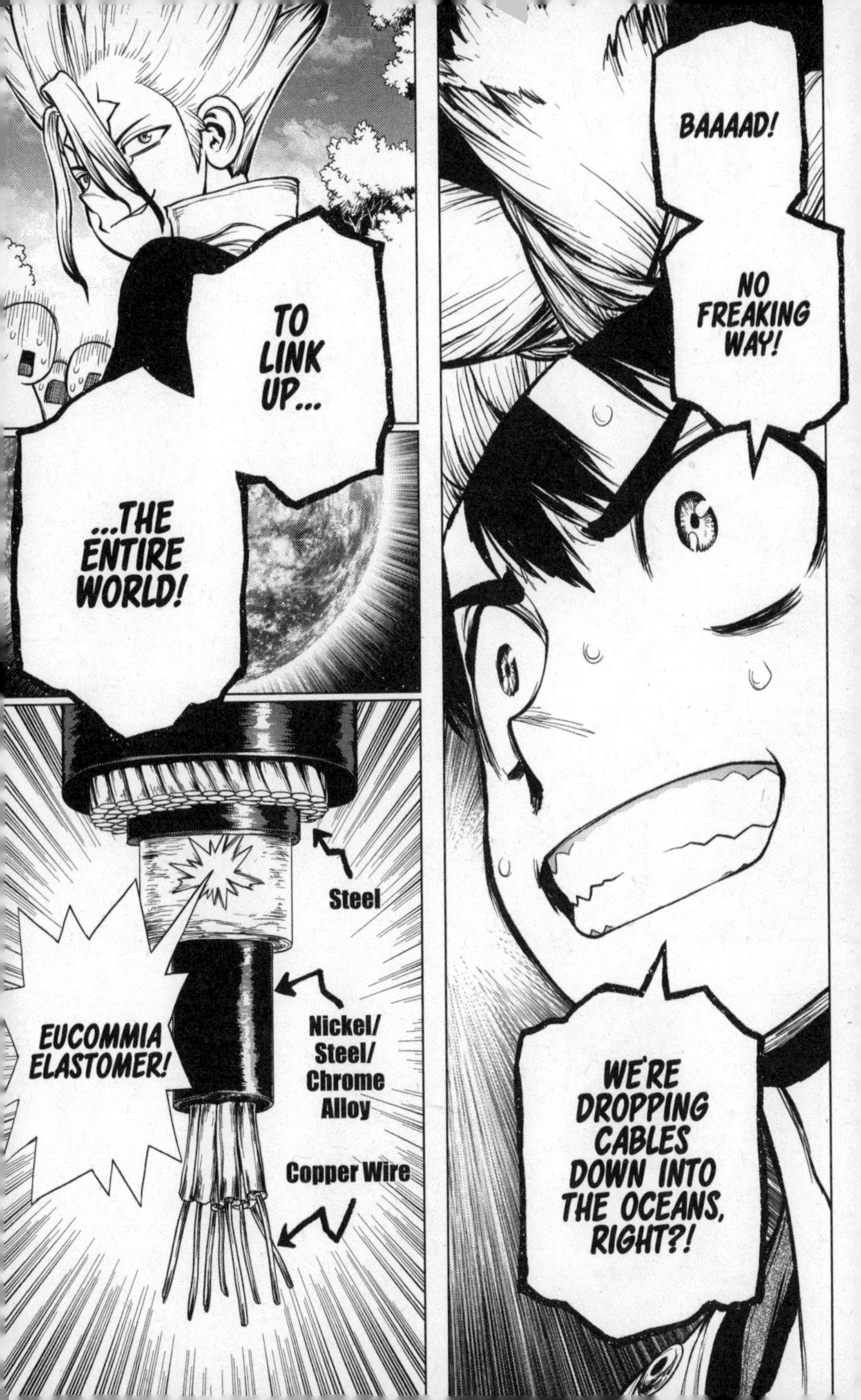
BAAAAD!
NO FREAKING WAY!
WE'RE DROPPING CABLES DOWN INTO THE OCEANS, RIGHT?!
TO LINK UP...
...THE ENTIRE WORLD!
Steel
Nickel/Steel/Chrome Alloy
Copper Wire
EUCOMMIA ELASTOMER!

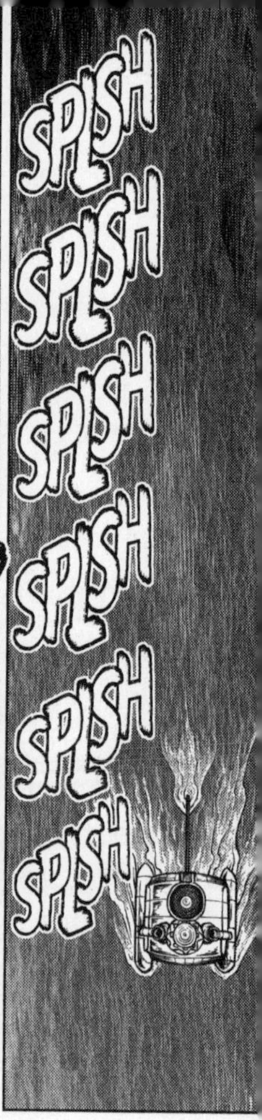
SPLISH
SPLISH
SPLISH
SPLISH
SPLISH
SPLISH
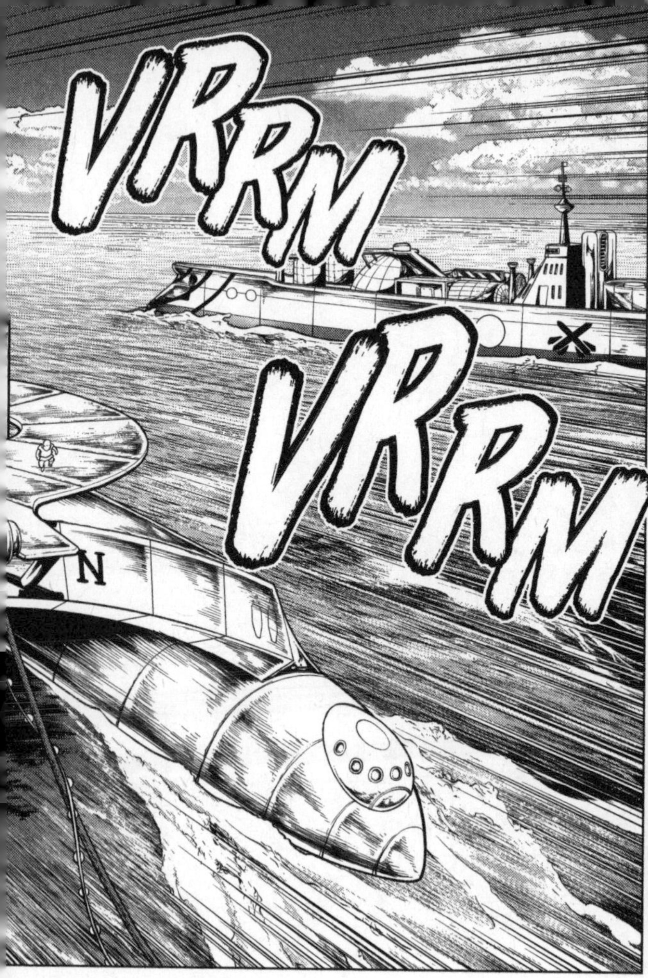
VRRM
VRRM
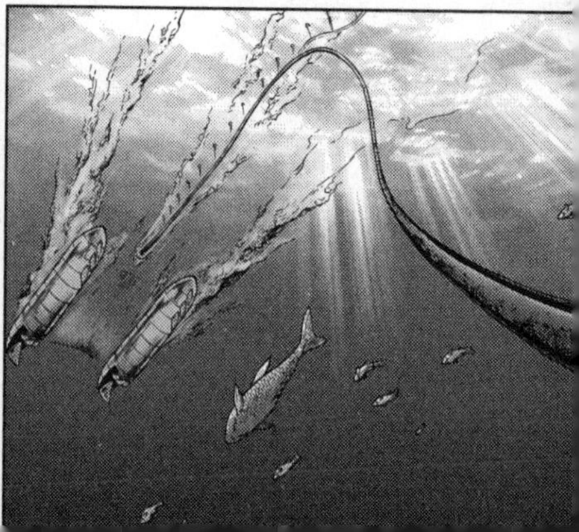
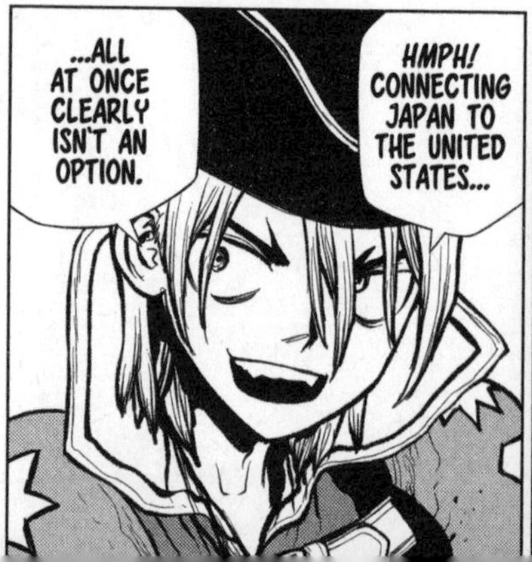
HMPH! CONNECTING JAPAN TO THE UNITED STATES...
...ALL AT ONCE CLEARLY ISN'T AN OPTION.

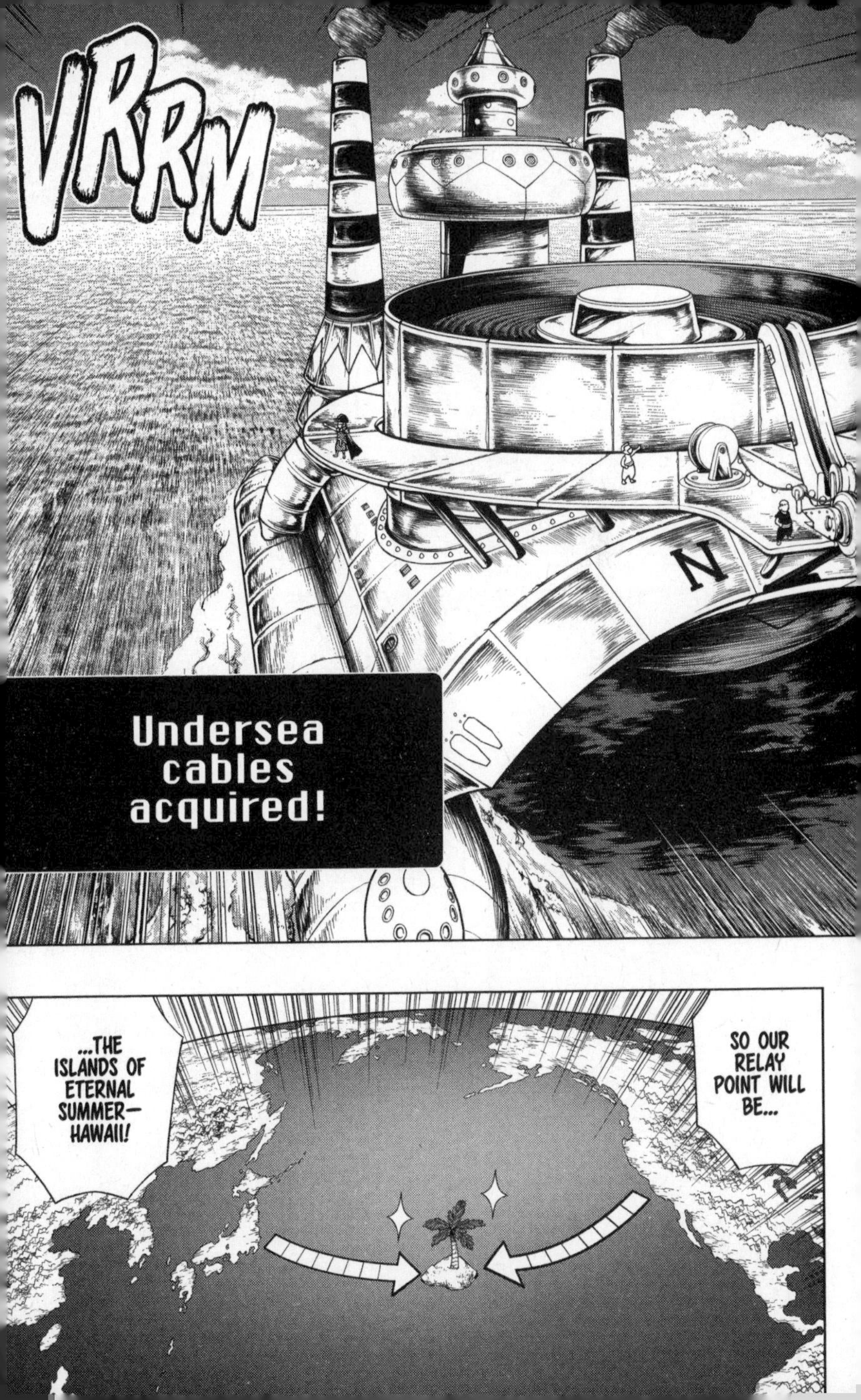
VRRM
Undersea cables acquired!
SO OUR RELAY POINT WILL BE...
...THE ISLANDS OF ETERNAL SUMMER—HAWAII!

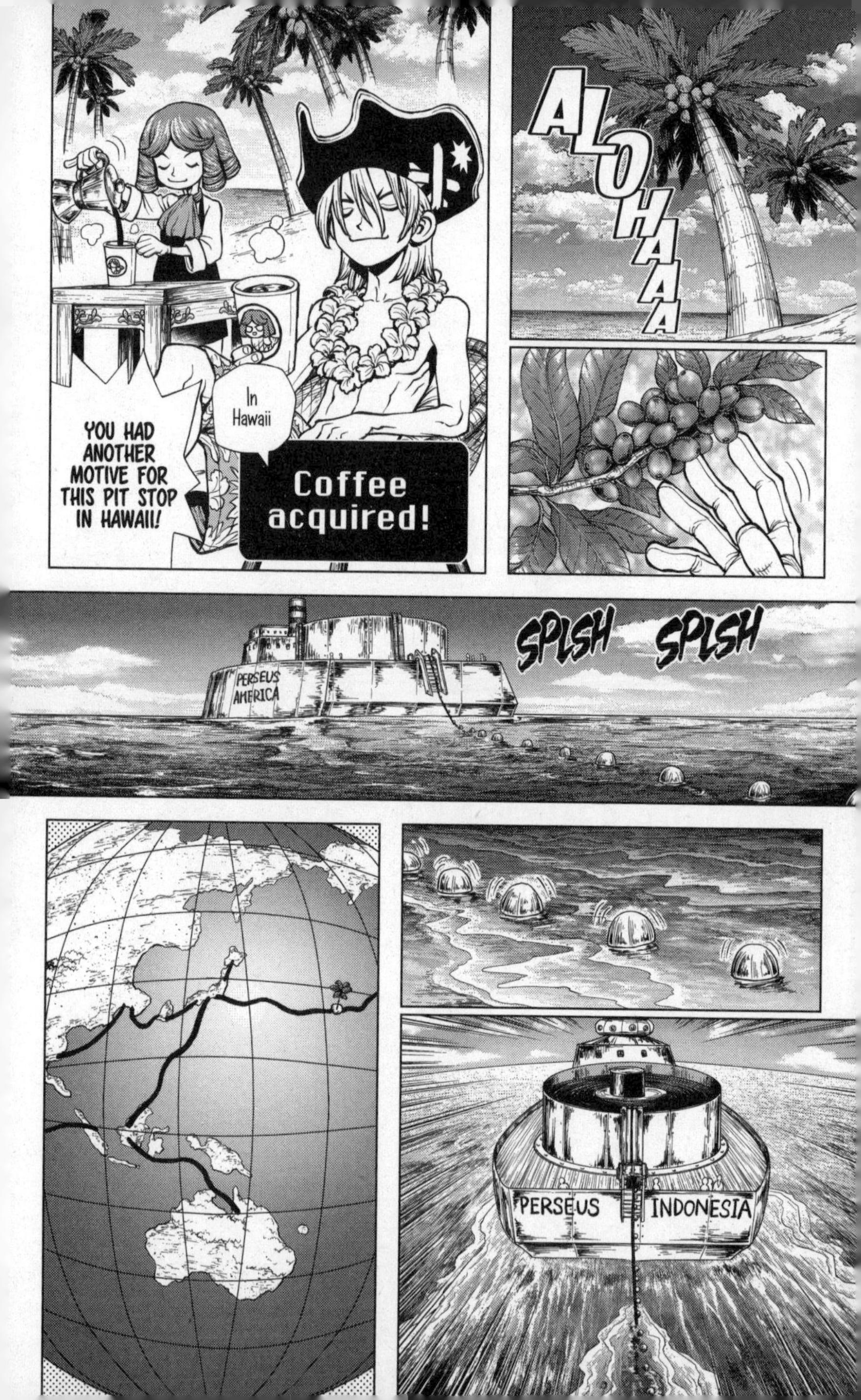

ALOHAAA
In Hawaii
Coffee acquired!
YOU HAD ANOTHER MOTIVE FOR THIS PIT STOP IN HAWAII!
SPLSH SPLSH
PERSEUS AMERICA
PERSEUS INDONESIA

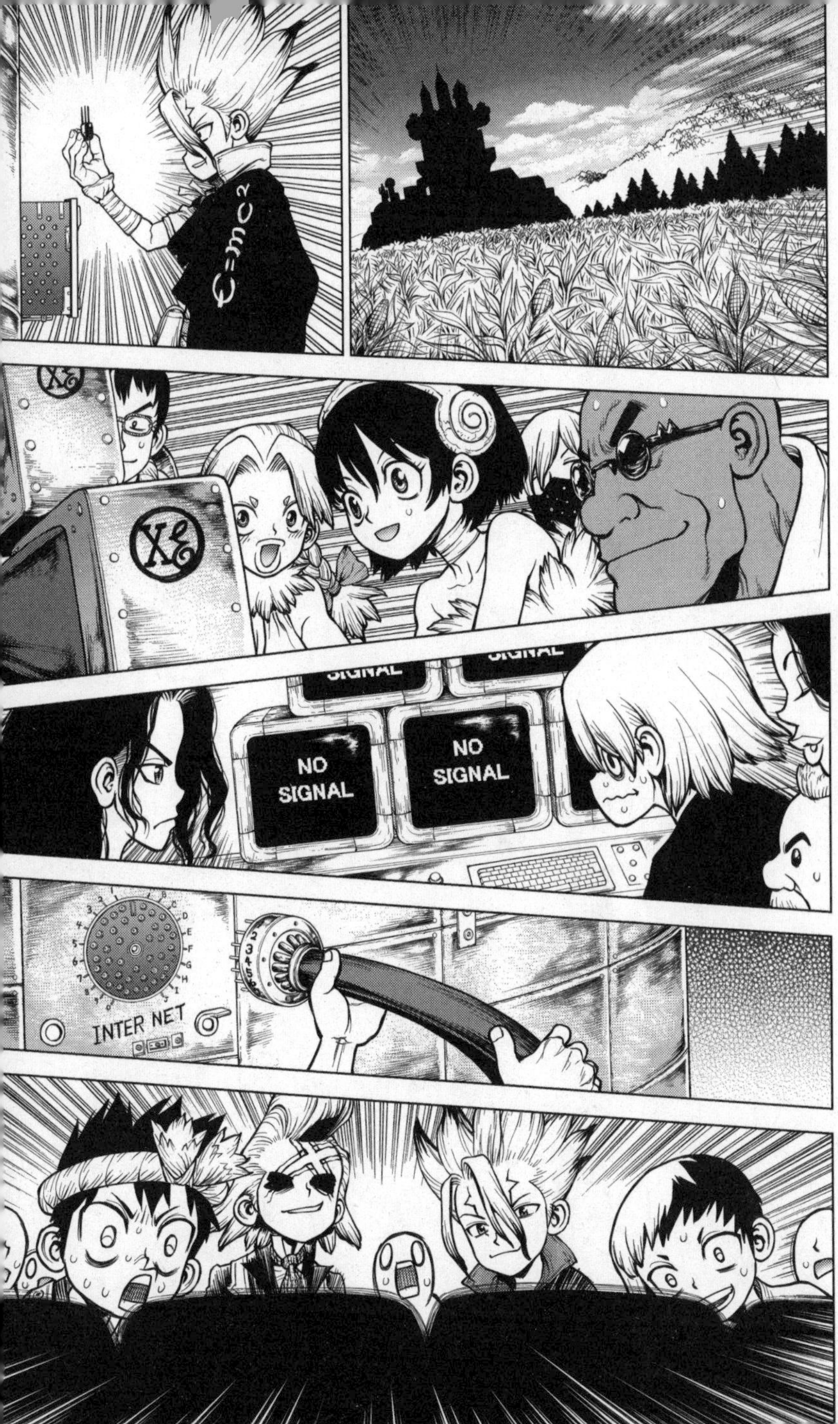

E=mc²
NO SIGNAL
NO SIGNAL
INTER NET

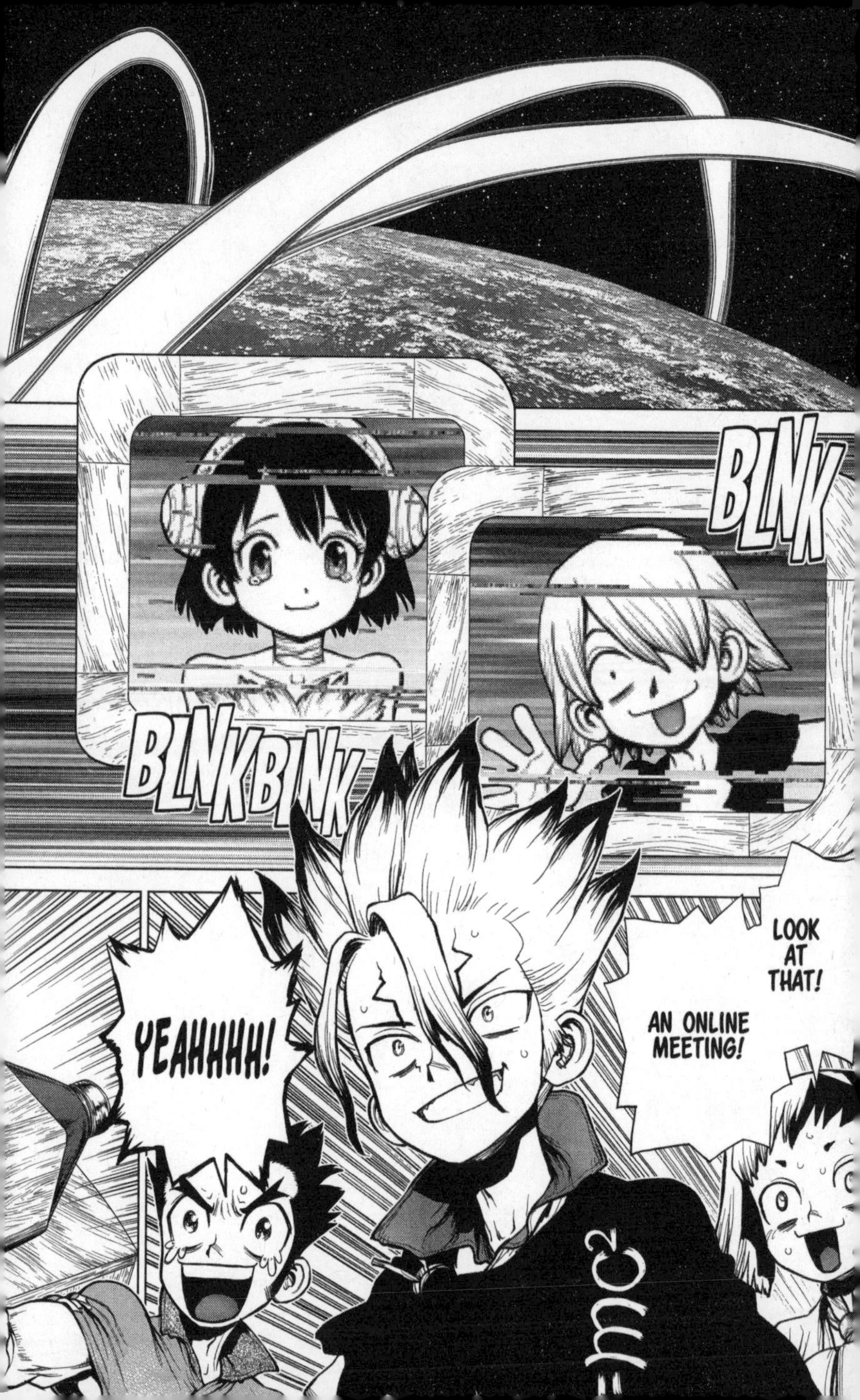
BLINK
BLINK BLINK
LOOK AT THAT!
AN ONLINE MEETING!
YEAHHHH!

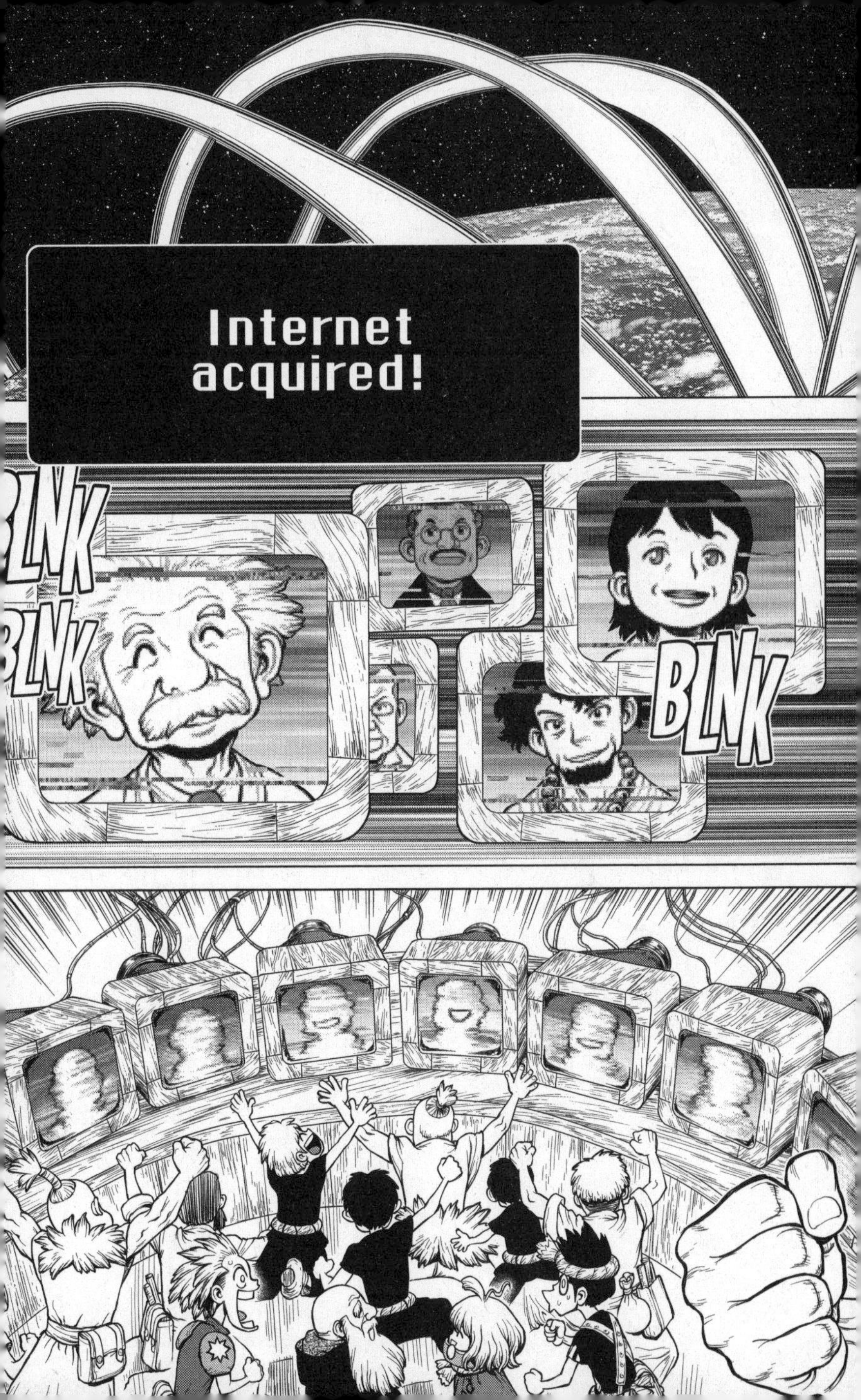
Internet acquired!
BLNK
BLNK
BLNK

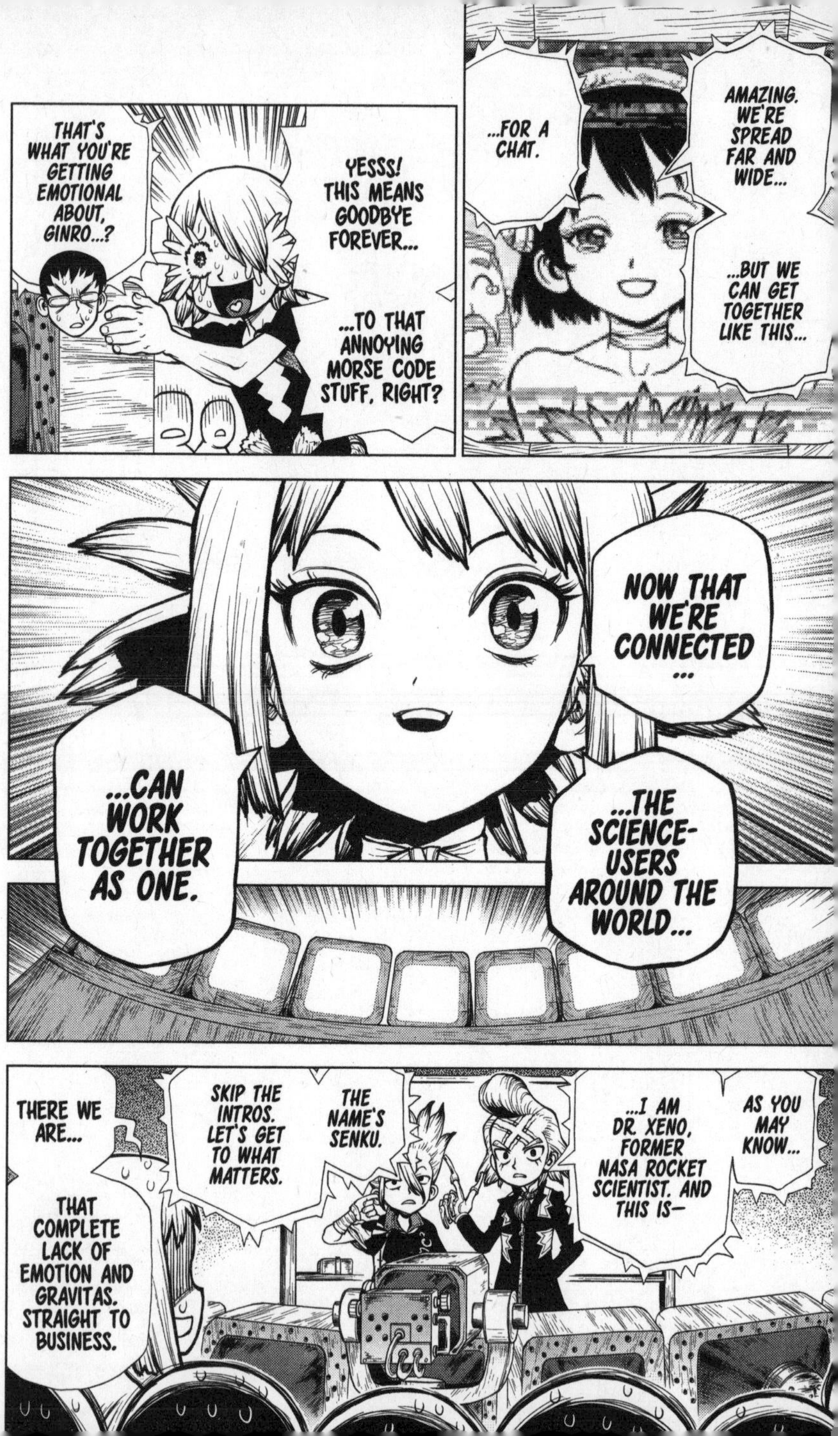
AMAZING. WE'RE SPREAD FAR AND WIDE...
...BUT WE CAN GET TOGETHER LIKE THIS...
...FOR A CHAT.
YESSS! THIS MEANS GOODBYE FOREVER...
...TO THAT ANNOYING MORSE CODE STUFF, RIGHT?
THAT'S WHAT YOU'RE GETTING EMOTIONAL ABOUT, GINRO...?
NOW THAT WE'RE CONNECTED...
...THE SCIENCE-USERS AROUND THE WORLD...
...CAN WORK TOGETHER AS ONE.
AS YOU MAY KNOW...
...I AM DR. XENO, FORMER NASA ROCKET SCIENTIST. AND THIS IS—
THE NAME'S SENKU.
SKIP THE INTROS. LET'S GET TO WHAT MATTERS.
THERE WE ARE...
THAT COMPLETE LACK OF EMOTION AND GRAVITAS. STRAIGHT TO BUSINESS.

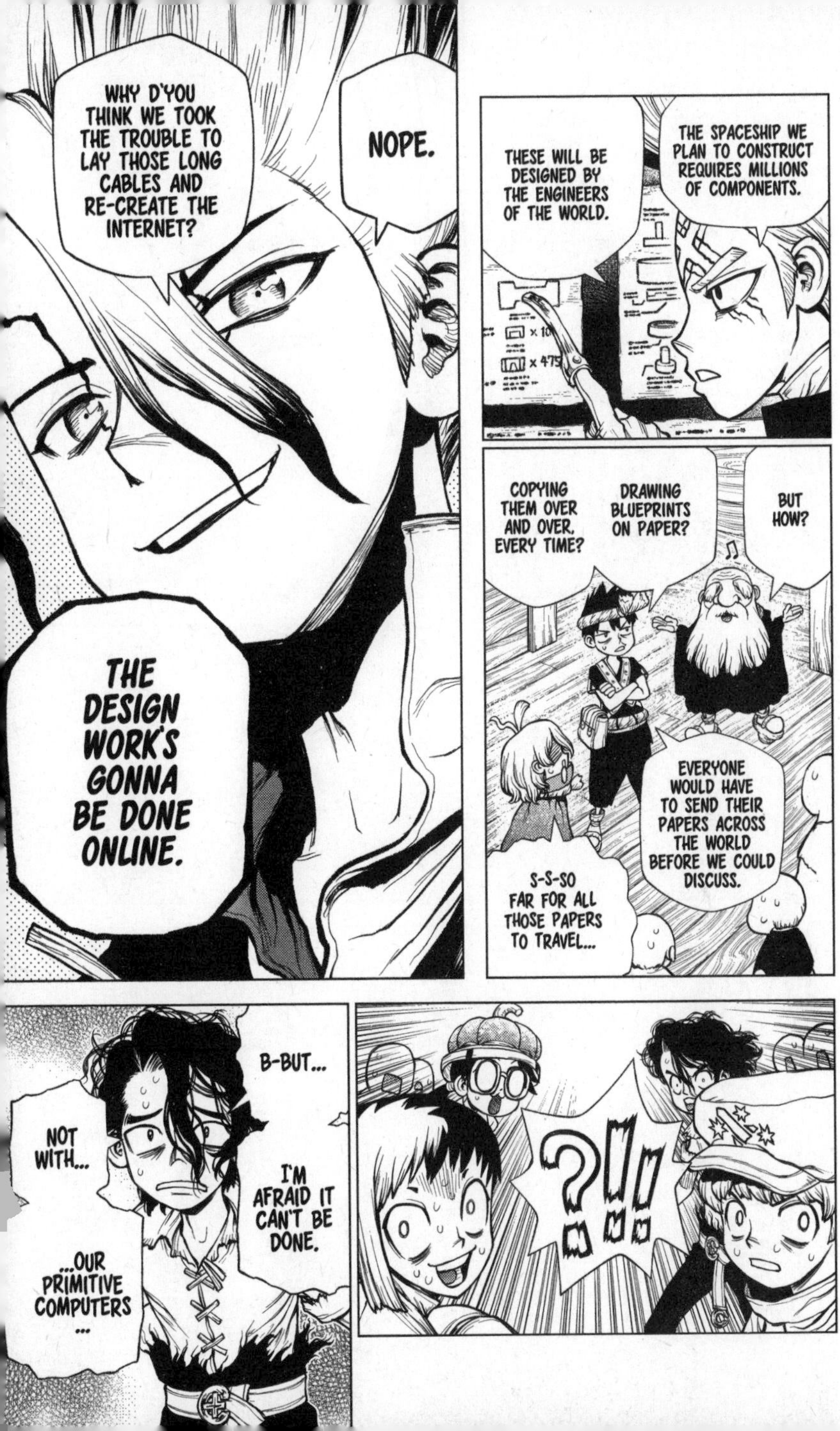
THE SPACESHIP WE PLAN TO CONSTRUCT REQUIRES MILLIONS OF COMPONENTS.
THESE WILL BE DESIGNED BY THE ENGINEERS OF THE WORLD.
BUT HOW?
DRAWING BLUEPRINTS ON PAPER?
COPYING THEM OVER AND OVER, EVERY TIME?
EVERYONE WOULD HAVE TO SEND THEIR PAPERS ACROSS THE WORLD BEFORE WE COULD DISCUSS.
S-S-SO FAR FOR ALL THOSE PAPERS TO TRAVEL...
NOPE.
WHY D'YOU THINK WE TOOK THE TROUBLE TO LAY THOSE LONG CABLES AND RE-CREATE THE INTERNET?
THE DESIGN WORK'S GONNA BE DONE ONLINE.
?!!
B-BUT...
I'M AFRAID IT CAN'T BE DONE.
NOT WITH...
...OUR PRIMITIVE COMPUTERS...

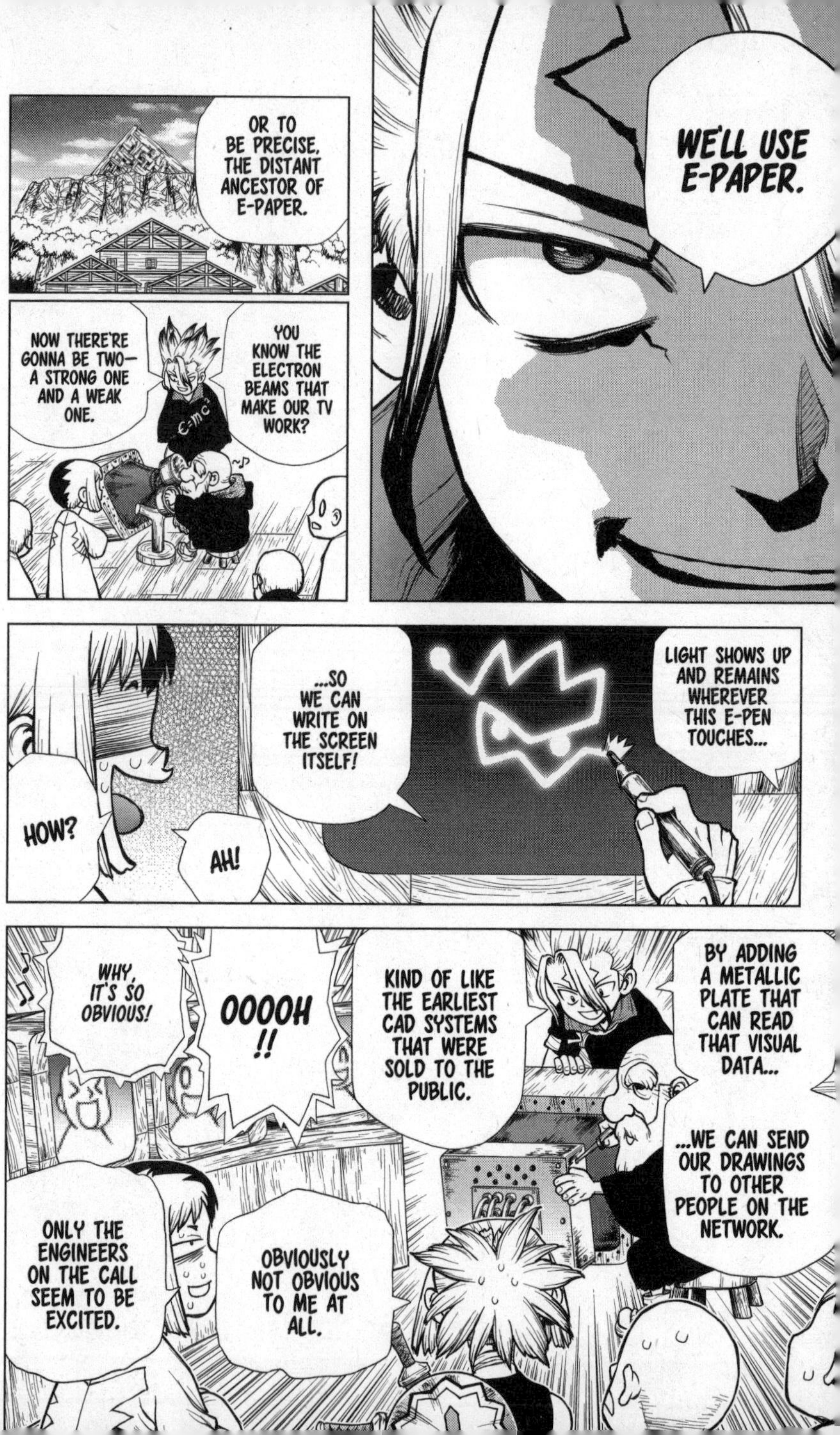
WE'LL USE E-PAPER.
OR TO BE PRECISE, THE DISTANT ANCESTOR OF E-PAPER.
YOU KNOW THE ELECTRON BEAMS THAT MAKE OUR TV WORK?
NOW THERE'RE GONNA BE TWO—A STRONG ONE AND A WEAK ONE.
LIGHT SHOWS UP AND REMAINS WHEREVER THIS E-PEN TOUCHES...
...SO WE CAN WRITE ON THE SCREEN ITSELF!
AH!
HOW?
BY ADDING A METALLIC PLATE THAT CAN READ THAT VISUAL DATA...
...WE CAN SEND OUR DRAWINGS TO OTHER PEOPLE ON THE NETWORK.
KIND OF LIKE THE EARLIEST CAD SYSTEMS THAT WERE SOLD TO THE PUBLIC.
OOOOH!!
WHY, IT'S SO OBVIOUS!
OBVIOUSLY NOT OBVIOUS TO ME AT ALL.
ONLY THE ENGINEERS ON THE CALL SEEM TO BE EXCITED.

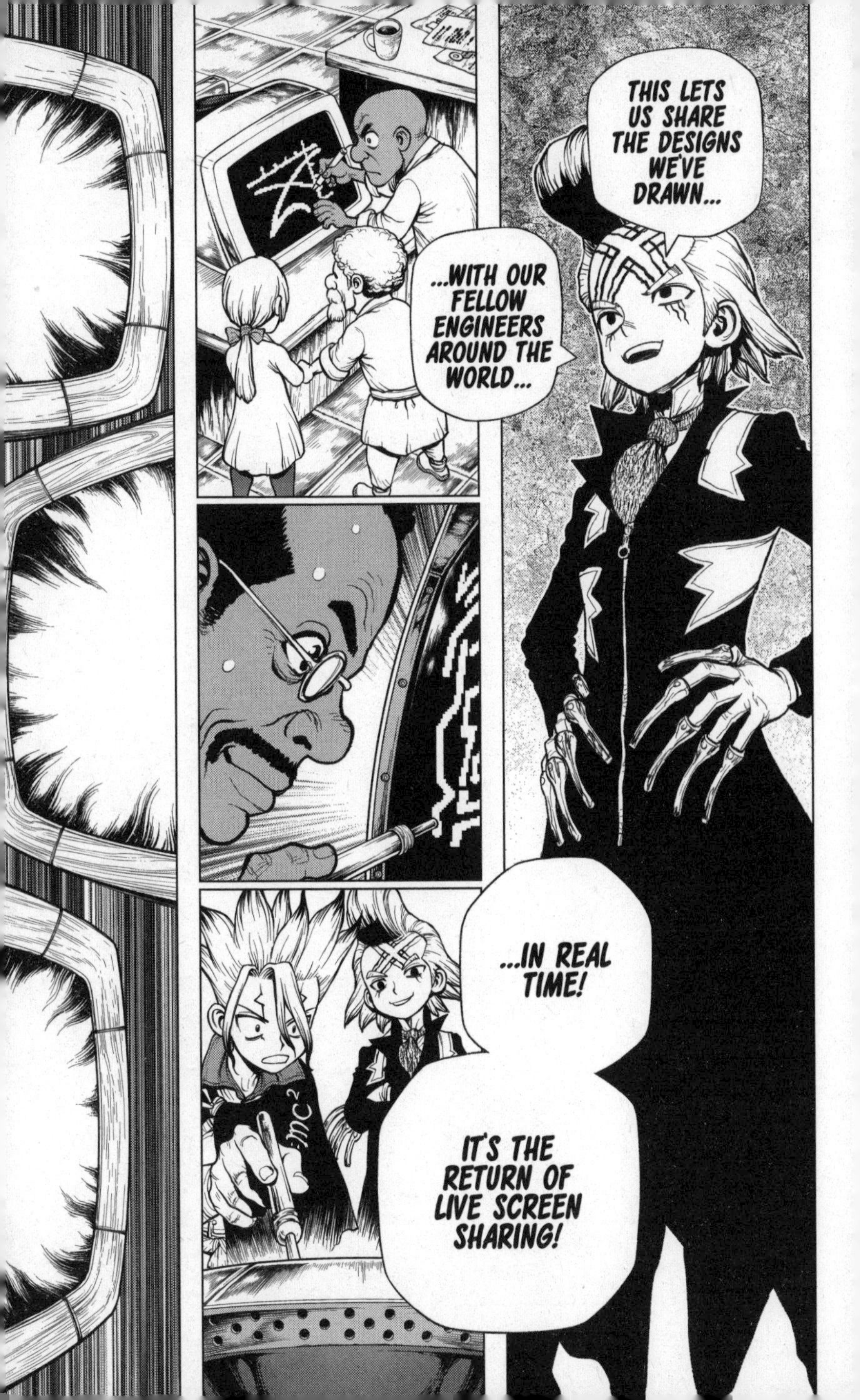
THIS LETS US SHARE THE DESIGNS WE'VE DRAWN...
...WITH OUR FELLOW ENGINEERS AROUND THE WORLD...
...IN REAL TIME!
IT'S THE RETURN OF LIVE SCREEN SHARING!

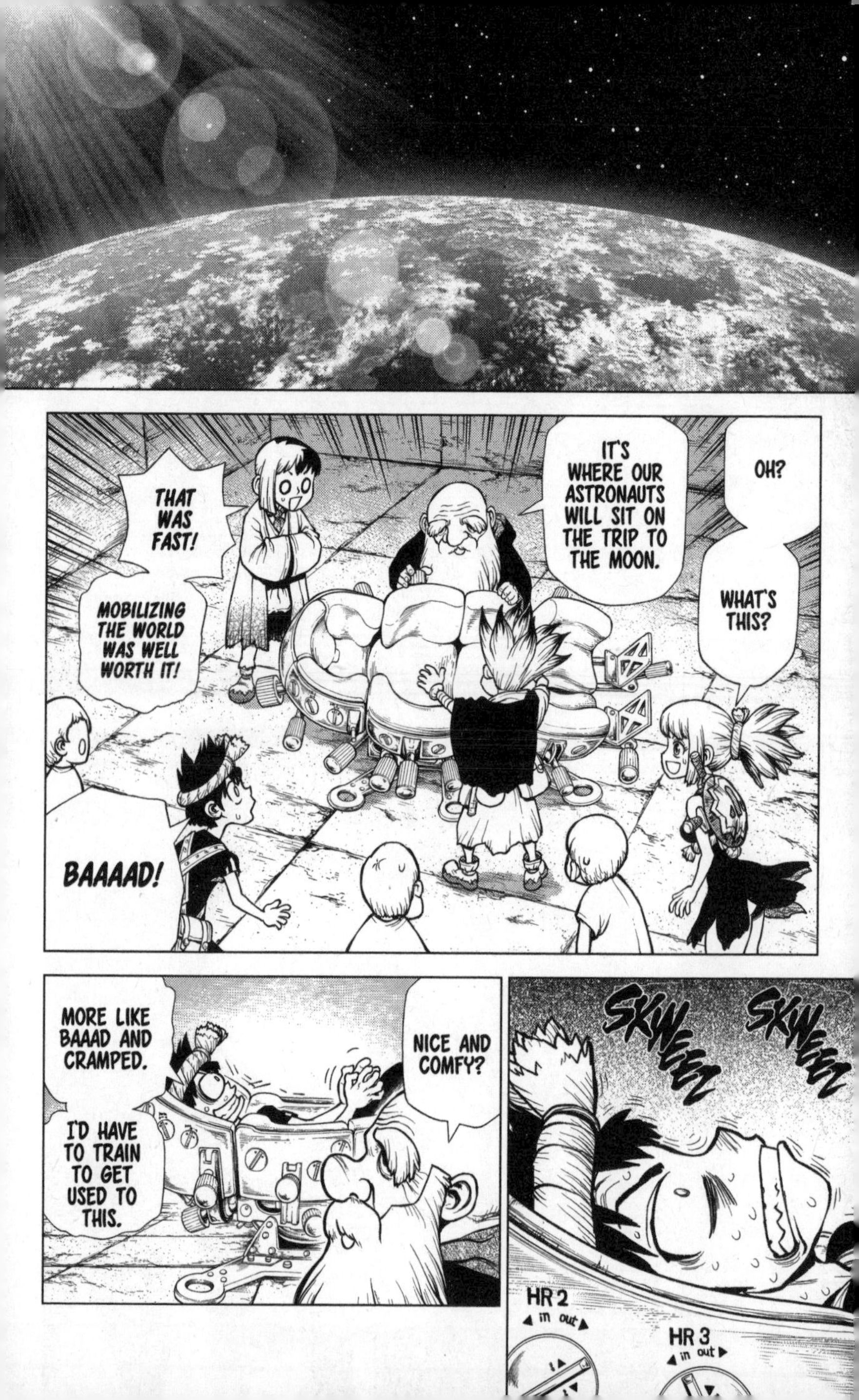
OH?
WHAT'S THIS?
IT'S WHERE OUR ASTRONAUTS WILL SIT ON THE TRIP TO THE MOON.
THAT WAS FAST!
MOBILIZING THE WORLD WAS WELL WORTH IT!
BAAAAD!
SKWEEE
SKWEEE
HR 2
in out
HR 3
in out
NICE AND COMFY?
MORE LIKE BAAAD AND CRAMPED.
I'D HAVE TO TRAIN TO GET USED TO THIS.

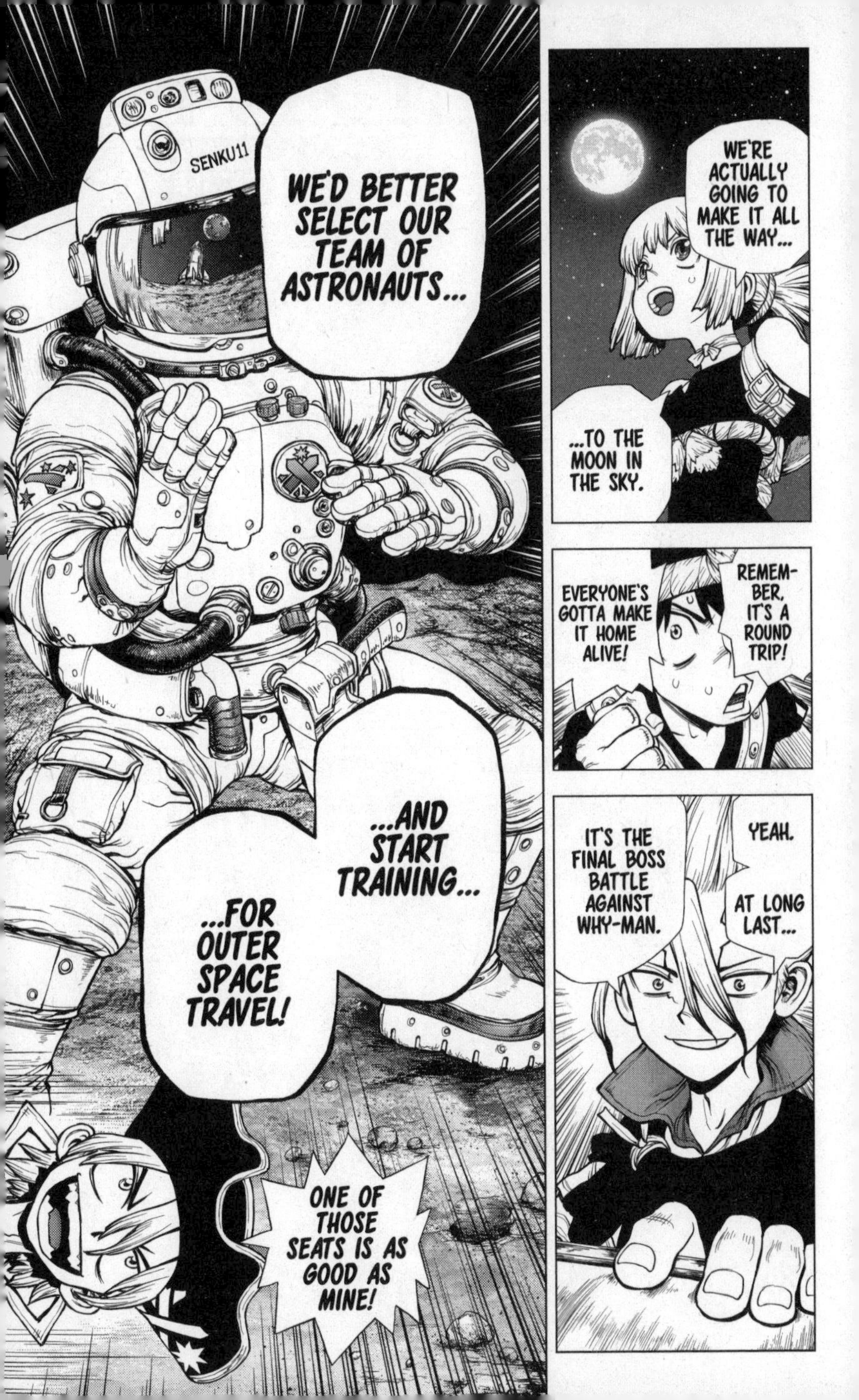
WE'RE ACTUALLY GOING TO MAKE IT ALL THE WAY...
...TO THE MOON IN THE SKY.
REMEMBER, IT'S A ROUND TRIP!
EVERYONE'S GOTTA MAKE IT HOME ALIVE!
YEAH.
AT LONG LAST...
IT'S THE FINAL BOSS BATTLE AGAINST WHY-MAN.
SENKU11
WE'D BETTER SELECT OUR TEAM OF ASTRONAUTS...
...AND START TRAINING...
...FOR OUTER SPACE TRAVEL!
ONE OF THOSE SEATS IS AS GOOD AS MINE!

SCHEDULE

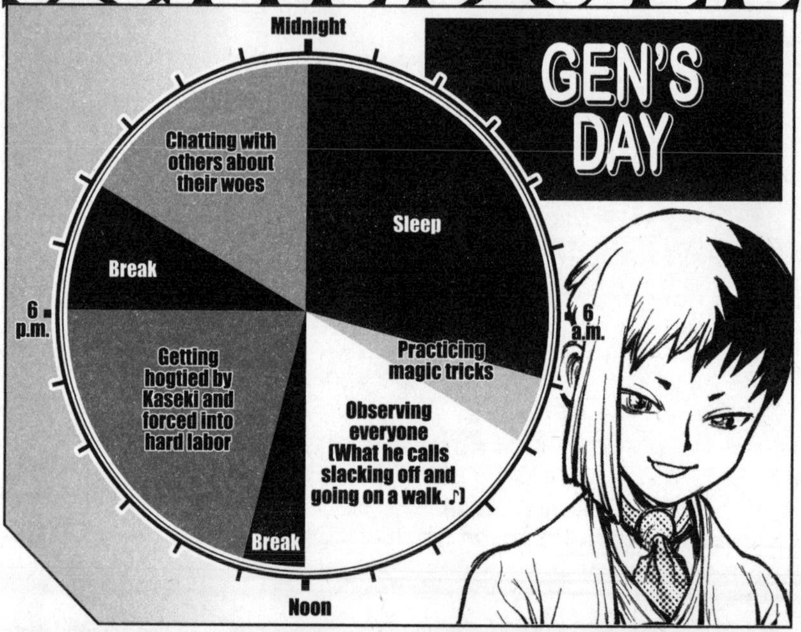
GEN'S DAY
Midnight
Sleep
Practicing magic tricks
Observing everyone (What he calls slacking off and going on a walk. ♪)
Break
Getting hogtied by Kaseki and forced into hard labor
Break
Chatting with others about their woes
6 a.m.
Noon
6 p.m.

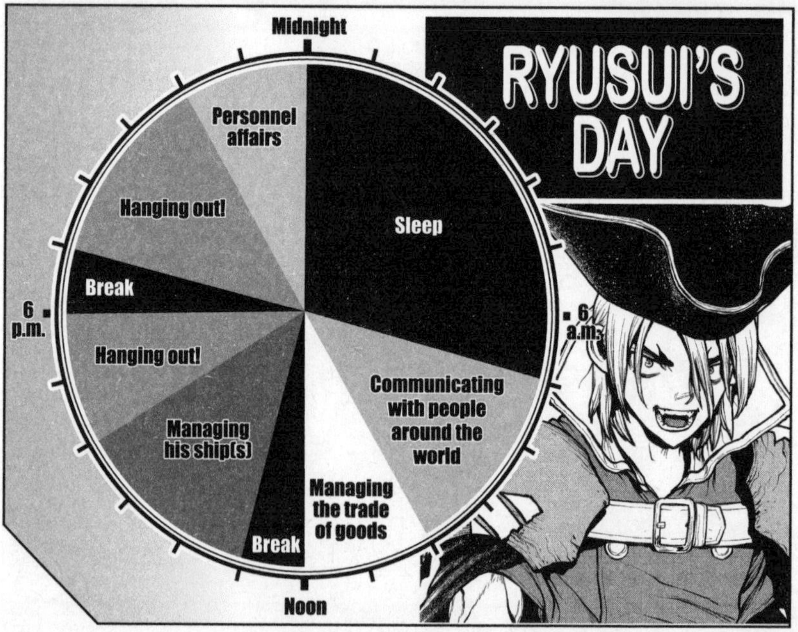
RYUSUI'S DAY
Midnight
Sleep
Communicating with people around the world
Managing the trade of goods
Break
Managing his ship(s)
Hanging out!
Break
Hanging out!
Personnel affairs
6 a.m.
Noon
6 p.m.

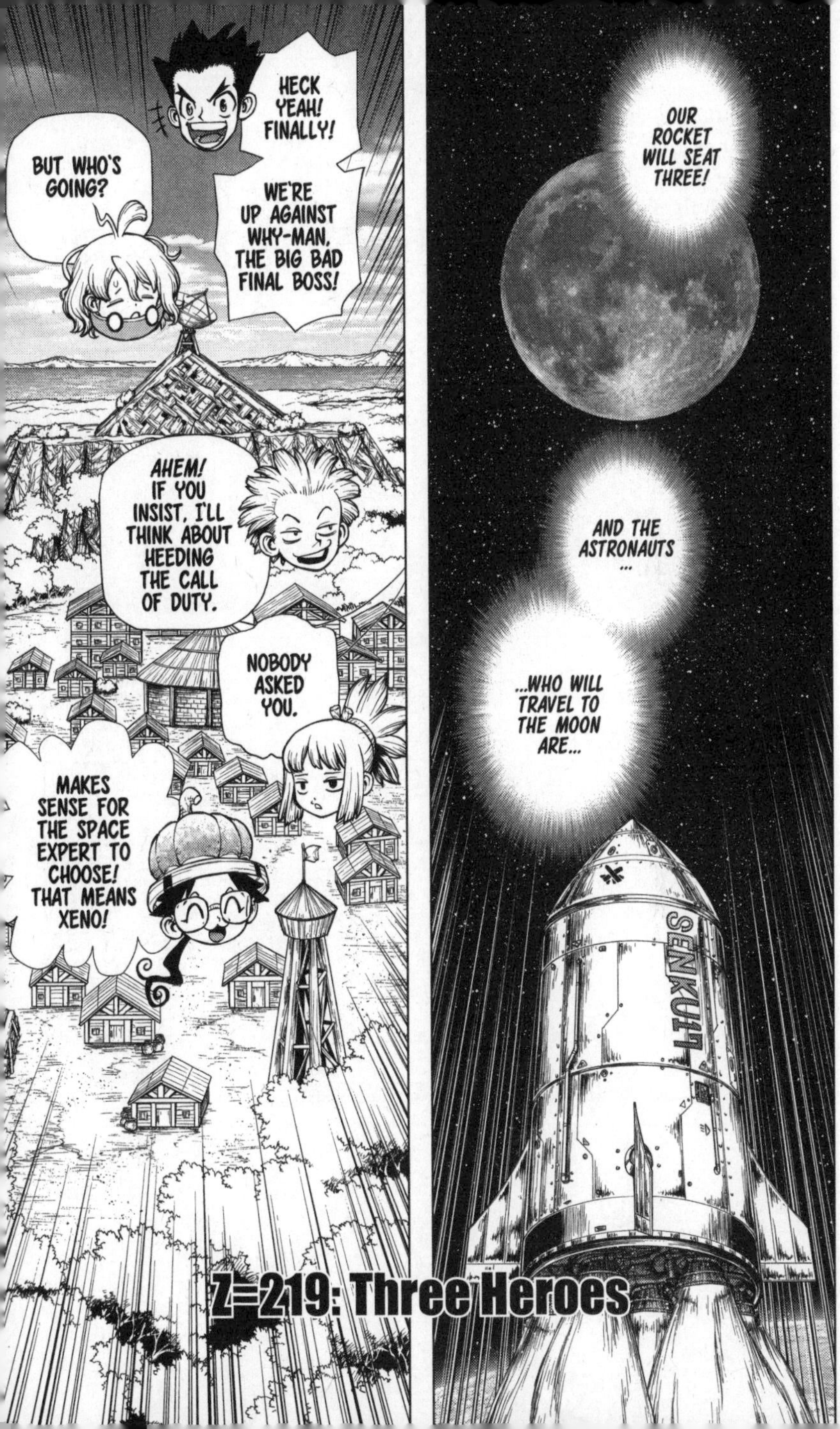
OUR ROCKET WILL SEAT THREE!
AND THE ASTRONAUTS ...
...WHO WILL TRAVEL TO THE MOON ARE...
SENKU
HECK YEAH! FINALLY!
WE'RE UP AGAINST WHY-MAN, THE BIG BAD FINAL BOSS!
BUT WHO'S GOING?
AHEM! IF YOU INSIST, I'LL THINK ABOUT HEEDING THE CALL OF DUTY.
NOBODY ASKED YOU.
MAKES SENSE FOR THE SPACE EXPERT TO CHOOSE! THAT MEANS XENO!

Z=219: Three Heroes

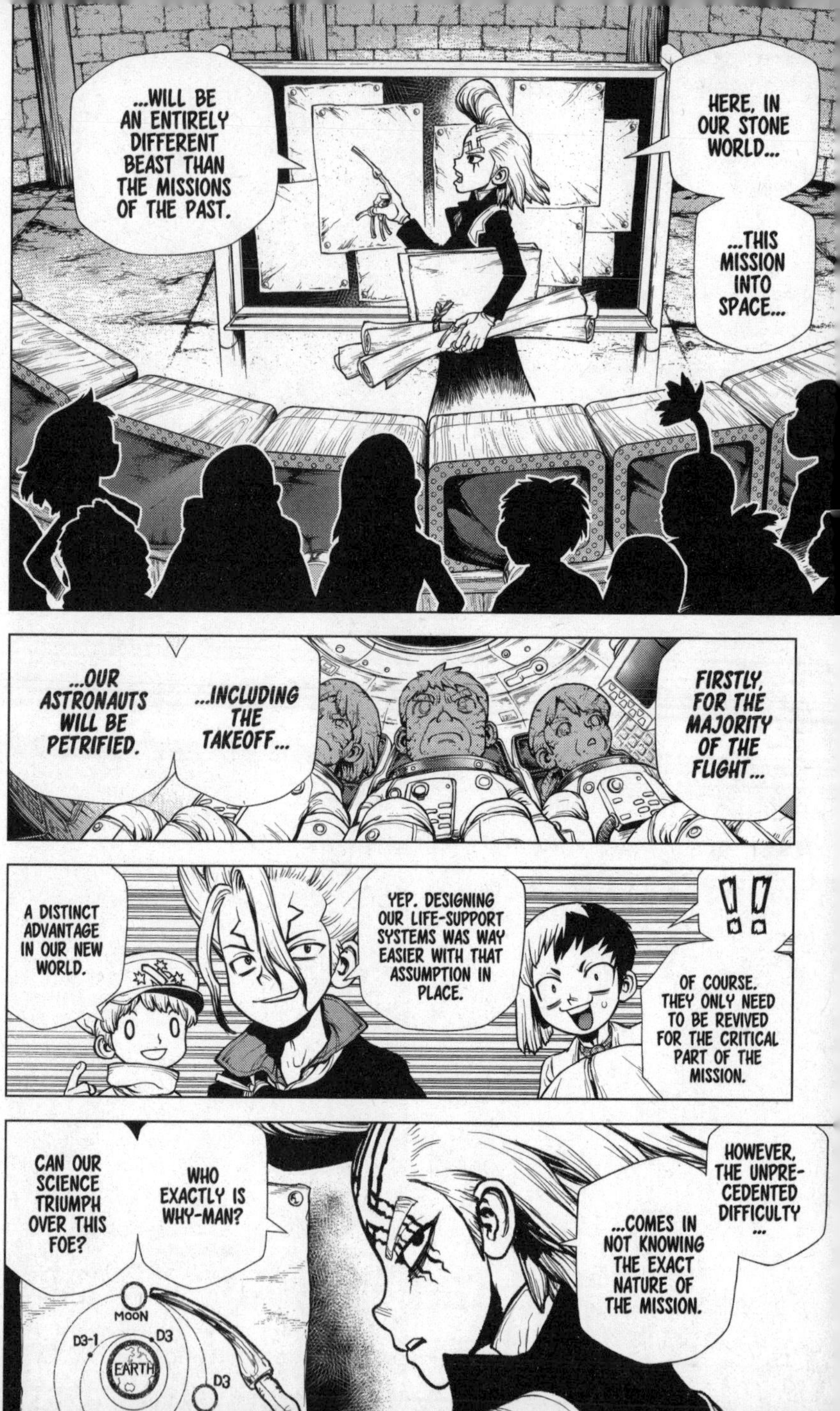
HERE, IN OUR STONE WORLD...
...THIS MISSION INTO SPACE...
...WILL BE AN ENTIRELY DIFFERENT BEAST THAN THE MISSIONS OF THE PAST.
FIRSTLY, FOR THE MAJORITY OF THE FLIGHT...
...INCLUDING THE TAKEOFF...
...OUR ASTRONAUTS WILL BE PETRIFIED.
!!
OF COURSE. THEY ONLY NEED TO BE REVIVED FOR THE CRITICAL PART OF THE MISSION.
YEP. DESIGNING OUR LIFE-SUPPORT SYSTEMS WAS WAY EASIER WITH THAT ASSUMPTION IN PLACE.
A DISTINCT ADVANTAGE IN OUR NEW WORLD.
HOWEVER, THE UNPRECEDENTED DIFFICULTY...
...COMES IN NOT KNOWING THE EXACT NATURE OF THE MISSION.
WHO EXACTLY IS WHY-MAN?
CAN OUR SCIENCE TRIUMPH OVER THIS FOE?
MOON
D3-1
D3
EARTH
D3

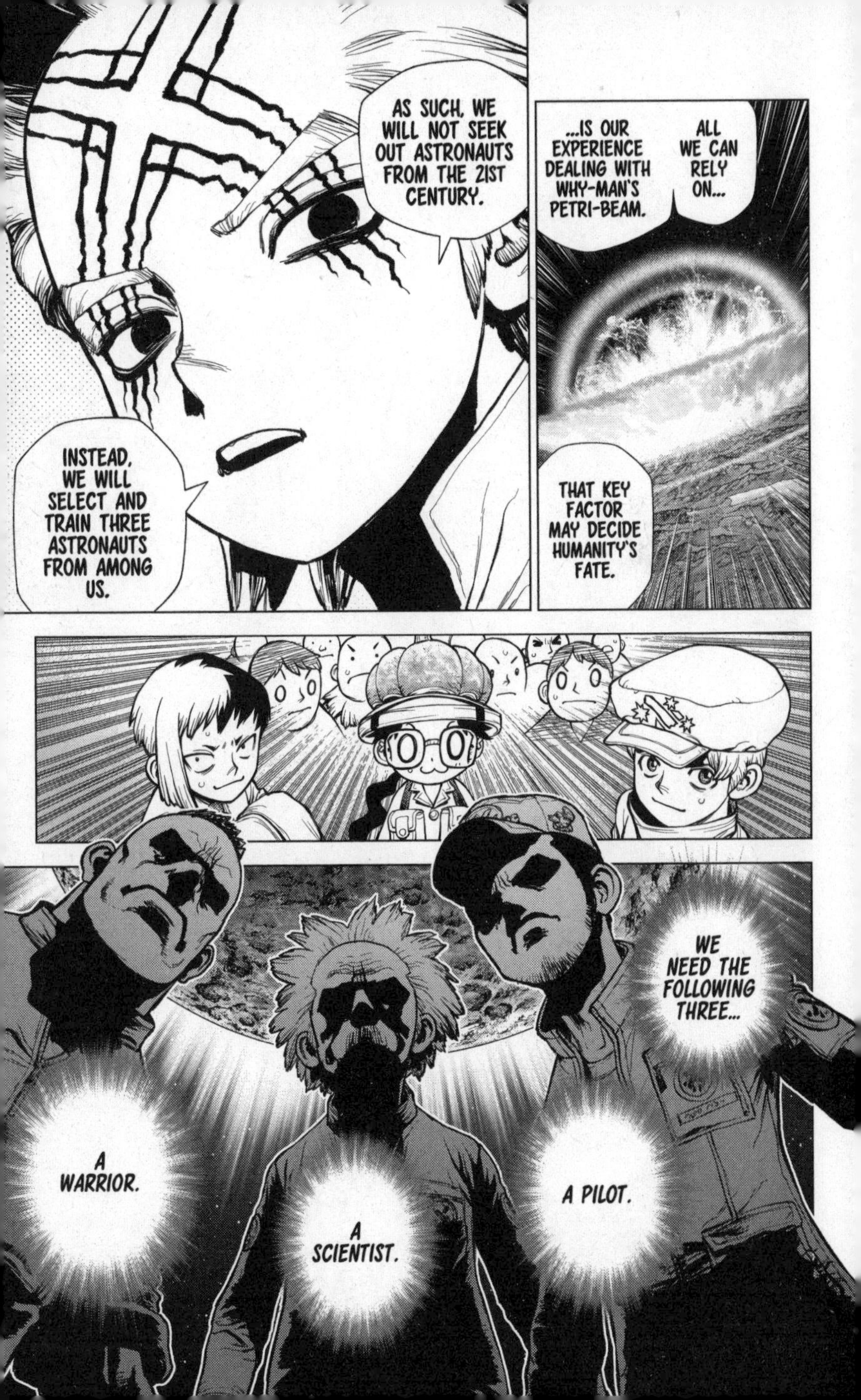
ALL WE CAN RELY ON...
...IS OUR EXPERIENCE DEALING WITH WHY-MAN'S PETRI-BEAM.
THAT KEY FACTOR MAY DECIDE HUMANITY'S FATE.
AS SUCH, WE WILL NOT SEEK OUT ASTRONAUTS FROM THE 21ST CENTURY.
INSTEAD, WE WILL SELECT AND TRAIN THREE ASTRONAUTS FROM AMONG US.
WE NEED THE FOLLOWING THREE...
A PILOT.
A SCIENTIST.
A WARRIOR.

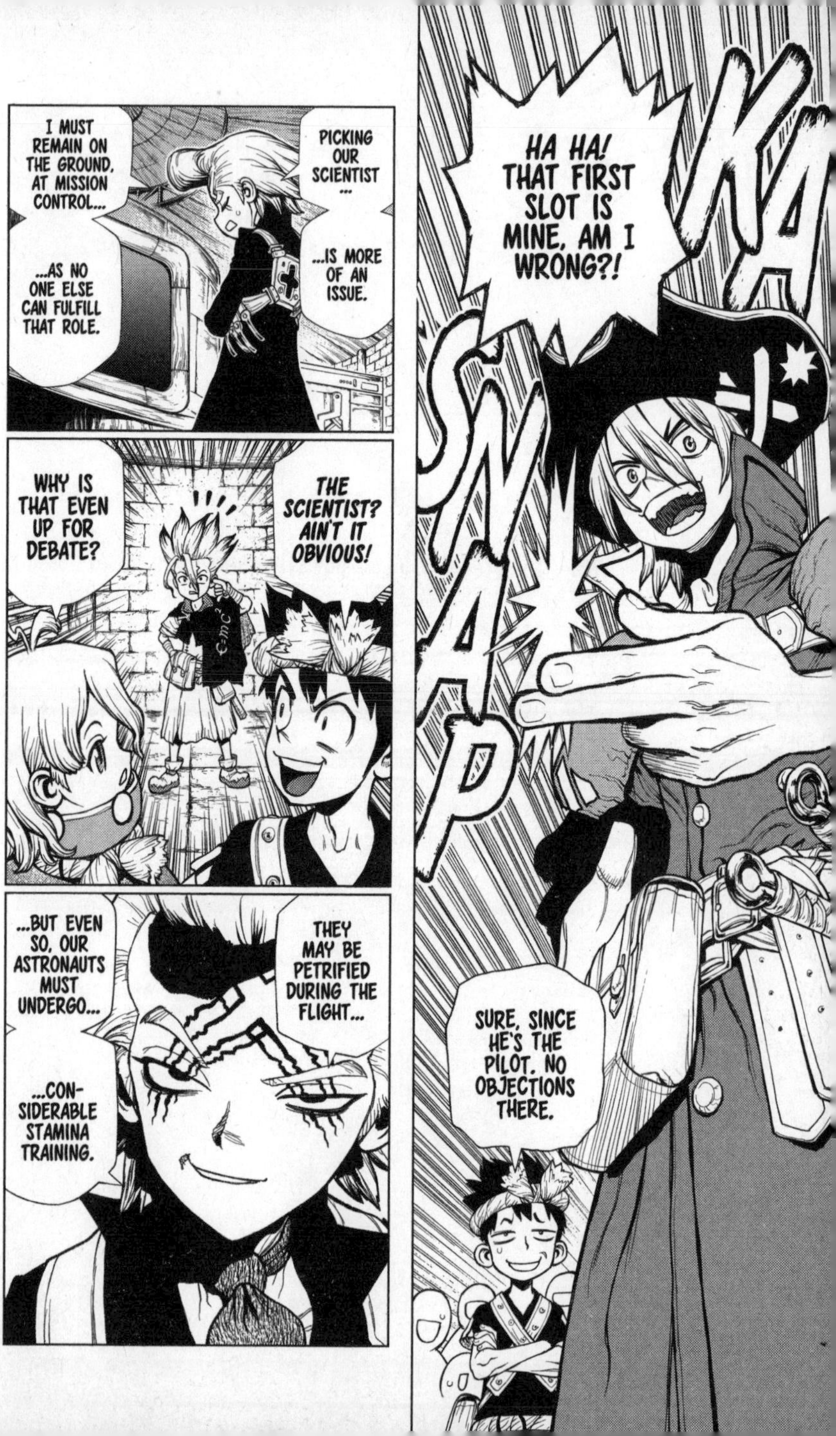

HA HA! THAT FIRST SLOT IS MINE, AM I WRONG?!
KA
SNAP
SURE, SINCE HE'S THE PILOT. NO OBJECTIONS THERE.
PICKING OUR SCIENTIST ...
...IS MORE OF AN ISSUE.
I MUST REMAIN ON THE GROUND, AT MISSION CONTROL...
...AS NO ONE ELSE CAN FULFILL THAT ROLE.
THE SCIENTIST? AIN'T IT OBVIOUS!
WHY IS THAT EVEN UP FOR DEBATE?
THEY MAY BE PETRIFIED DURING THE FLIGHT...
...BUT EVEN SO, OUR ASTRONAUTS MUST UNDERGO...
...CON- SIDERABLE STAMINA TRAINING.

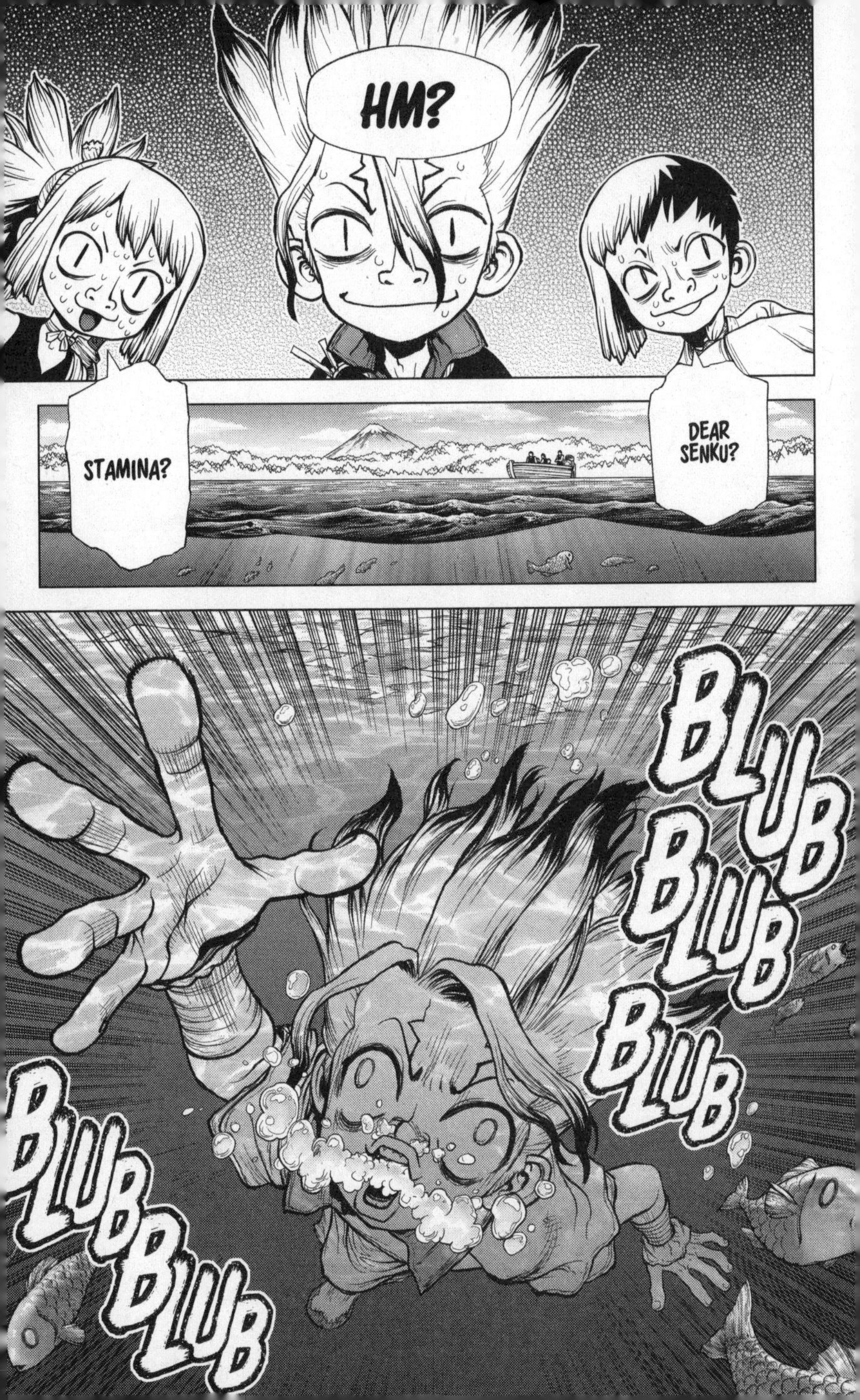
HM?
DEAR SENKU?
STAMINA?
BLUB BLUB BLUB
BLUB BLUB

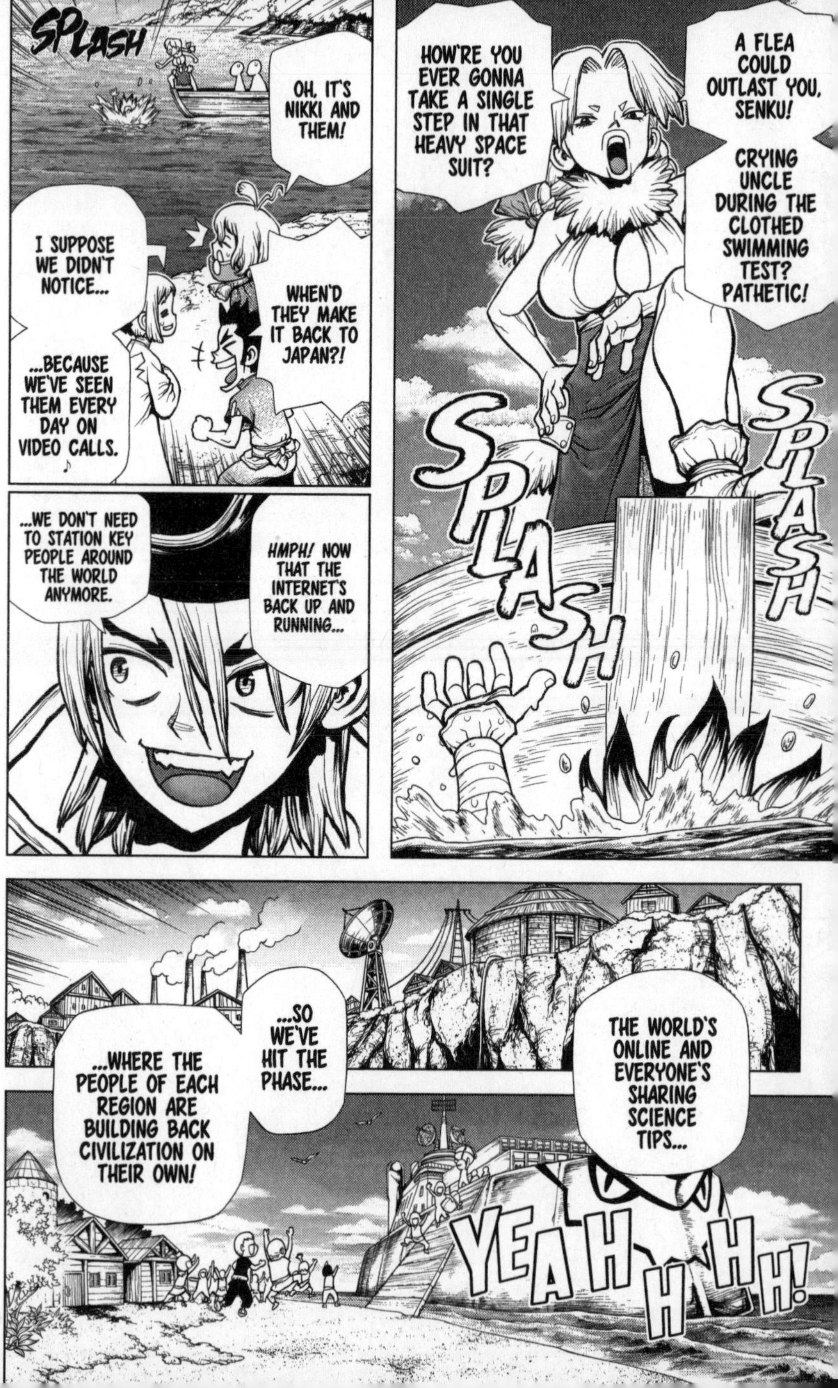
A FLEA COULD OUTLAST YOU, SENKU!
CRYING UNCLE DURING THE CLOTHED SWIMMING TEST? PATHETIC!
HOW'RE YOU EVER GONNA TAKE A SINGLE STEP IN THAT HEAVY SPACE SUIT?
SPLASH
SPLASH
SPLASH
OH, IT'S NIKKI AND THEM!
WHEN'D THEY MAKE IT BACK TO JAPAN?!
I SUPPOSE WE DIDN'T NOTICE...
...BECAUSE WE'VE SEEN THEM EVERY DAY ON VIDEO CALLS. ♪
HMPH! NOW THAT THE INTERNET'S BACK UP AND RUNNING...
...WE DON'T NEED TO STATION KEY PEOPLE AROUND THE WORLD ANYMORE.
THE WORLD'S ONLINE AND EVERYONE'S SHARING SCIENCE TIPS...
...SO WE'VE HIT THE PHASE...
...WHERE THE PEOPLE OF EACH REGION ARE BUILDING BACK CIVILIZATION ON THEIR OWN!
YEAHHHHH!

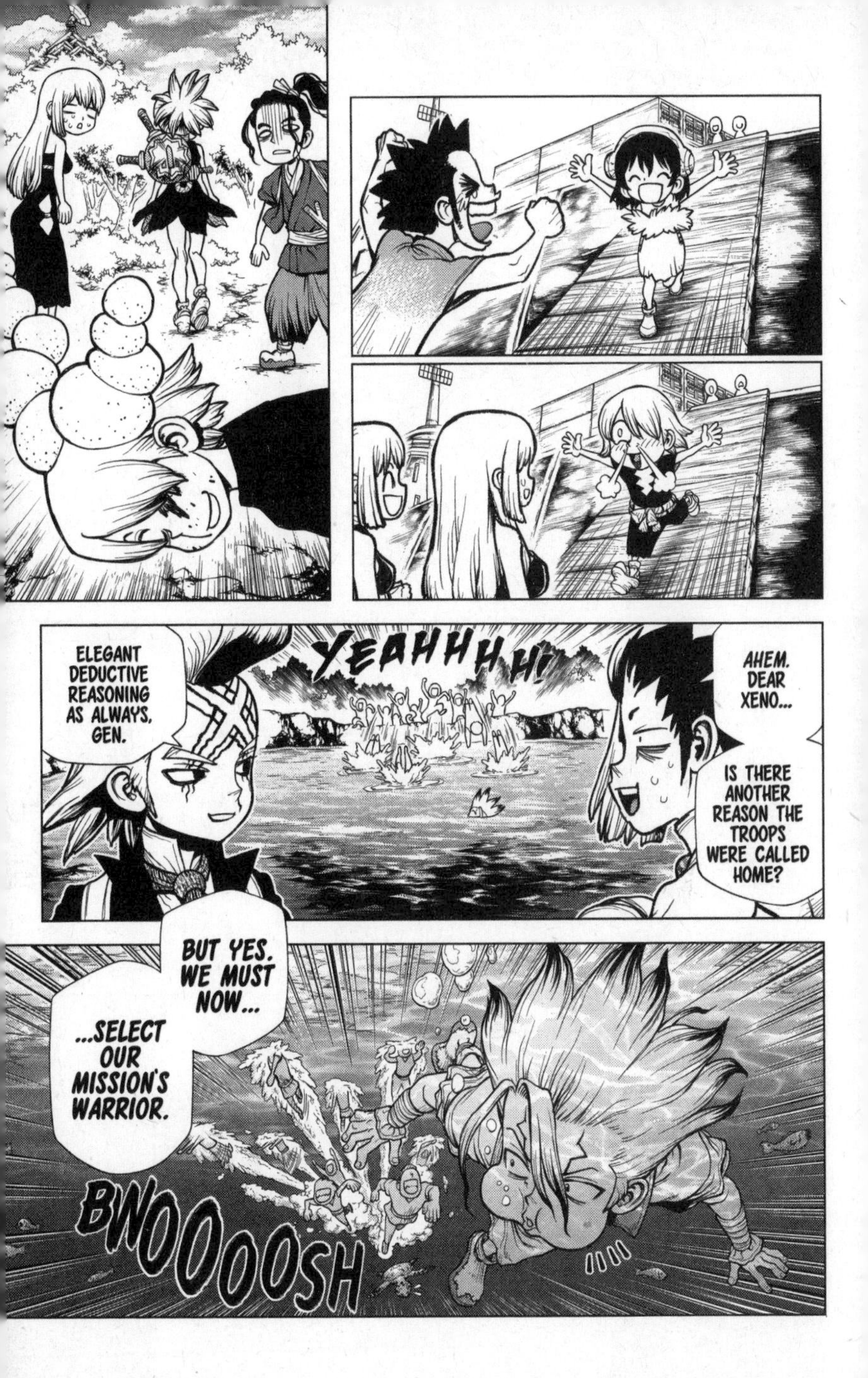
AHEM. DEAR XENO...
IS THERE ANOTHER REASON THE TROOPS WERE CALLED HOME?
YEAHHHHH!
ELEGANT DEDUCTIVE REASONING AS ALWAYS, GEN.
BUT YES. WE MUST NOW...
...SELECT OUR MISSION'S WARRIOR.
BWOOOOOSH

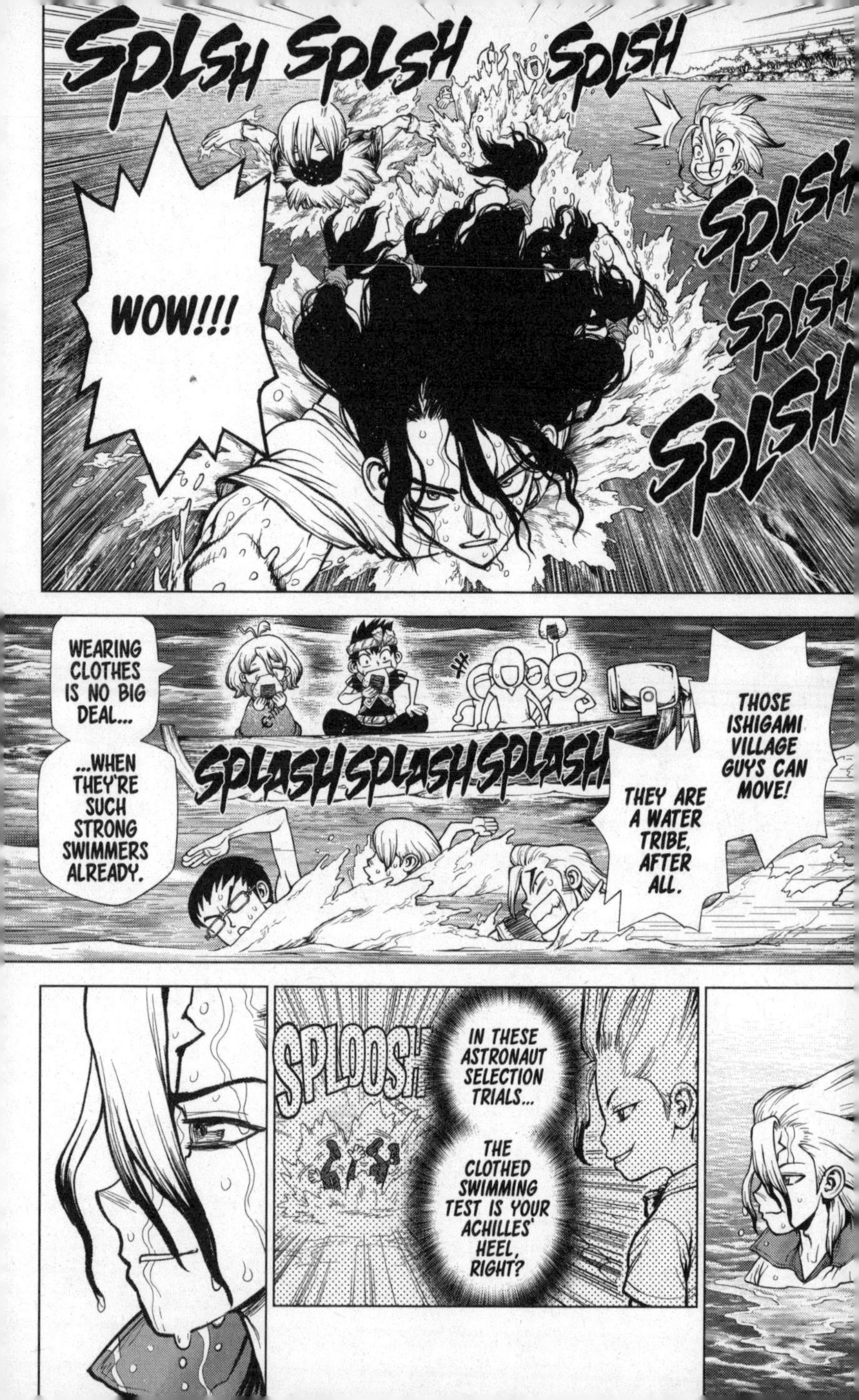
SPLSH SPLSH SPLSH
SPLSH SPLSH SPLSH
WOW!!!
THOSE ISHIGAMI VILLAGE GUYS CAN MOVE!
THEY ARE A WATER TRIBE, AFTER ALL.
SPLASH SPLASH SPLASH
WEARING CLOTHES IS NO BIG DEAL...
...WHEN THEY'RE SUCH STRONG SWIMMERS ALREADY.
SPLOOSH
IN THESE ASTRONAUT SELECTION TRIALS...
THE CLOTHED SWIMMING TEST IS YOUR ACHILLES' HEEL, RIGHT?

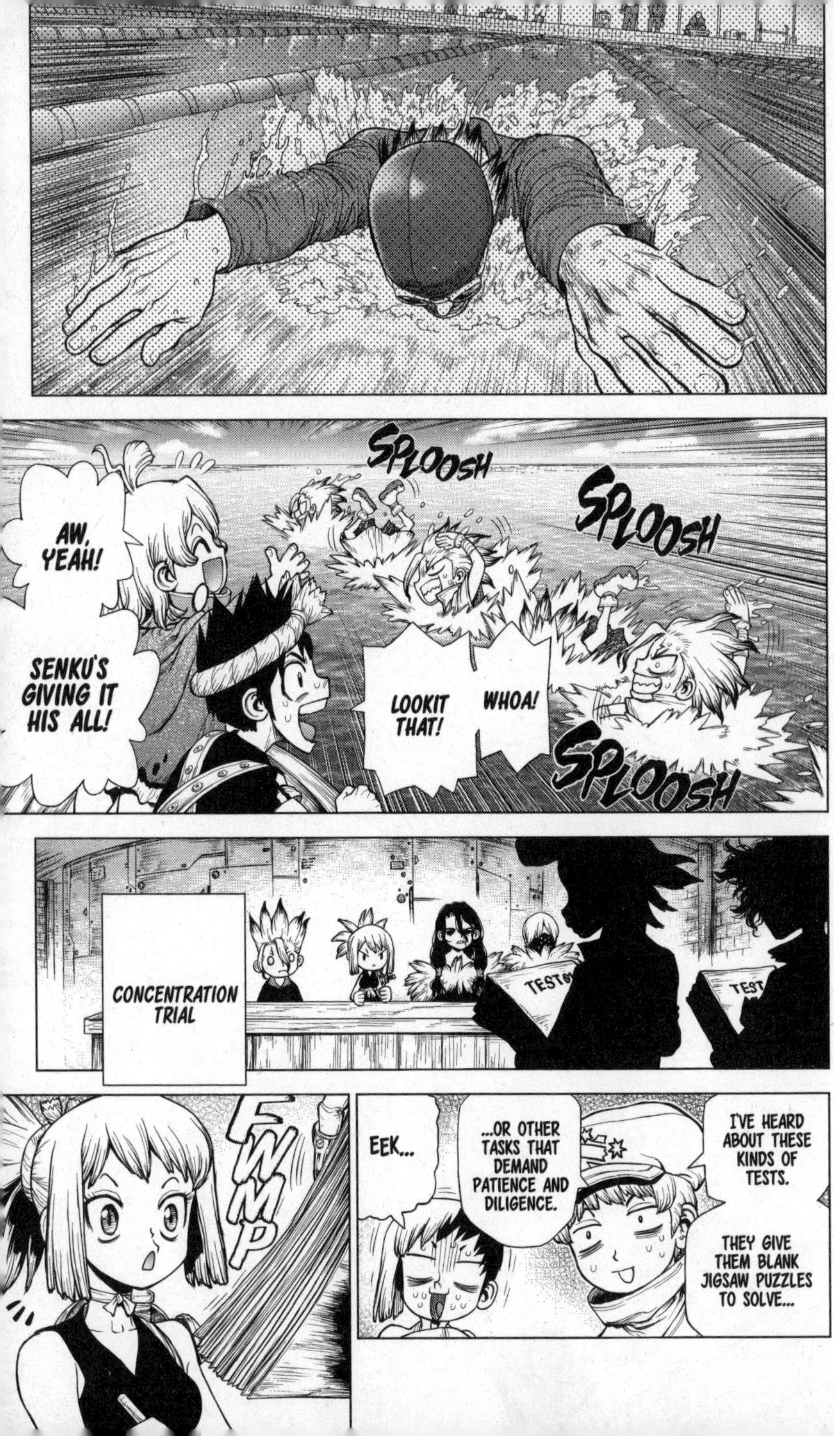
SPLOOSH
SPLOOSH
WHOA!
LOOKIT THAT!
SPLOOSH
AW, YEAH!
SENKU'S GIVING IT HIS ALL!
CONCENTRATION TRIAL
TEST
TEST
I'VE HEARD ABOUT THESE KINDS OF TESTS.
THEY GIVE THEM BLANK JIGSAW PUZZLES TO SOLVE...
...OR OTHER TASKS THAT DEMAND PATIENCE AND DILIGENCE.
EEK...
FWMP

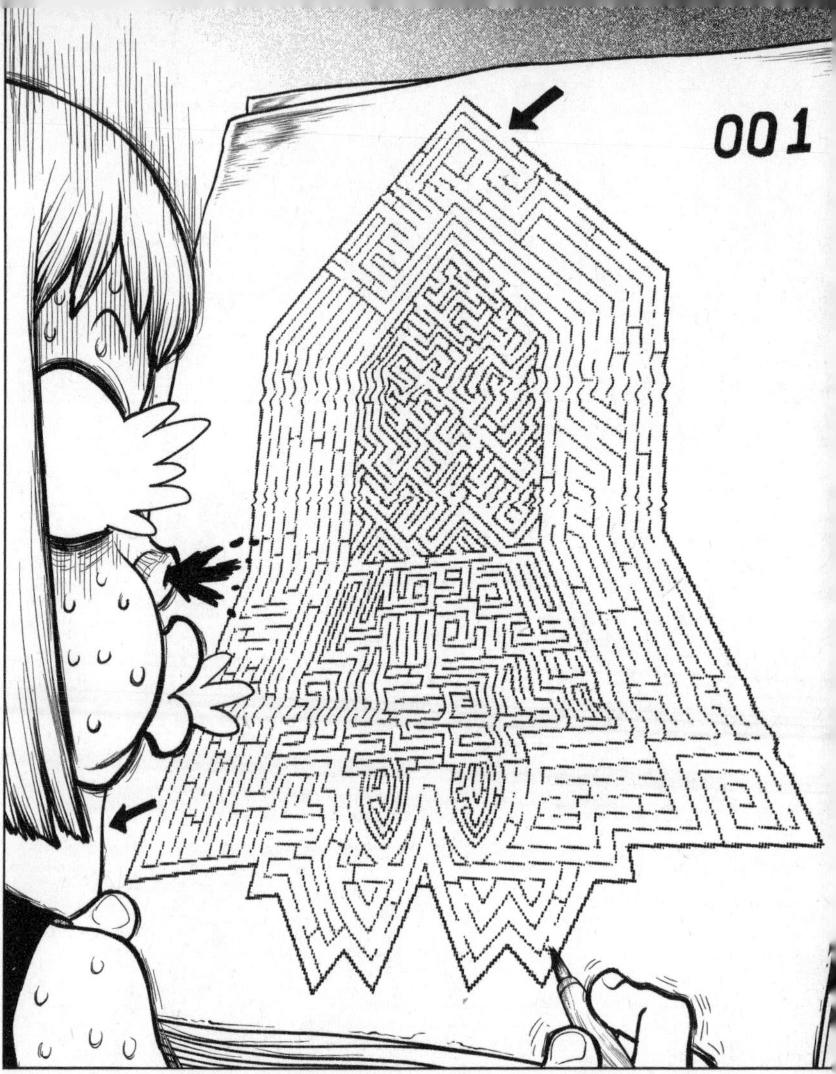
001

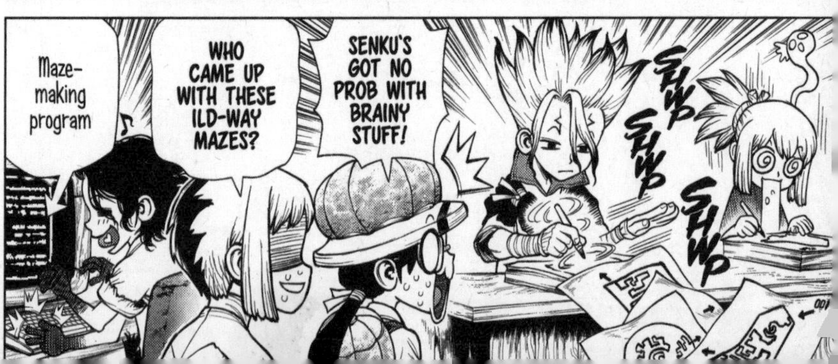
SHWP SHWP
SHWP SHWP
SENKU'S GOT NO PROB WITH BRAINY STUFF!
WHO CAME UP WITH THESE ILD-WAY MAZES?
Maze-making program

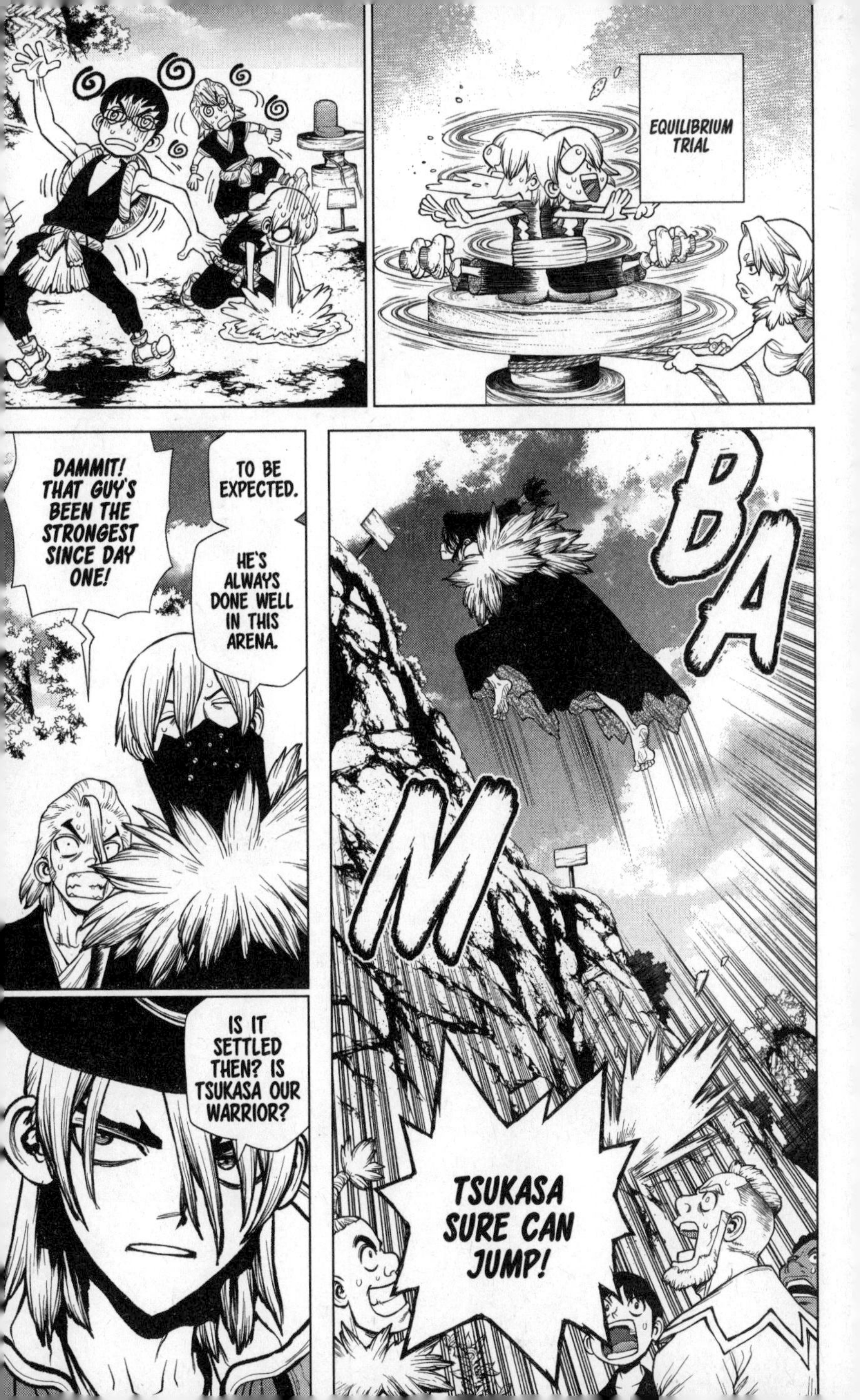
EQUILIBRIUM TRIAL
BAM
TSUKASA SURE CAN JUMP!
TO BE EXPECTED.
HE'S ALWAYS DONE WELL IN THIS ARENA.
DAMMIT! THAT GUY'S BEEN THE STRONGEST SINCE DAY ONE!
IS IT SETTLED THEN? IS TSUKASA OUR WARRIOR?

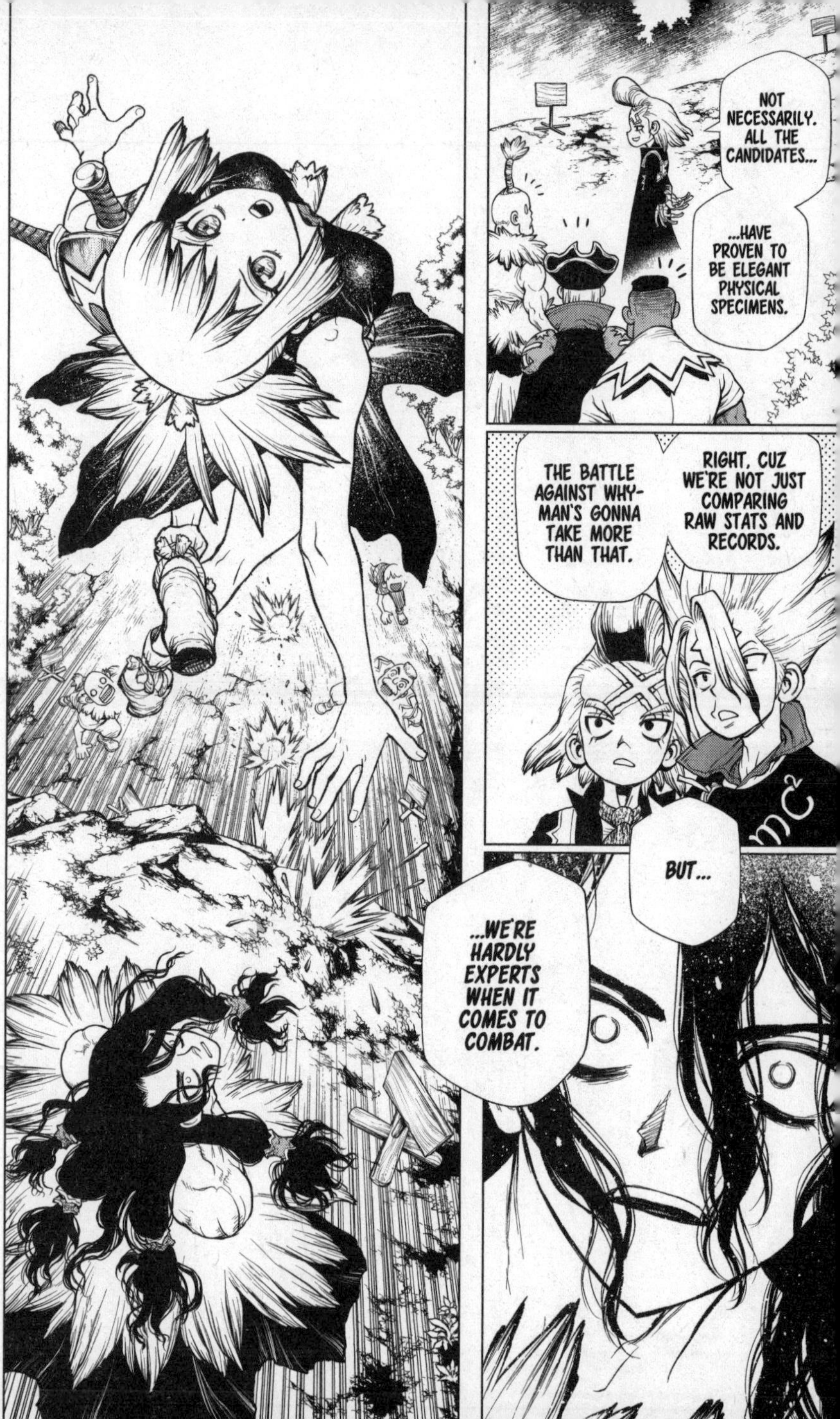
NOT NECESSARILY. ALL THE CANDIDATES...
...HAVE PROVEN TO BE ELEGANT PHYSICAL SPECIMENS.
RIGHT, CUZ WE'RE NOT JUST COMPARING RAW STATS AND RECORDS.
THE BATTLE AGAINST WHY-MAN'S GONNA TAKE MORE THAN THAT.
BUT...
...WE'RE HARDLY EXPERTS WHEN IT COMES TO COMBAT.

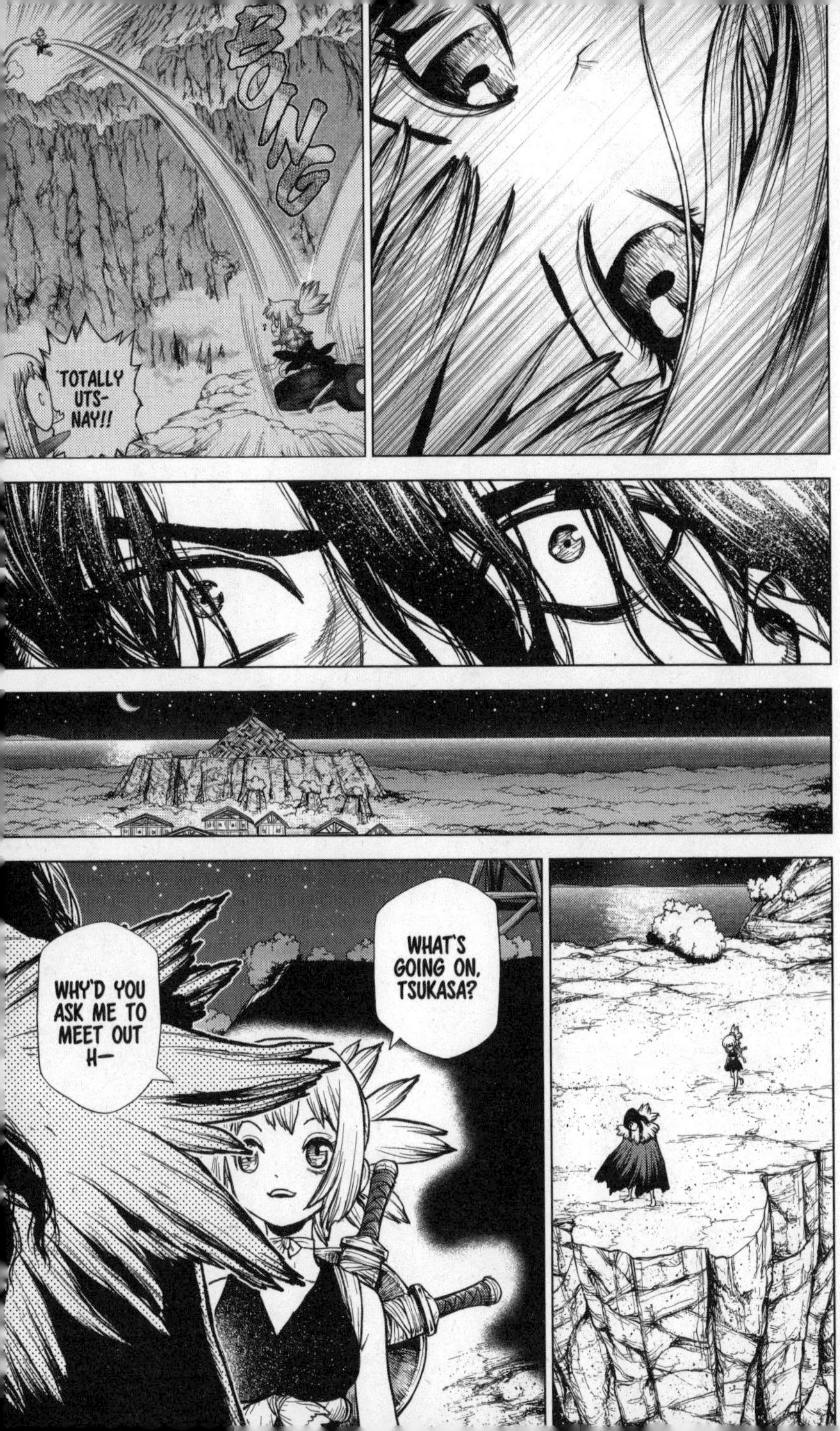
BOING
TOTALLY UTS-NAY!!
WHAT'S GOING ON, TSUKASA?
WHY'D YOU ASK ME TO MEET OUT H—

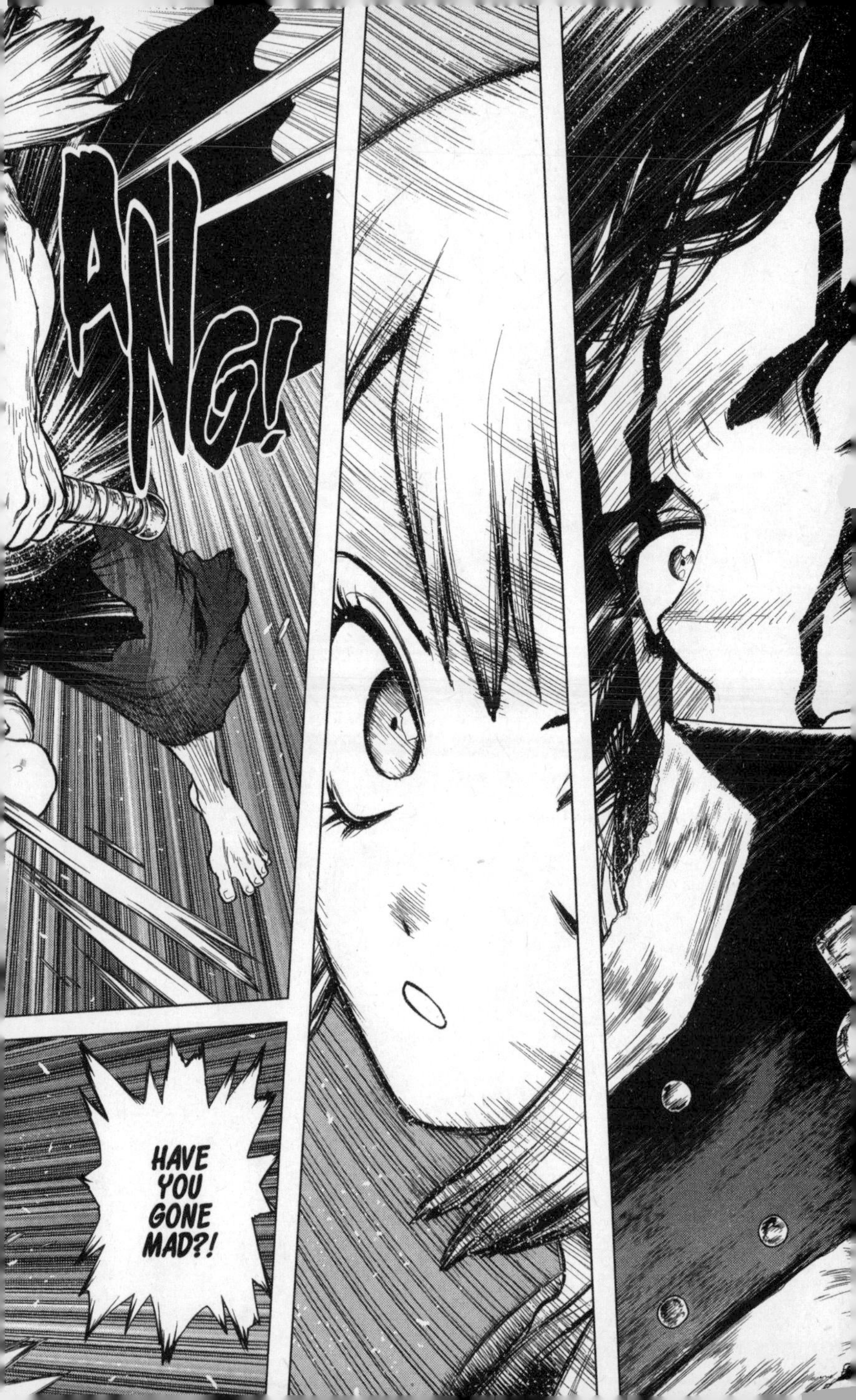
ANG!
HAVE YOU GONE MAD?!

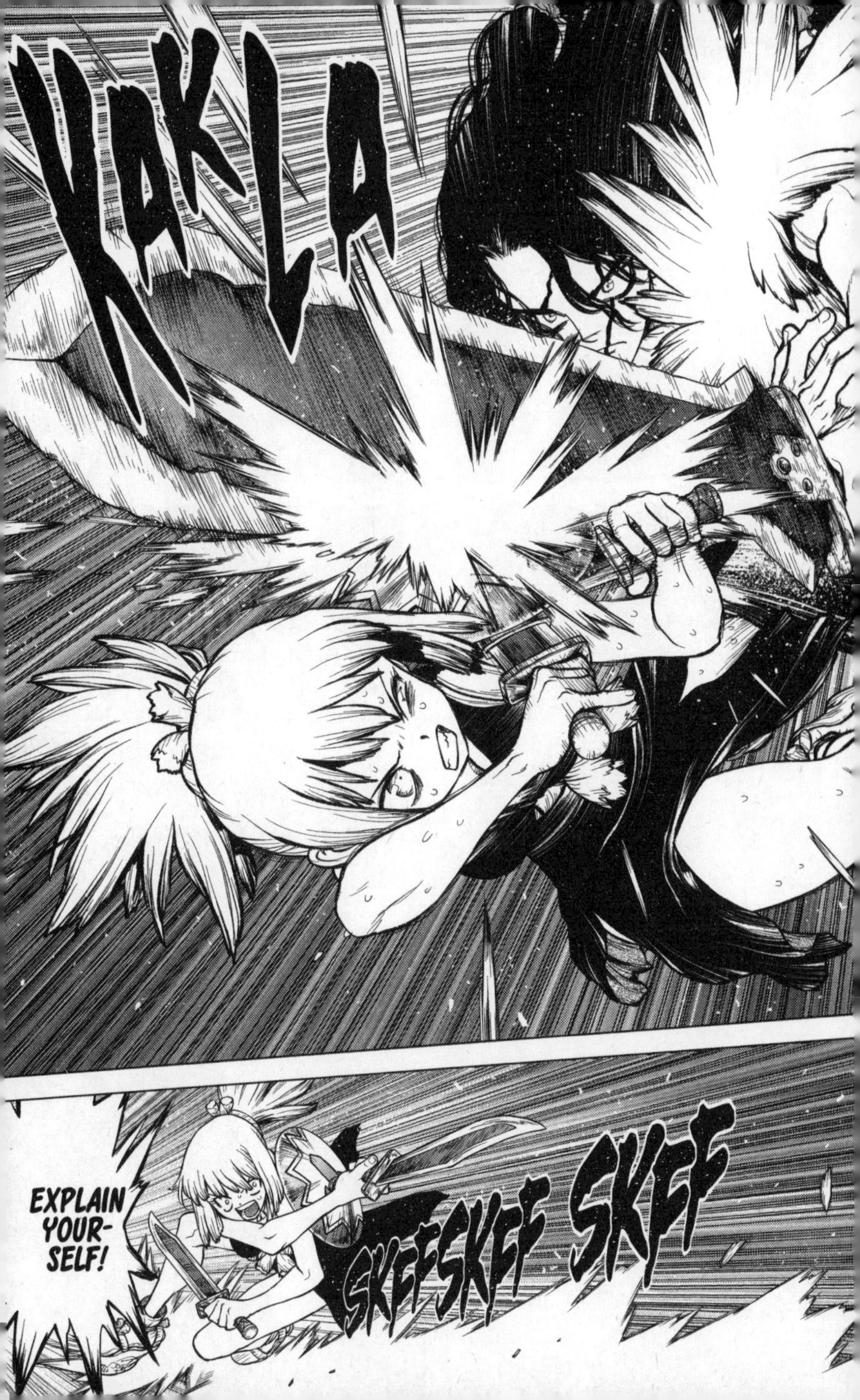
KAKLA
SKEFSKEF SKEF
EXPLAIN YOURSELF!

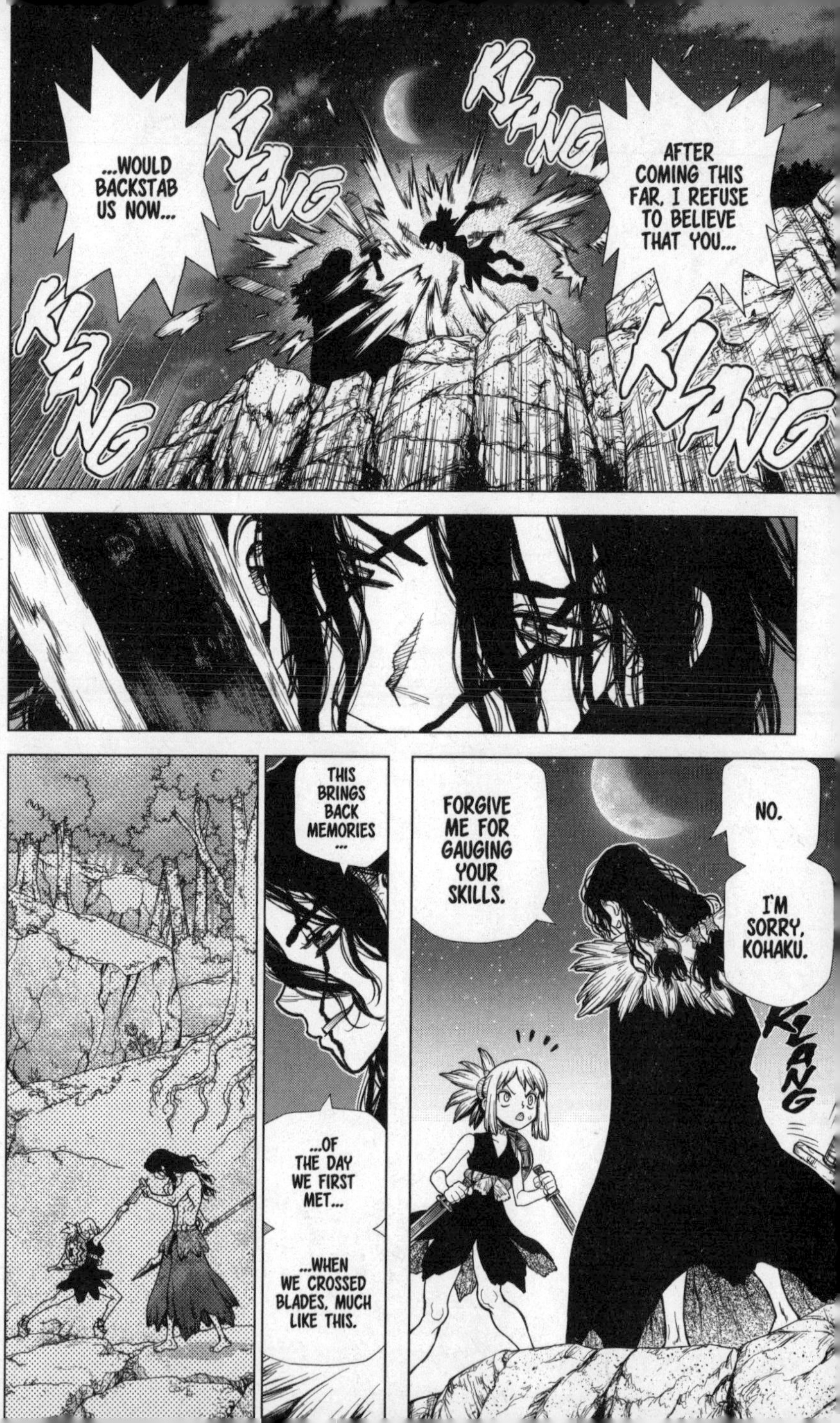
KLANG
AFTER COMING THIS FAR, I REFUSE TO BELIEVE THAT YOU...
KLANG
KLANG
...WOULD BACKSTAB US NOW...
KLANG
NO.
I'M SORRY, KOHAKU.
FORGIVE ME FOR GAUGING YOUR SKILLS.
KLANG
THIS BRINGS BACK MEMORIES...
...OF THE DAY WE FIRST MET...
...WHEN WE CROSSED BLADES, MUCH LIKE THIS.

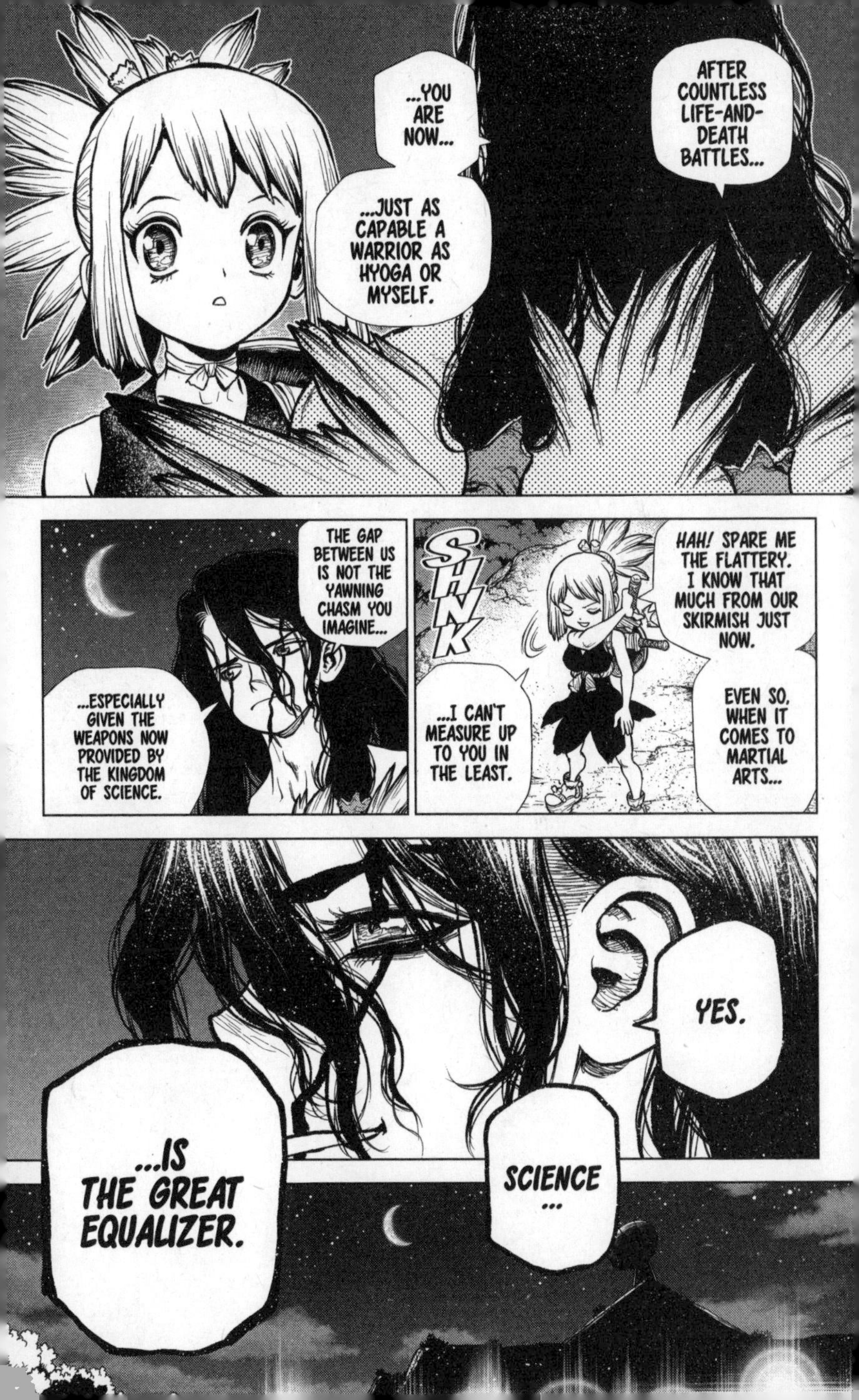
AFTER COUNTLESS LIFE-AND-DEATH BATTLES...
...YOU ARE NOW...
...JUST AS CAPABLE A WARRIOR AS HYOGA OR MYSELF.
HAH! SPARE ME THE FLATTERY. I KNOW THAT MUCH FROM OUR SKIRMISH JUST NOW.
SHNK
EVEN SO, WHEN IT COMES TO MARTIAL ARTS...
...I CAN'T MEASURE UP TO YOU IN THE LEAST.
THE GAP BETWEEN US IS NOT THE YAWNING CHASM YOU IMAGINE...
...ESPECIALLY GIVEN THE WEAPONS NOW PROVIDED BY THE KINGDOM OF SCIENCE.
YES.
SCIENCE ...
...IS THE GREAT EQUALIZER.

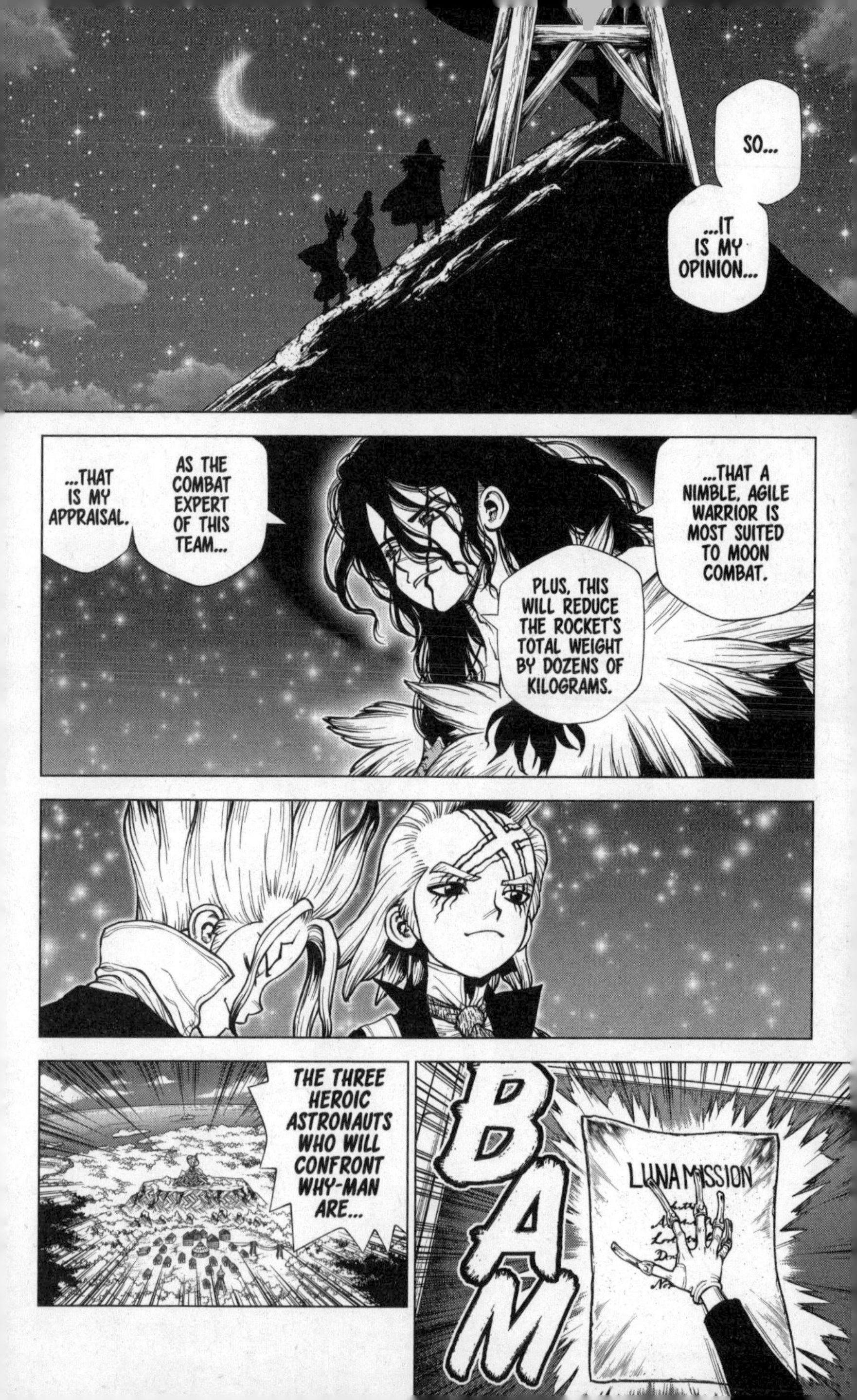
SO...
...IT IS MY OPINION...
...THAT A NIMBLE, AGILE WARRIOR IS MOST SUITED TO MOON COMBAT.
AS THE COMBAT EXPERT OF THIS TEAM...
...THAT IS MY APPRAISAL.
PLUS, THIS WILL REDUCE THE ROCKET'S TOTAL WEIGHT BY DOZENS OF KILOGRAMS.
BAM
LUNA MISSION
THE THREE HEROIC ASTRONAUTS WHO WILL CONFRONT WHY-MAN ARE...

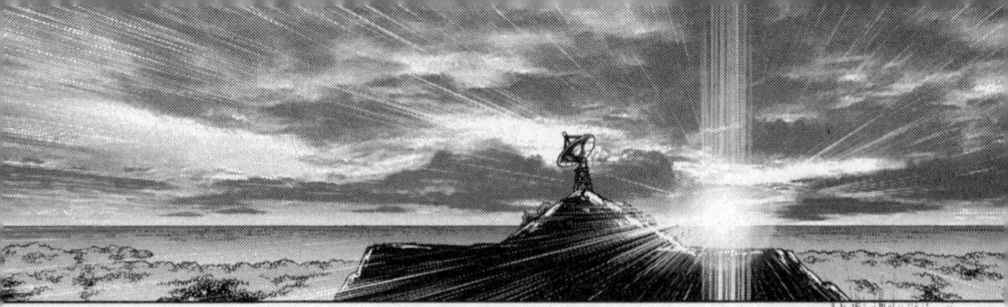
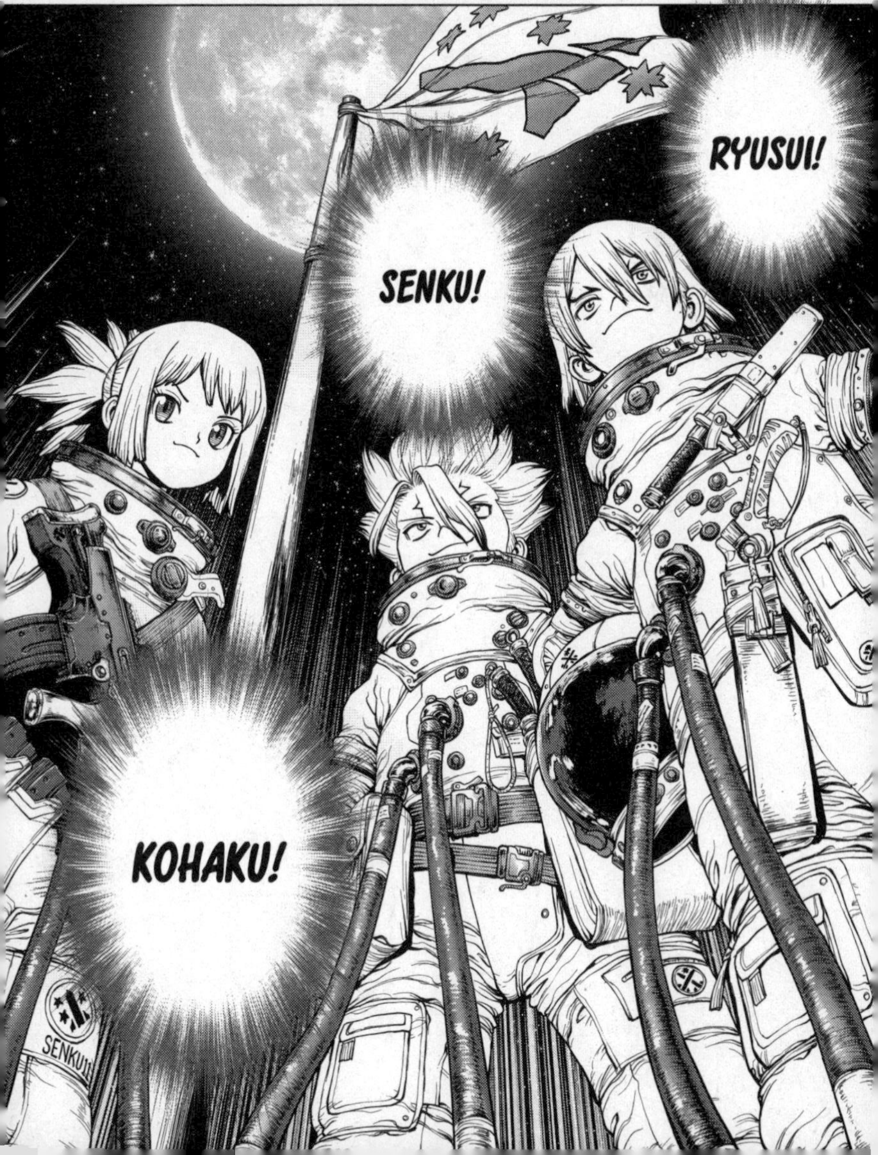
RYUSUI!
SENKU!
KOHAKU!

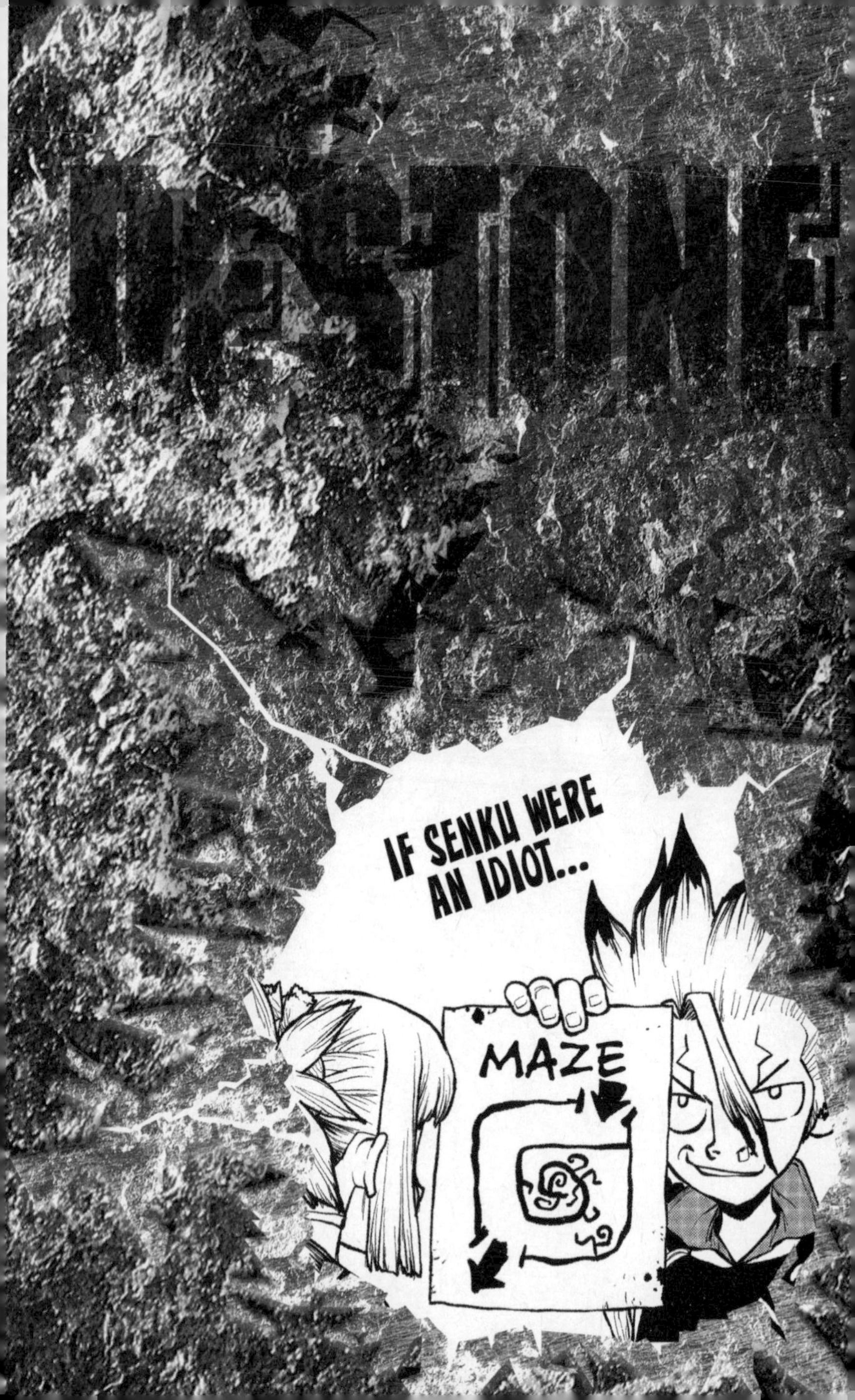
DR.STONE
IF SENKU WERE AN IDIOT...
MAZE

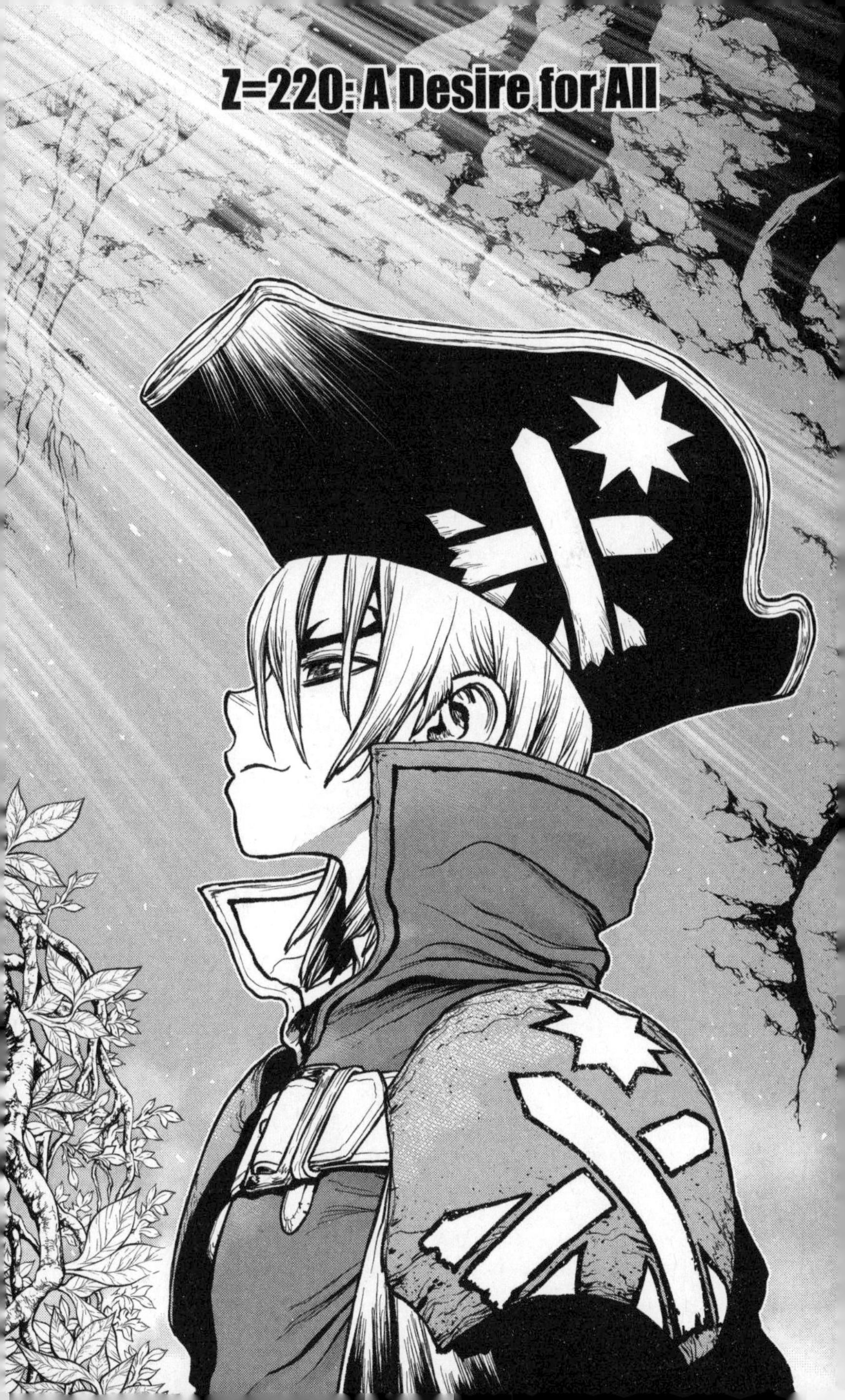
Z=220: A Desire for All

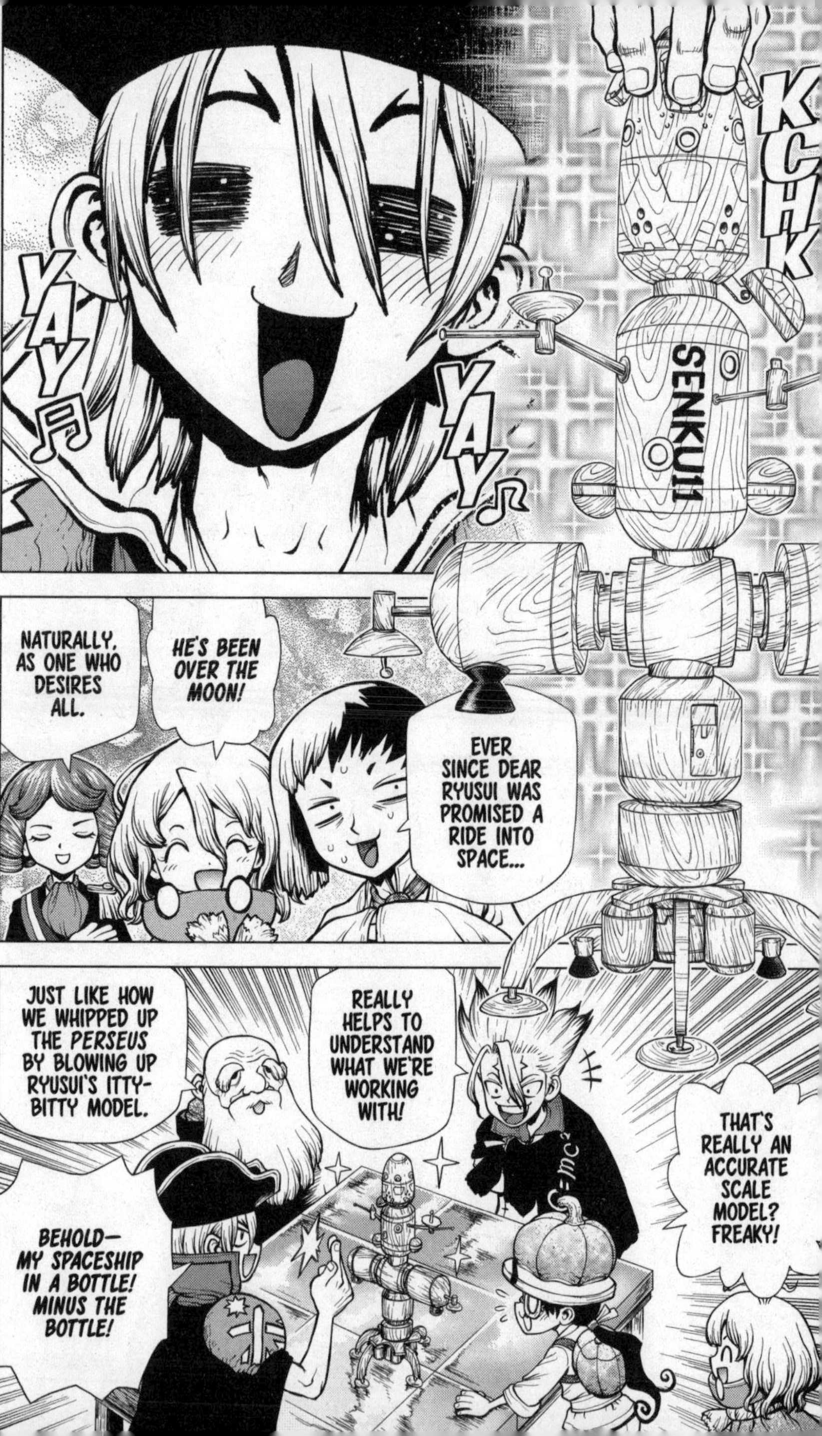
KCHK
SENKU11
YAY YAY♪
YAY YAY♪
EVER SINCE DEAR RYUSUI WAS PROMISED A RIDE INTO SPACE...
HE'S BEEN OVER THE MOON!
NATURALLY, AS ONE WHO DESIRES ALL.
THAT'S REALLY AN ACCURATE SCALE MODEL? FREAKY!
REALLY HELPS TO UNDERSTAND WHAT WE'RE WORKING WITH!
JUST LIKE HOW WE WHIPPED UP THE PERSEUS BY BLOWING UP RYUSUI'S ITTY-BITTY MODEL.
BEHOLD— MY SPACESHIP IN A BOTTLE! MINUS THE BOTTLE!

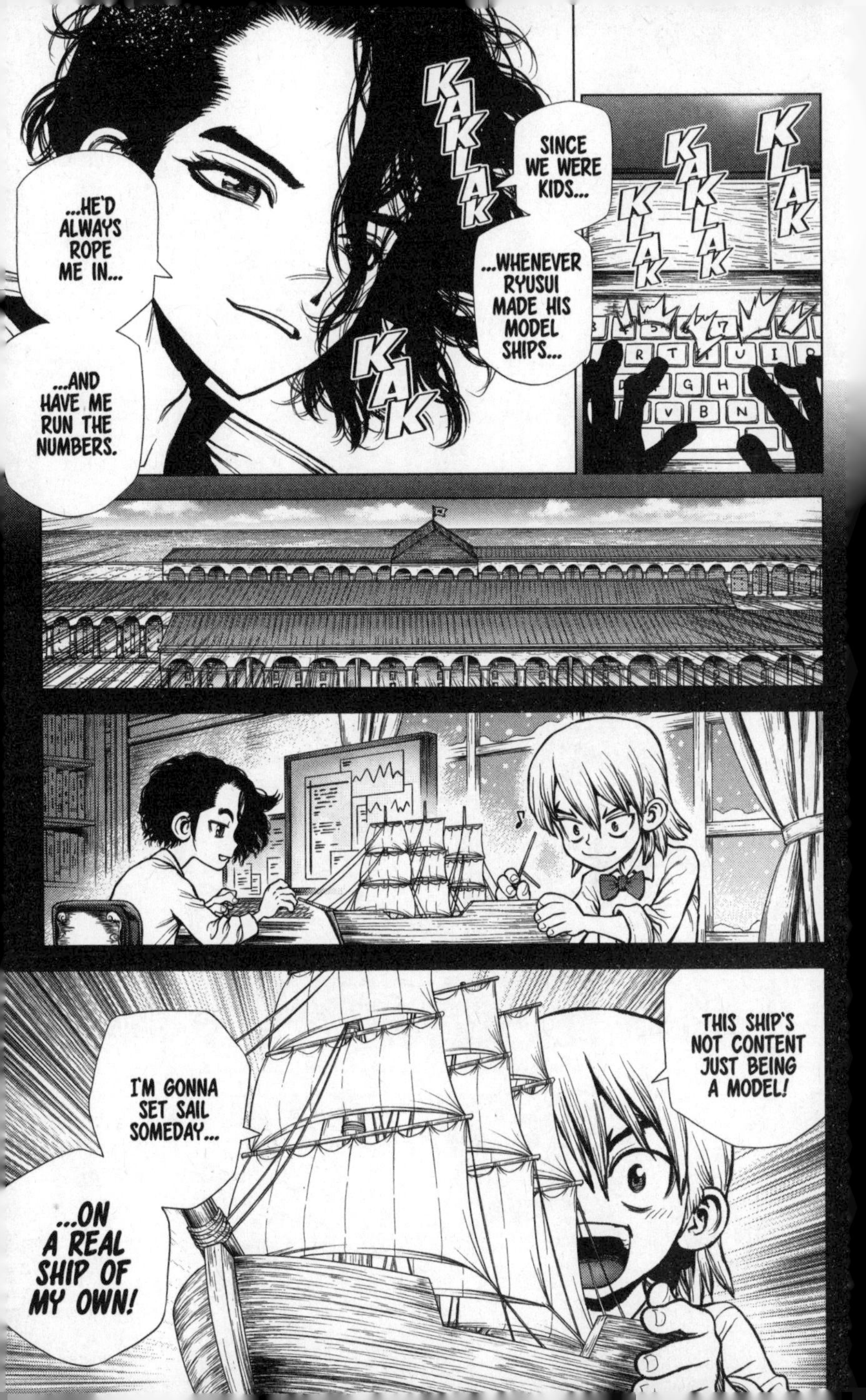
KLAK
KAKLAK
KLAK
KAKLAK
SINCE WE WERE KIDS...
...WHENEVER RYUSUI MADE HIS MODEL SHIPS...
...HE'D ALWAYS ROPE ME IN...
KAK
...AND HAVE ME RUN THE NUMBERS.
THIS SHIP'S NOT CONTENT JUST BEING A MODEL!
I'M GONNA SET SAIL SOMEDAY...
...ON A REAL SHIP OF MY OWN!

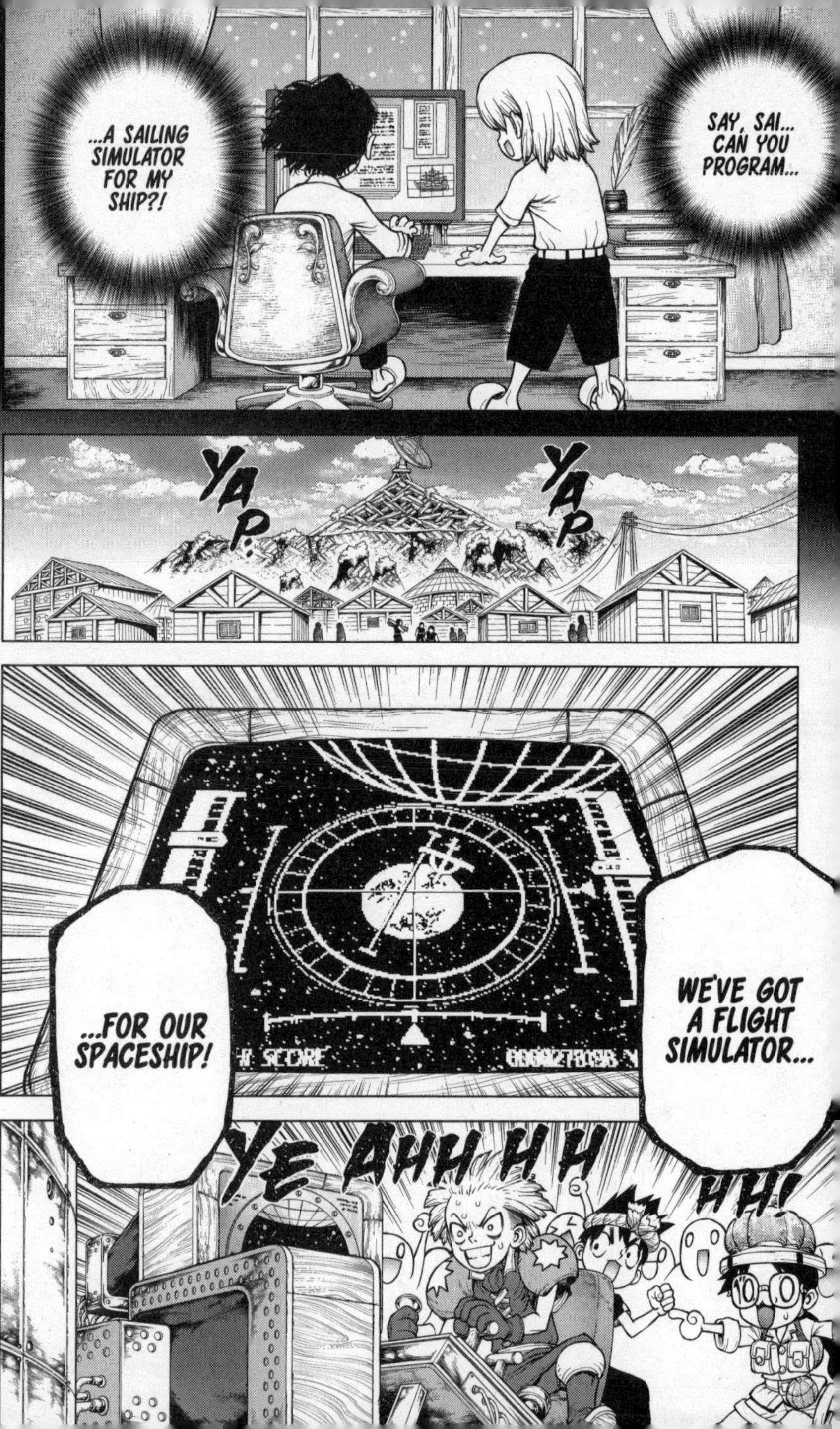
SAY, SAI... CAN YOU PROGRAM...
...A SAILING SIMULATOR FOR MY SHIP?!
YAP YAP
YAP YAP
WE'VE GOT A FLIGHT SIMULATOR...
...FOR OUR SPACESHIP!
SCORE
YEAHHHHHH!

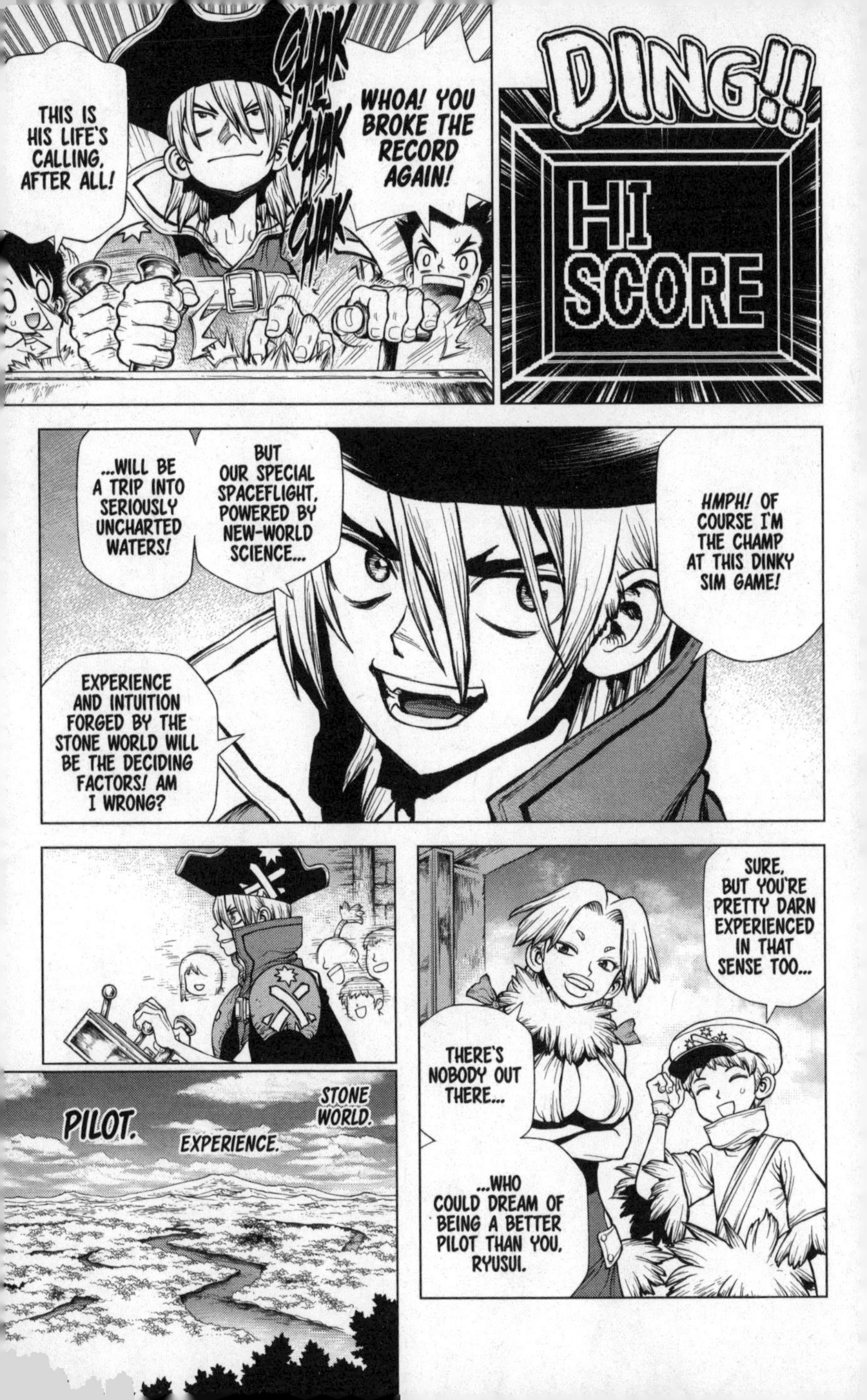
DING!!
HI SCORE
WHOA! YOU BROKE THE RECORD AGAIN!
CLAK CLAK CLAK CLAK
THIS IS HIS LIFE'S CALLING, AFTER ALL!
HMPH! OF COURSE I'M THE CHAMP AT THIS DINKY SIM GAME!
BUT OUR SPECIAL SPACEFLIGHT, POWERED BY NEW-WORLD SCIENCE...
...WILL BE A TRIP INTO SERIOUSLY UNCHARTED WATERS!
EXPERIENCE AND INTUITION FORGED BY THE STONE WORLD WILL BE THE DECIDING FACTORS! AM I WRONG?
SURE, BUT YOU'RE PRETTY DARN EXPERIENCED IN THAT SENSE TOO...
THERE'S NOBODY OUT THERE...
...WHO COULD DREAM OF BEING A BETTER PILOT THAN YOU, RYUSUI.
STONE WORLD.
PILOT.
EXPERIENCE.

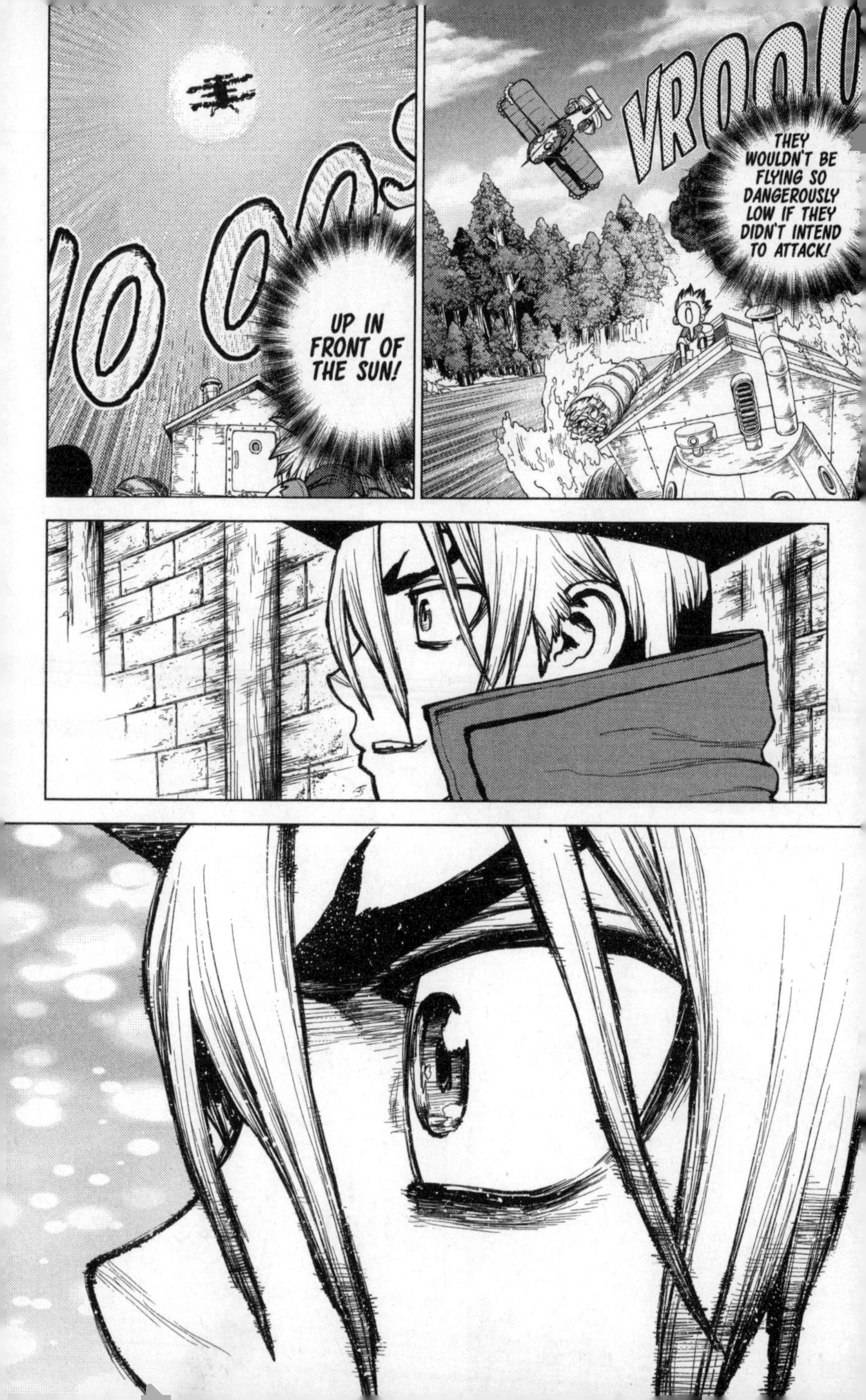
VROOO
THEY WOULDN'T BE FLYING SO DANGEROUSLY LOW IF THEY DIDN'T INTEND TO ATTACK!
UP IN FRONT OF THE SUN!

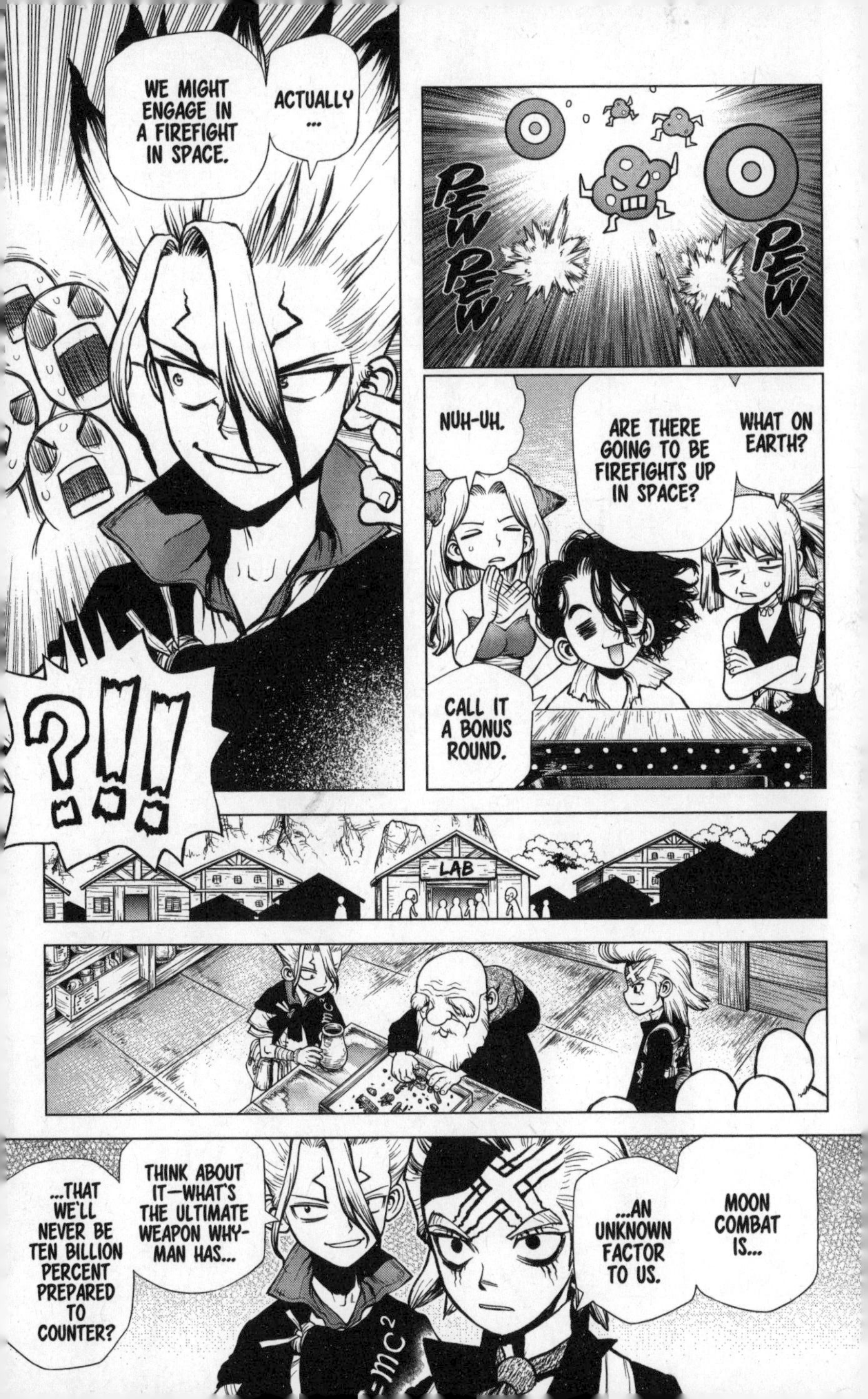
PEW
PEW PEW
WHAT ON EARTH?
ARE THERE GOING TO BE FIREFIGHTS UP IN SPACE?
NUH-UH.
CALL IT A BONUS ROUND.
ACTUALLY...
WE MIGHT ENGAGE IN A FIREFIGHT IN SPACE.
?!!
LAB
MOON COMBAT IS...
...AN UNKNOWN FACTOR TO US.
THINK ABOUT IT—WHAT'S THE ULTIMATE WEAPON WHY-MAN HAS...
...THAT WE'LL NEVER BE TEN BILLION PERCENT PREPARED TO COUNTER?

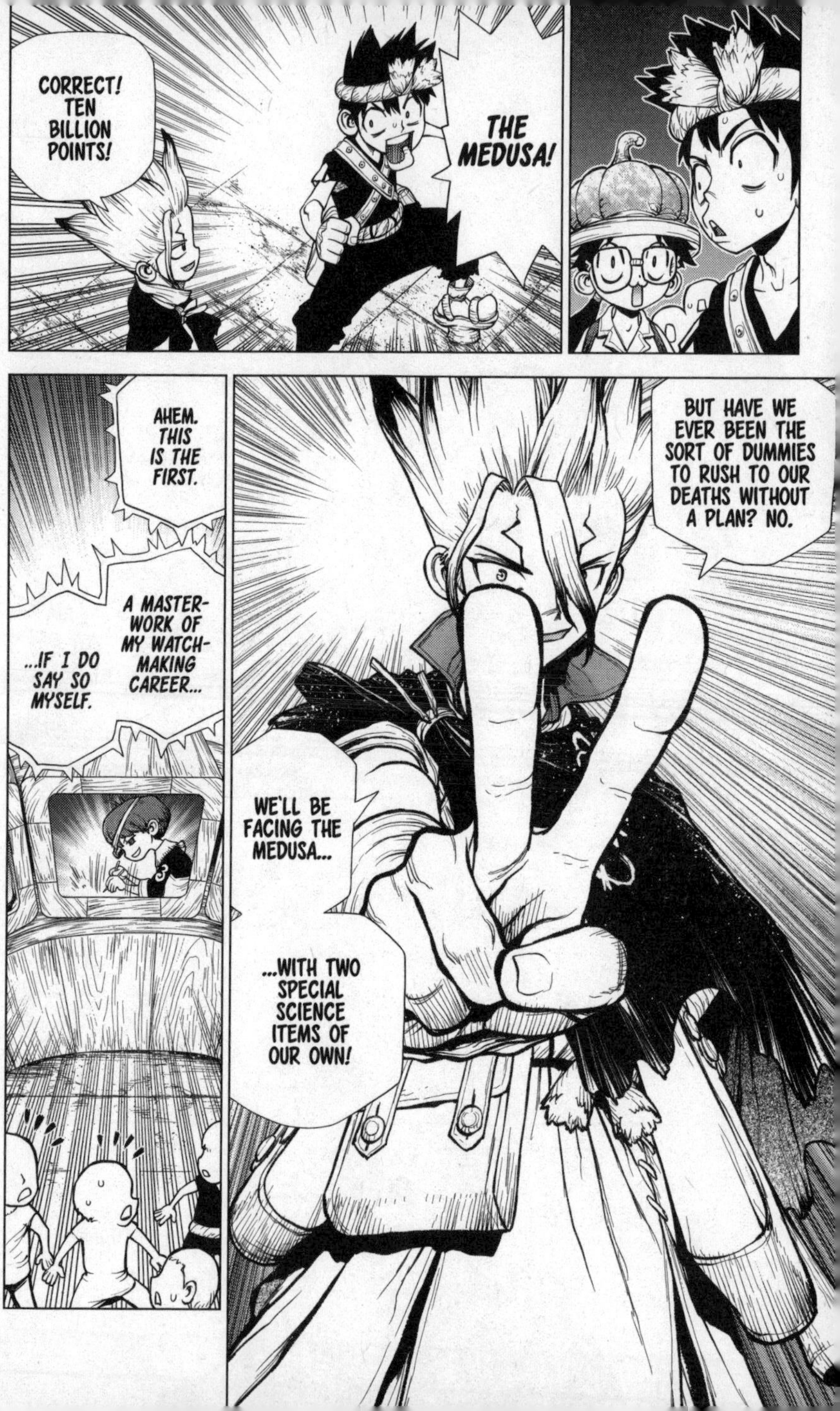
THE MEDUSA!
CORRECT! TEN BILLION POINTS!
BUT HAVE WE EVER BEEN THE SORT OF DUMMIES TO RUSH TO OUR DEATHS WITHOUT A PLAN? NO.
WE'LL BE FACING THE MEDUSA...
...WITH TWO SPECIAL SCIENCE ITEMS OF OUR OWN!
AHEM. THIS IS THE FIRST.
A MASTER-WORK OF MY WATCH-MAKING CAREER...
...IF I DO SAY SO MYSELF.

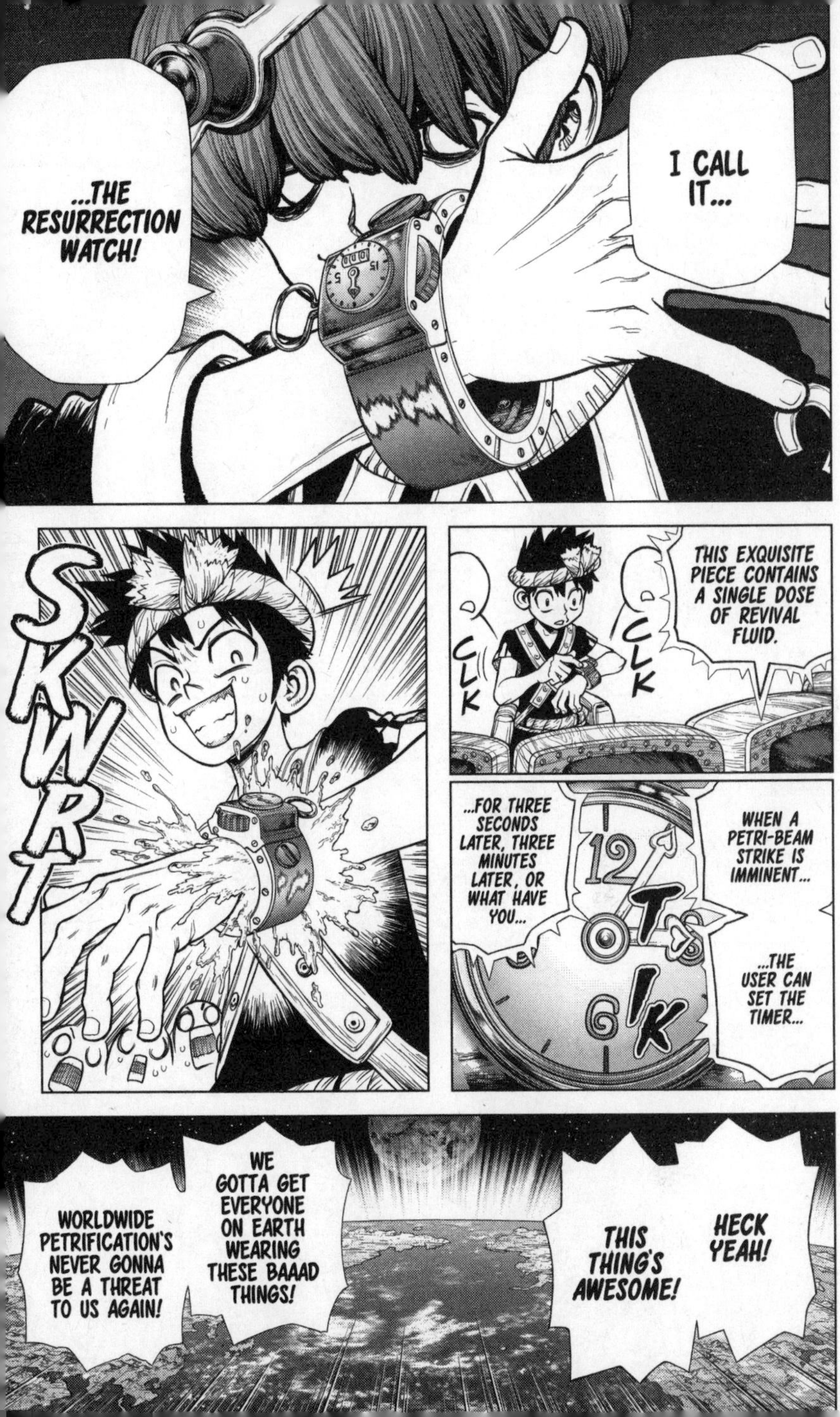
I CALL IT...
...THE RESURRECTION WATCH!
CLK
CLK
THIS EXQUISITE PIECE CONTAINS A SINGLE DOSE OF REVIVAL FLUID.
WHEN A PETRI-BEAM STRIKE IS IMMINENT...
...THE USER CAN SET THE TIMER...
...FOR THREE SECONDS LATER, THREE MINUTES LATER, OR WHAT HAVE YOU...
TIK
SKWRT
HECK YEAH!
THIS THING'S AWESOME!
WE GOTTA GET EVERYONE ON EARTH WEARING THESE BAAAD THINGS!
WORLDWIDE PETRIFICATION'S NEVER GONNA BE A THREAT TO US AGAIN!

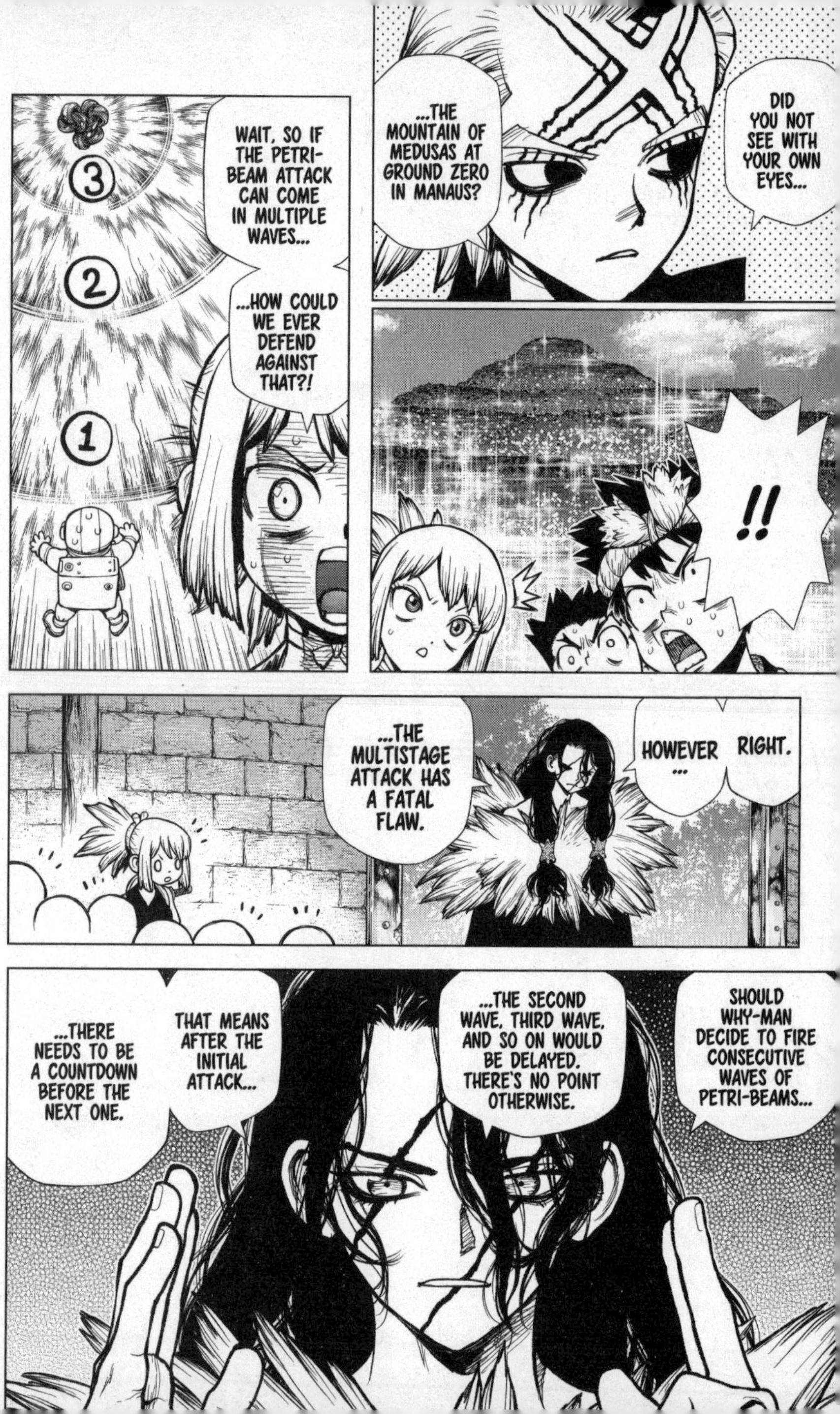
DID YOU NOT SEE WITH YOUR OWN EYES...
...THE MOUNTAIN OF MEDUSAS AT GROUND ZERO IN MANAUS?
!!
3
2
1
WAIT, SO IF THE PETRI-BEAM ATTACK CAN COME IN MULTIPLE WAVES...
...HOW COULD WE EVER DEFEND AGAINST THAT?!
RIGHT.
HOWEVER ...
...THE MULTISTAGE ATTACK HAS A FATAL FLAW.
SHOULD WHY-MAN DECIDE TO FIRE CONSECUTIVE WAVES OF PETRI-BEAMS...
...THE SECOND WAVE, THIRD WAVE, AND SO ON WOULD BE DELAYED. THERE'S NO POINT OTHERWISE.
THAT MEANS AFTER THE INITIAL ATTACK...
...THERE NEEDS TO BE A COUNTDOWN BEFORE THE NEXT ONE.

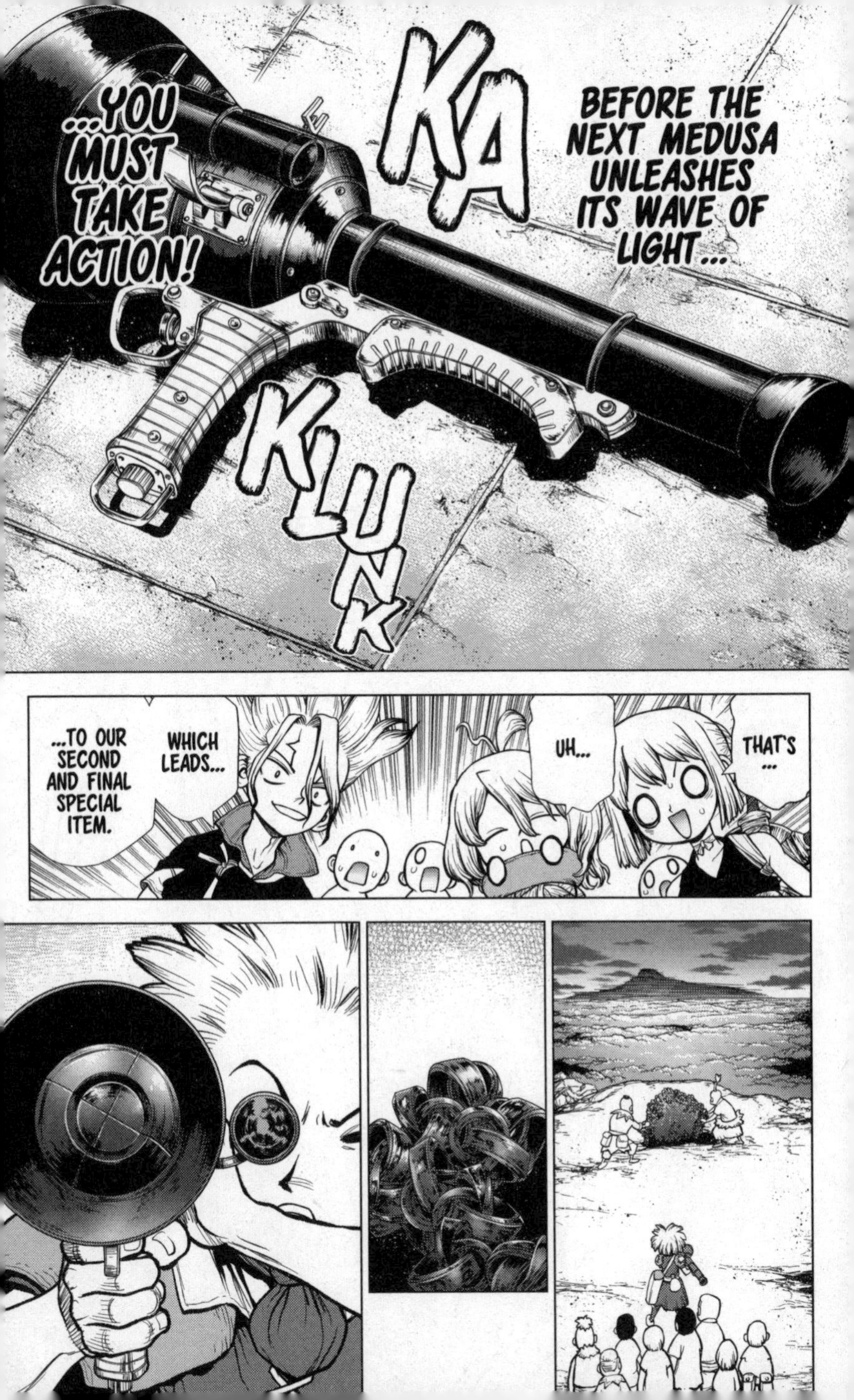
BEFORE THE NEXT MEDUSA UNLEASHES ITS WAVE OF LIGHT...
KA
...YOU MUST TAKE ACTION!
KLUNK
THAT'S ...
UH...
WHICH LEADS...
...TO OUR SECOND AND FINAL SPECIAL ITEM.

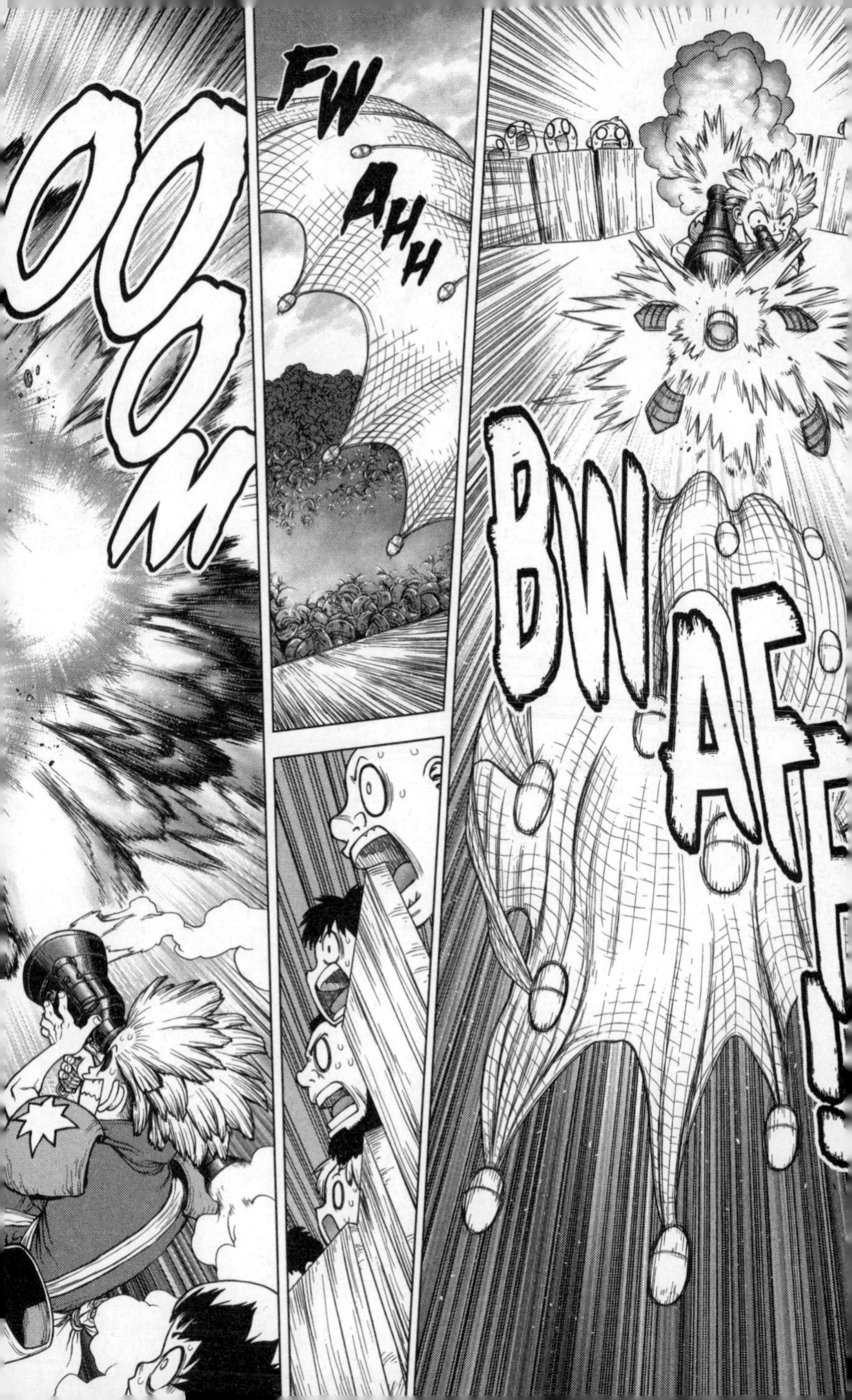
BWAF!
FWAHH
OOOM

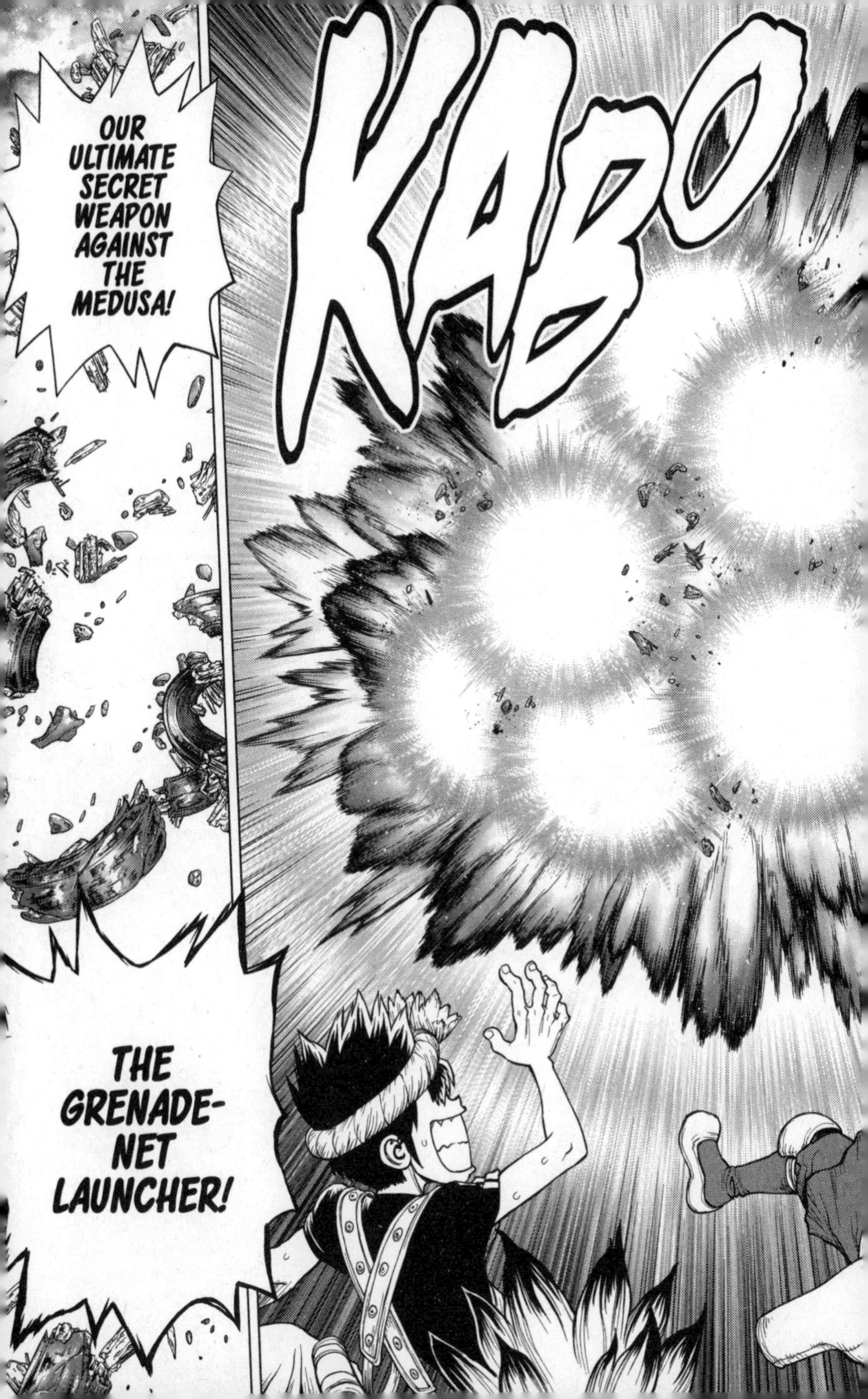
KABO
OUR ULTIMATE SECRET WEAPON AGAINST THE MEDUSA!
THE GRENADE-NET LAUNCHER!

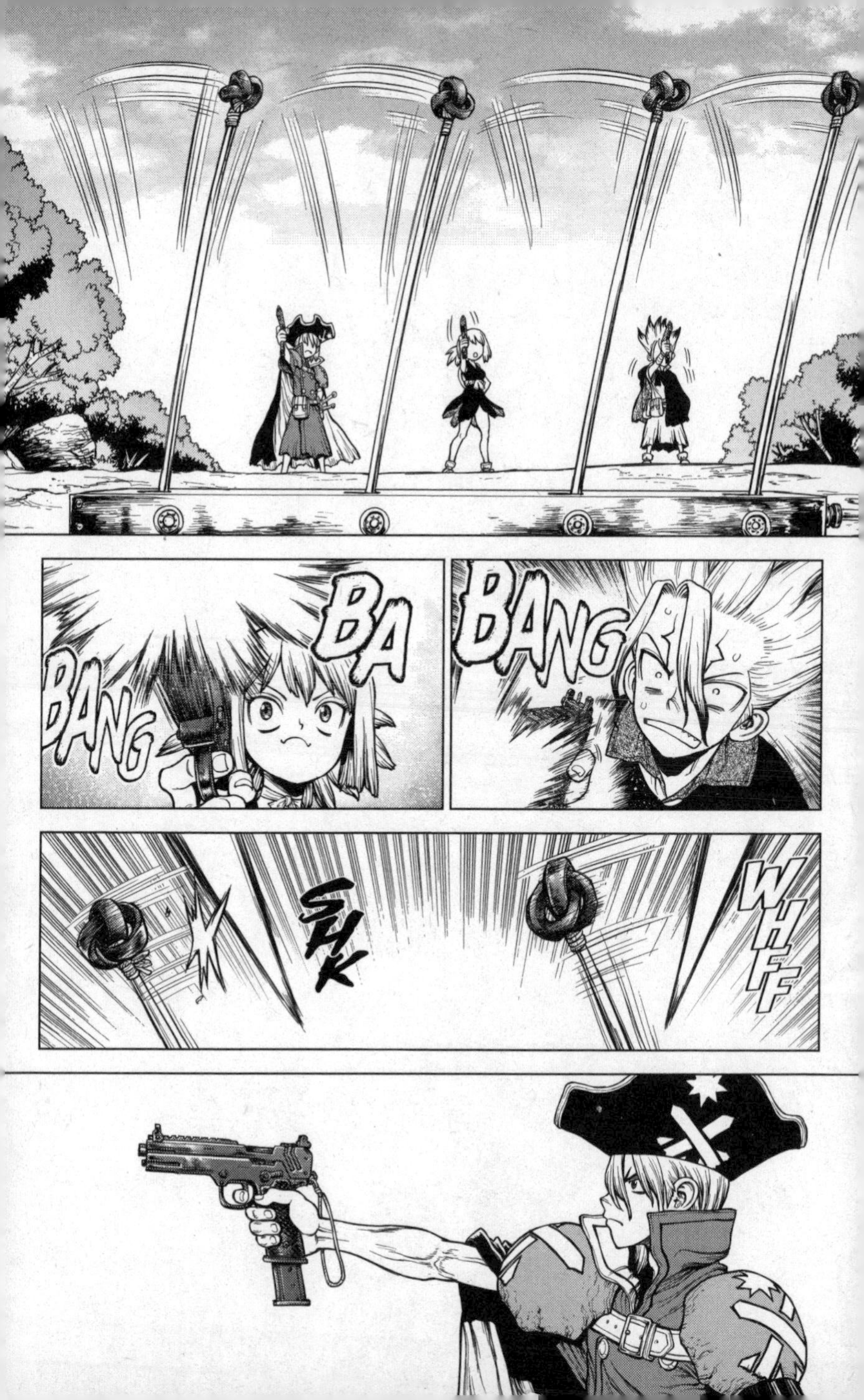
BANG
BA
BANG
WHFF
SHK

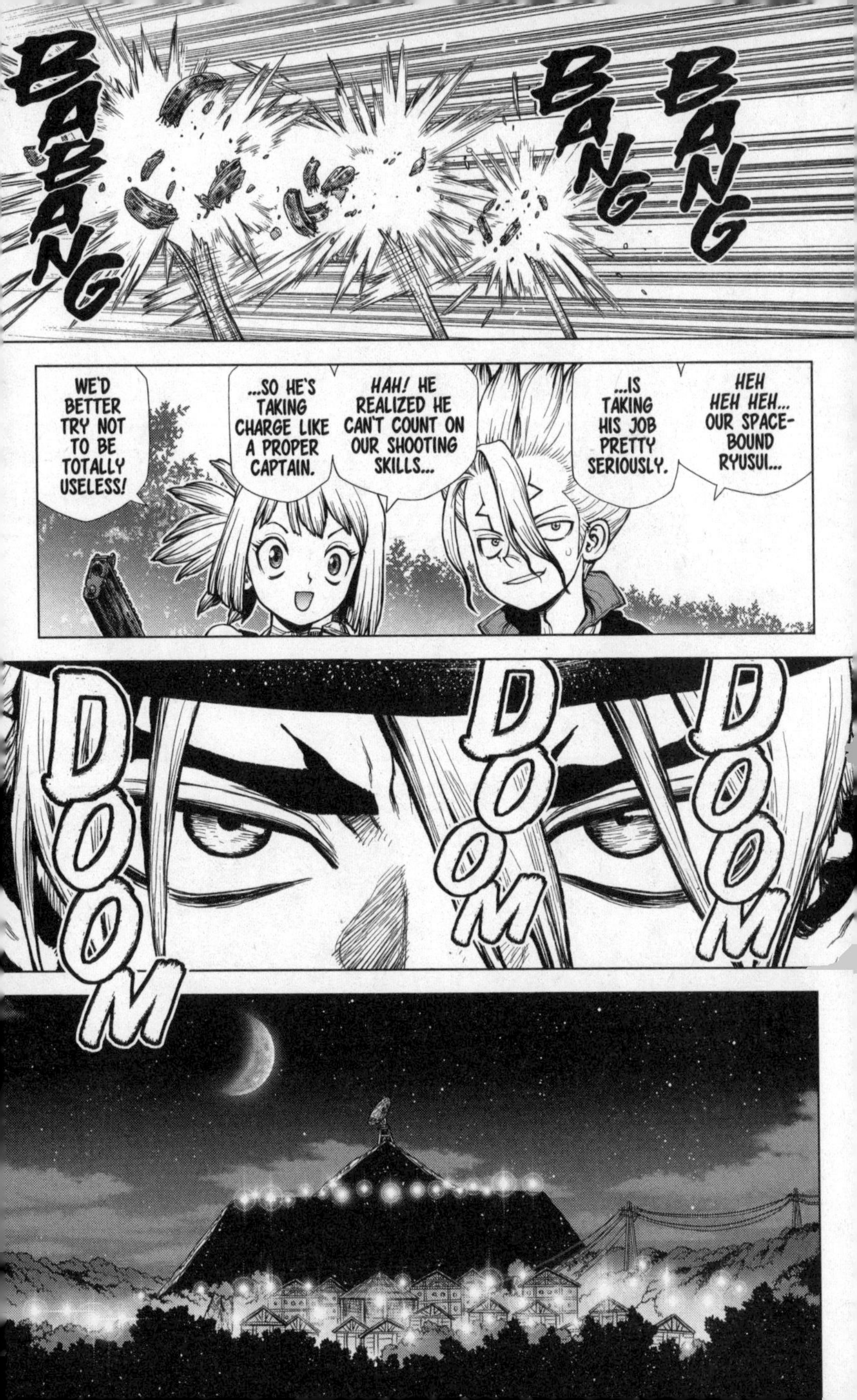
BANG
BANG
BABABANG
HEH HEH HEH... OUR SPACE-BOUND RYUSUI...
...IS TAKING HIS JOB PRETTY SERIOUSLY.
HAH! HE REALIZED HE CAN'T COUNT ON OUR SHOOTING SKILLS...
...SO HE'S TAKING CHARGE LIKE A PROPER CAPTAIN.
WE'D BETTER TRY NOT TO BE TOTALLY USELESS!
DOOM
DOOM
DOOM

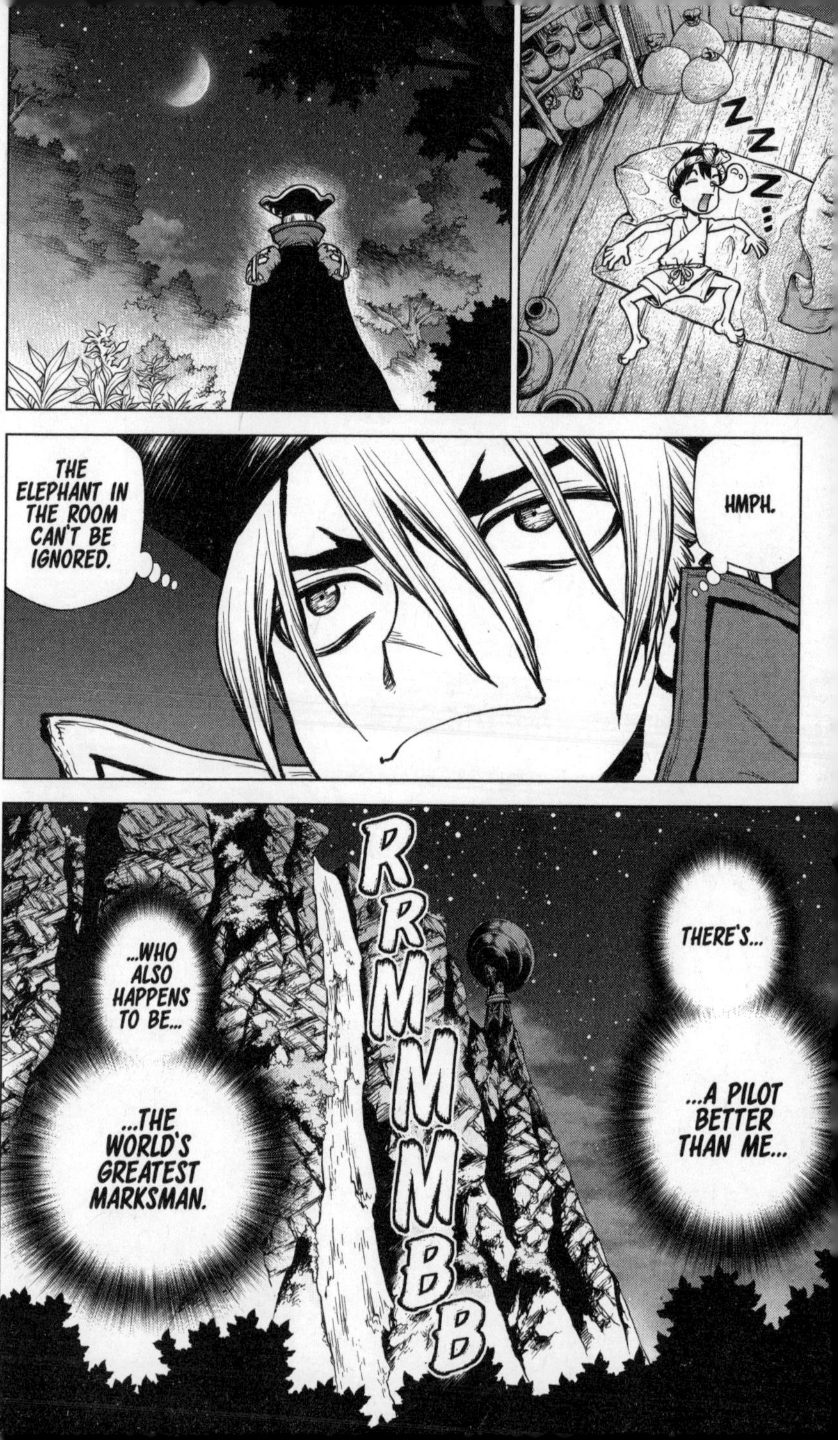

ZZZ...
HMPH.
THE ELEPHANT IN THE ROOM CAN'T BE IGNORED.
THERE'S...
...A PILOT BETTER THAN ME...
...WHO ALSO HAPPENS TO BE...
...THE WORLD'S GREATEST MARKSMAN.
RRMMMBB

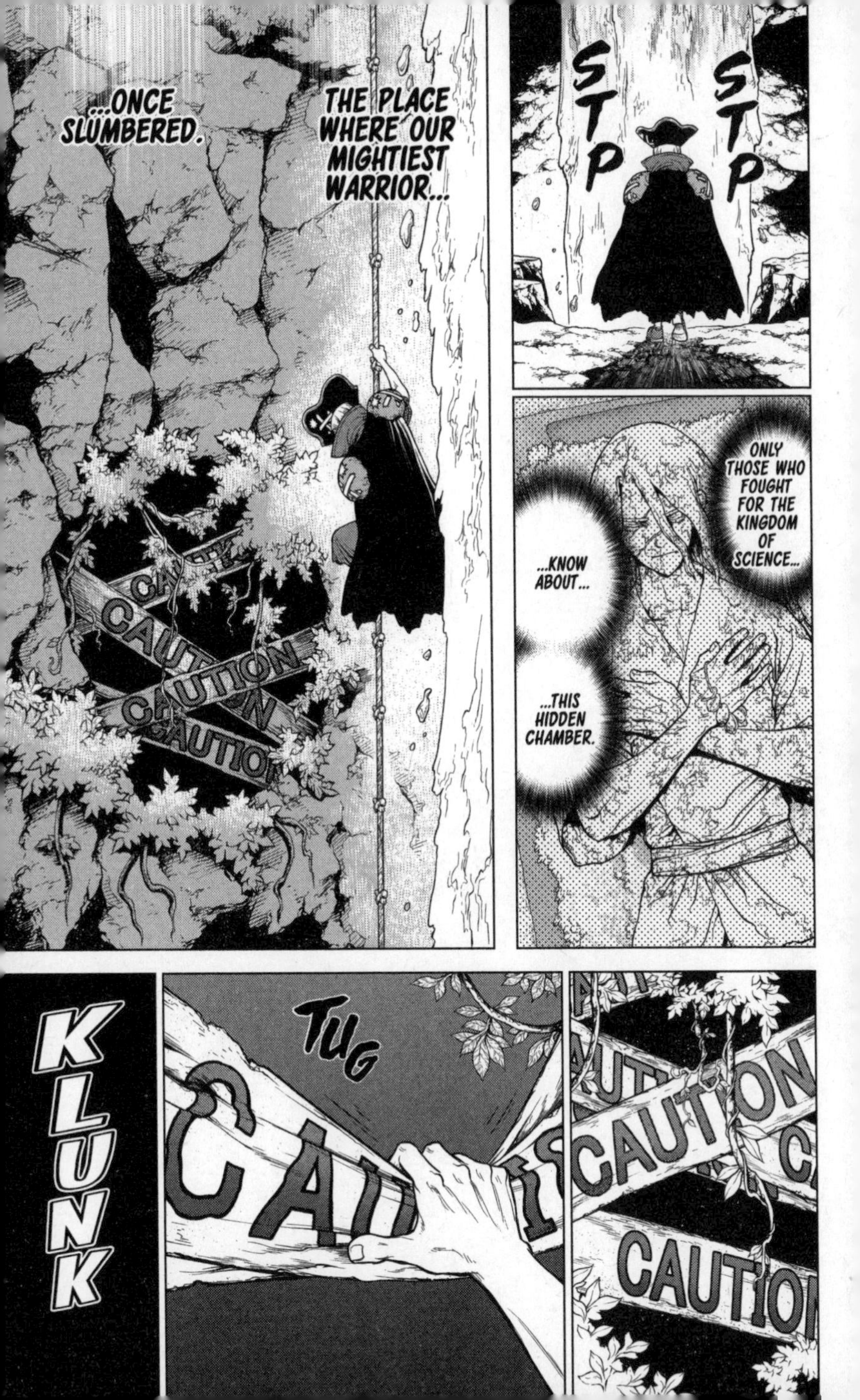
STP STP
ONLY THOSE WHO FOUGHT FOR THE KINGDOM OF SCIENCE...
...KNOW ABOUT...
...THIS HIDDEN CHAMBER.
THE PLACE WHERE OUR MIGHTIEST WARRIOR...
...ONCE SLUMBERED.
CAUTION
CAUTION
CAUTION
TUG
KLUNK

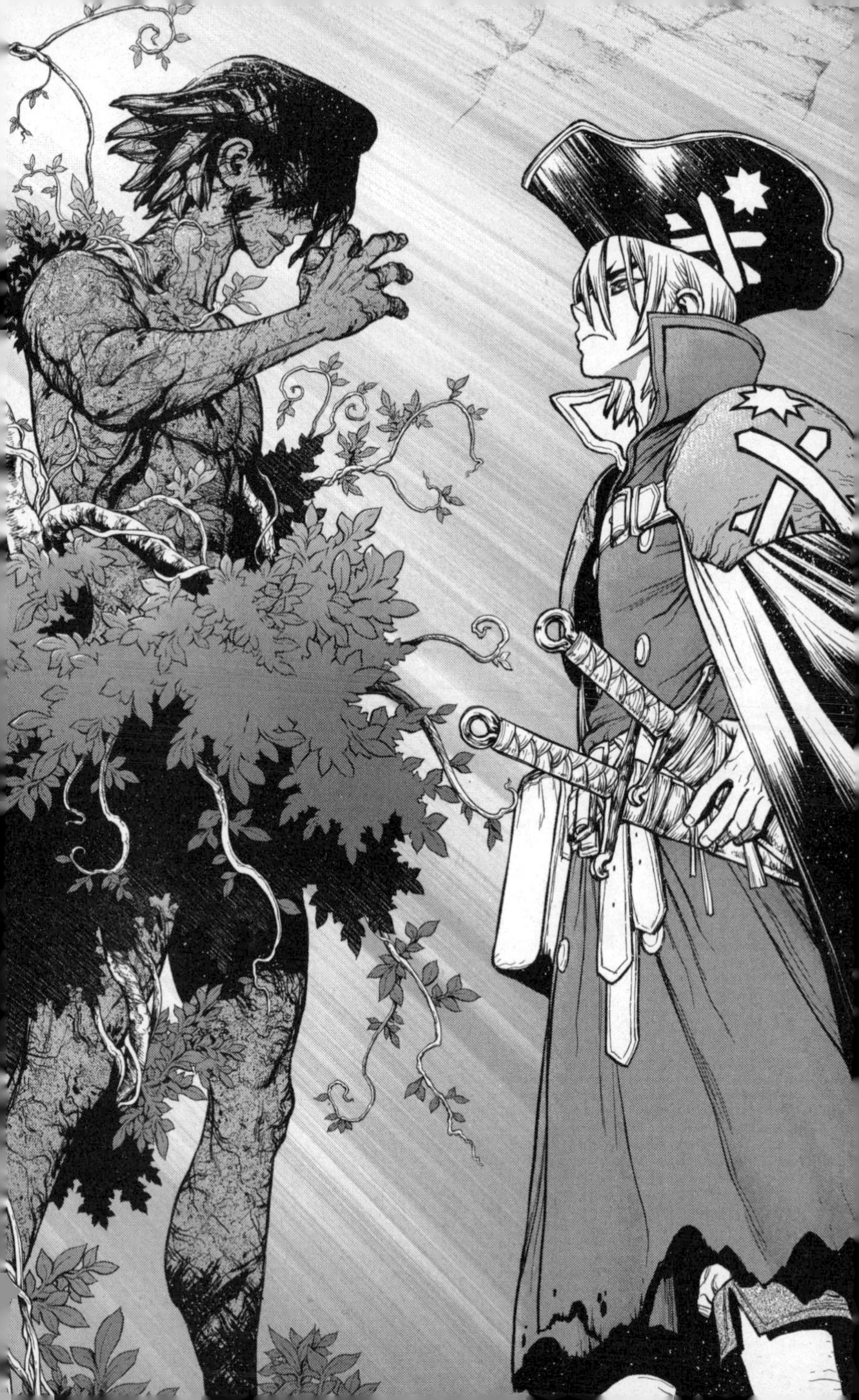

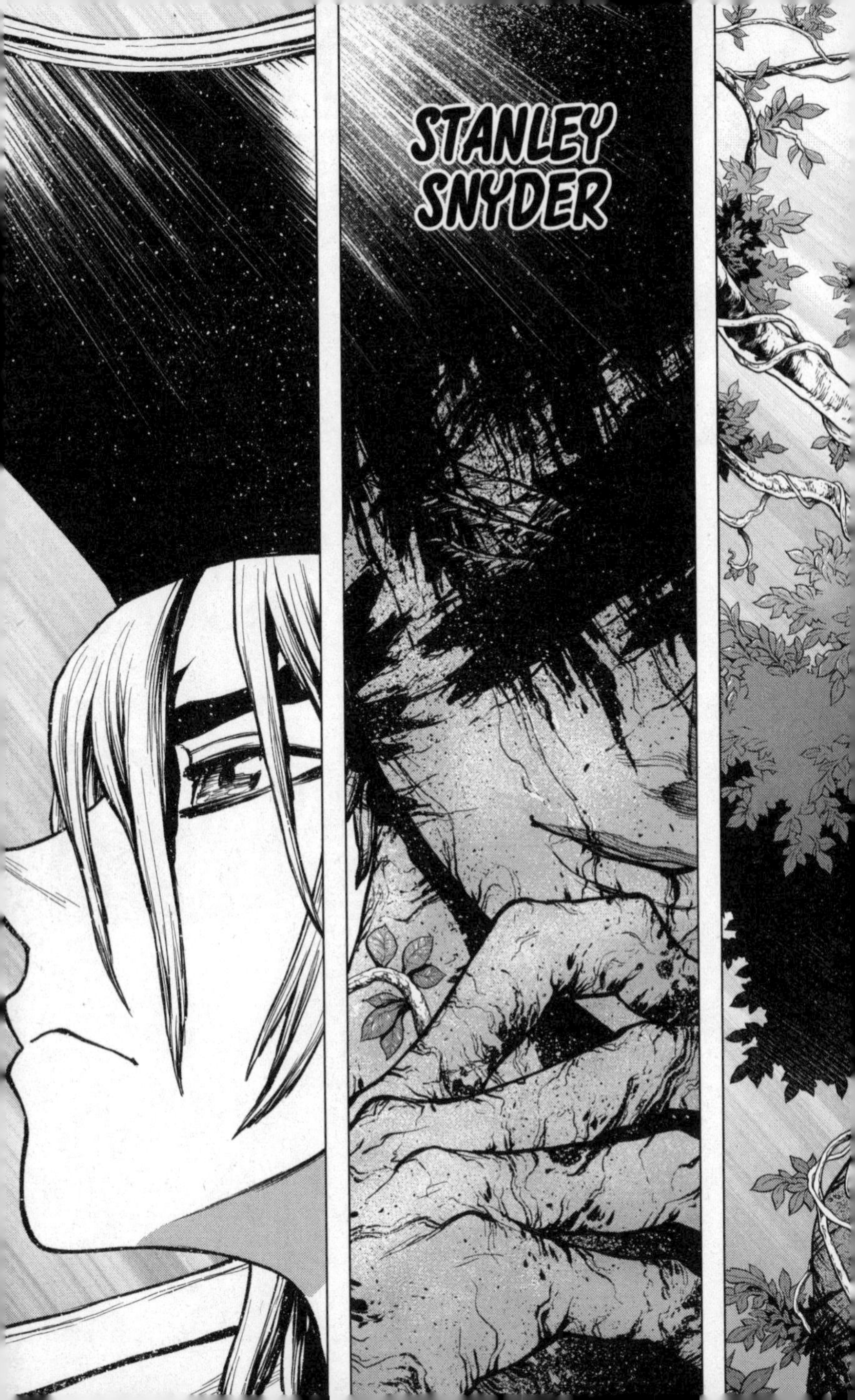
STANLEY SNYDER

SCHEDULE

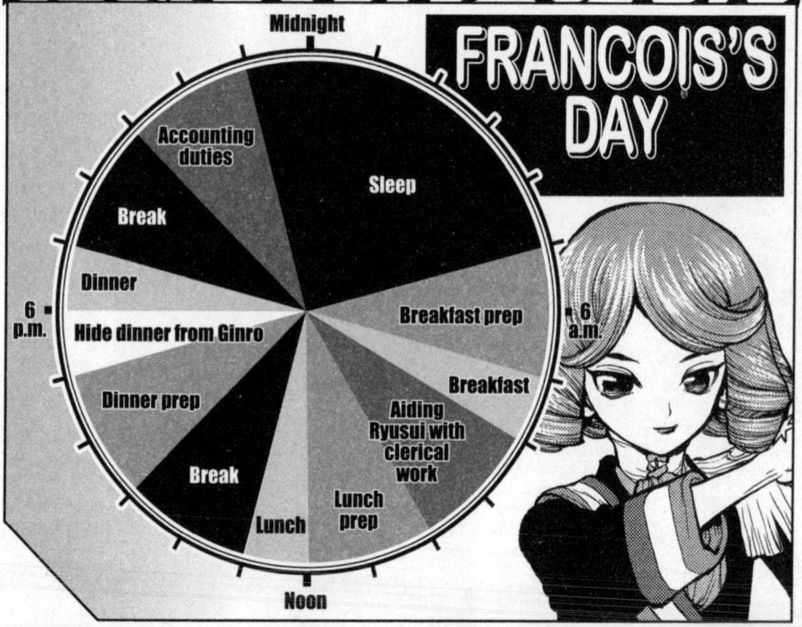
FRANCOIS'S DAY
Midnight
Sleep
Breakfast prep
6 a.m.
Breakfast
Aiding Ryusui with clerical work
Lunch prep
Noon
Lunch
Break
Dinner prep
Hide dinner from Ginro
6 p.m.
Dinner
Break
Accounting duties

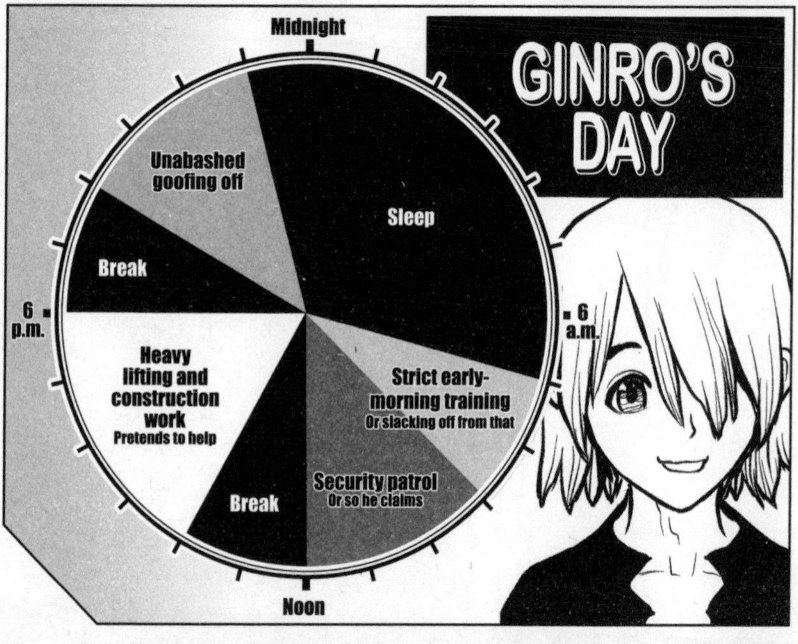
GINRO'S DAY
Midnight
Sleep
6 a.m.
Strict early-morning training
Or slacking off from that
Security patrol
Or so he claims
Noon
Break
Heavy lifting and construction work
Pretends to help
6 p.m.
Break
Unabashed goofing off

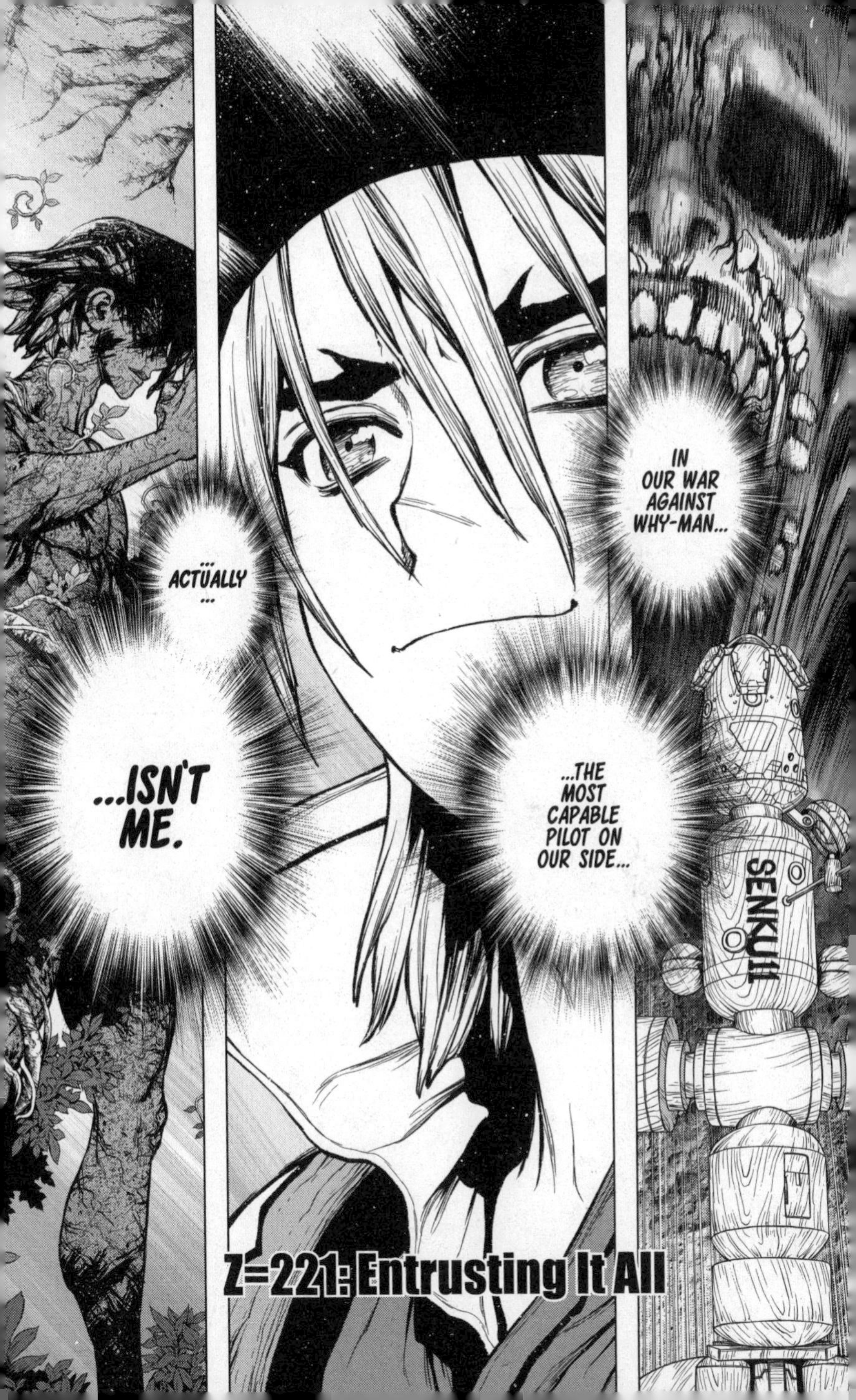
IN OUR WAR AGAINST WHY-MAN...
...THE MOST CAPABLE PILOT ON OUR SIDE...
SENKU II
...ACTUALLY...
...ISN'T ME.

Z=221: Entrusting It All

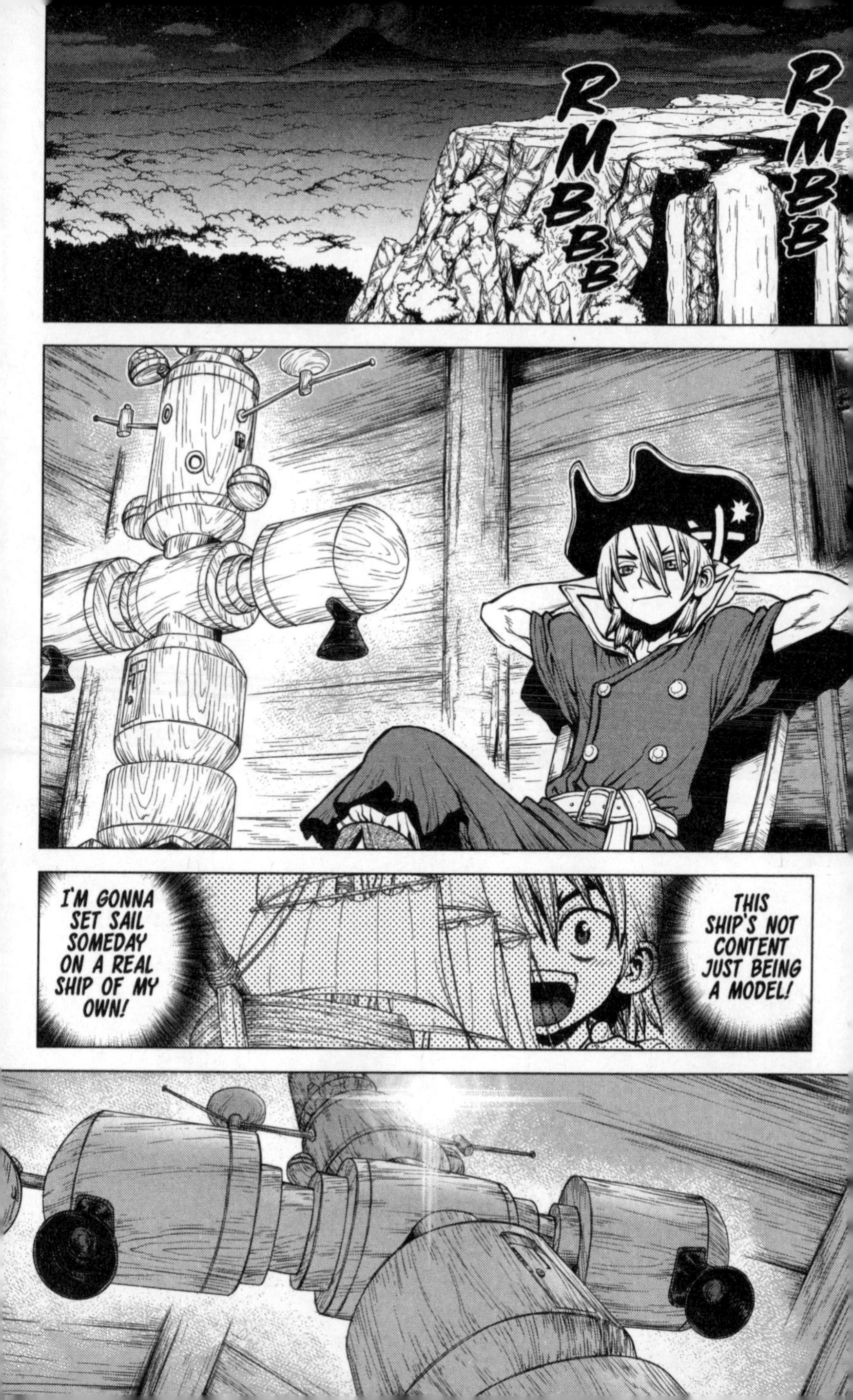
RMBB
RMBBB
THIS SHIP'S NOT CONTENT JUST BEING A MODEL!
I'M GONNA SET SAIL SOMEDAY ON A REAL SHIP OF MY OWN!

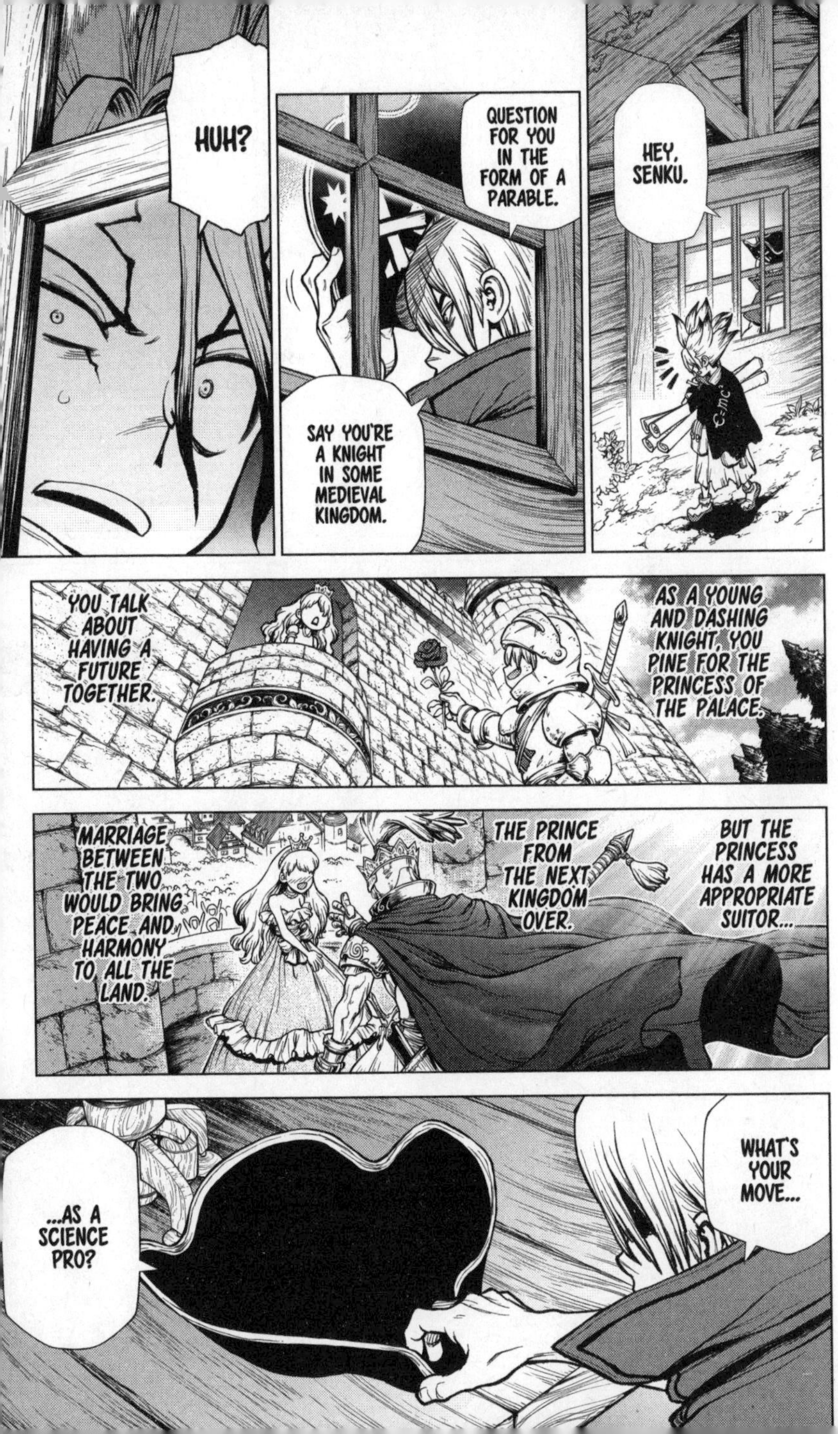
HEY, SENKU.
QUESTION FOR YOU IN THE FORM OF A PARABLE.
SAY YOU'RE A KNIGHT IN SOME MEDIEVAL KINGDOM.
HUH?
AS A YOUNG AND DASHING KNIGHT, YOU PINE FOR THE PRINCESS OF THE PALACE.
YOU TALK ABOUT HAVING A FUTURE TOGETHER.
BUT THE PRINCESS HAS A MORE APPROPRIATE SUITOR...
THE PRINCE FROM THE NEXT KINGDOM OVER.
MARRIAGE BETWEEN THE TWO WOULD BRING PEACE AND HARMONY TO ALL THE LAND.
WHAT'S YOUR MOVE...
...AS A SCIENCE PRO?

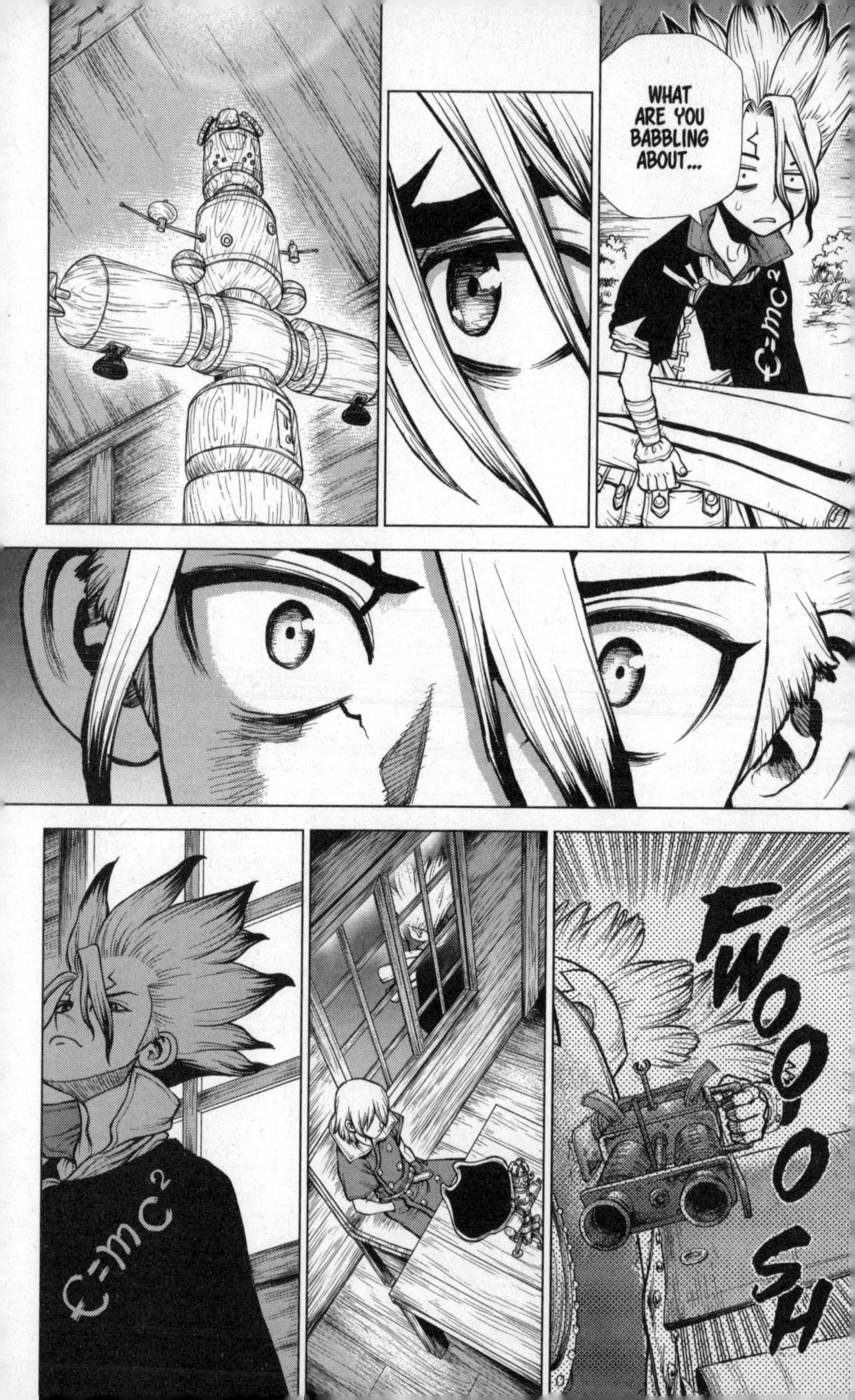
WHAT ARE YOU BABBLING ABOUT...
E=mc²
E=mc²
FWOOOOSH

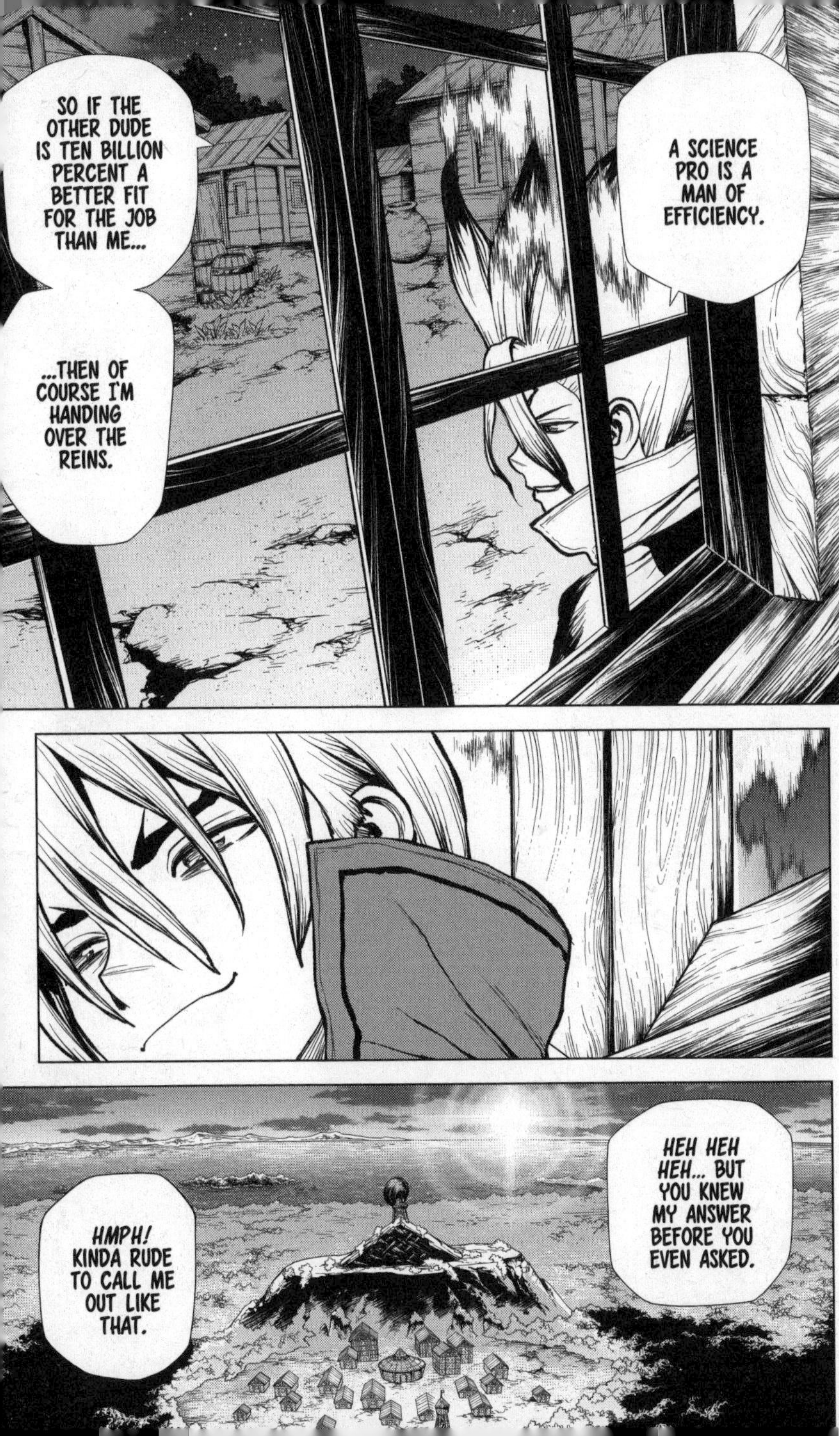
A SCIENCE PRO IS A MAN OF EFFICIENCY.
SO IF THE OTHER DUDE IS TEN BILLION PERCENT A BETTER FIT FOR THE JOB THAN ME...
...THEN OF COURSE I'M HANDING OVER THE REINS.
HEH HEH HEH... BUT YOU KNEW MY ANSWER BEFORE YOU EVEN ASKED.
HMPH! KINDA RUDE TO CALL ME OUT LIKE THAT.

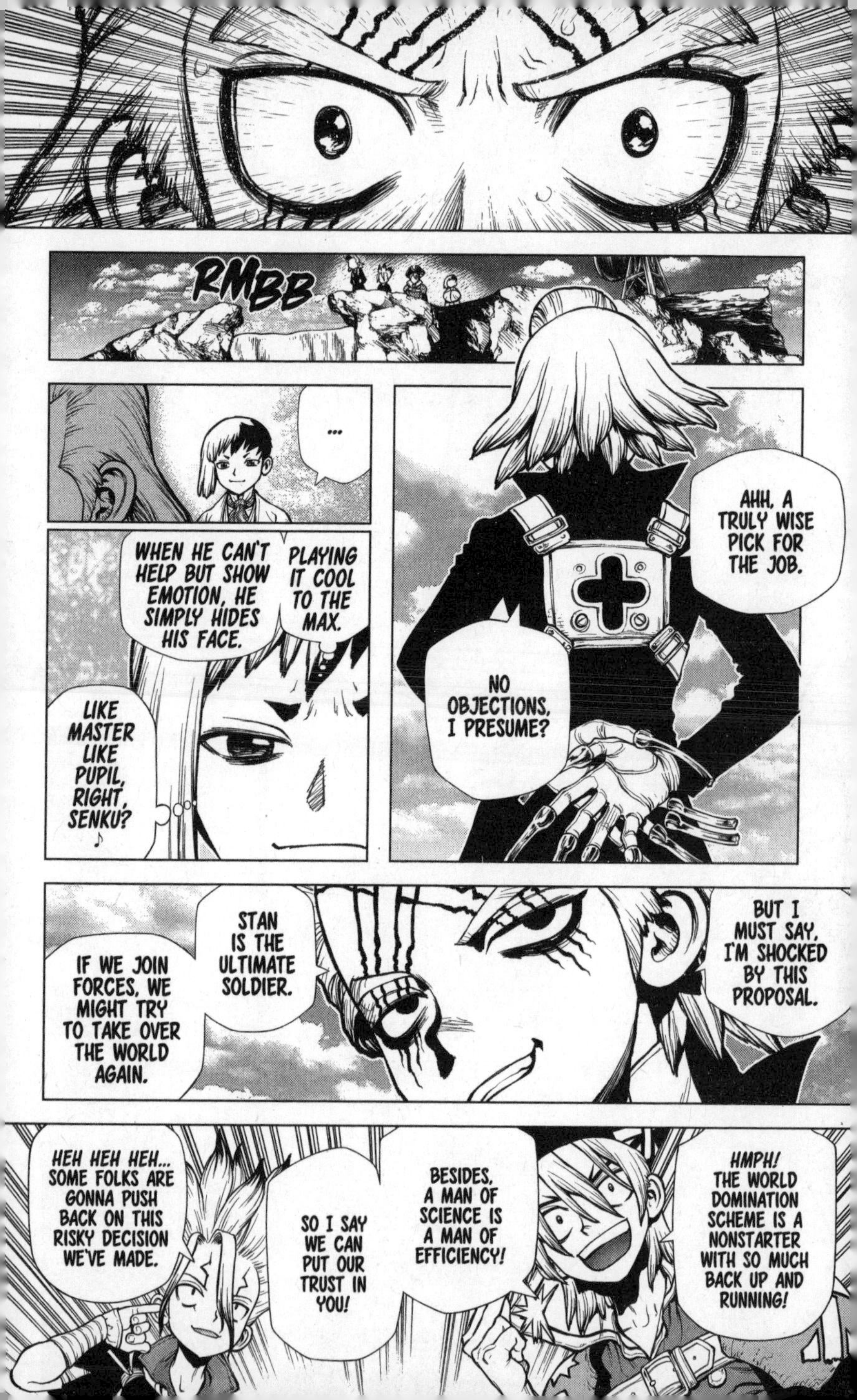
RMBB
AHH, A TRULY WISE PICK FOR THE JOB.
NO OBJECTIONS, I PRESUME?
...
PLAYING IT COOL TO THE MAX.
WHEN HE CAN'T HELP BUT SHOW EMOTION, HE SIMPLY HIDES HIS FACE.
LIKE MASTER LIKE PUPIL, RIGHT, SENKU? ♪
BUT I MUST SAY, I'M SHOCKED BY THIS PROPOSAL.
STAN IS THE ULTIMATE SOLDIER.
IF WE JOIN FORCES, WE MIGHT TRY TO TAKE OVER THE WORLD AGAIN.
HMPH! THE WORLD DOMINATION SCHEME IS A NONSTARTER WITH SO MUCH BACK UP AND RUNNING!
BESIDES, A MAN OF SCIENCE IS A MAN OF EFFICIENCY!
SO I SAY WE CAN PUT OUR TRUST IN YOU!
HEH HEH HEH... SOME FOLKS ARE GONNA PUSH BACK ON THIS RISKY DECISION WE'VE MADE.

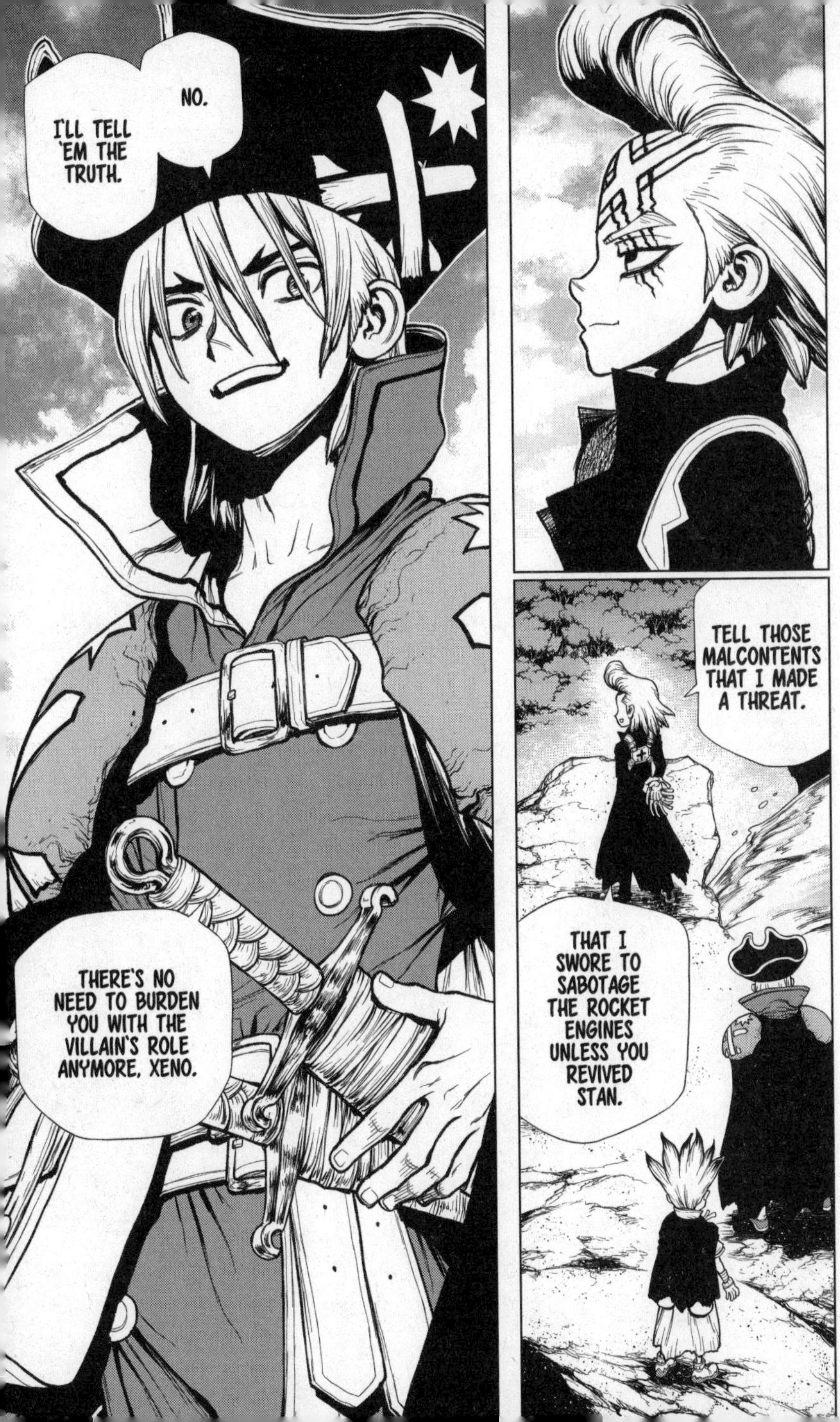
TELL THOSE MALCONTENTS THAT I MADE A THREAT.
THAT I SWORE TO SABOTAGE THE ROCKET ENGINES UNLESS YOU REVIVED STAN.
NO.
I'LL TELL 'EM THE TRUTH.
THERE'S NO NEED TO BURDEN YOU WITH THE VILLAIN'S ROLE ANYMORE, XENO.

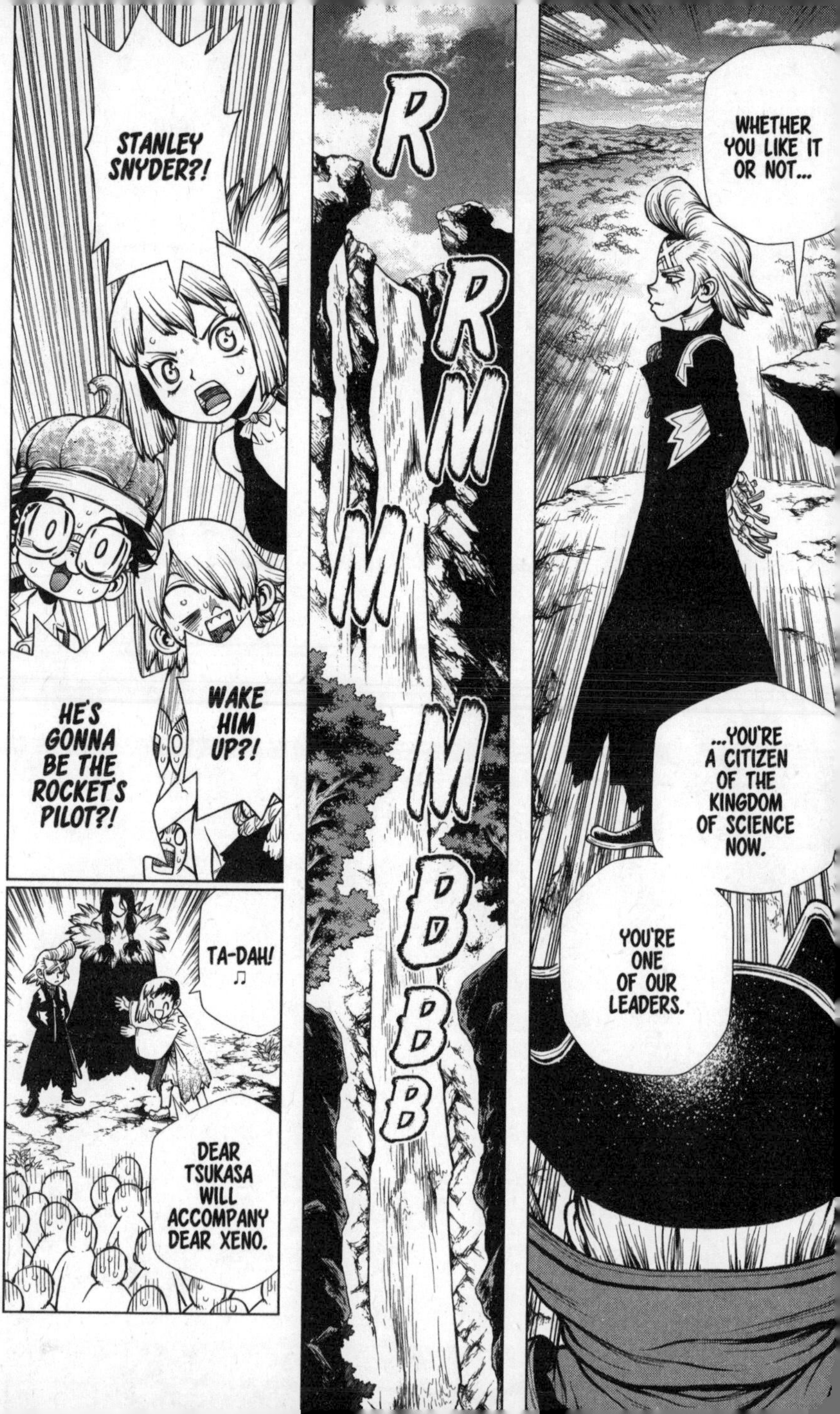
WHETHER YOU LIKE IT OR NOT...
...YOU'RE A CITIZEN OF THE KINGDOM OF SCIENCE NOW.
YOU'RE ONE OF OUR LEADERS.
RRMMMBBB
STANLEY SNYDER?!
WAKE HIM UP?!
HE'S GONNA BE THE ROCKET'S PILOT?!
TA-DAH! ♫
DEAR TSUKASA WILL ACCOMPANY DEAR XENO.

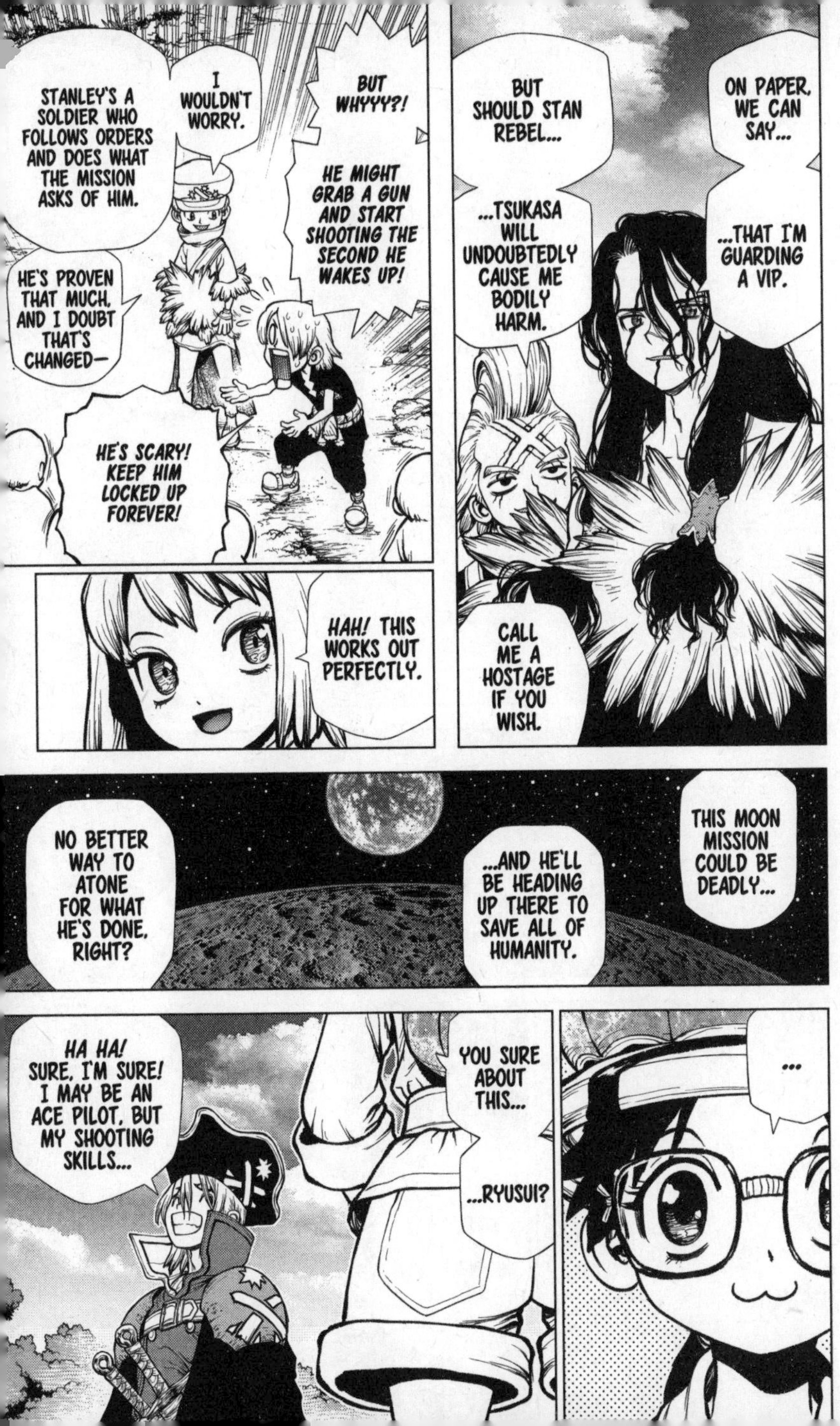
ON PAPER, WE CAN SAY...
...THAT I'M GUARDING A VIP.
BUT SHOULD STAN REBEL...
...TSUKASA WILL UNDOUBTEDLY CAUSE ME BODILY HARM.
CALL ME A HOSTAGE IF YOU WISH.
BUT WHYYY?!
HE MIGHT GRAB A GUN AND START SHOOTING THE SECOND HE WAKES UP!
I WOULDN'T WORRY.
STANLEY'S A SOLDIER WHO FOLLOWS ORDERS AND DOES WHAT THE MISSION ASKS OF HIM.
HE'S PROVEN THAT MUCH, AND I DOUBT THAT'S CHANGED—
HE'S SCARY! KEEP HIM LOCKED UP FOREVER!
HAH! THIS WORKS OUT PERFECTLY.
THIS MOON MISSION COULD BE DEADLY...
...AND HE'LL BE HEADING UP THERE TO SAVE ALL OF HUMANITY.
NO BETTER WAY TO ATONE FOR WHAT HE'S DONE, RIGHT?
...
YOU SURE ABOUT THIS...
...RYUSUI?
HA HA! SURE, I'M SURE! I MAY BE AN ACE PILOT, BUT MY SHOOTING SKILLS...

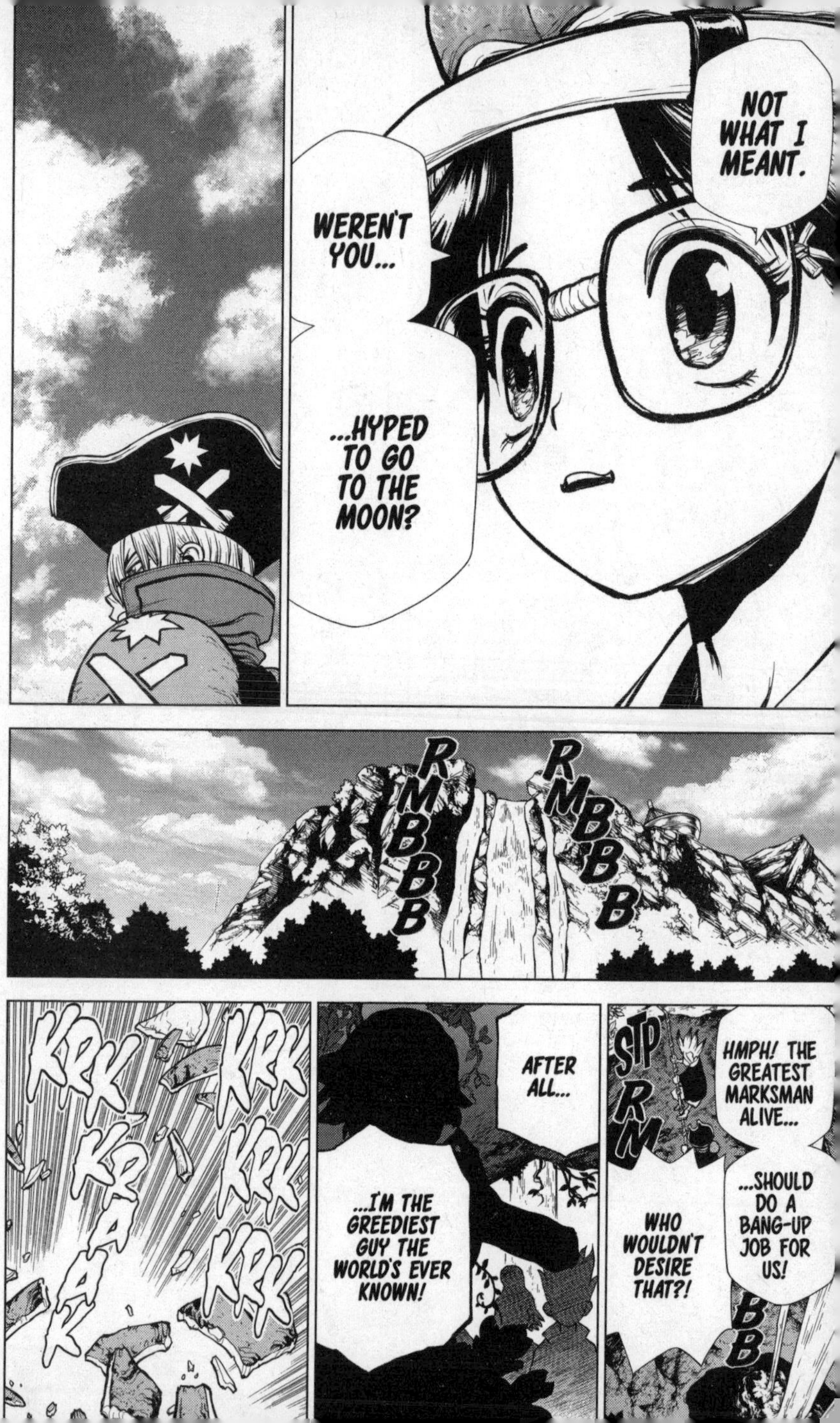
NOT WHAT I MEANT.
WEREN'T YOU...
...HYPED TO GO TO THE MOON?
RMBBB
RMBBB
HMPH! THE GREATEST MARKSMAN ALIVE...
STP
RM
...SHOULD DO A BANG-UP JOB FOR US!
WHO WOULDN'T DESIRE THAT?!
BB
AFTER ALL...
...I'M THE GREEDIEST GUY THE WORLD'S EVER KNOWN!
KRK
KRK
KRK
KRK
KRAAK

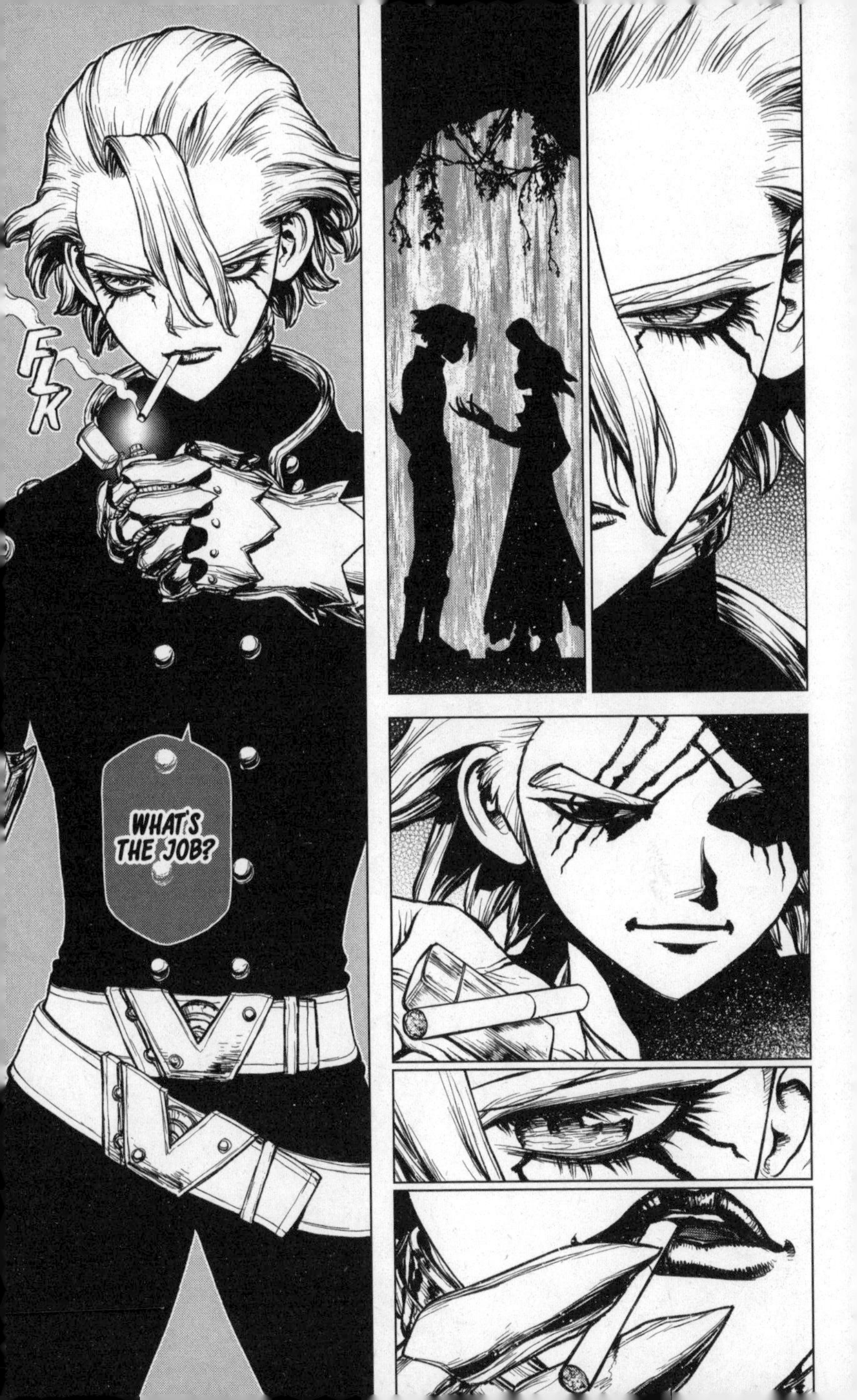

FLK
WHAT'S THE JOB?

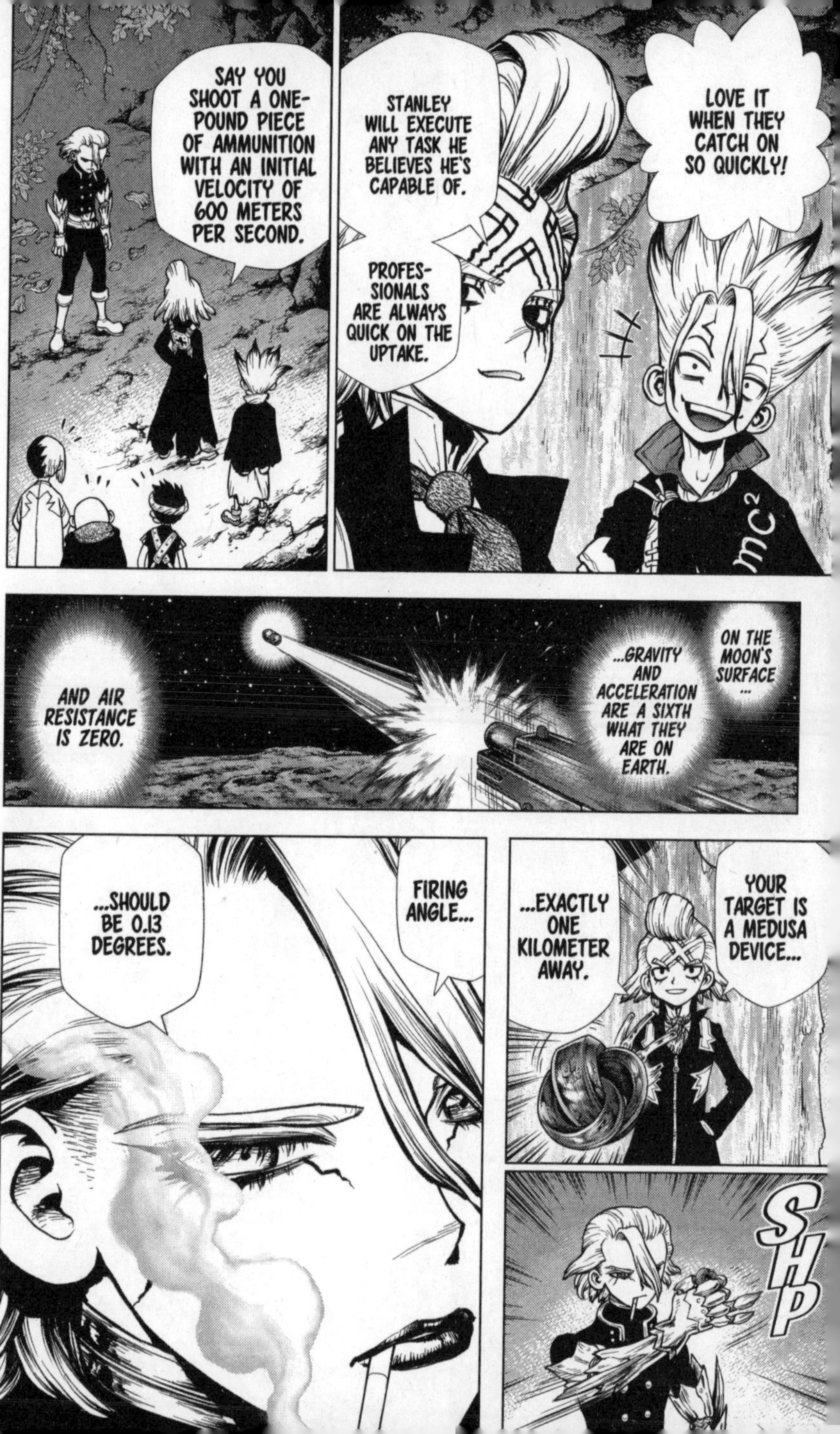
LOVE IT WHEN THEY CATCH ON SO QUICKLY!
STANLEY WILL EXECUTE ANY TASK HE BELIEVES HE'S CAPABLE OF.
PROFES-SIONALS ARE ALWAYS QUICK ON THE UPTAKE.
SAY YOU SHOOT A ONE-POUND PIECE OF AMMUNITION WITH AN INITIAL VELOCITY OF 600 METERS PER SECOND.
ON THE MOON'S SURFACE...
...GRAVITY AND ACCELERATION ARE A SIXTH WHAT THEY ARE ON EARTH.
AND AIR RESISTANCE IS ZERO.
YOUR TARGET IS A MEDUSA DEVICE...
...EXACTLY ONE KILOMETER AWAY.
FIRING ANGLE...
...SHOULD BE 0.13 DEGREES.
SHP

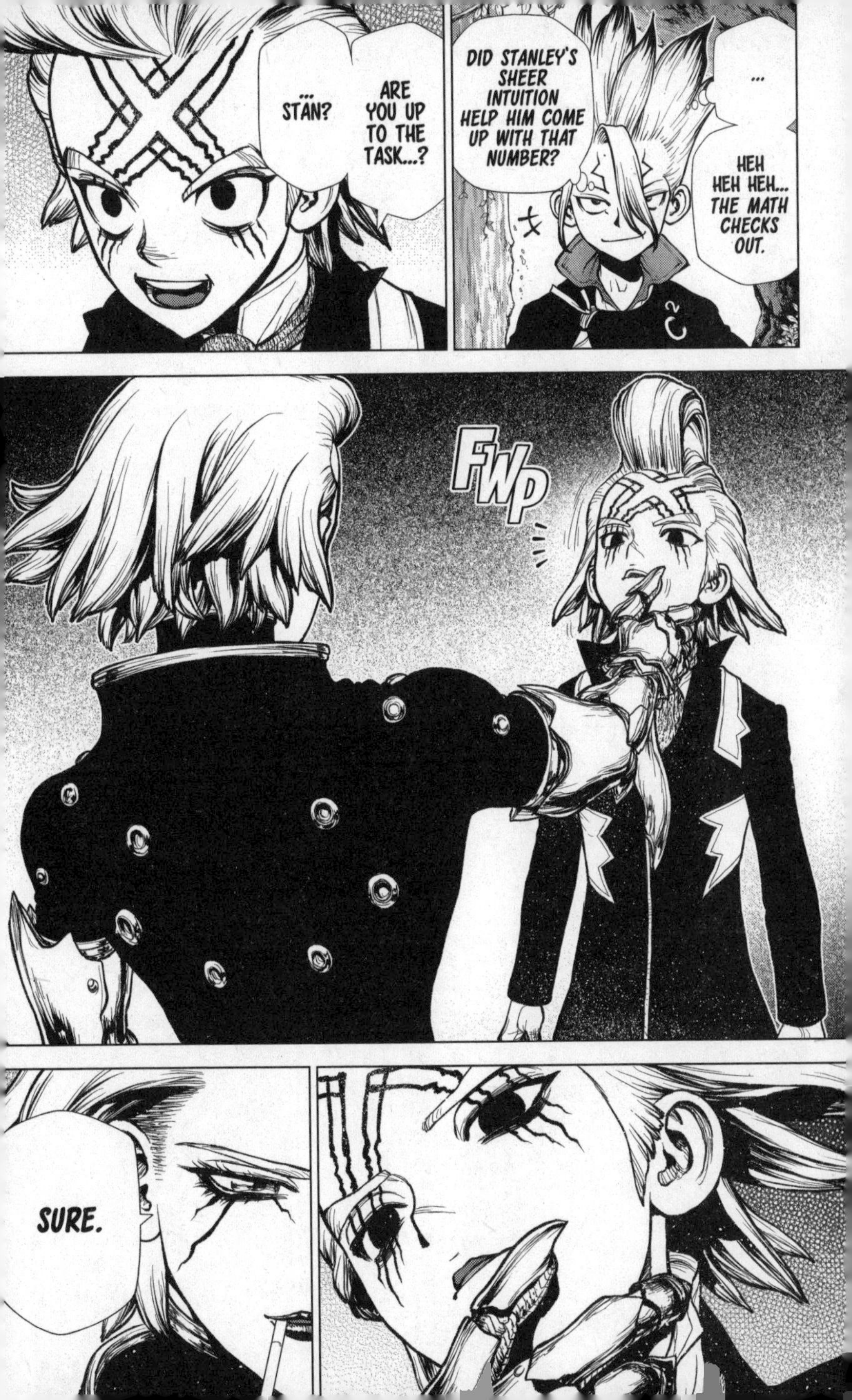
...
DID STANLEY'S SHEER INTUITION HELP HIM COME UP WITH THAT NUMBER?
HEH HEH HEH... THE MATH CHECKS OUT.
ARE YOU UP TO THE TASK...?
... STAN?
FWP
SURE.

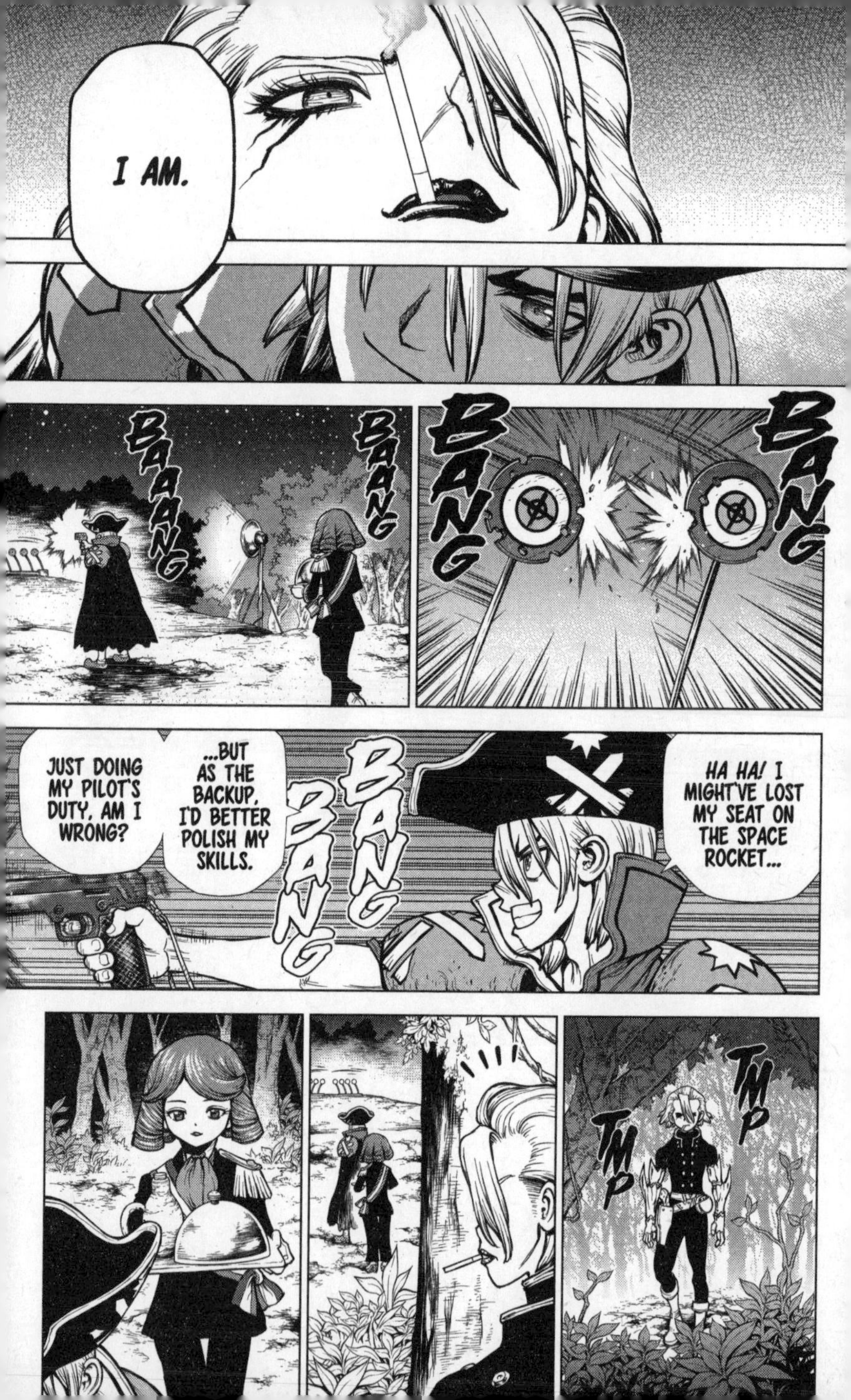
I AM.
BANG
BANG
BAAANG
BAAANG
HA HA! I MIGHT'VE LOST MY SEAT ON THE SPACE ROCKET...
BANG
BANG
...BUT AS THE BACKUP, I'D BETTER POLISH MY SKILLS.
JUST DOING MY PILOT'S DUTY, AM I WRONG?
TMP
TMP

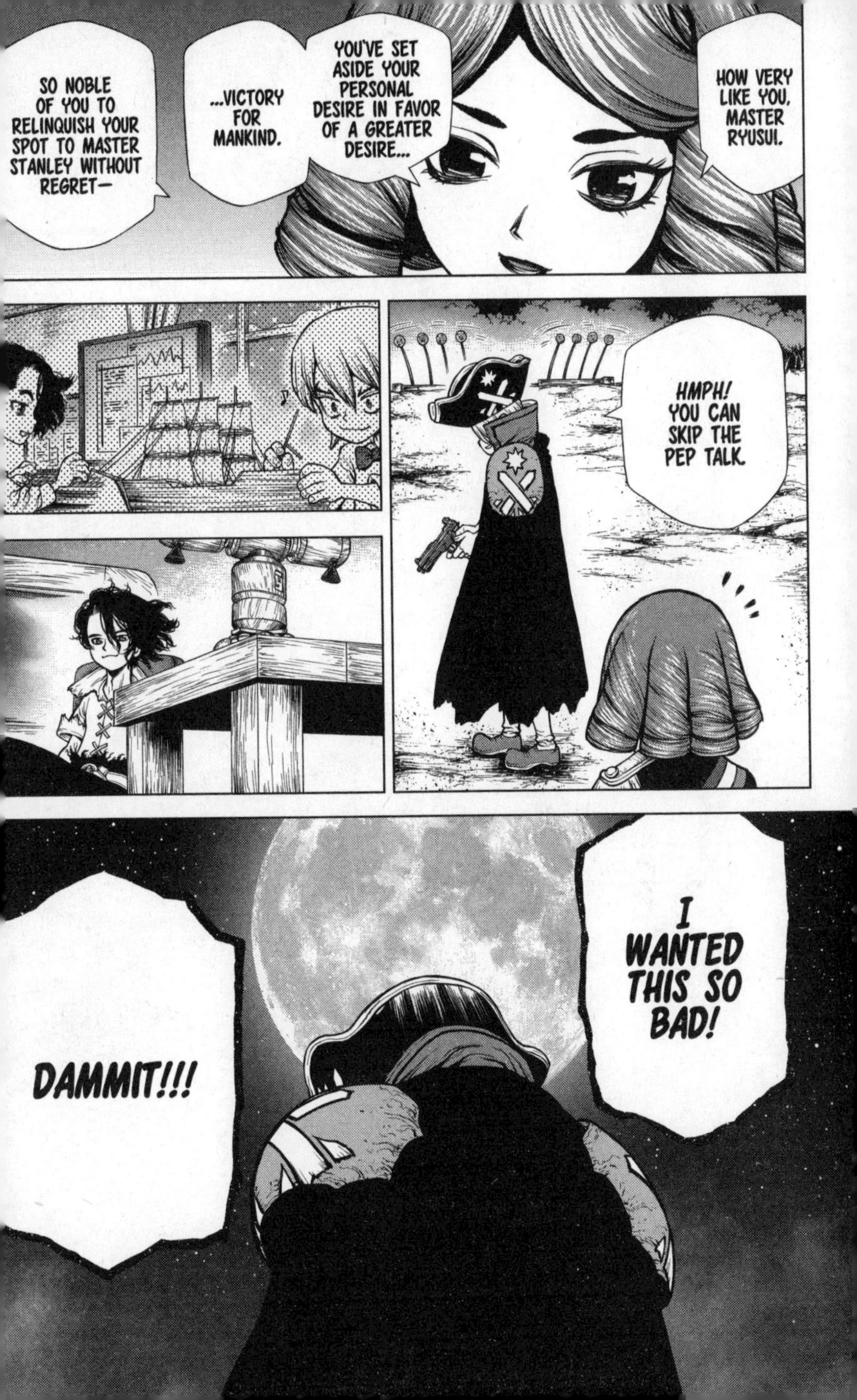
HOW VERY LIKE YOU, MASTER RYUSUI.
YOU'VE SET ASIDE YOUR PERSONAL DESIRE IN FAVOR OF A GREATER DESIRE...
...VICTORY FOR MANKIND.
SO NOBLE OF YOU TO RELINQUISH YOUR SPOT TO MASTER STANLEY WITHOUT REGRET—
HMPH! YOU CAN SKIP THE PEP TALK.
I WANTED THIS SO BAD!
DAMMIT!!!

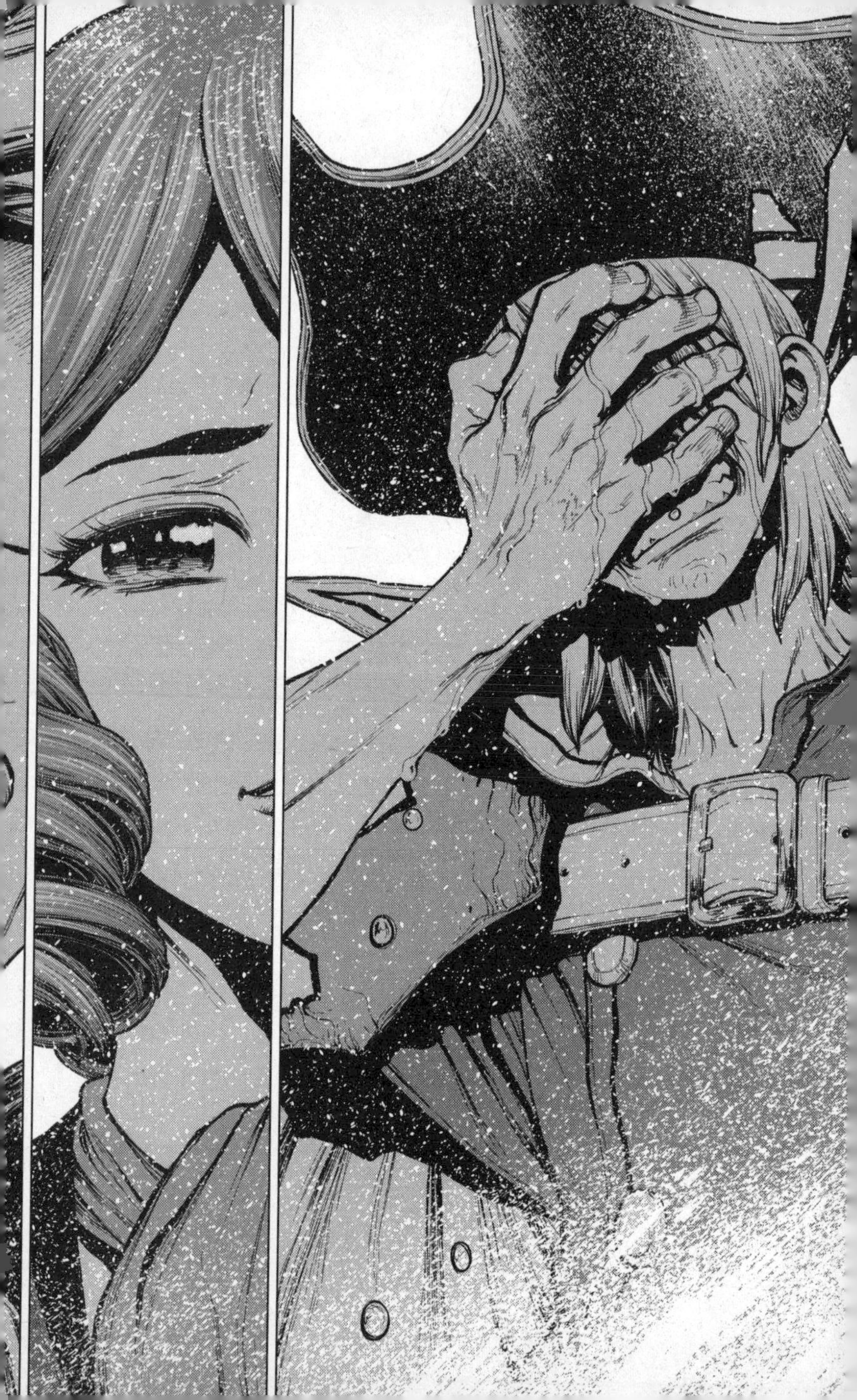

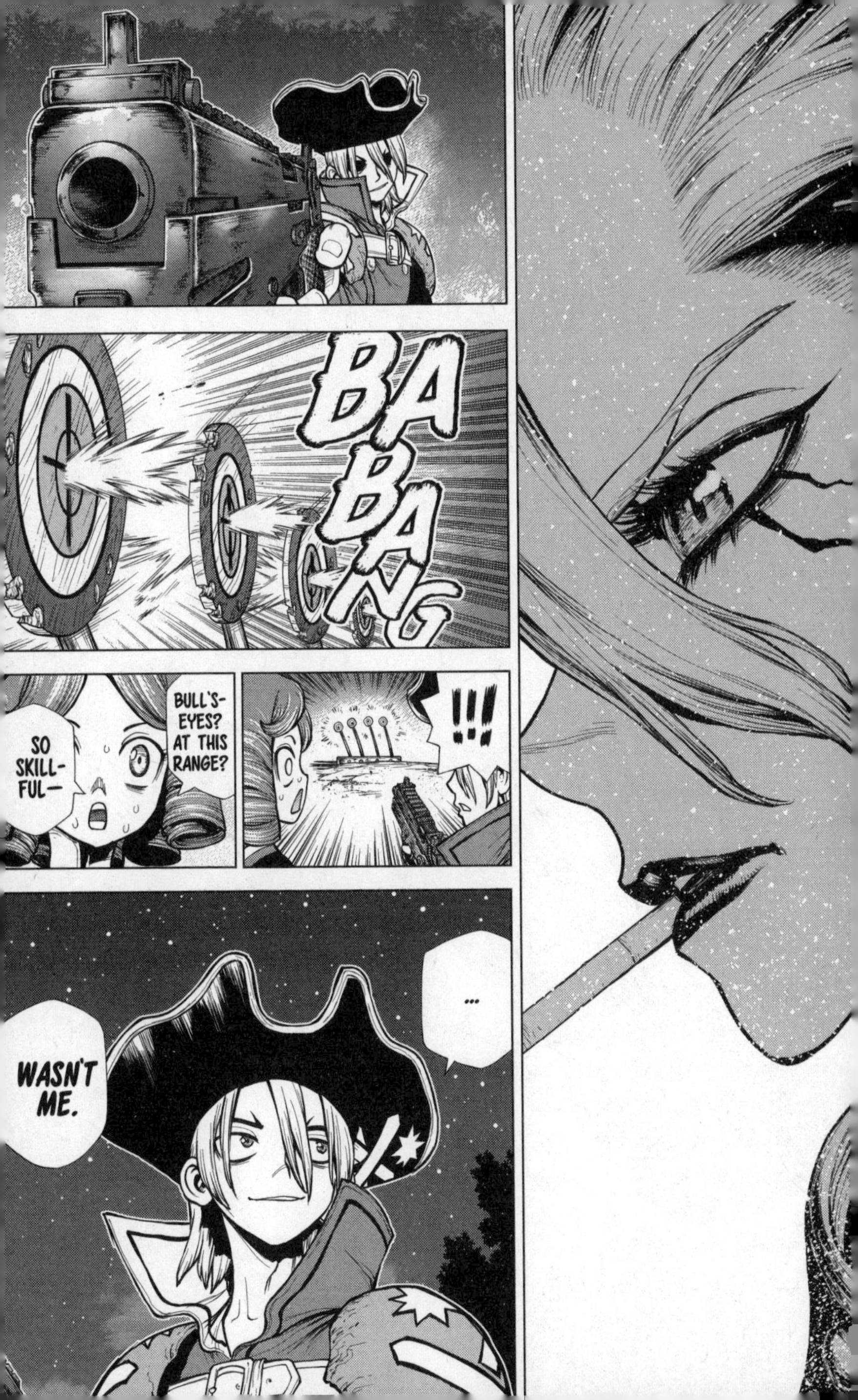
BA
BA
BANG
!!!
BULL'S-EYES? AT THIS RANGE?
SO SKILL-FUL—
...
WASN'T ME.

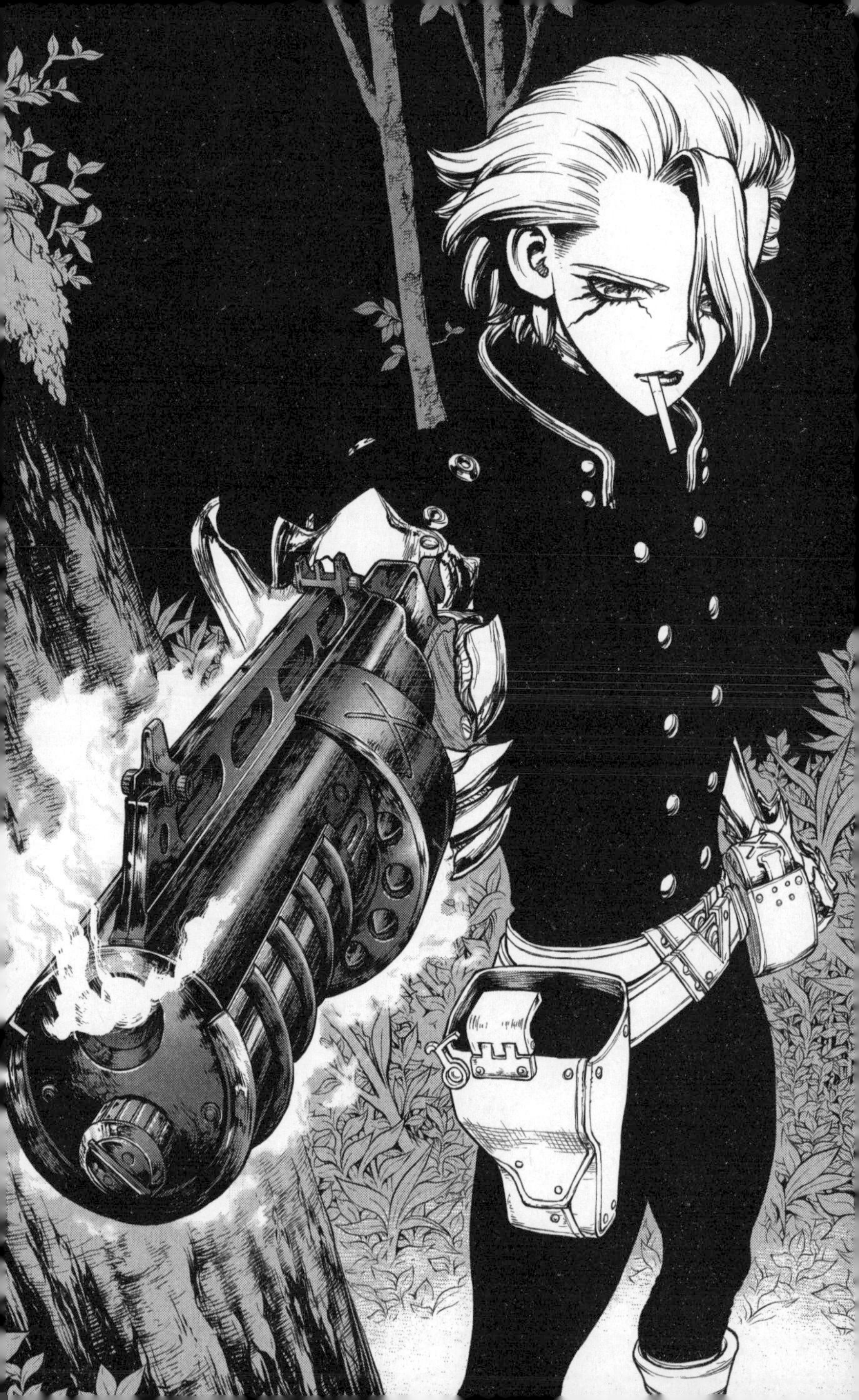

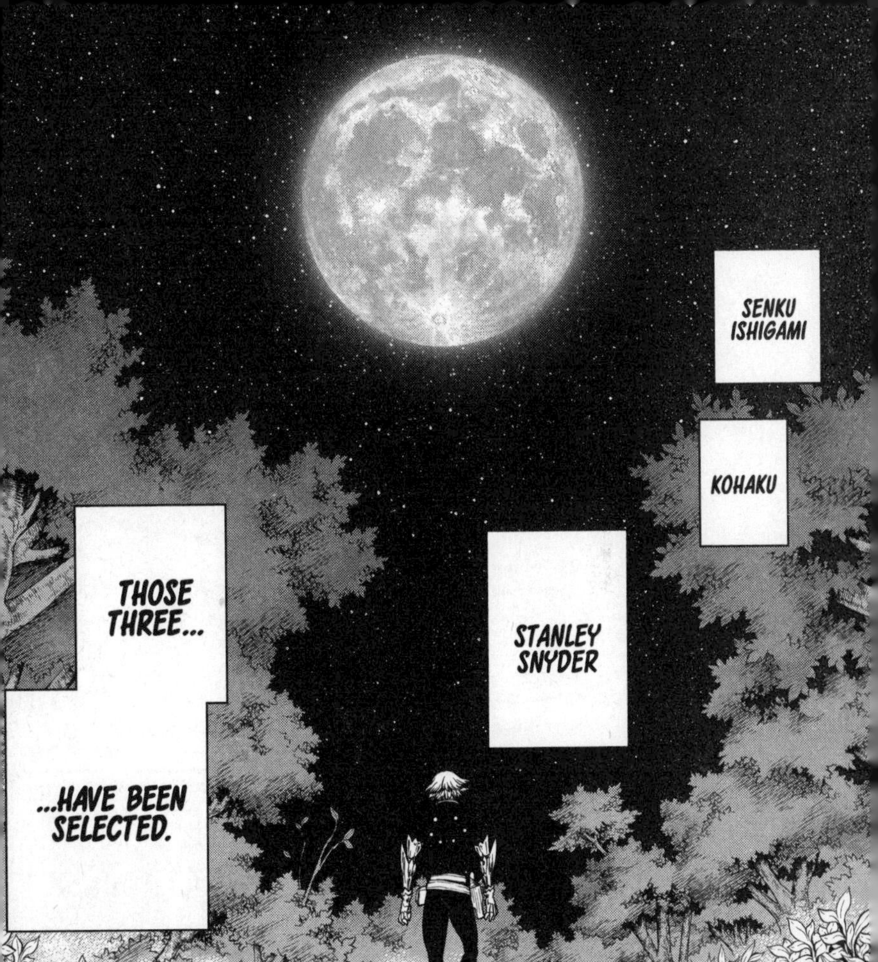
SENKU ISHIGAMI
KOHAKU
STANLEY SNYDER
THOSE THREE...
...HAVE BEEN SELECTED.
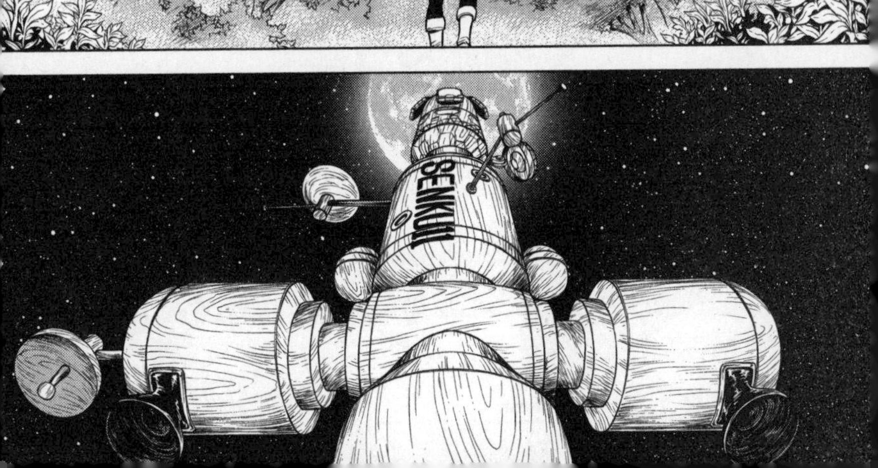
SENKUU

SCHEDULE

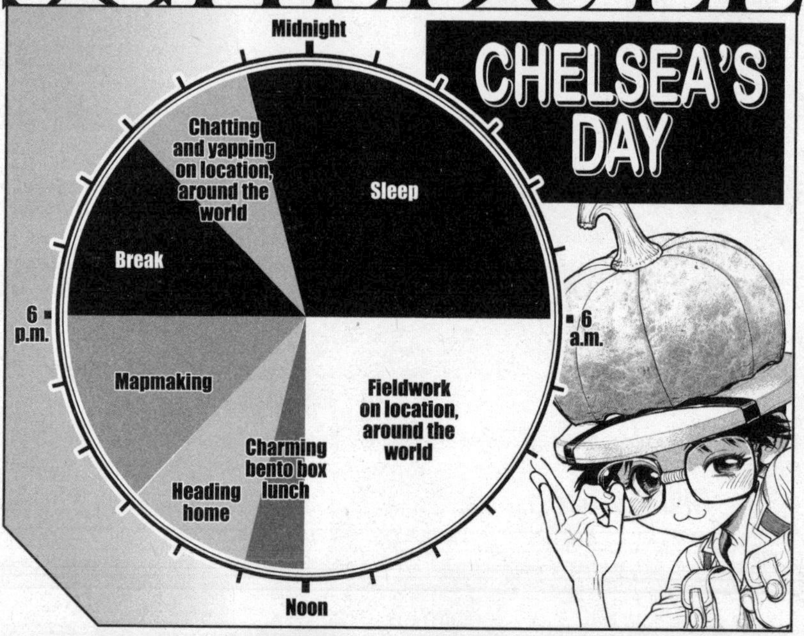
CHELSEA'S DAY
Midnight
6 a.m.
Noon
6 p.m.
Sleep
Fieldwork on location, around the world
Charming bento box lunch
Heading home
Mapmaking
Break
Chatting and yapping on location, around the world

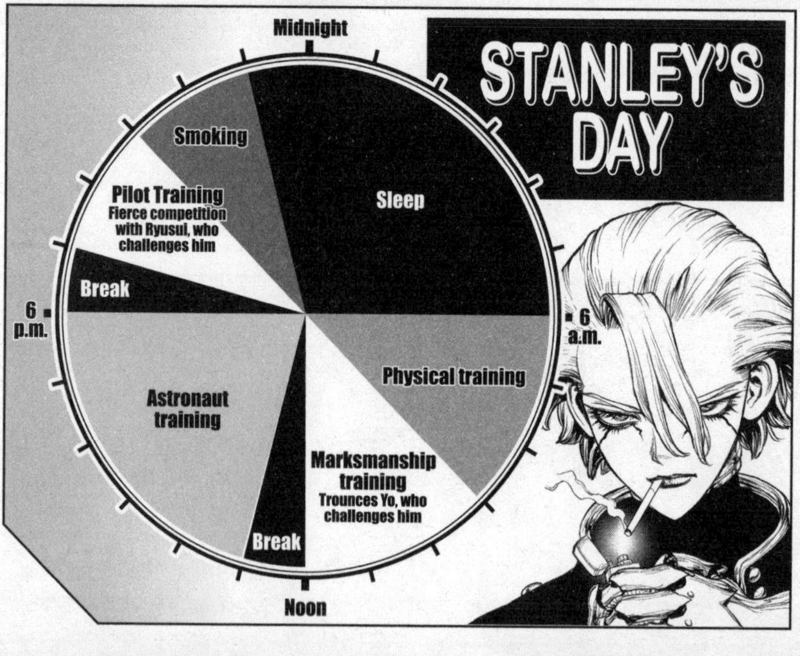
STANLEY'S DAY
Midnight
6 a.m.
Noon
6 p.m.
Sleep
Physical training
Marksmanship training
Trounces Yo, who challenges him
Break
Astronaut training
Break
Pilot Training
Fierce competition with Ryusui, who challenges him
Smoking

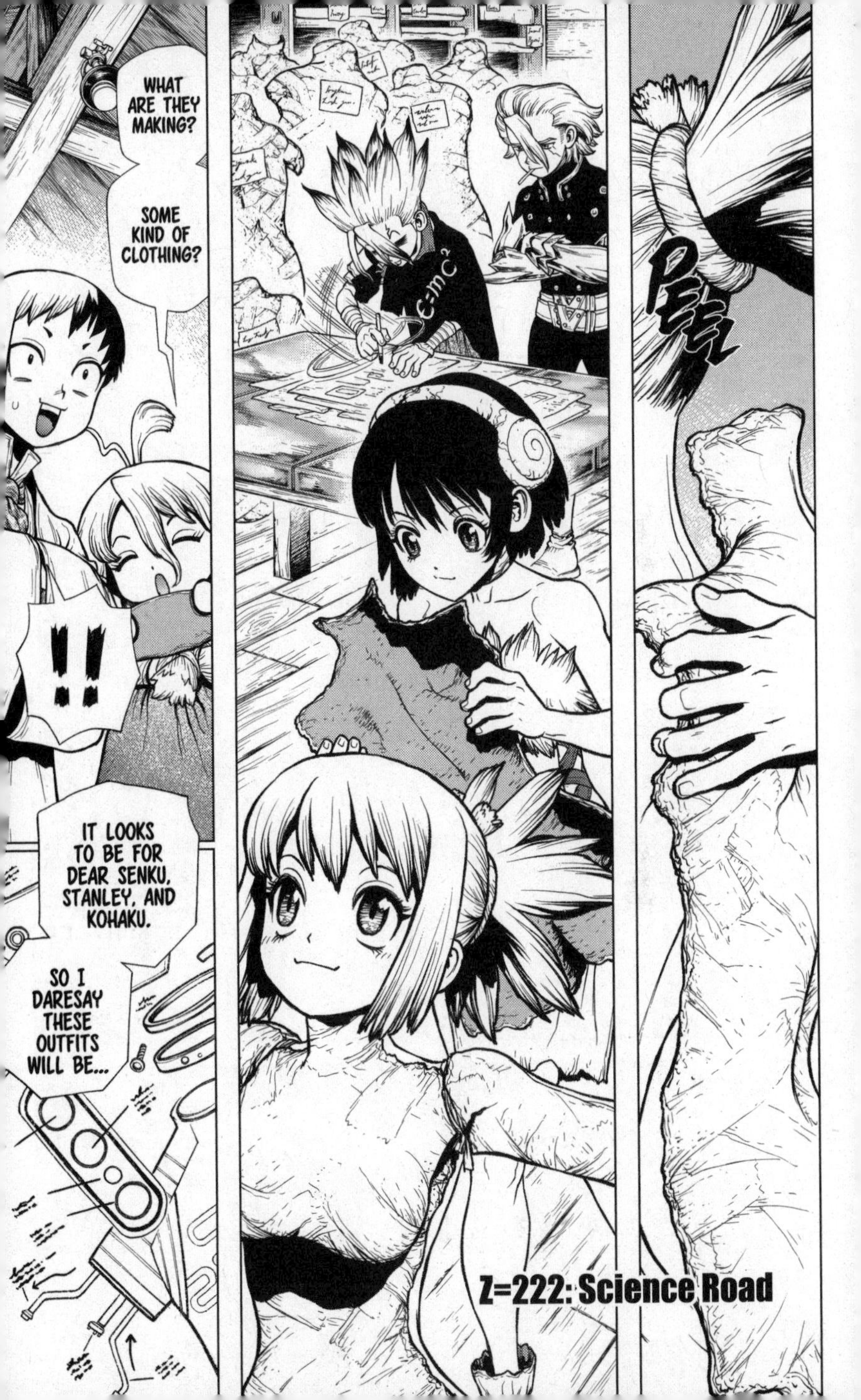
PEEL
Z=222: Science Road
WHAT ARE THEY MAKING?
SOME KIND OF CLOTHING?
!!
IT LOOKS TO BE FOR DEAR SENKU, STANLEY, AND KOHAKU.
SO I DARESAY THESE OUTFITS WILL BE...

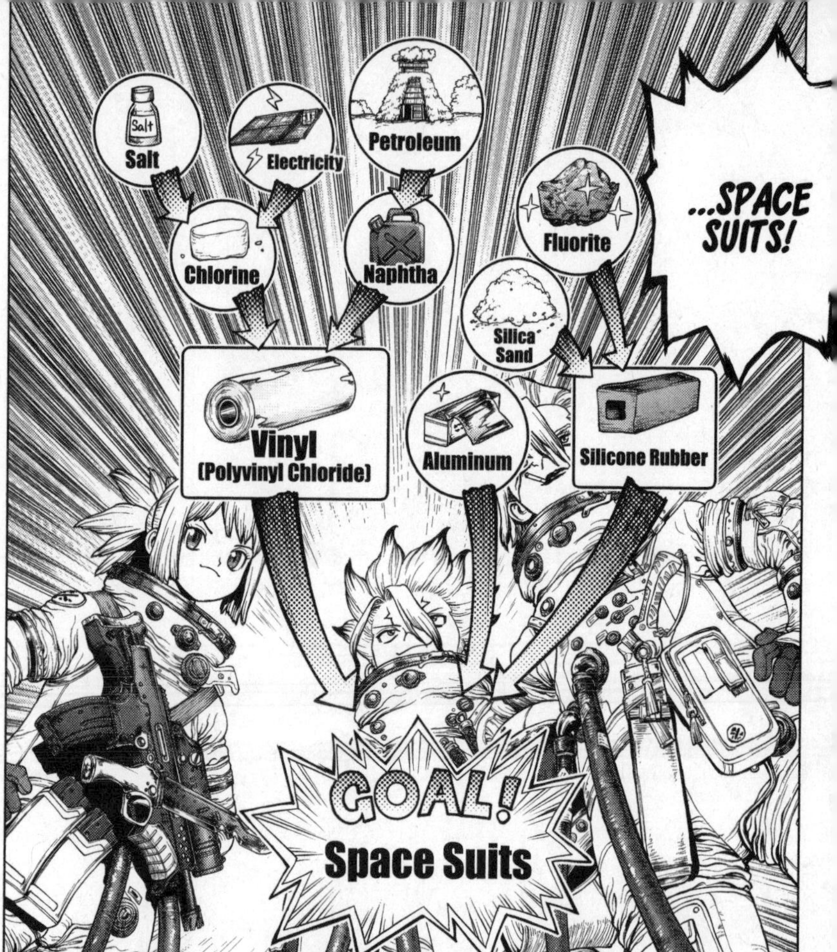
...SPACE SUITS!
Petroleum
Electricity
Salt
Fluorite
Naphtha
Chlorine
Silica Sand
Silicone Rubber
Aluminum
Vinyl (Polyvinyl Chloride)
GOAL!
Space Suits
SENKU

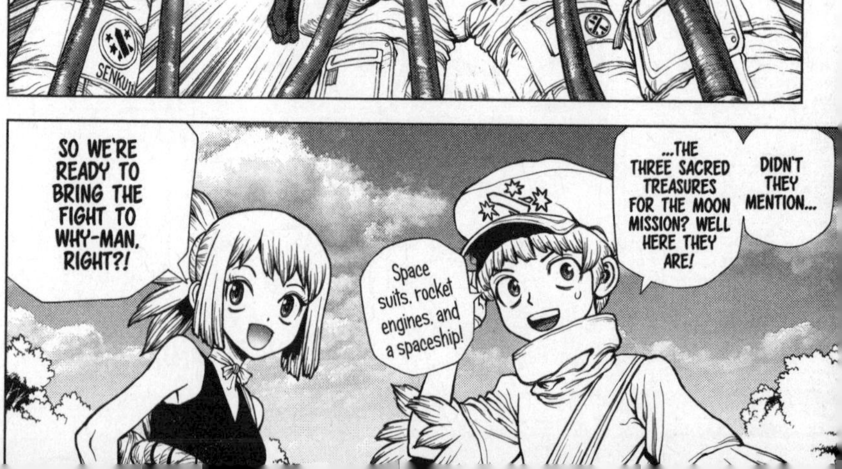
DIDN'T THEY MENTION...
...THE THREE SACRED TREASURES FOR THE MOON MISSION? WELL HERE THEY ARE!
Space suits, rocket engines, and a spaceship!
SO WE'RE READY TO BRING THE FIGHT TO WHY-MAN, RIGHT?!

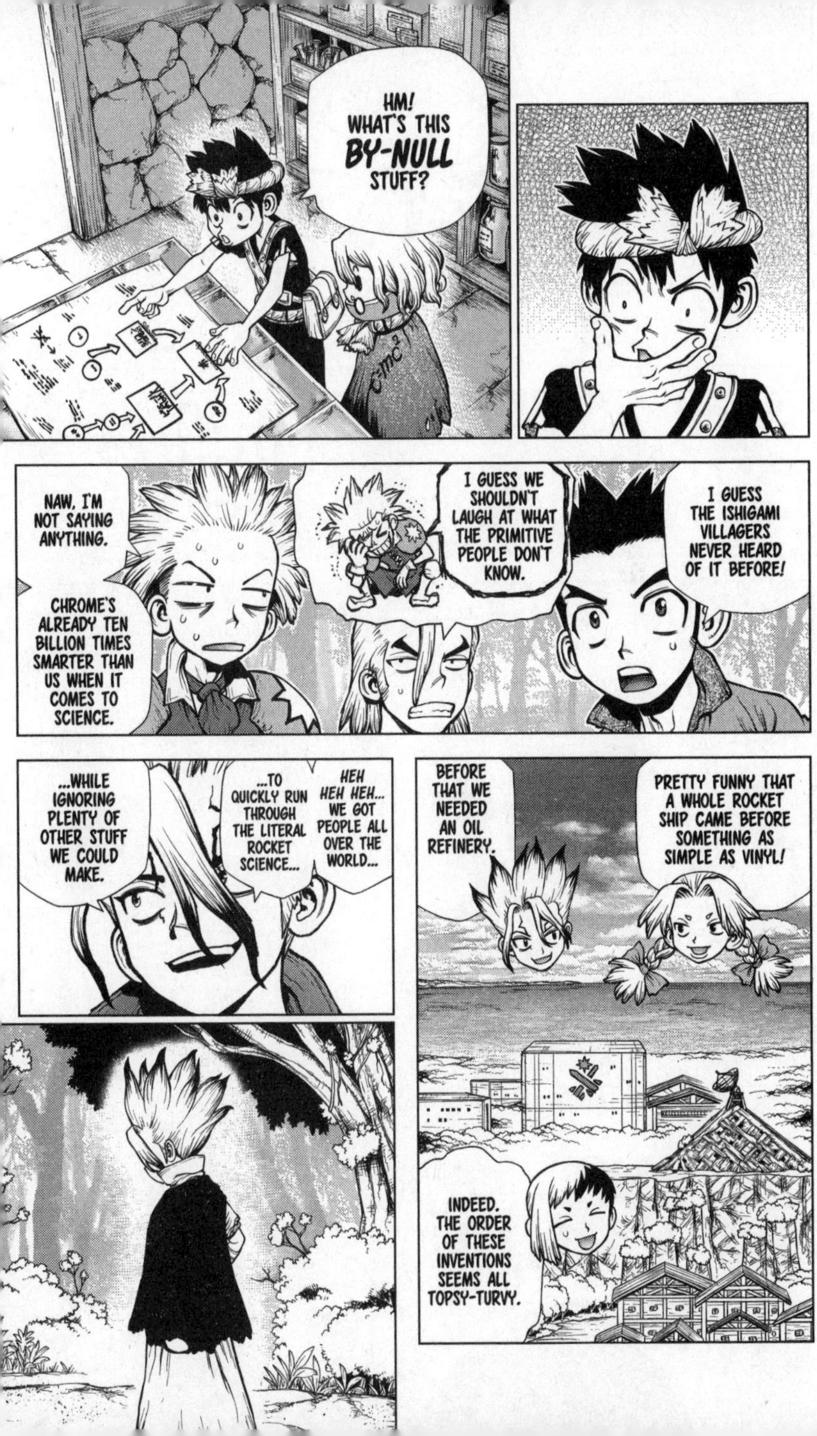
HM! WHAT'S THIS BY-NULL STUFF?
I GUESS THE ISHIGAMI VILLAGERS NEVER HEARD OF IT BEFORE!
I GUESS WE SHOULDN'T LAUGH AT WHAT THE PRIMITIVE PEOPLE DON'T KNOW.
NAW, I'M NOT SAYING ANYTHING.
CHROME'S ALREADY TEN BILLION TIMES SMARTER THAN US WHEN IT COMES TO SCIENCE.
PRETTY FUNNY THAT A WHOLE ROCKET SHIP CAME BEFORE SOMETHING AS SIMPLE AS VINYL!
BEFORE THAT WE NEEDED AN OIL REFINERY.
INDEED. THE ORDER OF THESE INVENTIONS SEEMS ALL TOPSY-TURVY.
HEH HEH HEH... WE GOT PEOPLE ALL OVER THE WORLD...
...TO QUICKLY RUN THROUGH THE LITERAL ROCKET SCIENCE...
...WHILE IGNORING PLENTY OF OTHER STUFF WE COULD MAKE.

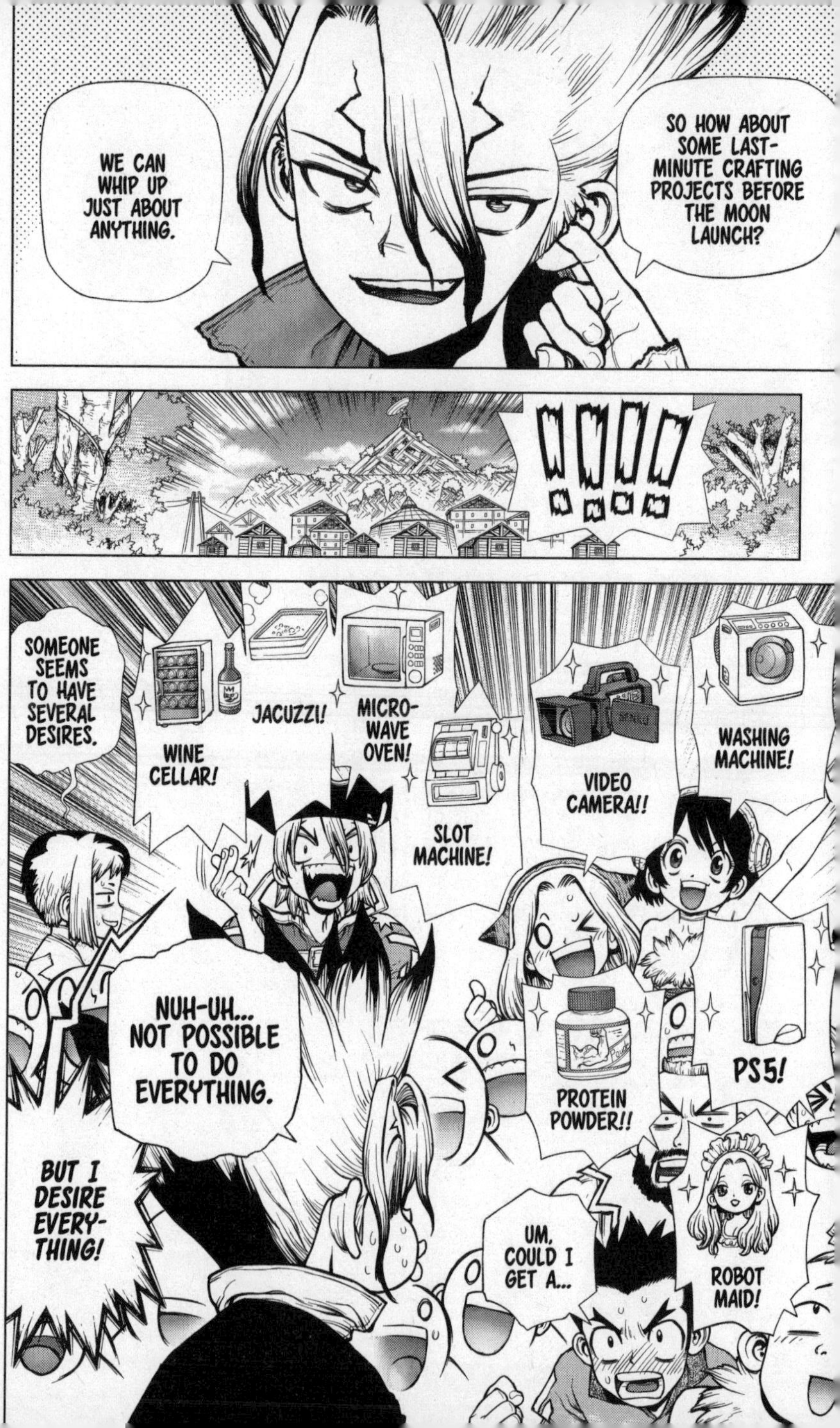
SO HOW ABOUT SOME LAST-MINUTE CRAFTING PROJECTS BEFORE THE MOON LAUNCH?
WE CAN WHIP UP JUST ABOUT ANYTHING.
WASHING MACHINE!
VIDEO CAMERA!!
SLOT MACHINE!
MICRO-WAVE OVEN!
JACUZZI!
WINE CELLAR!
SOMEONE SEEMS TO HAVE SEVERAL DESIRES.
PS5!
PROTEIN POWDER!!
NUH-UH... NOT POSSIBLE TO DO EVERYTHING.
ROBOT MAID!
UM, COULD I GET A...
BUT I DESIRE EVERY-THING!

Z=222: Science Road

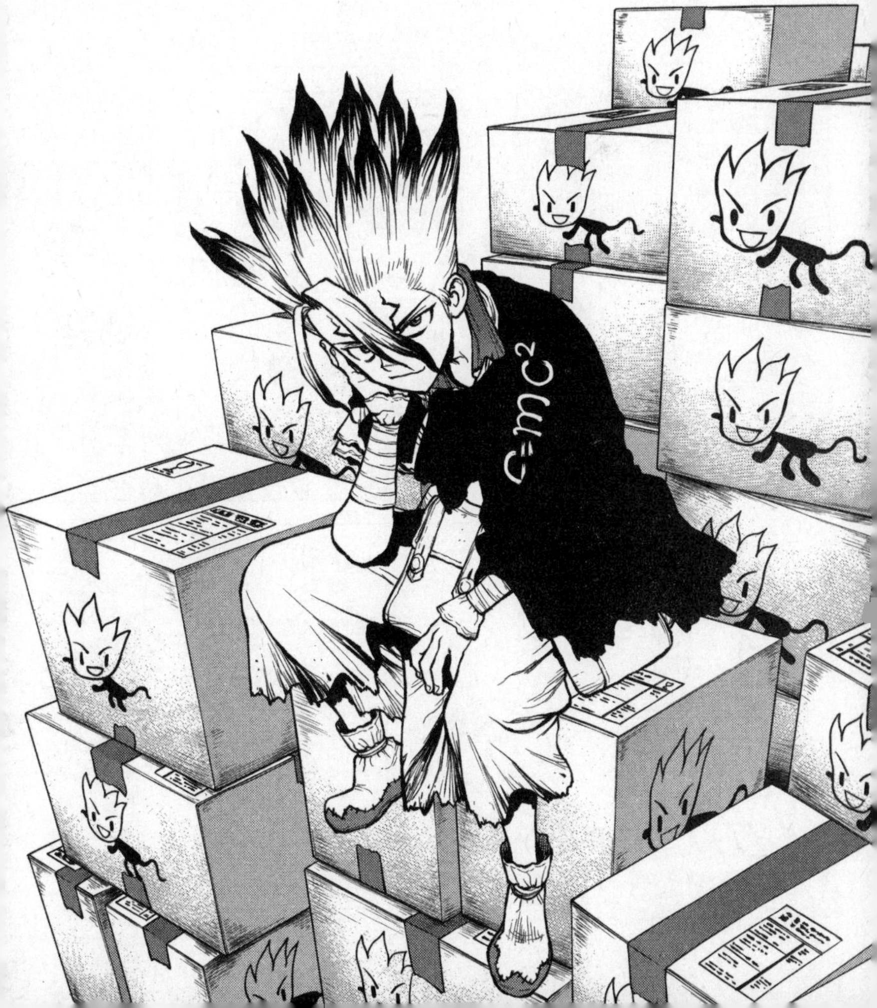
$E=mc^2$

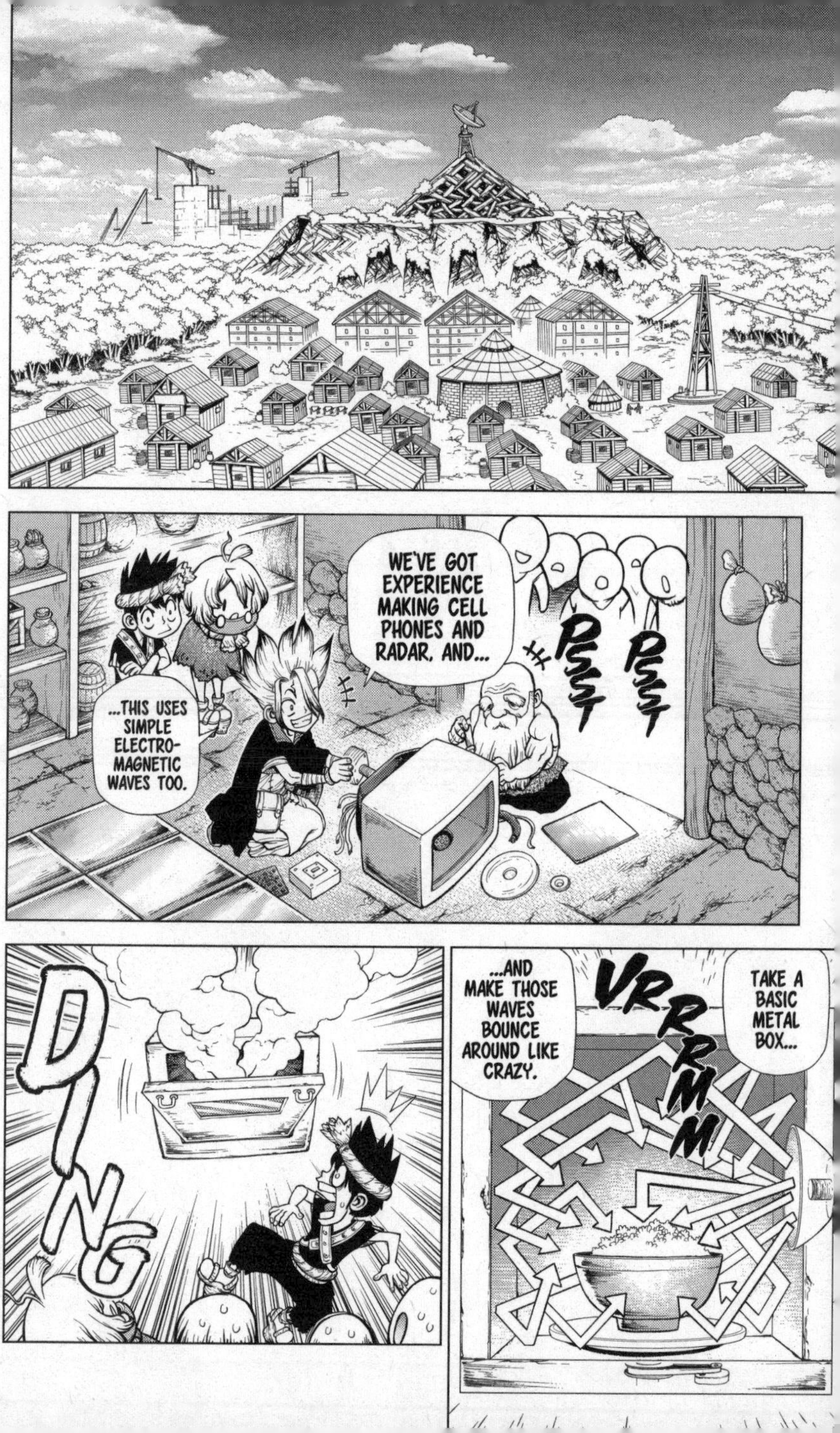
WE'VE GOT EXPERIENCE MAKING CELL PHONES AND RADAR, AND...
PSSST
PSSST
...THIS USES SIMPLE ELECTRO-MAGNETIC WAVES TOO.
TAKE A BASIC METAL BOX...
VRRRMM
...AND MAKE THOSE WAVES BOUNCE AROUND LIKE CRAZY.
DING

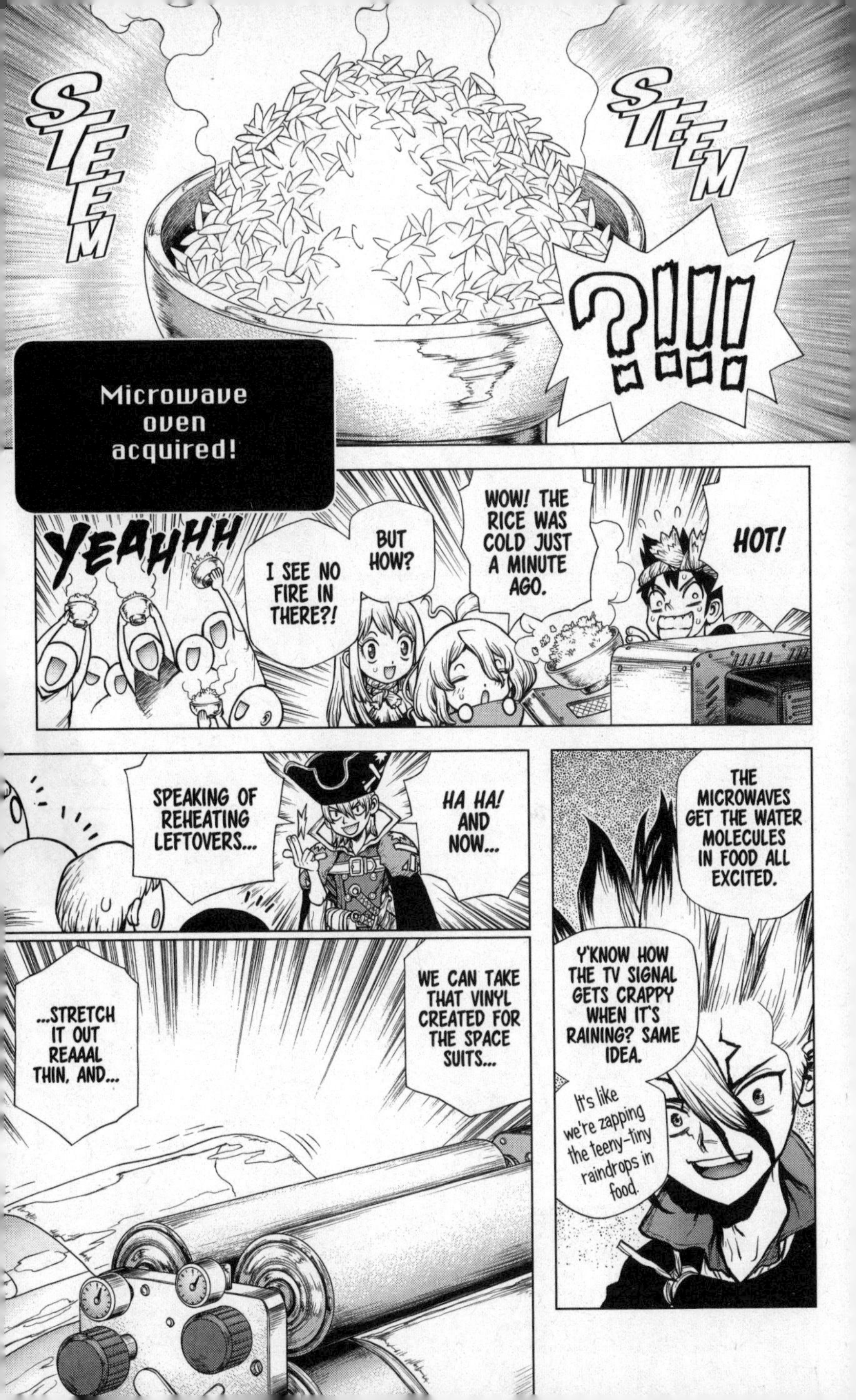
STEEM
?!!!
STEEM
Microwave oven acquired!
HOT!
WOW! THE RICE WAS COLD JUST A MINUTE AGO.
BUT HOW?
I SEE NO FIRE IN THERE?!
YEAHHH
THE MICROWAVES GET THE WATER MOLECULES IN FOOD ALL EXCITED.
Y'KNOW HOW THE TV SIGNAL GETS CRAPPY WHEN IT'S RAINING? SAME IDEA.
It's like we're zapping the teeny-tiny raindrops in food.
HA HA! AND NOW...
SPEAKING OF REHEATING LEFTOVERS...
WE CAN TAKE THAT VINYL CREATED FOR THE SPACE SUITS...
...STRETCH IT OUT REAAAL THIN, AND...

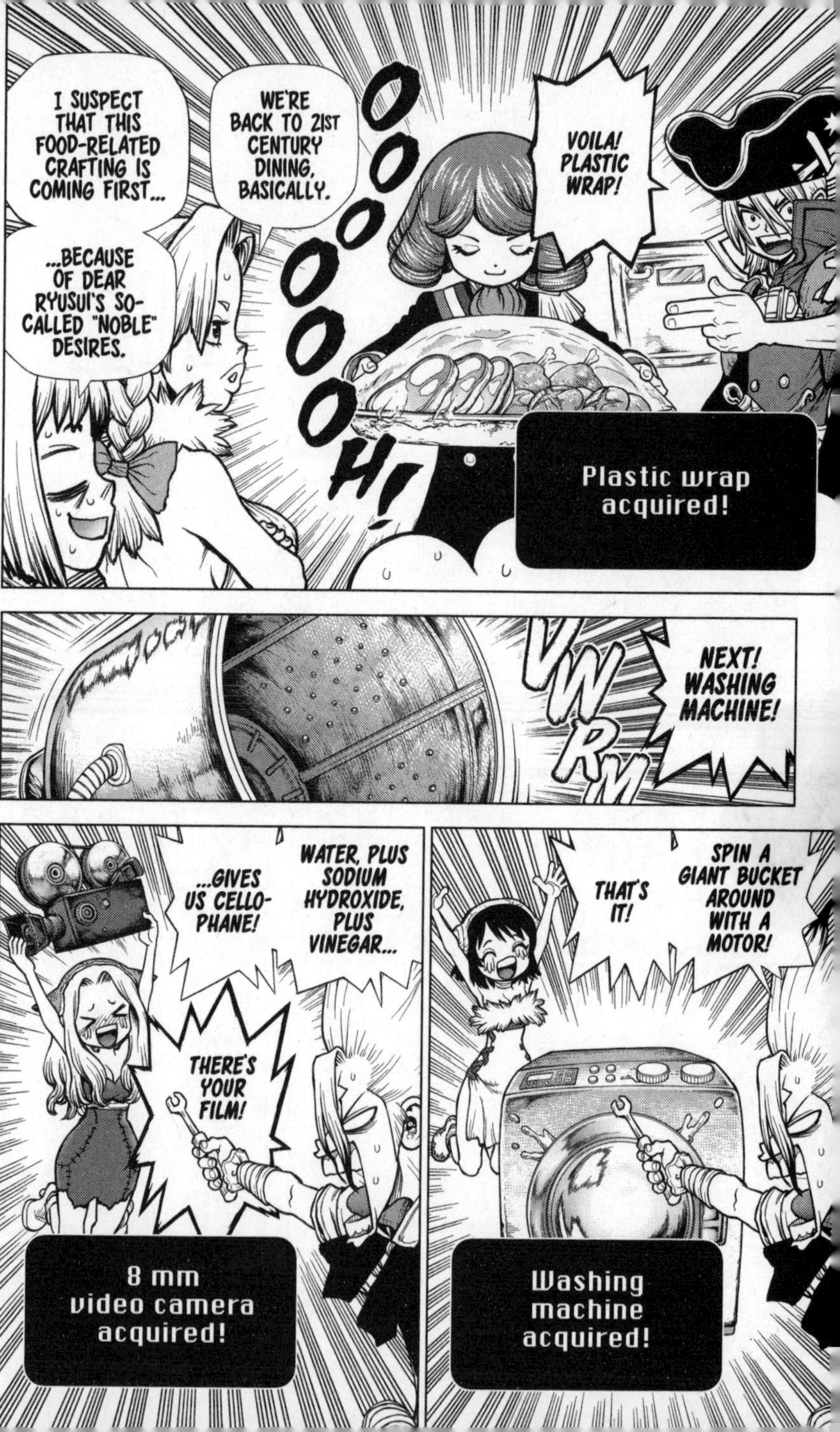
VOILA! PLASTIC WRAP!
OOOOOOOH!
WE'RE BACK TO 21ST CENTURY DINING, BASICALLY.
I SUSPECT THAT THIS FOOD-RELATED CRAFTING IS COMING FIRST...
...BECAUSE OF DEAR RYUSUI'S SO-CALLED "NOBLE" DESIRES.
Plastic wrap acquired!
NEXT! WASHING MACHINE!
VWRM
SPIN A GIANT BUCKET AROUND WITH A MOTOR!
THAT'S IT!
Washing machine acquired!
WATER, PLUS SODIUM HYDROXIDE, PLUS VINEGAR...
...GIVES US CELLO-PHANE!
THERE'S YOUR FILM!
8 mm video camera acquired!

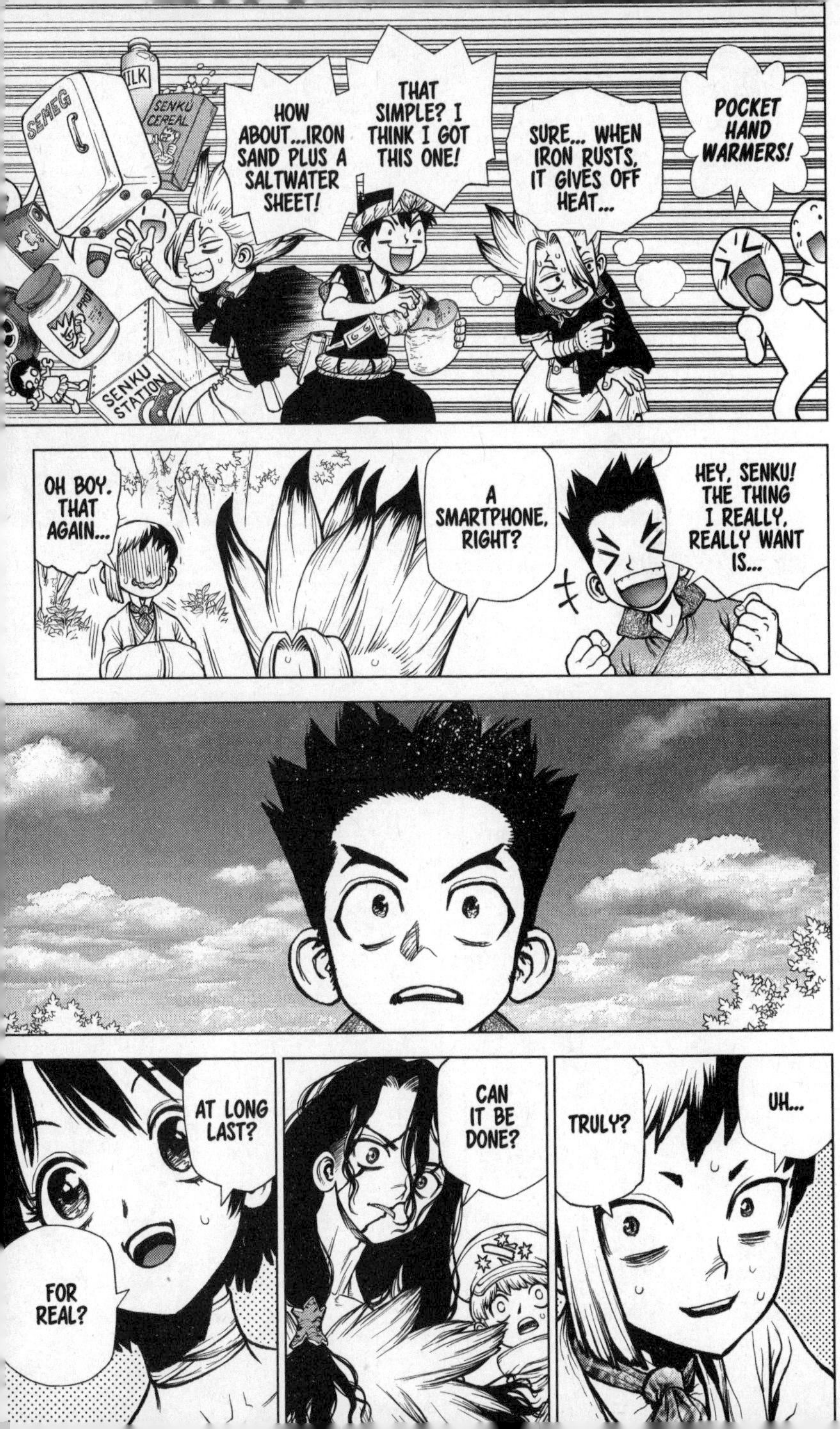
POCKET HAND WARMERS!
SURE... WHEN IRON RUSTS, IT GIVES OFF HEAT...
THAT SIMPLE? I THINK I GOT THIS ONE!
HOW ABOUT...IRON SAND PLUS A SALTWATER SHEET!
SENKU CEREAL
SEMEG
SENKU STATION
HEY, SENKU! THE THING I REALLY, REALLY WANT IS...
A SMARTPHONE, RIGHT?
OH BOY. THAT AGAIN...
UH...
TRULY?
CAN IT BE DONE?
AT LONG LAST?
FOR REAL?

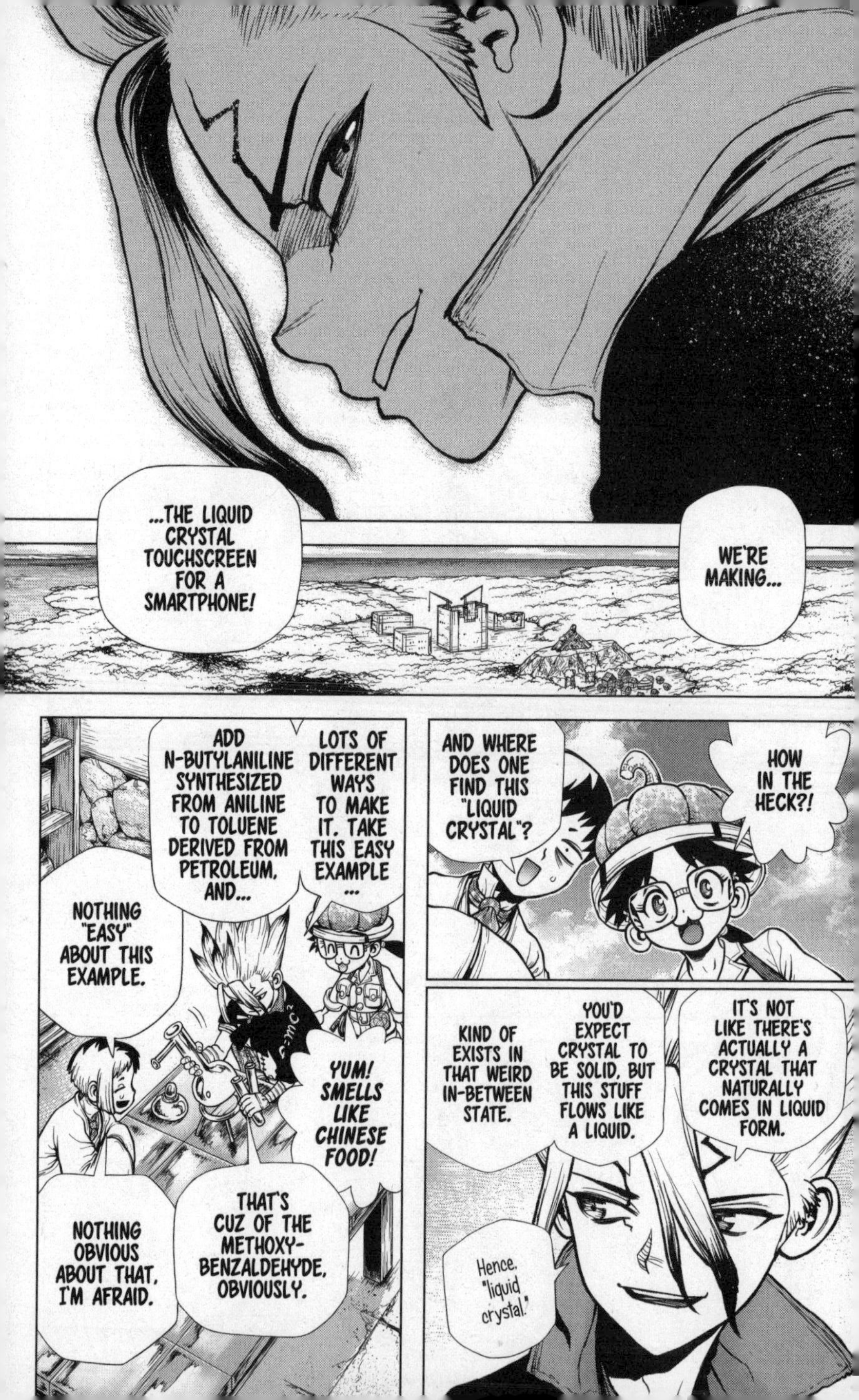
WE'RE MAKING...
...THE LIQUID CRYSTAL TOUCHSCREEN FOR A SMARTPHONE!
HOW IN THE HECK?!
AND WHERE DOES ONE FIND THIS "LIQUID CRYSTAL"?
IT'S NOT LIKE THERE'S ACTUALLY A CRYSTAL THAT NATURALLY COMES IN LIQUID FORM.
YOU'D EXPECT CRYSTAL TO BE SOLID, BUT THIS STUFF FLOWS LIKE A LIQUID.
KIND OF EXISTS IN THAT WEIRD IN-BETWEEN STATE.
Hence, "liquid crystal."
LOTS OF DIFFERENT WAYS TO MAKE IT. TAKE THIS EASY EXAMPLE...
ADD N-BUTYLANILINE SYNTHESIZED FROM ANILINE TO TOLUENE DERIVED FROM PETROLEUM, AND...
NOTHING "EASY" ABOUT THIS EXAMPLE.
YUM! SMELLS LIKE CHINESE FOOD!
THAT'S CUZ OF THE METHOXY-BENZALDEHYDE, OBVIOUSLY.
NOTHING OBVIOUS ABOUT THAT, I'M AFRAID.

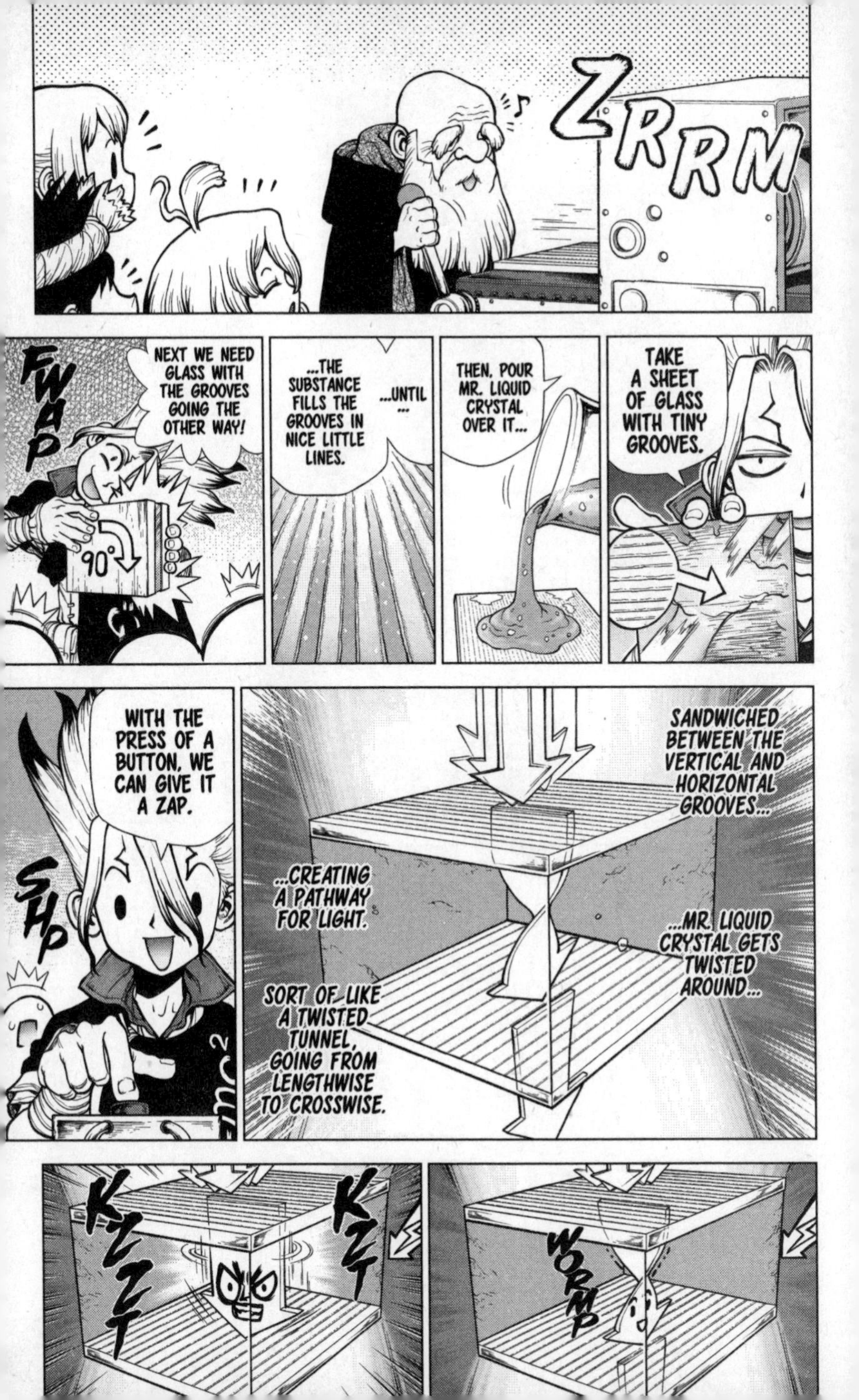
ZRRRM
TAKE A SHEET OF GLASS WITH TINY GROOVES.
THEN, POUR MR. LIQUID CRYSTAL OVER IT...
...UNTIL ...
...THE SUBSTANCE FILLS THE GROOVES IN NICE LITTLE LINES.
NEXT WE NEED GLASS WITH THE GROOVES GOING THE OTHER WAY!
FWAP
90°
SANDWICHED BETWEEN THE VERTICAL AND HORIZONTAL GROOVES...
...MR. LIQUID CRYSTAL GETS TWISTED AROUND...
...CREATING A PATHWAY FOR LIGHT.
SORT OF LIKE A TWISTED TUNNEL, GOING FROM LENGTHWISE TO CROSSWISE.
WITH THE PRESS OF A BUTTON, WE CAN GIVE IT A ZAP.
SHP
WORMP
KZZT
KZZZT

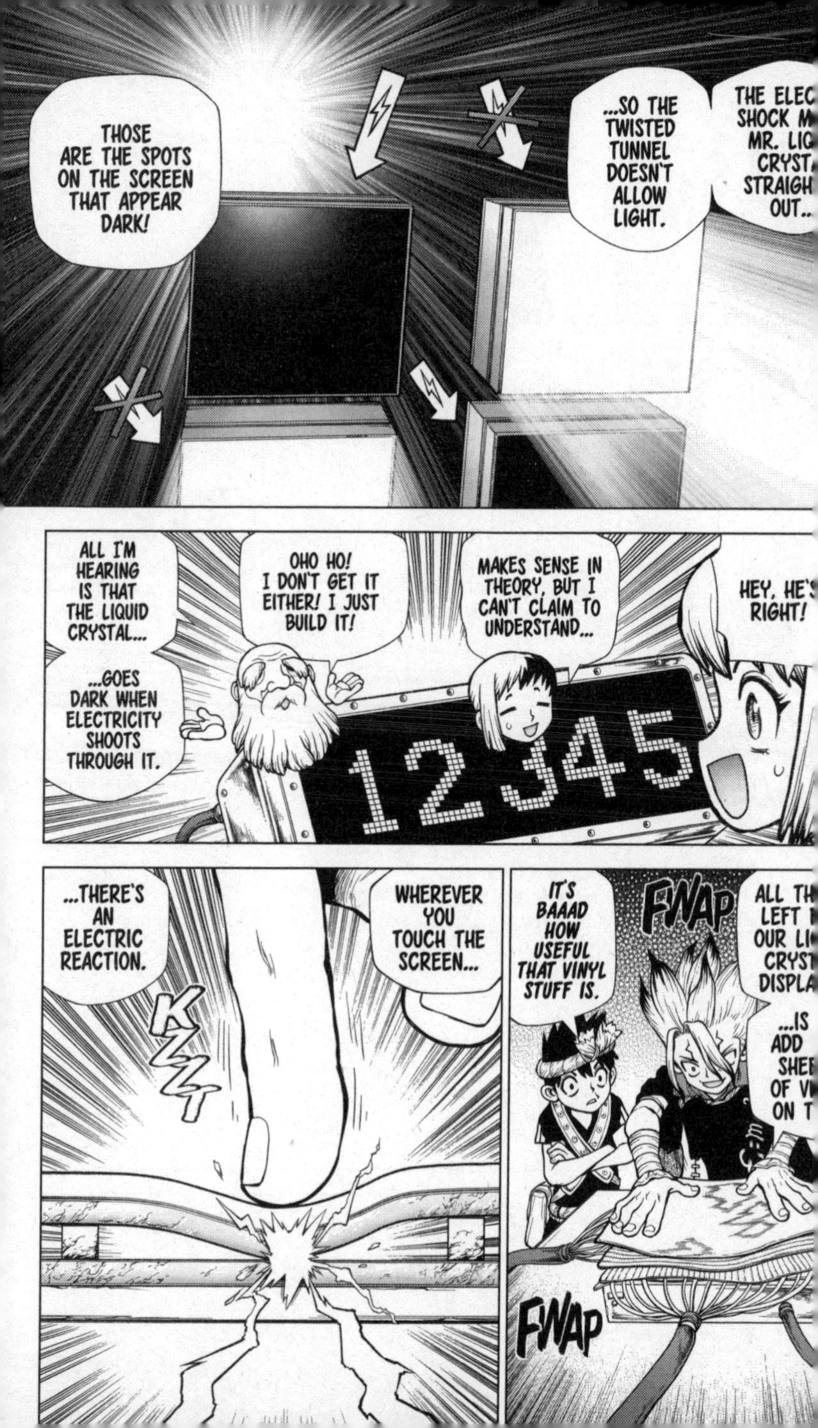
THE ELEC SHOCK M MR. LIG CRYST STRAIGH OUT...
...SO THE TWISTED TUNNEL DOESN'T ALLOW LIGHT.
THOSE ARE THE SPOTS ON THE SCREEN THAT APPEAR DARK!
HEY, HE'S RIGHT!
MAKES SENSE IN THEORY, BUT I CAN'T CLAIM TO UNDERSTAND...
12345
OHO HO! I DON'T GET IT EITHER! I JUST BUILD IT!
ALL I'M HEARING IS THAT THE LIQUID CRYSTAL...
...GOES DARK WHEN ELECTRICITY SHOOTS THROUGH IT.
ALL TH LEFT OUR LI CRYST DISPLA
...IS ADD SHE OF V ON T
FWAP
IT'S BAAAD HOW USEFUL THAT VINYL STUFF IS.
FWAP
WHEREVER YOU TOUCH THE SCREEN...
...THERE'S AN ELECTRIC REACTION.
KZZT

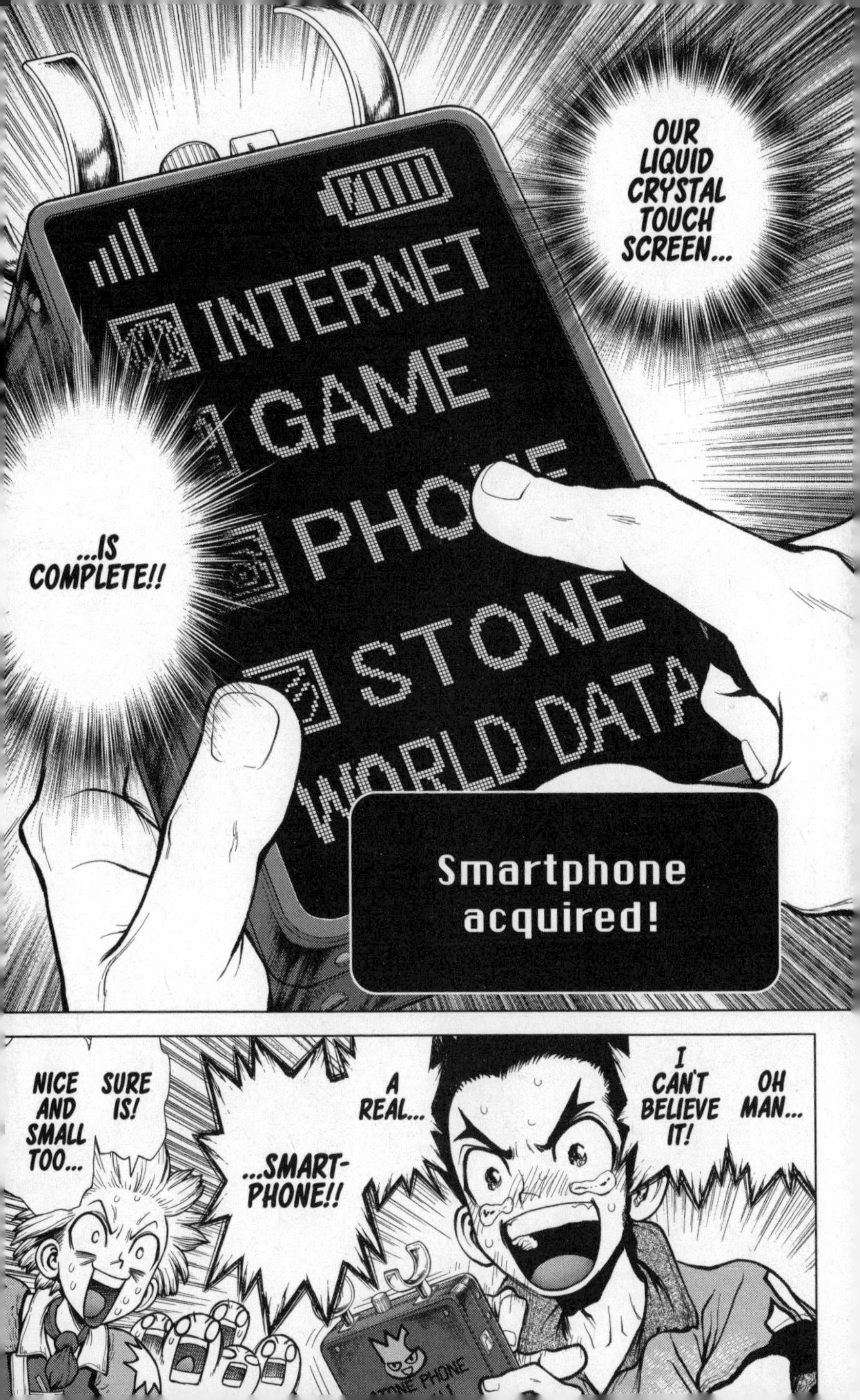
OUR LIQUID CRYSTAL TOUCH SCREEN...
INTERNET
GAME
PHONE
STONE WORLD DATA
...IS COMPLETE!!
Smartphone acquired!
OH MAN...
I CAN'T BELIEVE IT!
A REAL...
...SMART-PHONE!!
SURE IS!
NICE AND SMALL TOO...

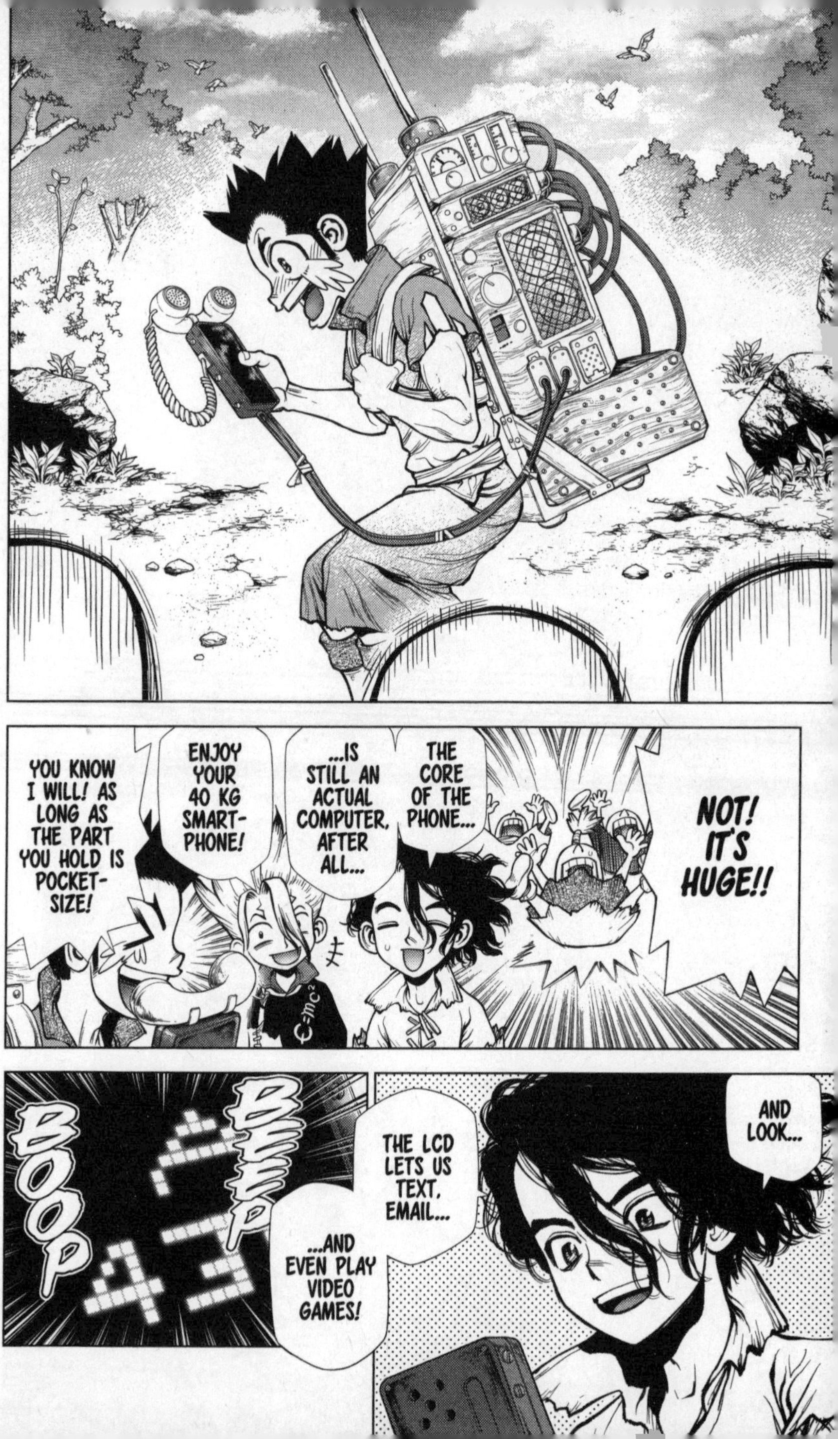
NOT! IT'S HUGE!!
THE CORE OF THE PHONE...
...IS STILL AN ACTUAL COMPUTER, AFTER ALL...
ENJOY YOUR 40 KG SMART-PHONE!
YOU KNOW I WILL! AS LONG AS THE PART YOU HOLD IS POCKET-SIZE!
AND LOOK...
THE LCD LETS US TEXT, EMAIL...
...AND EVEN PLAY VIDEO GAMES!
BEEP
BOOP

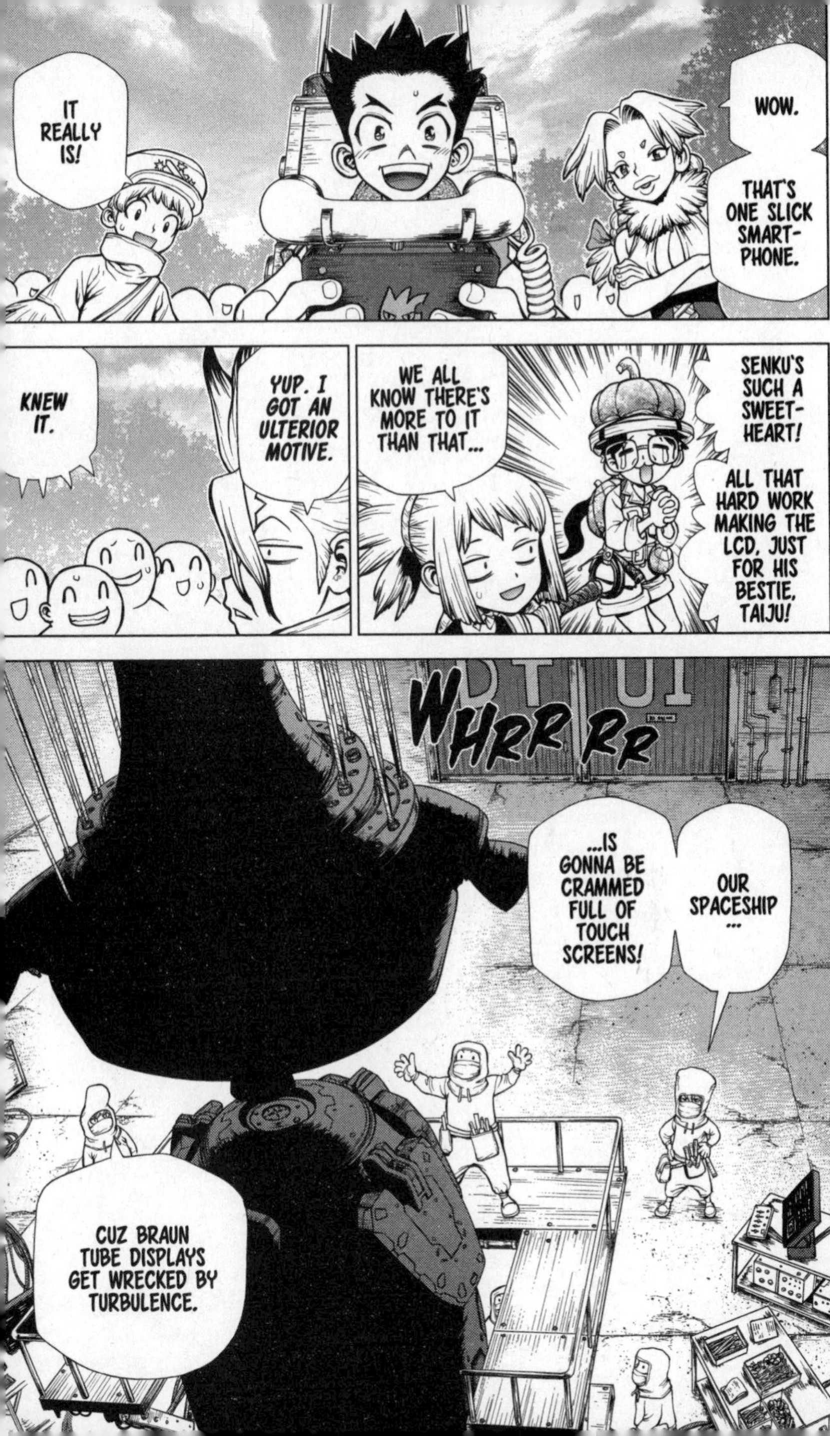
WOW.
THAT'S ONE SLICK SMARTPHONE.
IT REALLY IS!
SENKU'S SUCH A SWEETHEART!
ALL THAT HARD WORK MAKING THE LCD, JUST FOR HIS BESTIE, TAIJU!
WE ALL KNOW THERE'S MORE TO IT THAN THAT...
YUP. I GOT AN ULTERIOR MOTIVE.
KNEW IT.
WHRRRR
OUR SPACESHIP...
...IS GONNA BE CRAMMED FULL OF TOUCH SCREENS!
CUZ BRAUN TUBE DISPLAYS GET WRECKED BY TURBULENCE.

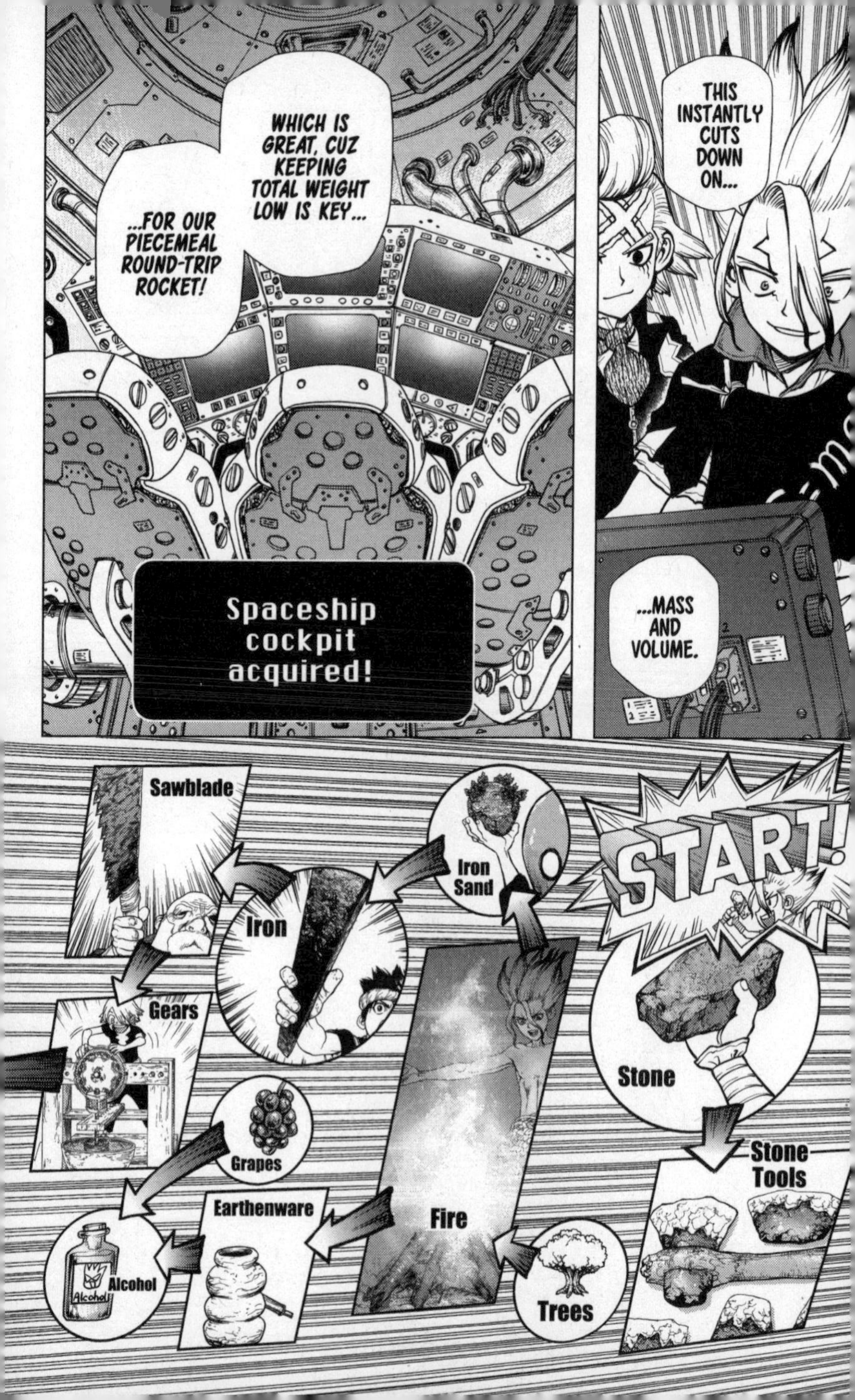
THIS INSTANTLY CUTS DOWN ON...
...MASS AND VOLUME.
WHICH IS GREAT, CUZ KEEPING TOTAL WEIGHT LOW IS KEY...
...FOR OUR PIECEMEAL ROUND-TRIP ROCKET!
Spaceship cockpit acquired!
START!
Stone
Stone Tools
Trees
Fire
Iron Sand
Iron
Sawblade
Gears
Grapes
Earthenware
Alcohol
Alcohol

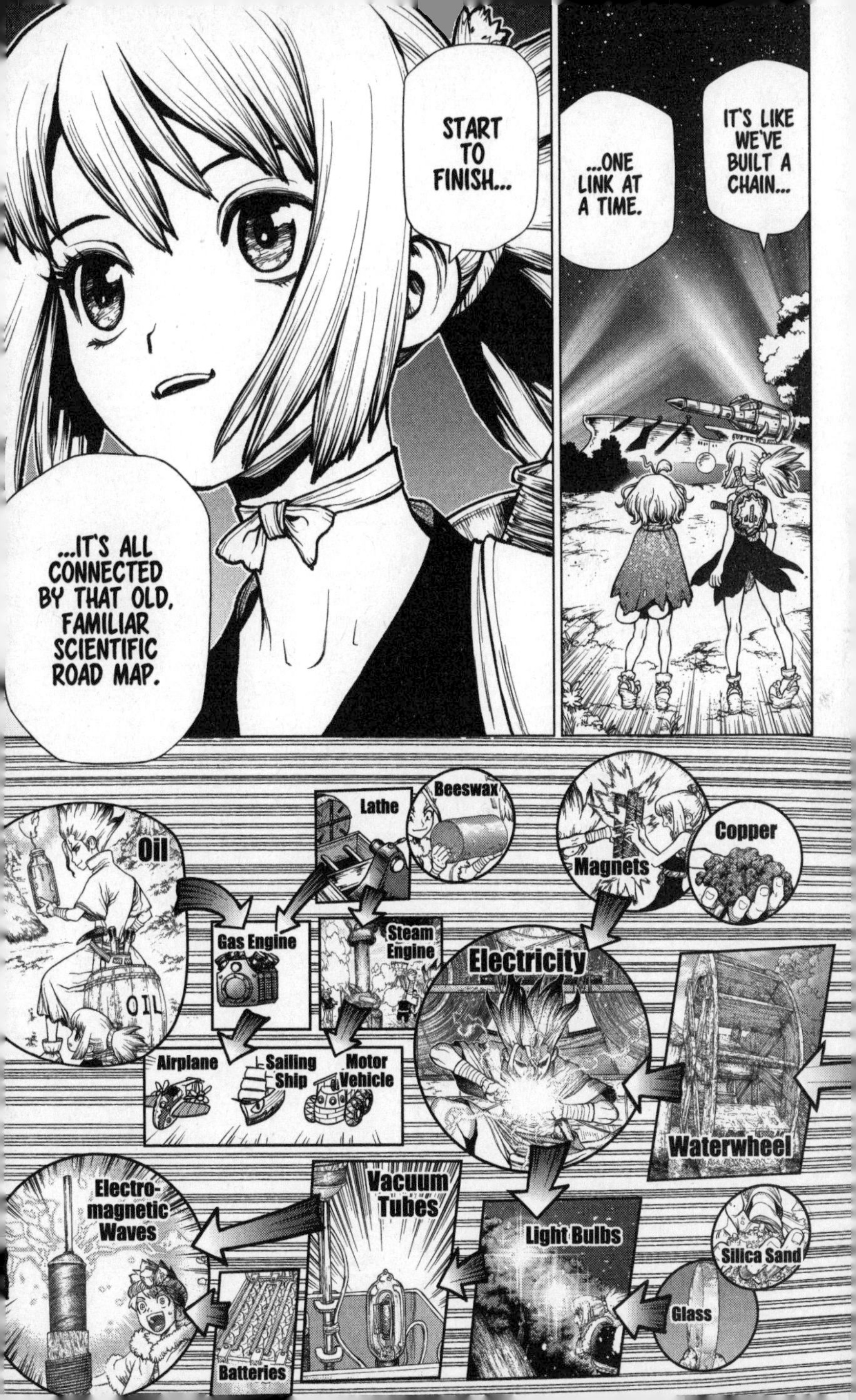
IT'S LIKE WE'VE BUILT A CHAIN...
...ONE LINK AT A TIME.
START TO FINISH...
...IT'S ALL CONNECTED BY THAT OLD, FAMILIAR SCIENTIFIC ROAD MAP.
Copper
Magnets
Beeswax
Lathe
Oil
OIL
Gas Engine
Steam Engine
Electricity
Waterwheel
Motor Vehicle
Sailing Ship
Airplane
Silica Sand
Light Bulbs
Vacuum Tubes
Electro-magnetic Waves
Glass
Batteries

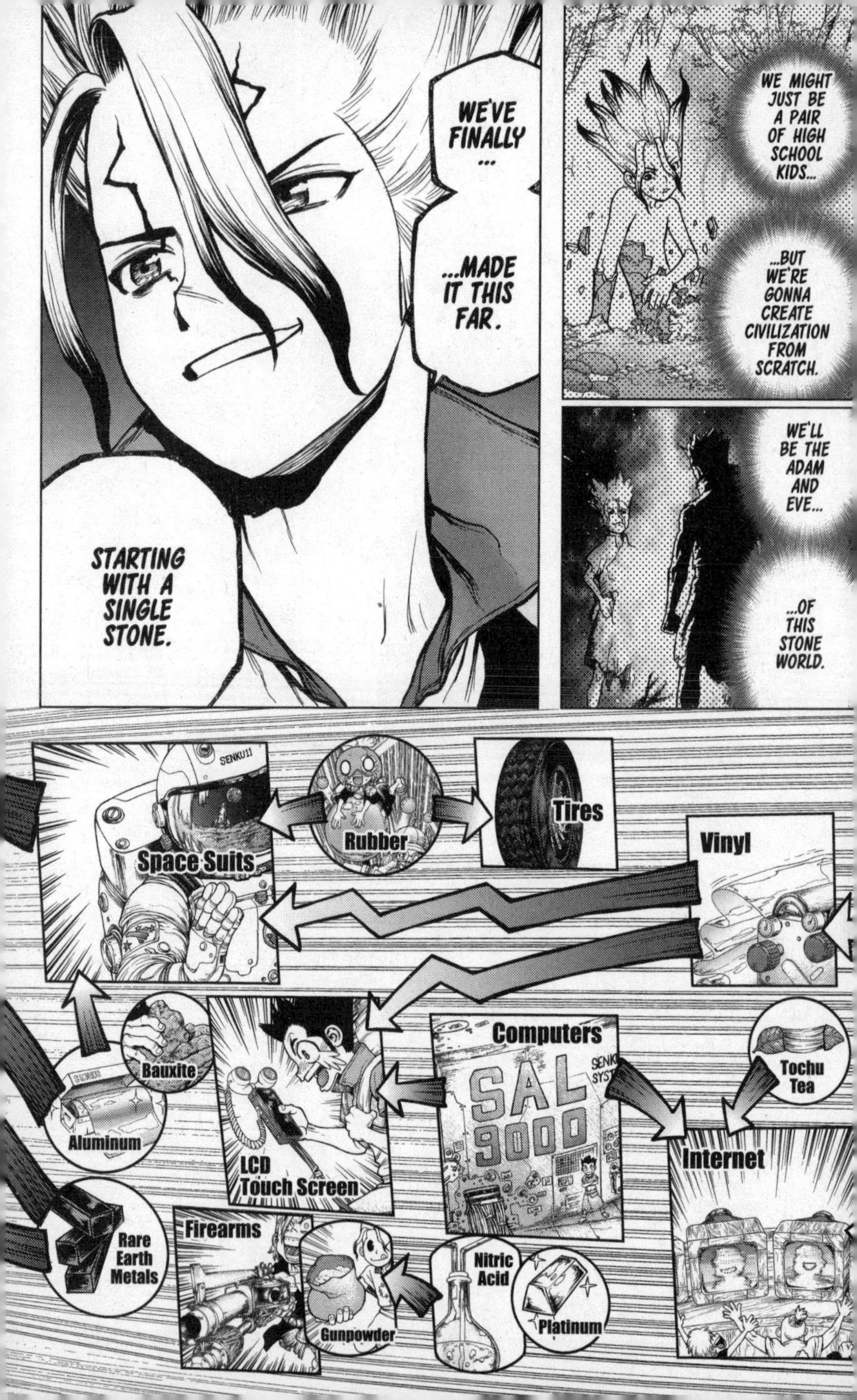

WE MIGHT JUST BE A PAIR OF HIGH SCHOOL KIDS...
...BUT WE'RE GONNA CREATE CIVILIZATION FROM SCRATCH.
WE'LL BE THE ADAM AND EVE...
...OF THIS STONE WORLD.
WE'VE FINALLY...
...MADE IT THIS FAR.
STARTING WITH A SINGLE STONE.
Vinyl
Tires
Rubber
SENKU11
Space Suits
Tochu Tea
Internet
Computers
SAL 9000
LCD Touch Screen
Bauxite
Aluminum
Platinum
Nitric Acid
Gunpowder
Firearms
Rare Earth Metals

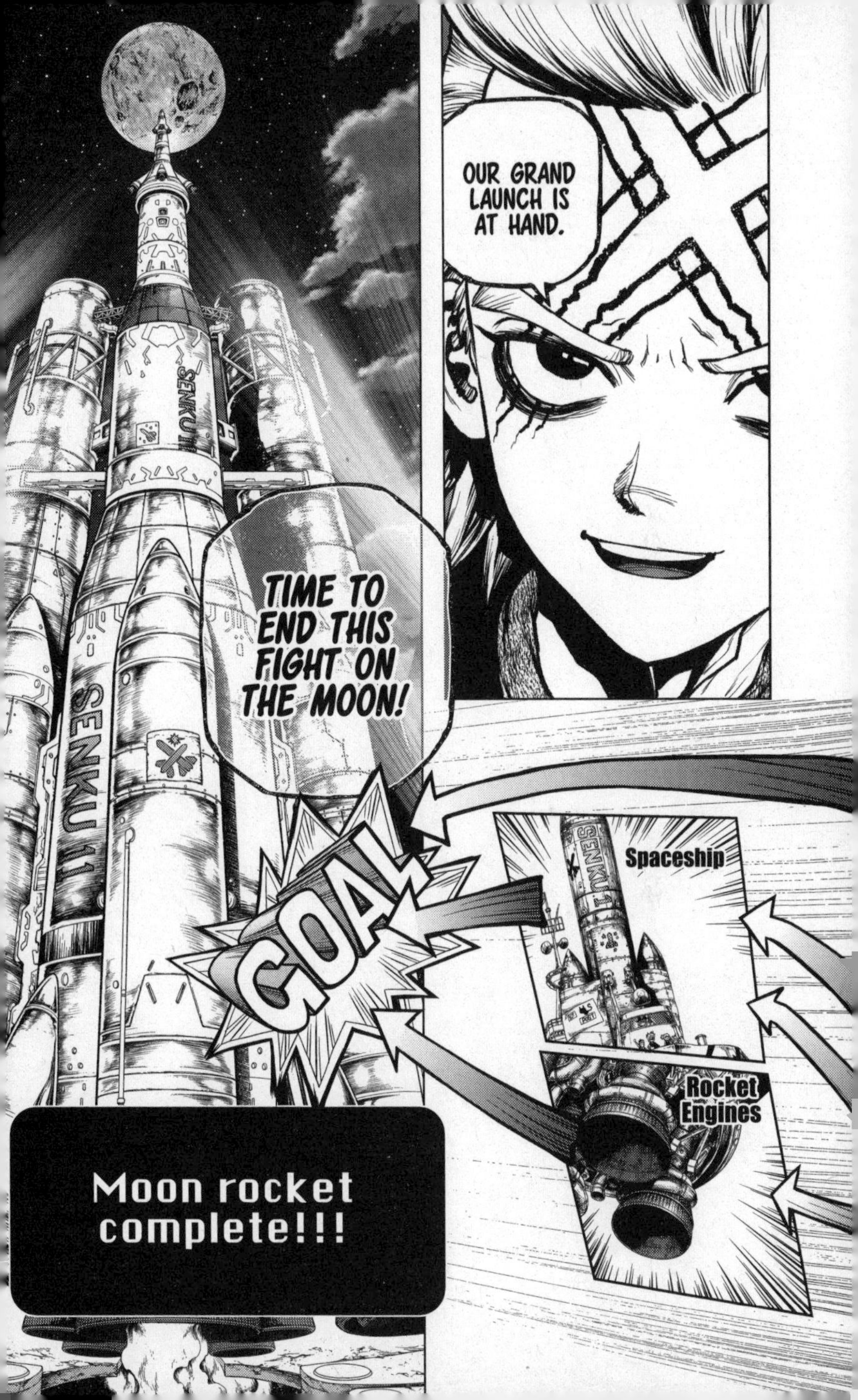
OUR GRAND LAUNCH IS AT HAND.
Spaceship
Rocket Engines
GOAL
TIME TO END THIS FIGHT ON THE MOON!
Moon rocket complete!!!

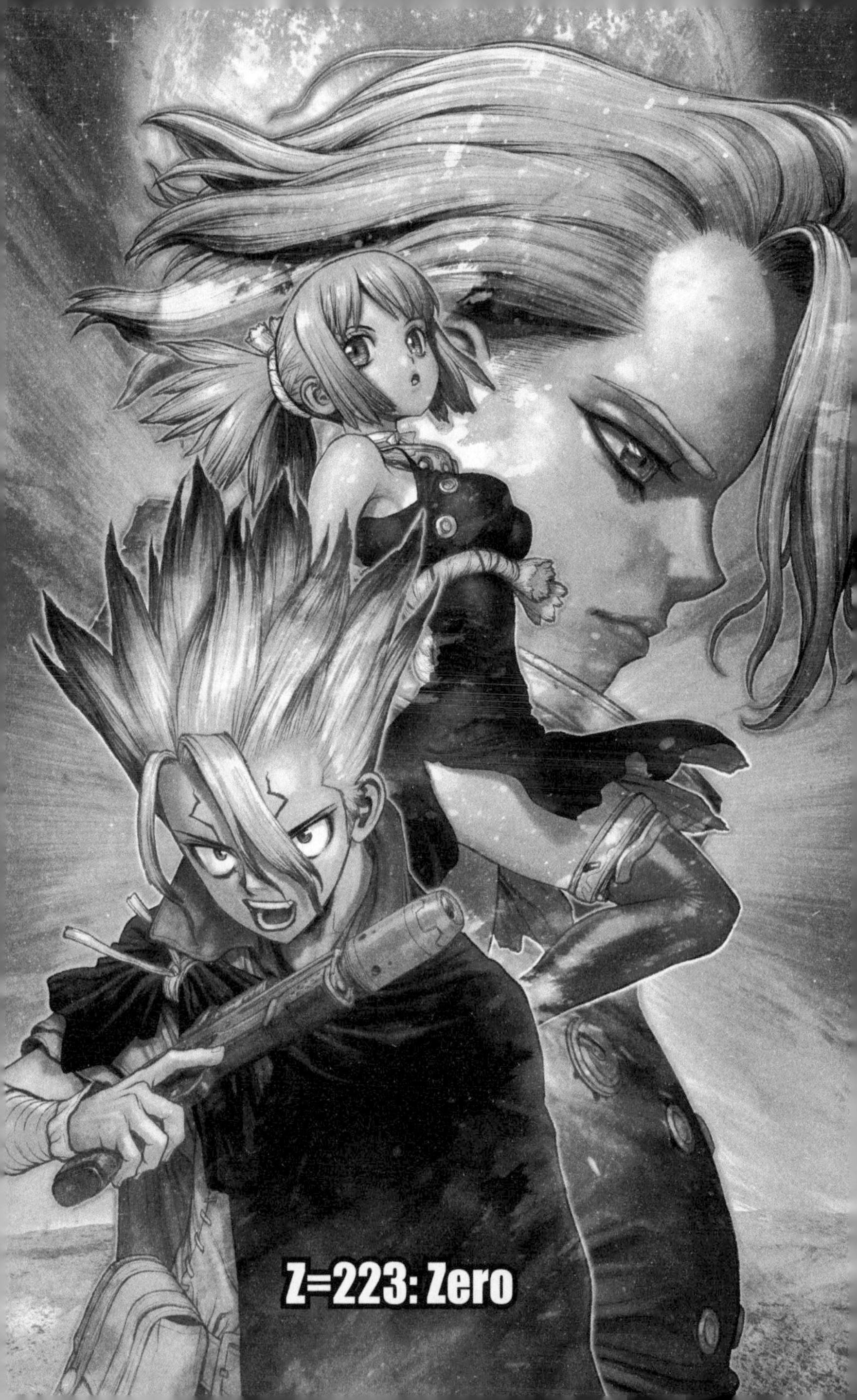
Z=223: Zero

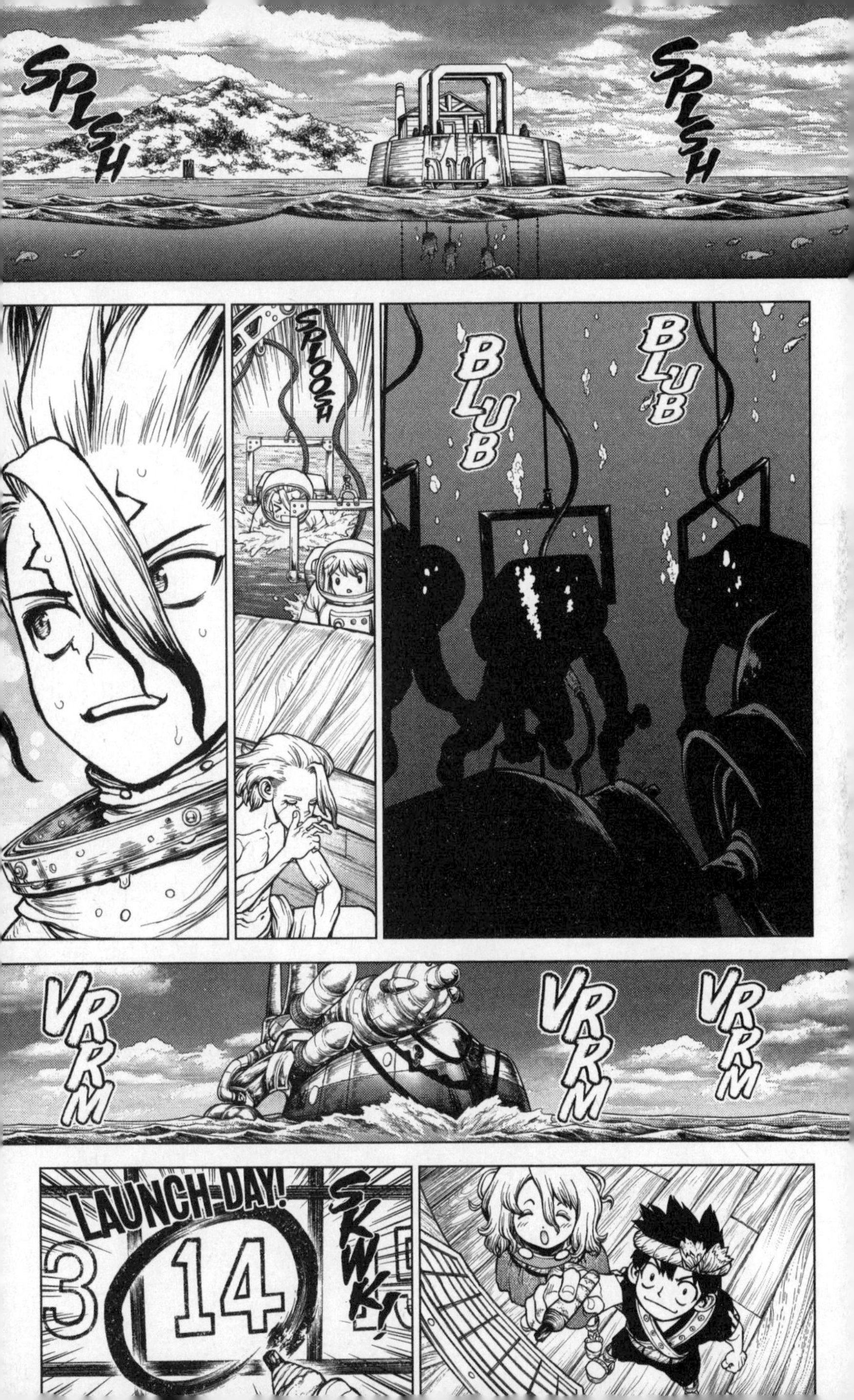
SPLSH
SPLSH
BLUB
BLUB
SPLOOSH
VRRM
VRRM
VRRM
SKWK!
LAUNCH DAY!
3
14

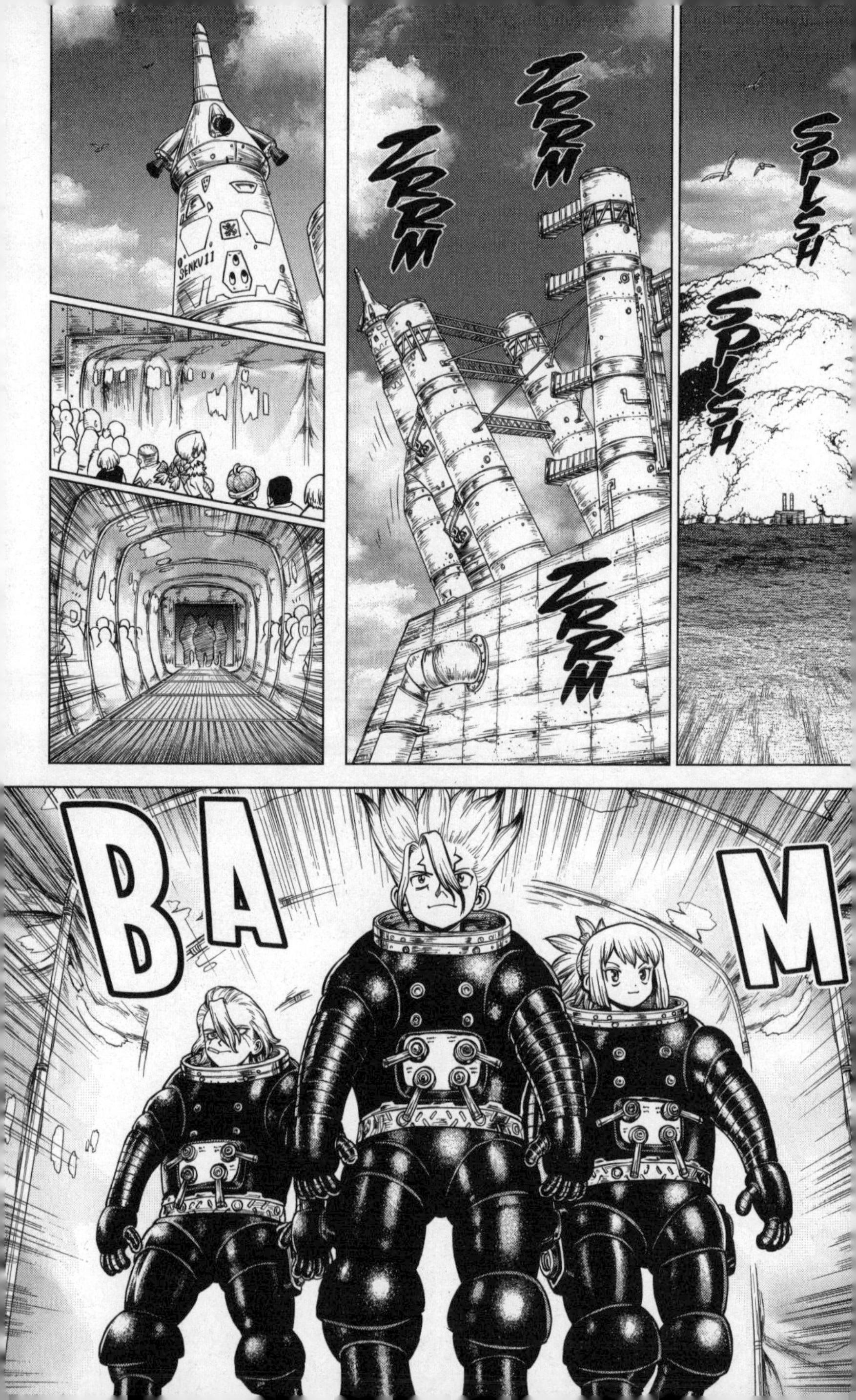
SPLSH
SPLSH
ZRRM
ZRRM
ZRRM
SENKU 11
BAM

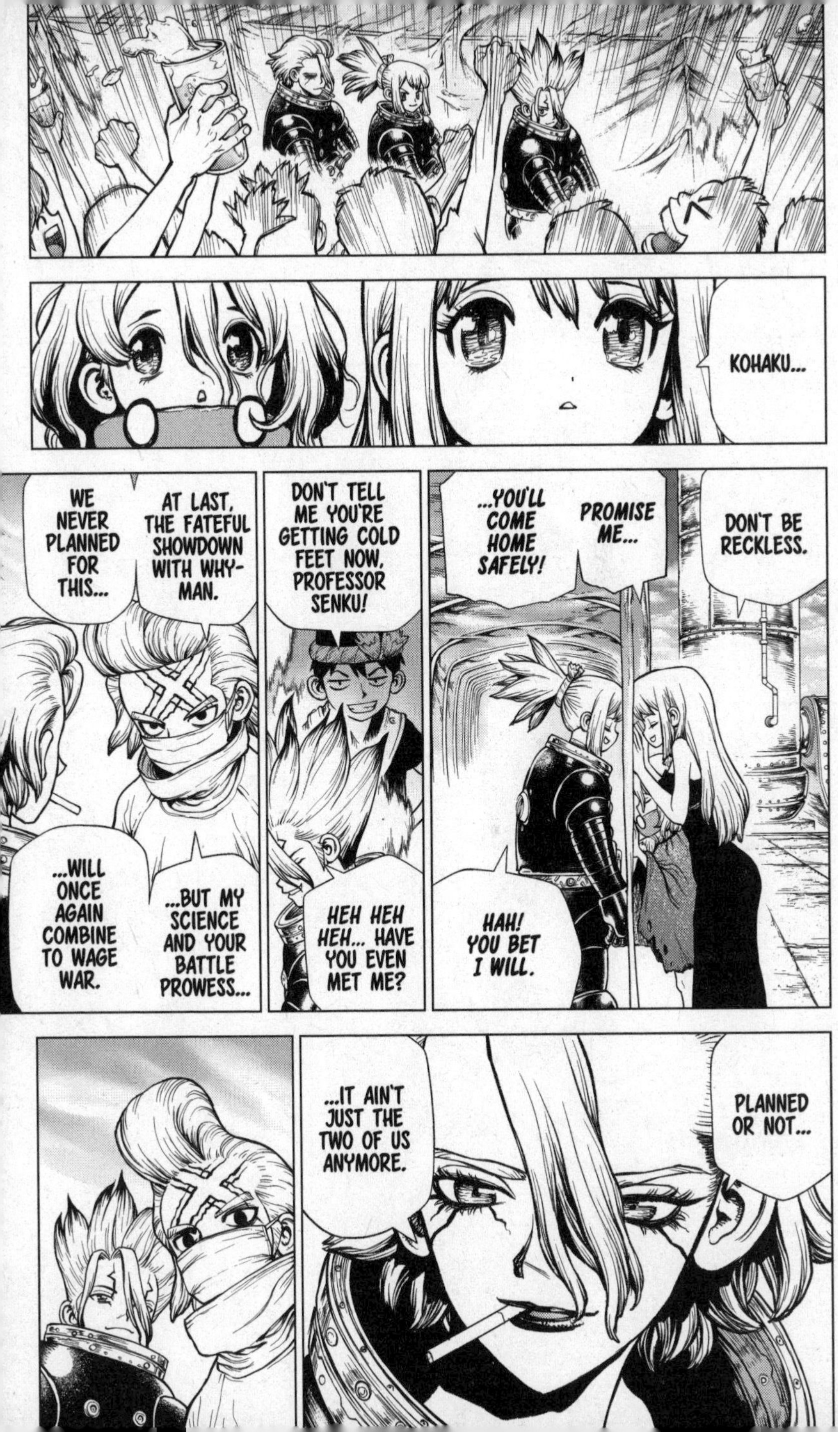
KOHAKU...
DON'T BE RECKLESS.
PROMISE ME...
...YOU'LL COME HOME SAFELY!
HAH! YOU BET I WILL.
DON'T TELL ME YOU'RE GETTING COLD FEET NOW, PROFESSOR SENKU!
HEH HEH HEH... HAVE YOU EVEN MET ME?
AT LAST, THE FATEFUL SHOWDOWN WITH WHY-MAN.
WE NEVER PLANNED FOR THIS...
...BUT MY SCIENCE AND YOUR BATTLE PROWESS...
...WILL ONCE AGAIN COMBINE TO WAGE WAR.
PLANNED OR NOT...
...IT AIN'T JUST THE TWO OF US ANYMORE.

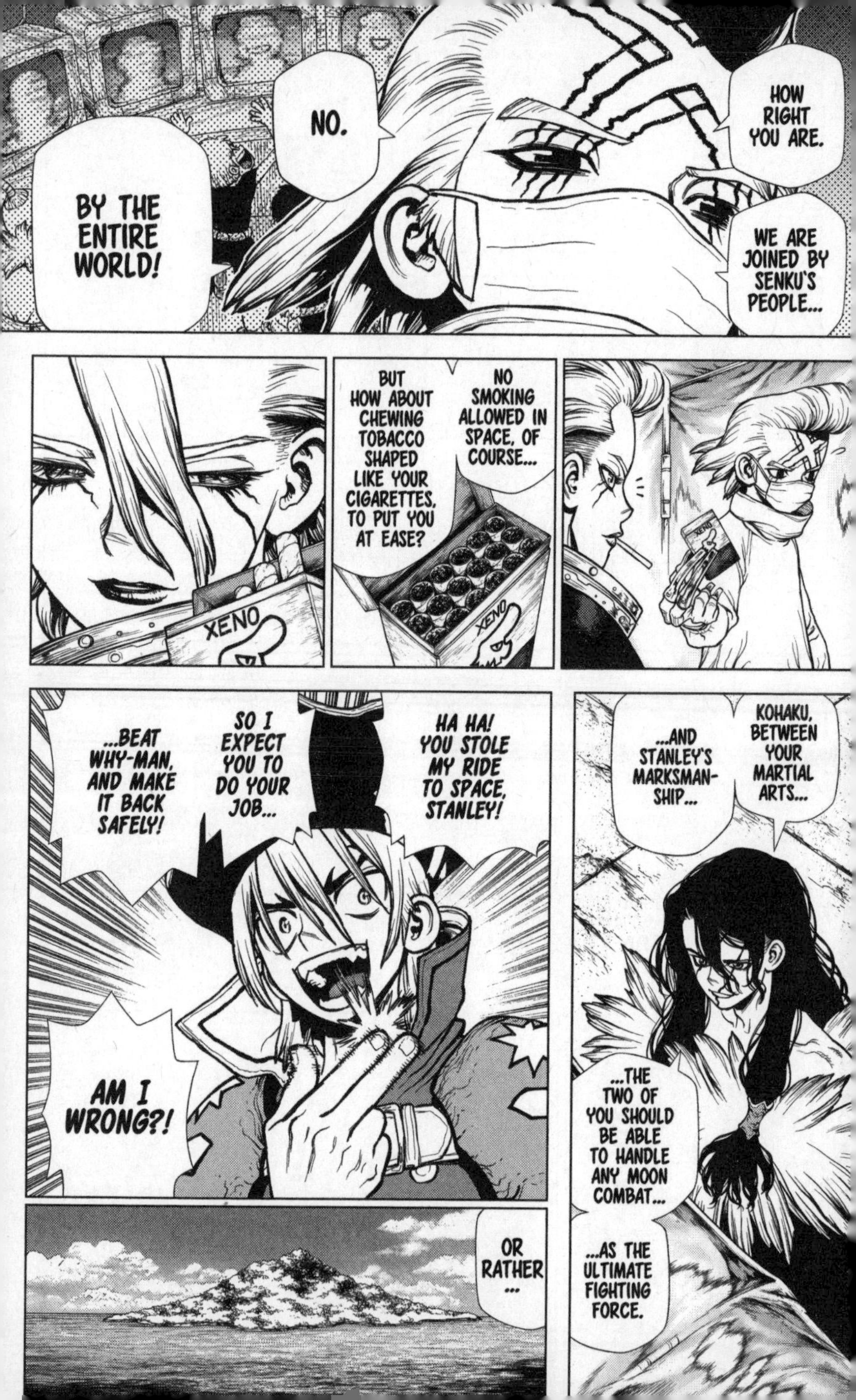
HOW RIGHT YOU ARE.
WE ARE JOINED BY SENKU'S PEOPLE...
NO.
BY THE ENTIRE WORLD!
NO SMOKING ALLOWED IN SPACE, OF COURSE...
BUT HOW ABOUT CHEWING TOBACCO SHAPED LIKE YOUR CIGARETTES, TO PUT YOU AT EASE?
XENO
XENO
XENO
KOHAKU, BETWEEN YOUR MARTIAL ARTS...
...AND STANLEY'S MARKSMAN-SHIP...
...THE TWO OF YOU SHOULD BE ABLE TO HANDLE ANY MOON COMBAT...
...AS THE ULTIMATE FIGHTING FORCE.
HA HA! YOU STOLE MY RIDE TO SPACE, STANLEY!
SO I EXPECT YOU TO DO YOUR JOB...
...BEAT WHY-MAN, AND MAKE IT BACK SAFELY!
AM I WRONG?!
OR RATHER...

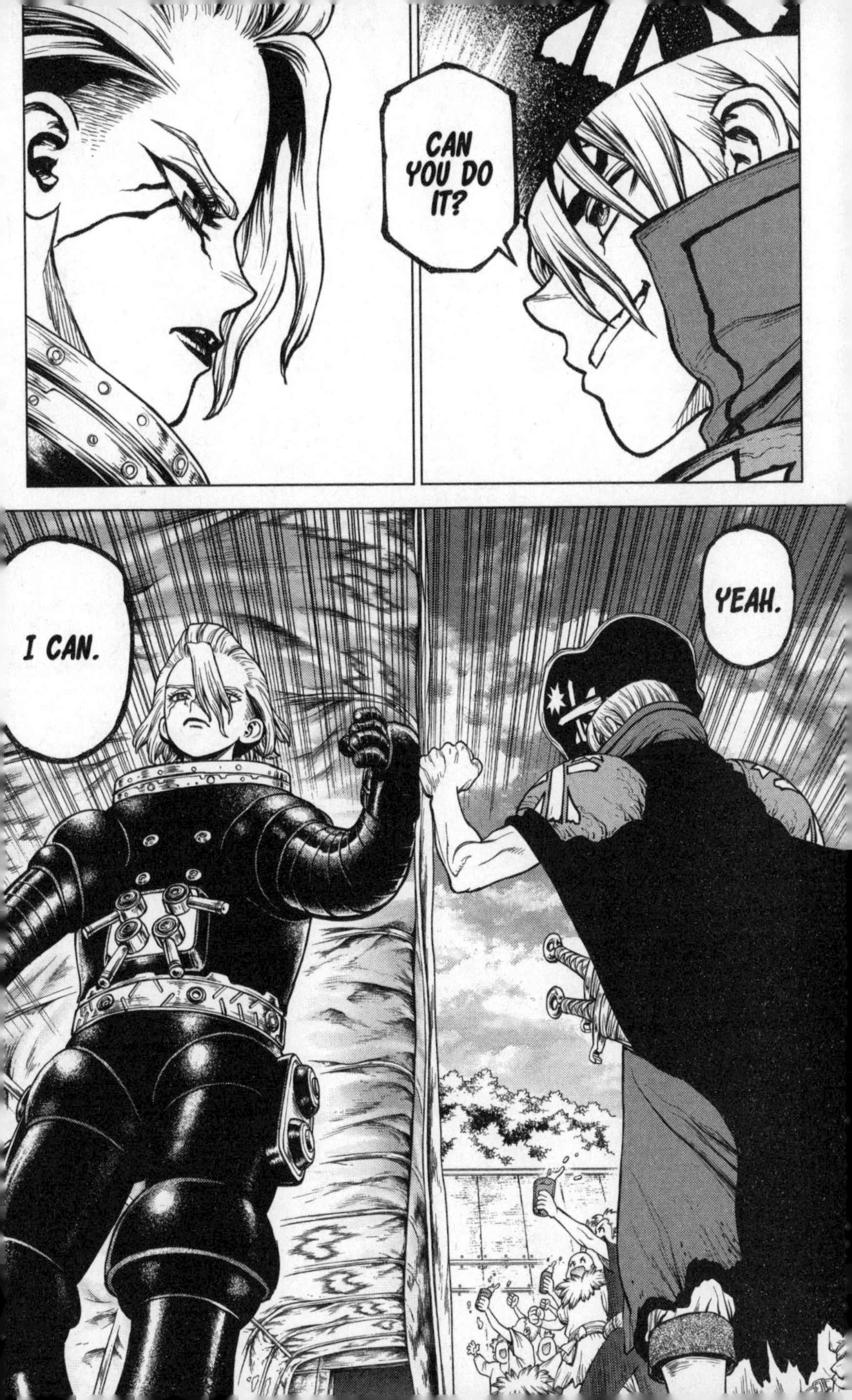
CAN YOU DO IT?
YEAH.
I CAN.

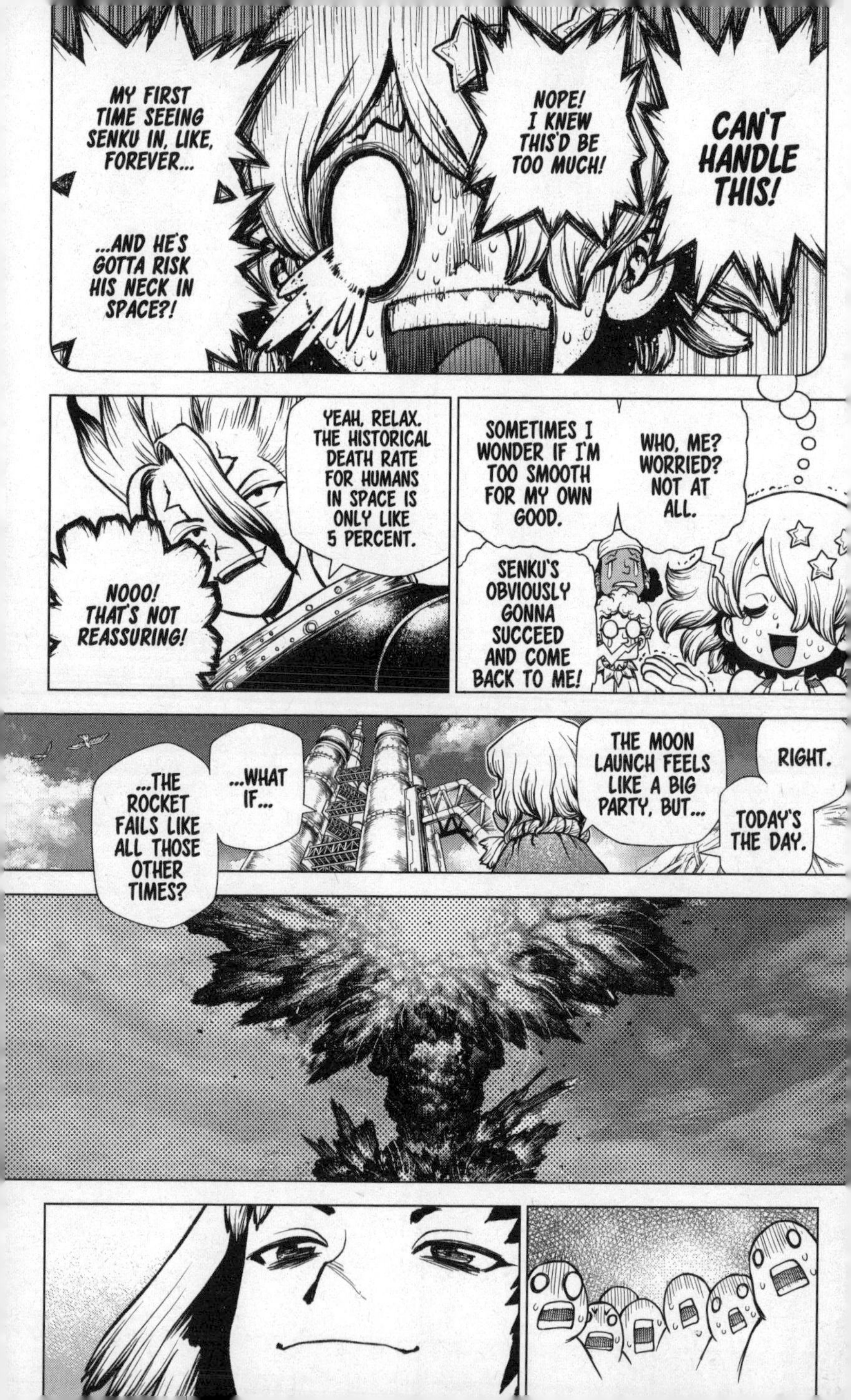
CAN'T HANDLE THIS!
NOPE! I KNEW THIS'D BE TOO MUCH!
MY FIRST TIME SEEING SENKU IN, LIKE, FOREVER...
...AND HE'S GOTTA RISK HIS NECK IN SPACE?!
WHO, ME? WORRIED? NOT AT ALL.
SOMETIMES I WONDER IF I'M TOO SMOOTH FOR MY OWN GOOD.
SENKU'S OBVIOUSLY GONNA SUCCEED AND COME BACK TO ME!
YEAH, RELAX. THE HISTORICAL DEATH RATE FOR HUMANS IN SPACE IS ONLY LIKE 5 PERCENT.
NOOO! THAT'S NOT REASSURING!
RIGHT.
TODAY'S THE DAY.
THE MOON LAUNCH FEELS LIKE A BIG PARTY, BUT...
...WHAT IF...
...THE ROCKET FAILS LIKE ALL THOSE OTHER TIMES?

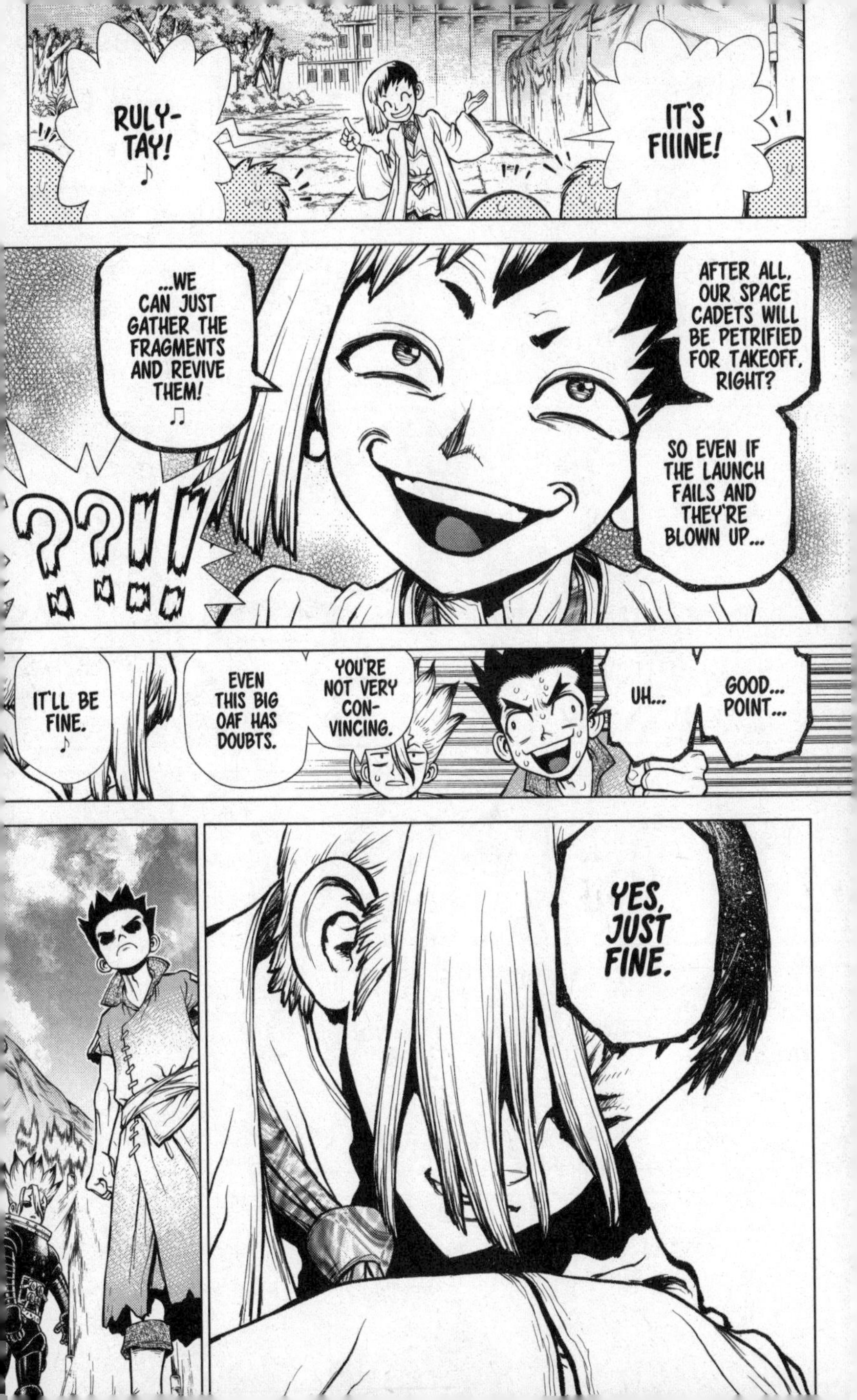
IT'S FIIINE!
RULY-TAY! ♪
AFTER ALL, OUR SPACE CADETS WILL BE PETRIFIED FOR TAKEOFF, RIGHT?
SO EVEN IF THE LAUNCH FAILS AND THEY'RE BLOWN UP...
...WE CAN JUST GATHER THE FRAGMENTS AND REVIVE THEM! ♫
??!!
UH... GOOD... POINT...
YOU'RE NOT VERY CON-VINCING.
EVEN THIS BIG OAF HAS DOUBTS.
IT'LL BE FINE. ♪
YES, JUST FINE.

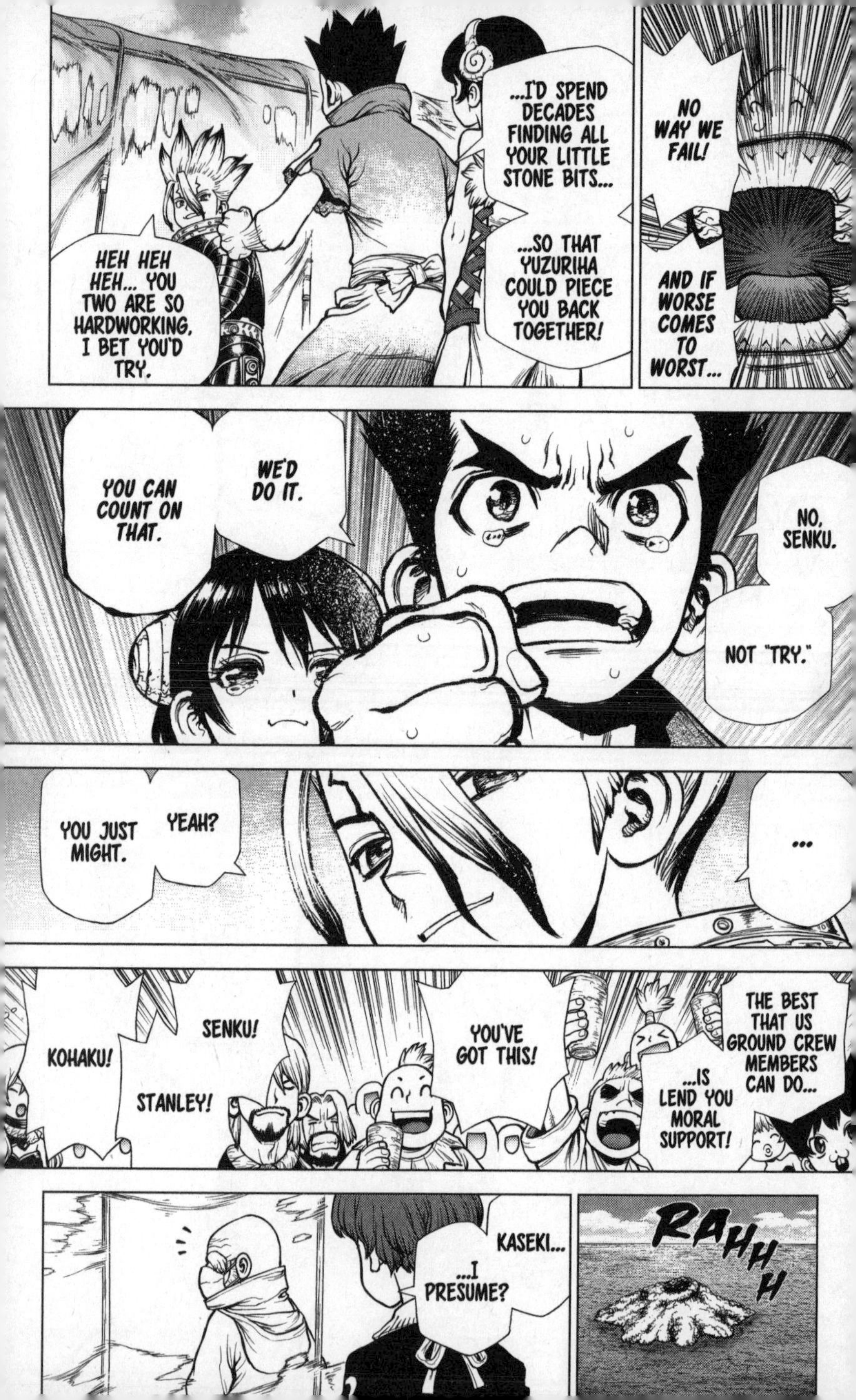
NO WAY WE FAIL!
AND IF WORSE COMES TO WORST...
...I'D SPEND DECADES FINDING ALL YOUR LITTLE STONE BITS...
...SO THAT YUZURIHA COULD PIECE YOU BACK TOGETHER!
HEH HEH HEH... YOU TWO ARE SO HARDWORKING. I BET YOU'D TRY.
NO, SENKU.
NOT "TRY."
WE'D DO IT.
YOU CAN COUNT ON THAT.
...
YEAH?
YOU JUST MIGHT.
THE BEST THAT US GROUND CREW MEMBERS CAN DO...
...IS LEND YOU MORAL SUPPORT!
YOU'VE GOT THIS!
SENKU!
STANLEY!
KOHAKU!
RAHHH
KASEKI...
...I PRESUME?

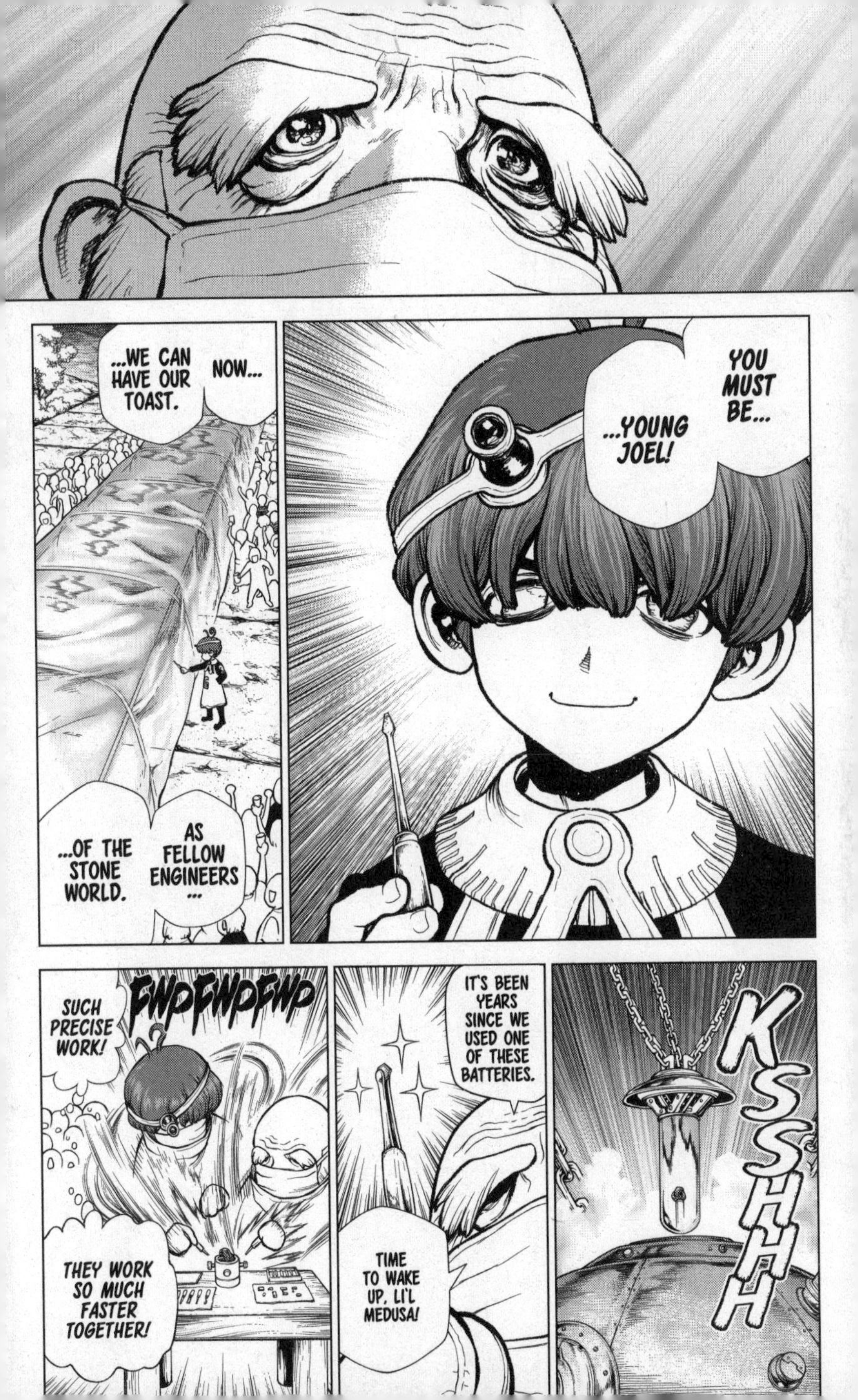
YOU MUST BE...
...YOUNG JOEL!
NOW...
...WE CAN HAVE OUR TOAST.
AS FELLOW ENGINEERS...
...OF THE STONE WORLD.
KSSHHHH
IT'S BEEN YEARS SINCE WE USED ONE OF THESE BATTERIES.
TIME TO WAKE UP, LI'L MEDUSA!
FWPFWPFWP
SUCH PRECISE WORK!
THEY WORK SO MUCH FASTER TOGETHER!

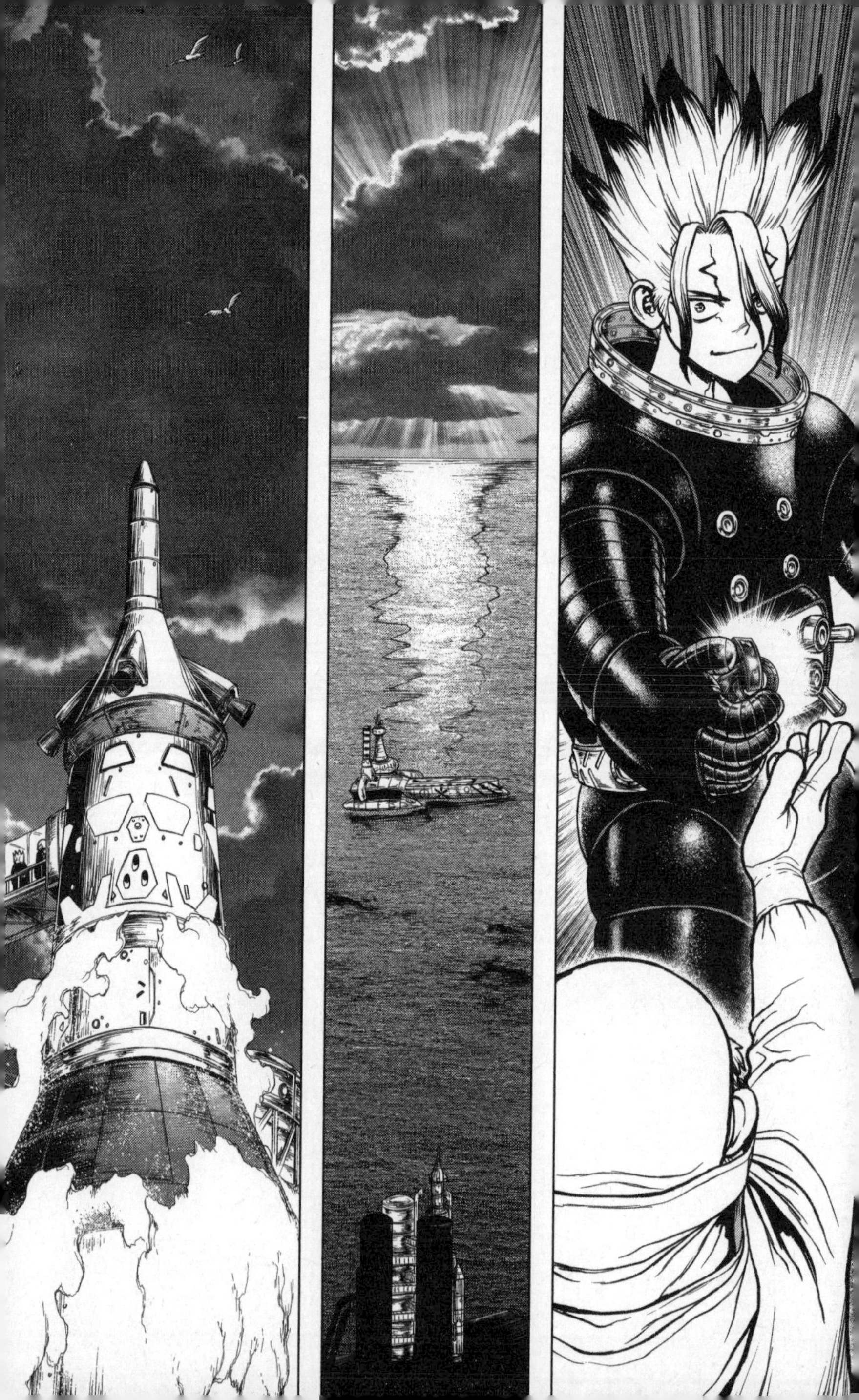

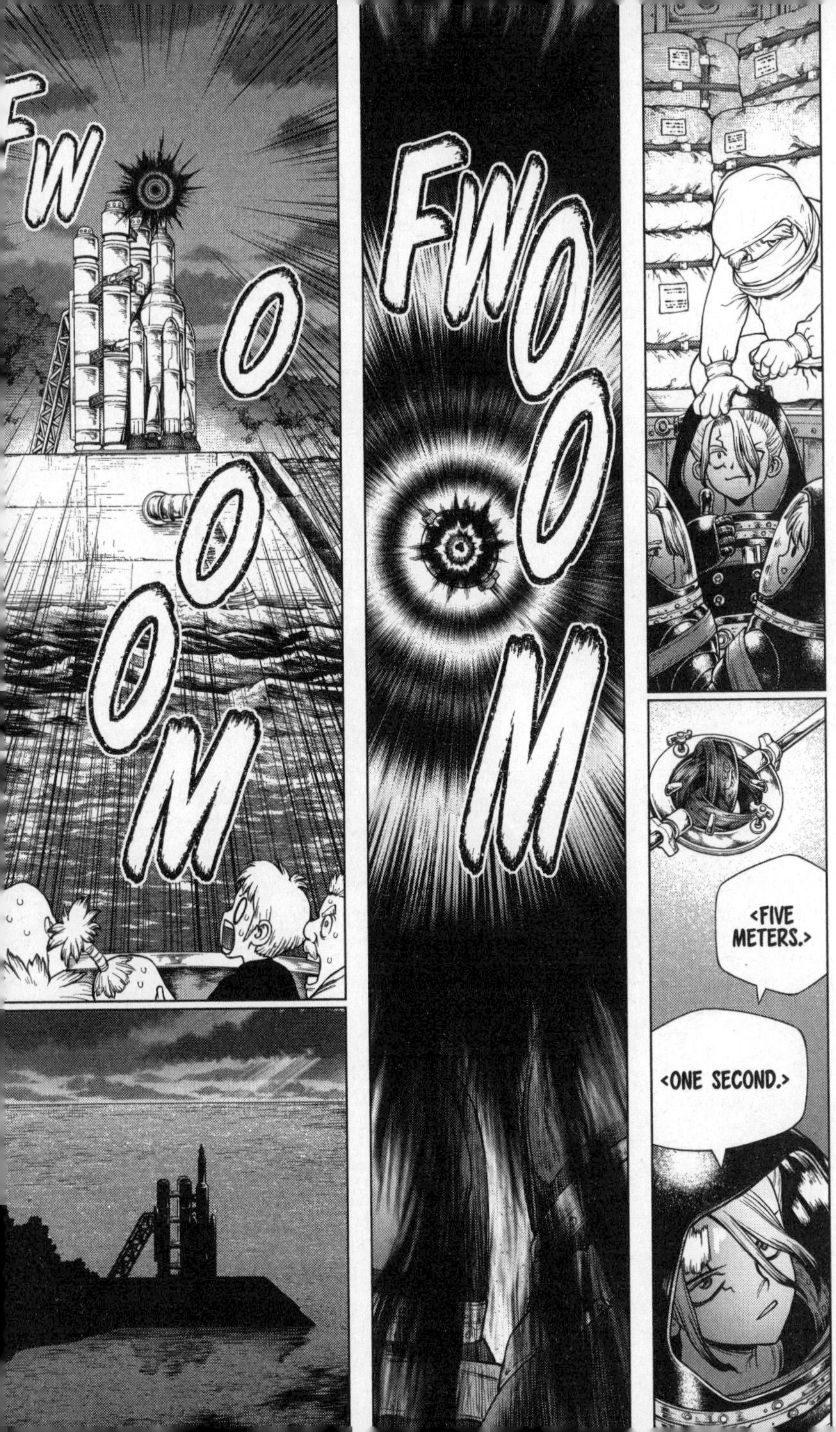
<FIVE METERS.>
<ONE SECOND.>
FWOOOM
FWOOOOM

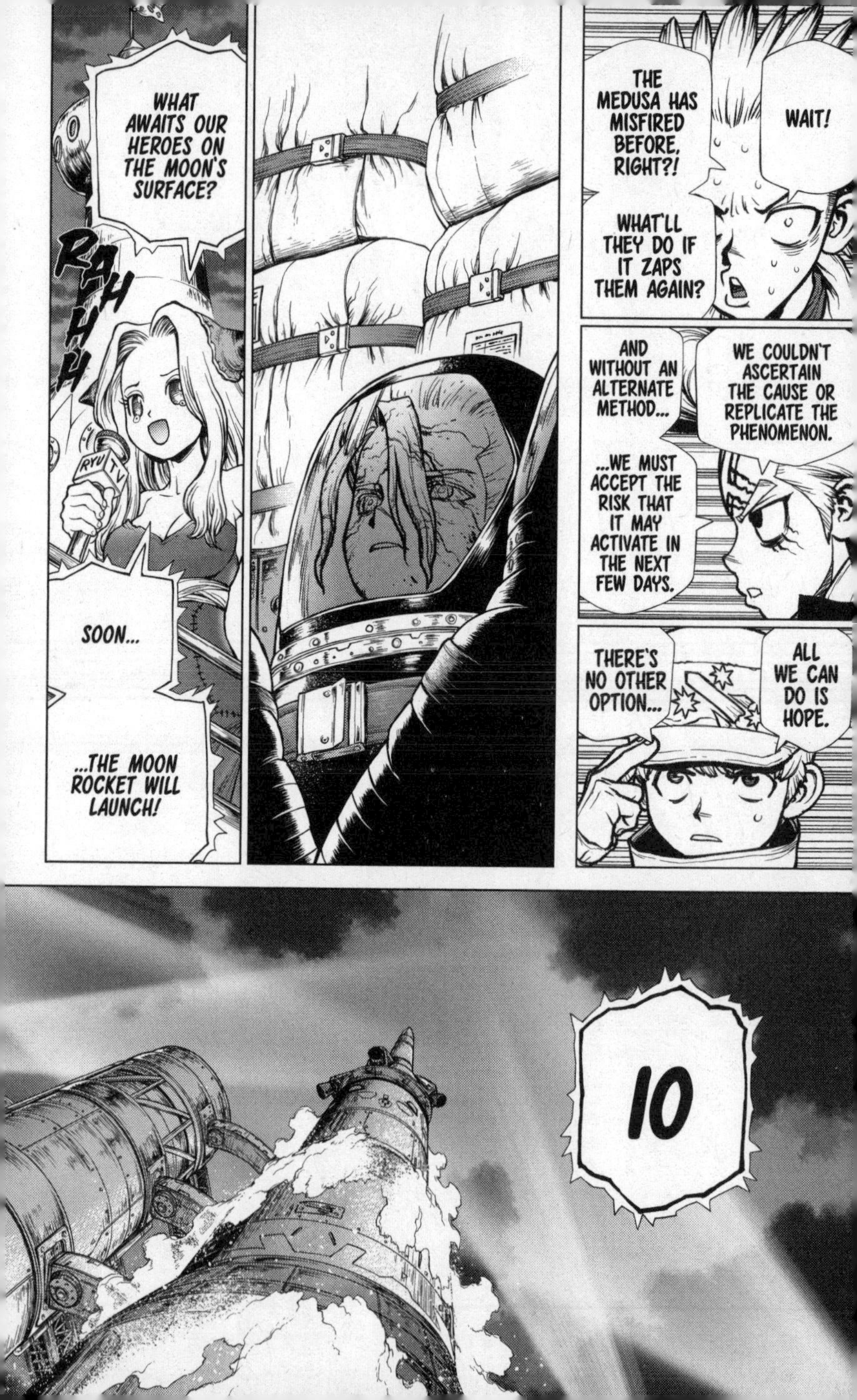
WAIT!
THE MEDUSA HAS MISFIRED BEFORE, RIGHT?!
WHAT'LL THEY DO IF IT ZAPS THEM AGAIN?
WE COULDN'T ASCERTAIN THE CAUSE OR REPLICATE THE PHENOMENON.
AND WITHOUT AN ALTERNATE METHOD...
...WE MUST ACCEPT THE RISK THAT IT MAY ACTIVATE IN THE NEXT FEW DAYS.
ALL WE CAN DO IS HOPE.
THERE'S NO OTHER OPTION...
WHAT AWAITS OUR HEROES ON THE MOON'S SURFACE?
RAHHHH
RYU TV
SOON...
...THE MOON ROCKET WILL LAUNCH!
10

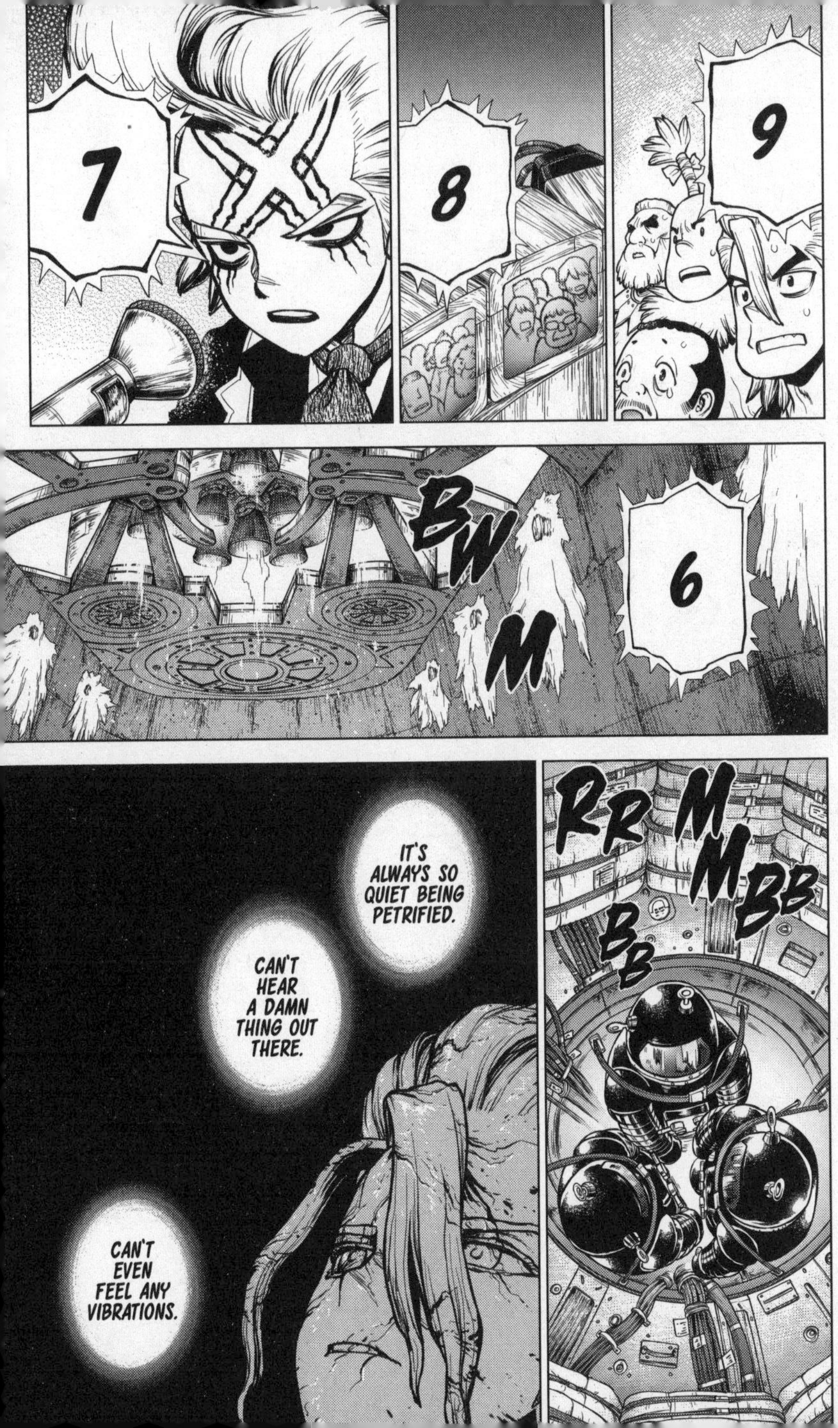
9
8
7
6
BWM
RRMMBB
BB
IT'S ALWAYS SO QUIET BEING PETRIFIED.
CAN'T HEAR A DAMN THING OUT THERE.
CAN'T EVEN FEEL ANY VIBRATIONS.

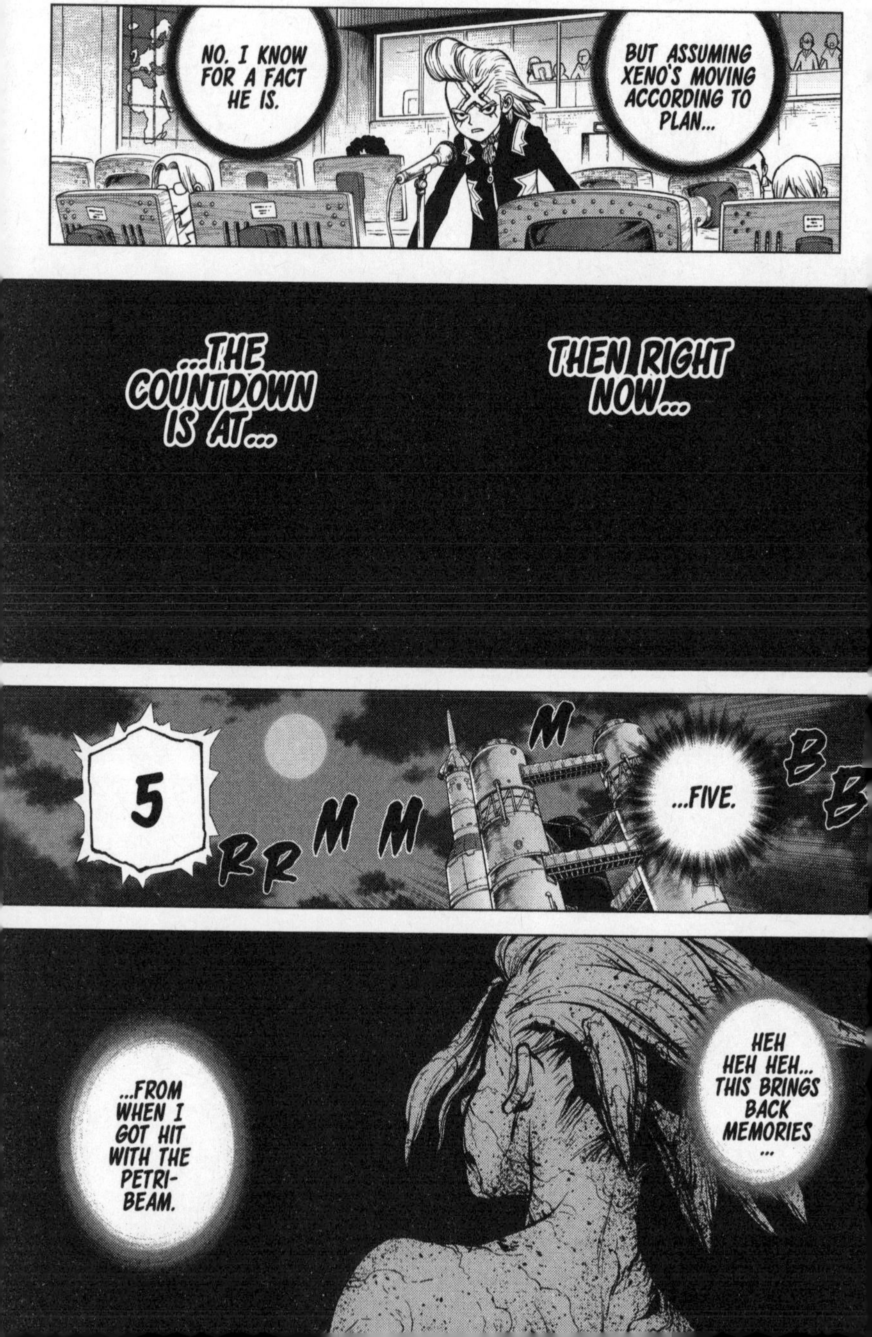
BUT ASSUMING XENO'S MOVING ACCORDING TO PLAN...
NO. I KNOW FOR A FACT HE IS.
THEN RIGHT NOW...
...THE COUNTDOWN IS AT...
BB
...FIVE.
M
RRMMM
5
HEH HEH HEH... THIS BRINGS BACK MEMORIES...
...FROM WHEN I GOT HIT WITH THE PETRI-BEAM.

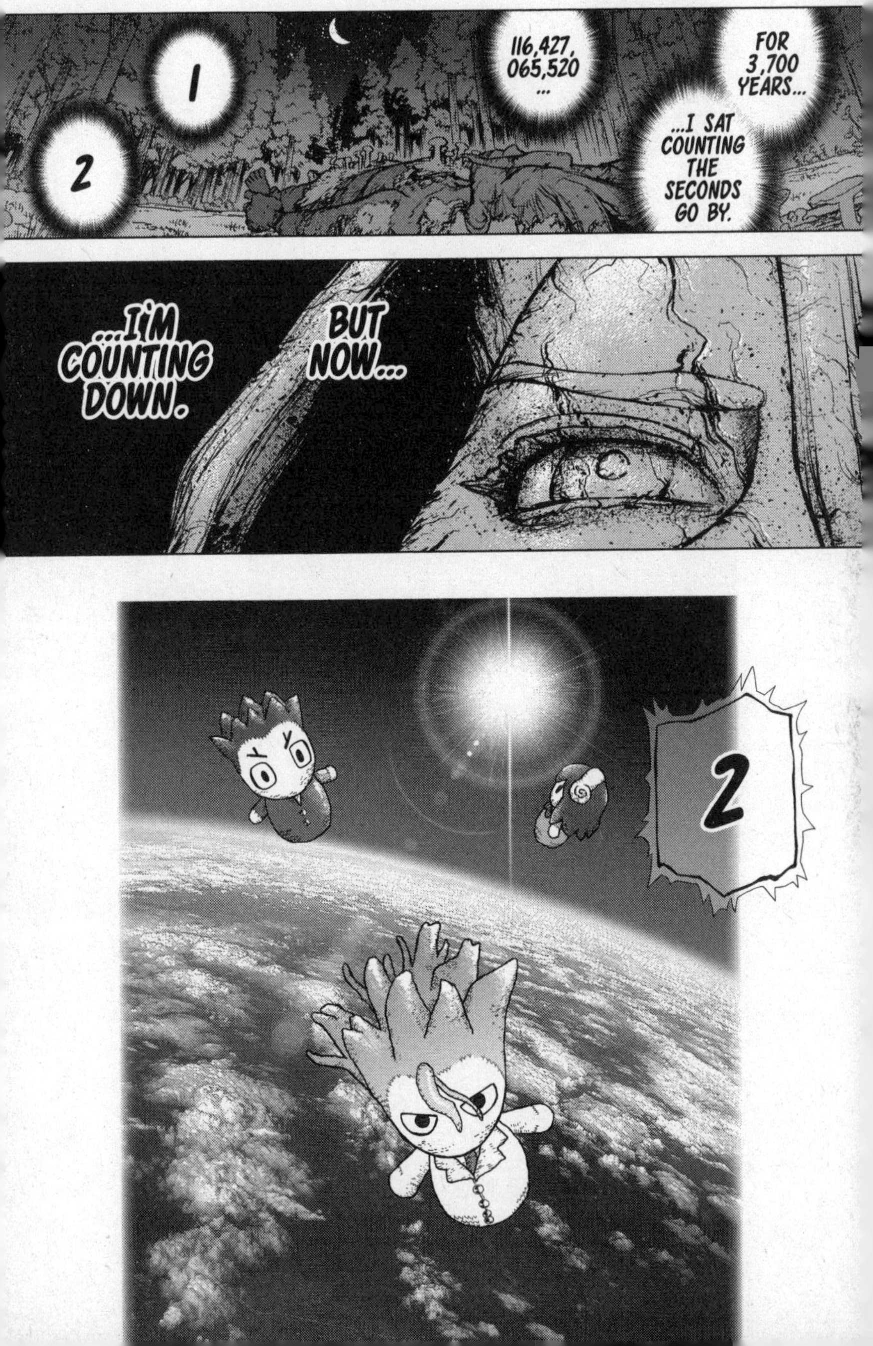
FOR 3,700 YEARS...
...I SAT COUNTING THE SECONDS GO BY.
116,427,065,520 ...
1
2
BUT NOW...
...I'M COUNTING DOWN.
2

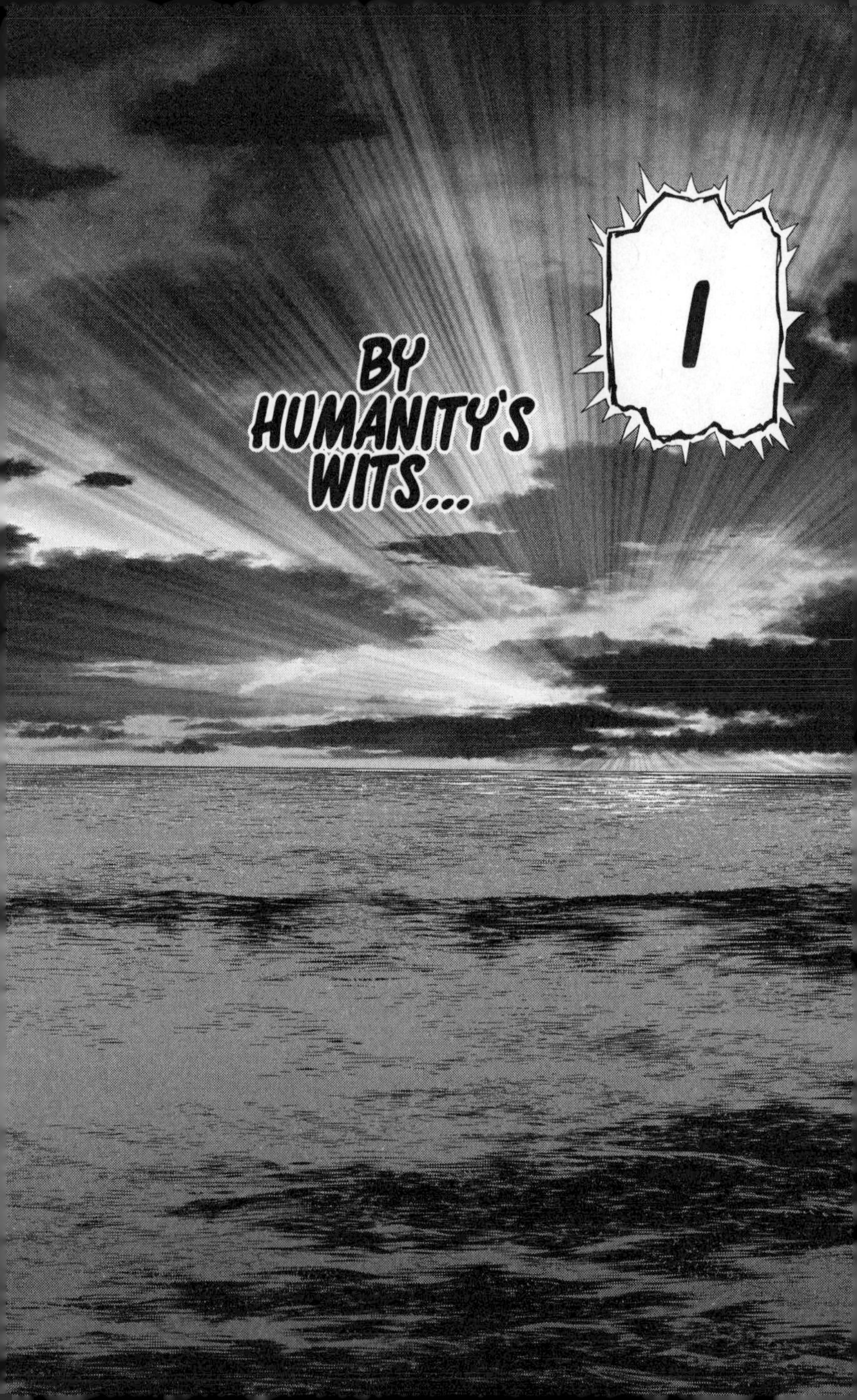
!
BY HUMANITY'S WITS...

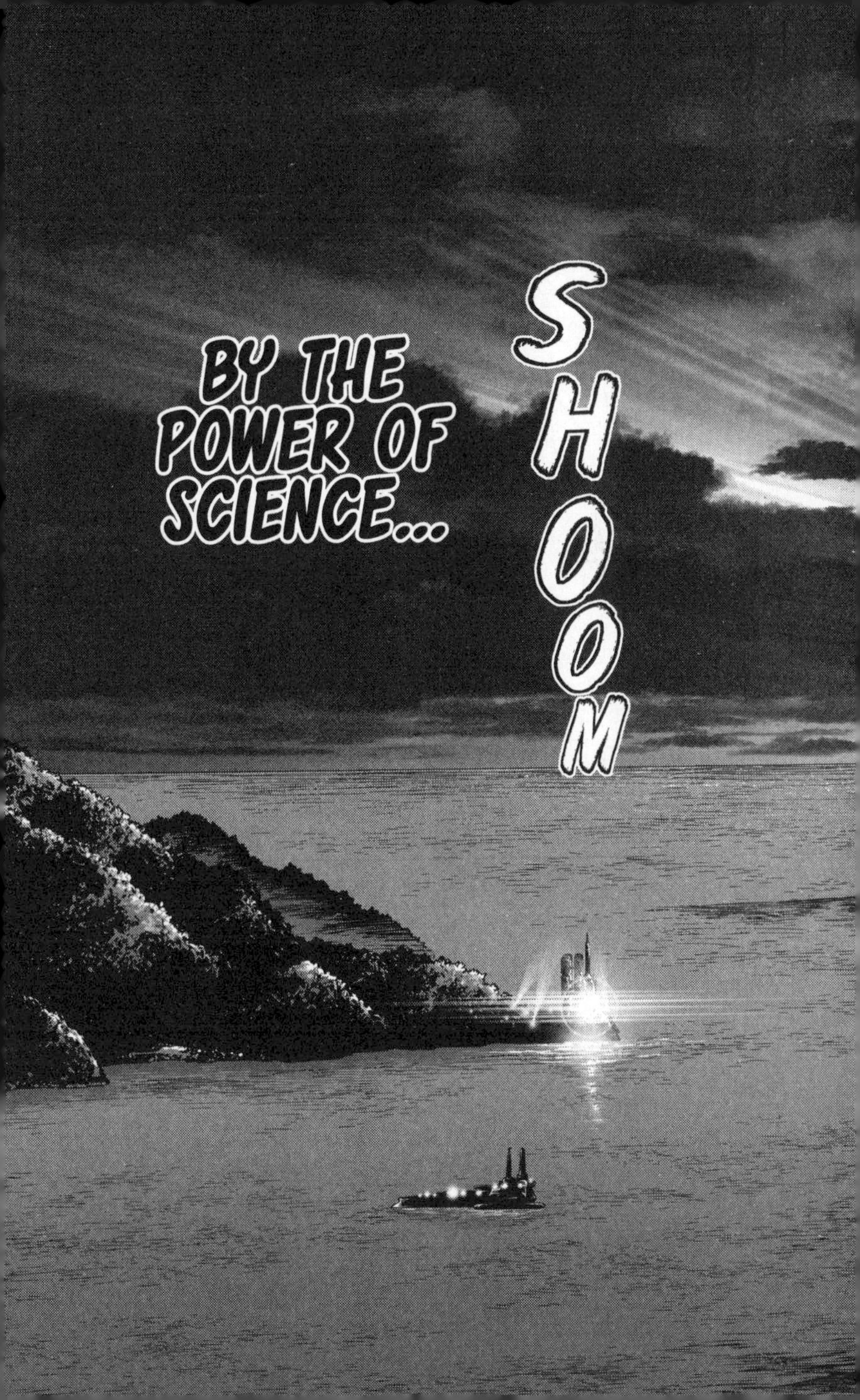
SHOOM
BY THE POWER OF SCIENCE...

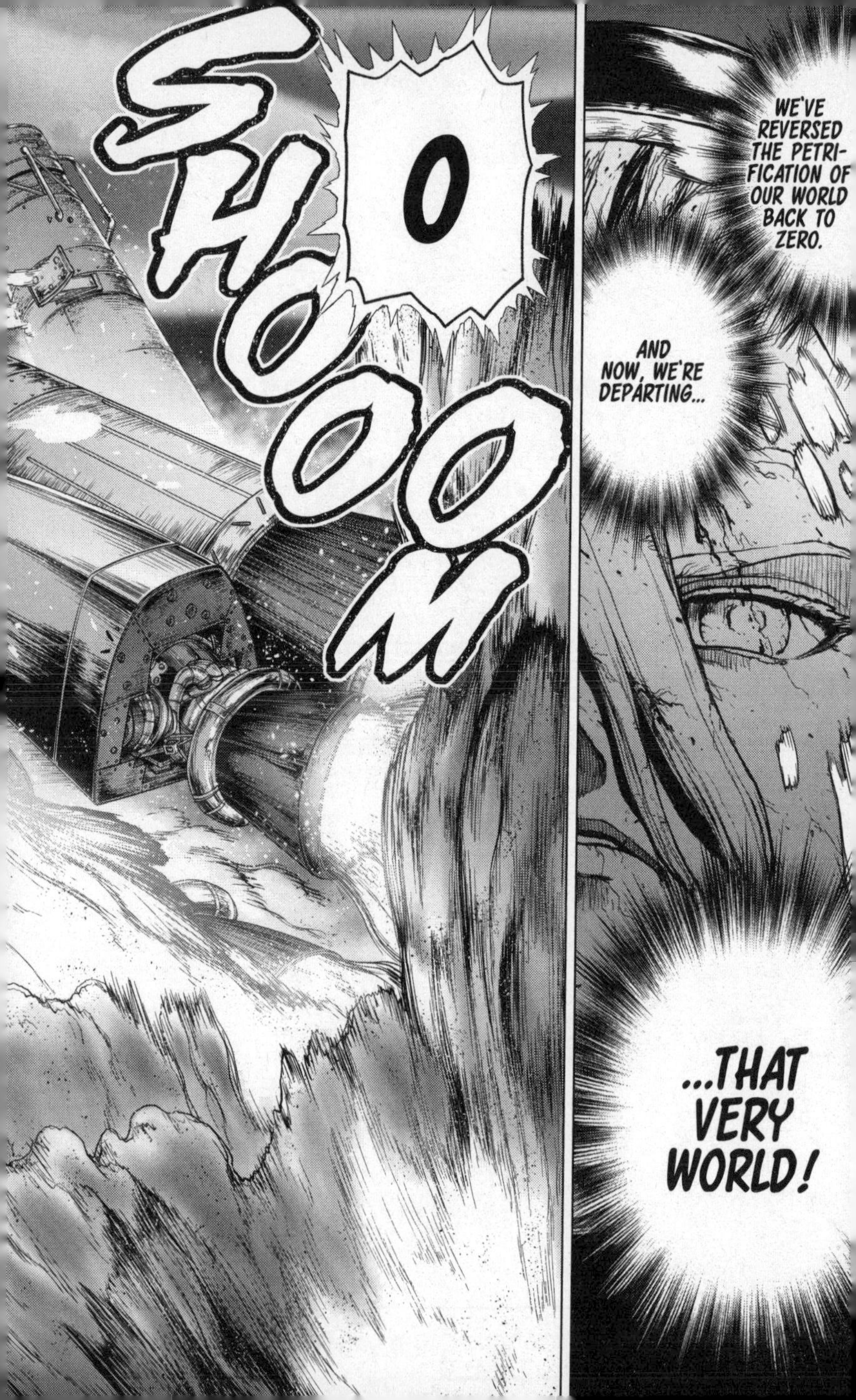
WE'VE REVERSED THE PETRI-FICATION OF OUR WORLD BACK TO ZERO.
AND NOW, WE'RE DEPARTING...
...THAT VERY WORLD!
SHOOOOOM

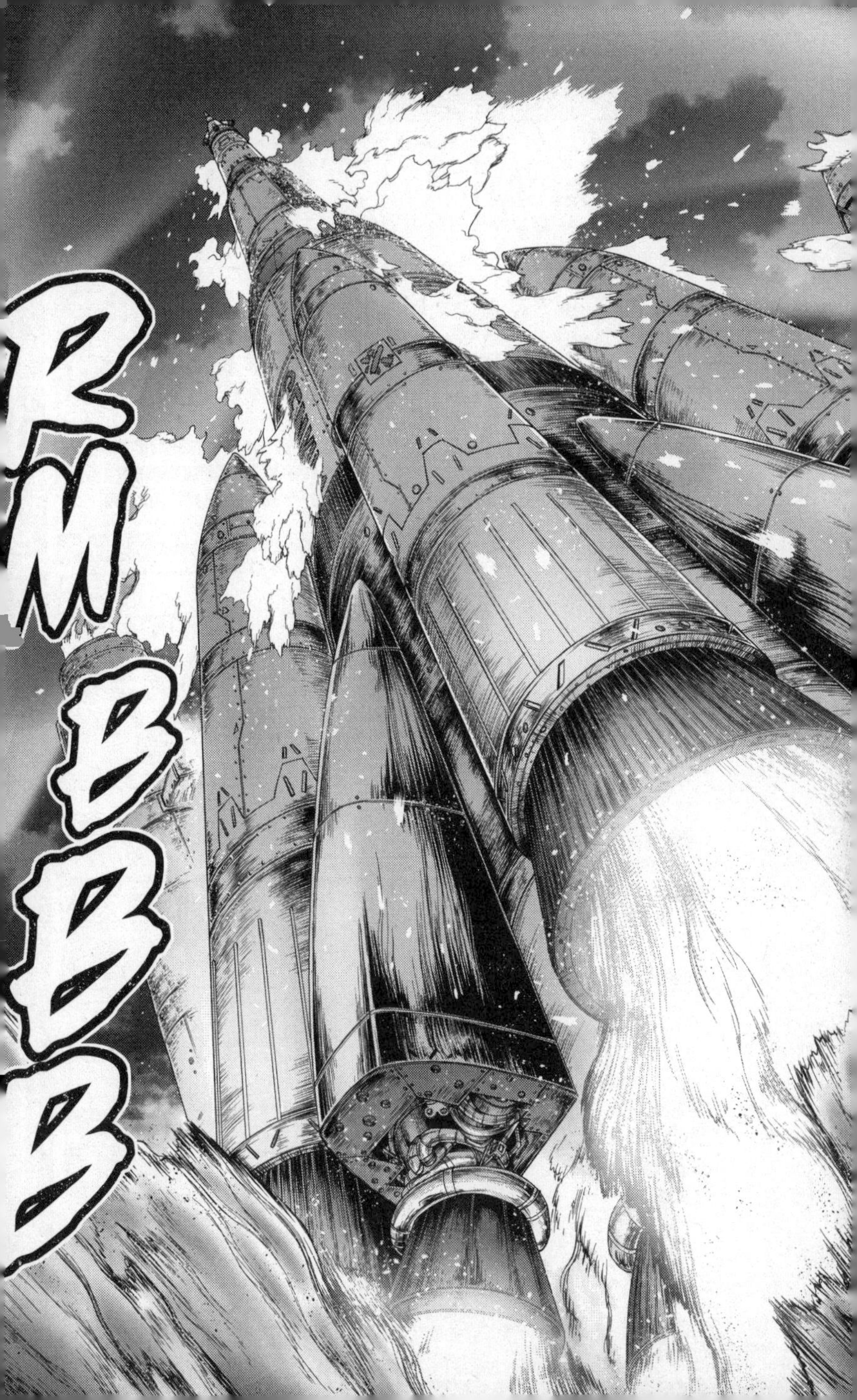
RMBBB

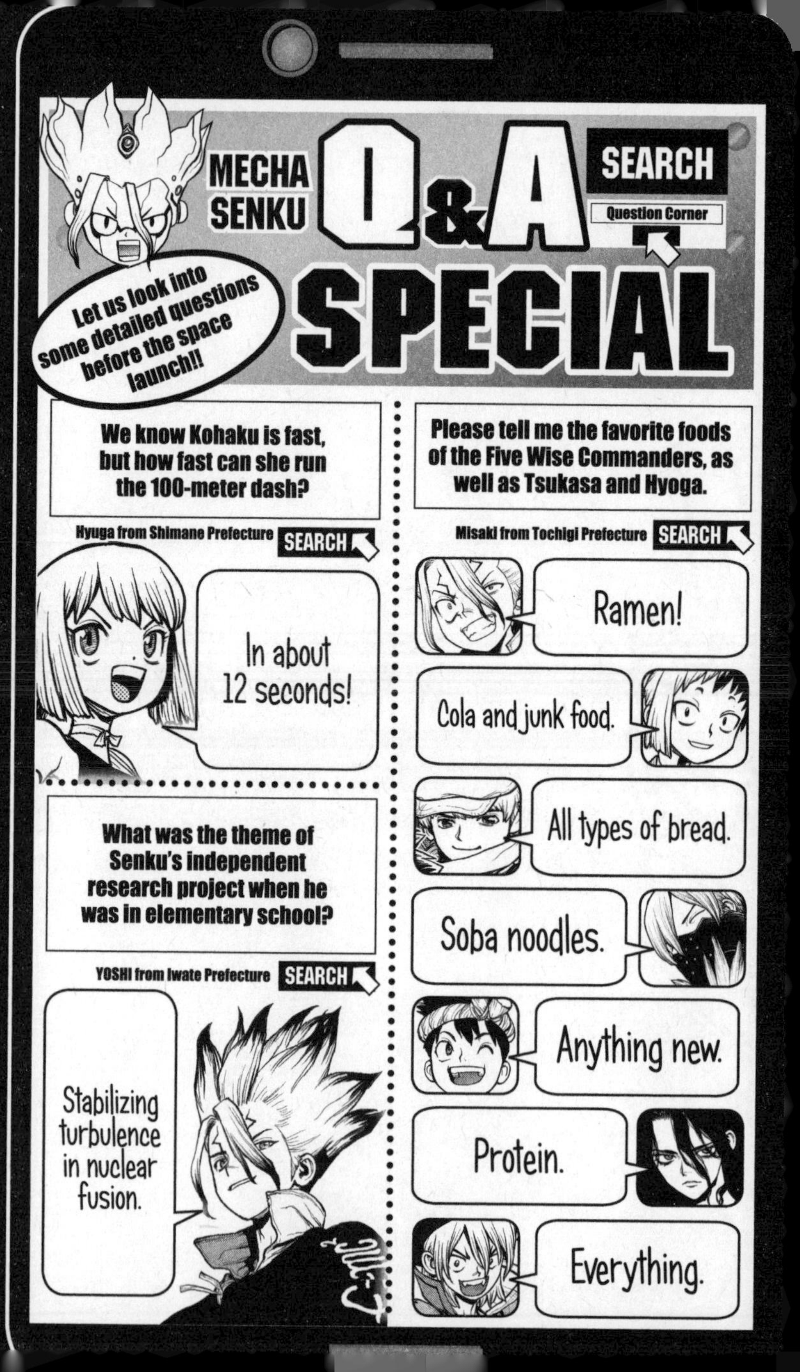
MECHA SENKU
Q&A
SEARCH
Question Corner
SPECIAL
Let us look into some detailed questions before the space launch!!
Please tell me the favorite foods of the Five Wise Commanders, as well as Tsukasa and Hyoga.
Misaki from Tochigi Prefecture
SEARCH
Ramen!
Cola and junk food.
All types of bread.
Soba noodles.
Anything new.
Protein.
Everything.
We know Kohaku is fast, but how fast can she run the 100-meter dash?
Hyuga from Shimane Prefecture
SEARCH
In about 12 seconds!
What was the theme of Senku's independent research project when he was in elementary school?
YOSHI from Iwate Prefecture
SEARCH
Stabilizing turbulence in nuclear fusion.

When did Senku, Taiju, and Yuzuriha start hanging out?

K.M. from Tokyo **SEARCH**

Senku and Taiju became friends in third grade, while Taiju and Yuzuriha were in the same class in fifth grade.

However, because of Taiju's feelings for Yuzuriha, they did not hang out as a trio until their first year of middle school.

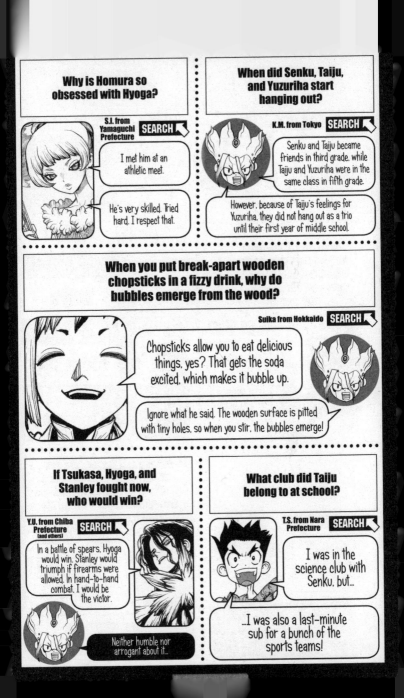

Why is Homura so obsessed with Hyoga?

S.I. from Yamaguchi Prefecture **SEARCH**

I met him at an athletic meet.

He's very skilled. Tried hard. I respect that.

When you put break-apart wooden chopsticks in a fizzy drink, why do bubbles emerge from the wood?

Suika from Hokkaido **SEARCH**

Chopsticks allow you to eat delicious things, yes? That gets the soda excited, which makes it bubble up.

Ignore what he said. The wooden surface is pitted with tiny holes, so when you stir, the bubbles emerge!

What club did Taiju belong to at school?

T.S. from Nara Prefecture **SEARCH**

I was in the science club with Senku, but...

...I was also a last-minute sub for a bunch of the sports teams!

If Tsukasa, Hyoga, and Stanley fought now, who would win?

Y.U. from Chiba Prefecture (and others) **SEARCH**

In a battle of spears, Hyoga would win. Stanley would triumph if firearms were allowed. In hand-to-hand combat, I would be the victor.

Neither humble nor arrogant about it...

How good are the characters at singing?

Suemitsu from Ibaraki Prefecture SEARCH

Here are the top three!

1st **Lillian**

2nd **Ukyo**

3rd **Amaryllis**

Worst of the Worst **Yo**

Kohaku and Stanley are two of the astronauts, but can they even communicate? One speaks Japanese and the other English, right?

Hikari from Saitama Prefecture SEARCH

Trace amounts of English were preserved among the language of Ishigami Village. Kohaku has always mixed a bit of English into her speech, including the words for numbers.

Neither is against the idea of learning a few new words here and there!

How does Moz have so much luck with the ladies?

S.S. from Fukuoka Prefecture SEARCH

Confidence.

Amaryllis is the most beautiful woman on the island, but how does she show off her beauty to the world?

S.H. from Kanagawa Prefecture SEARCH

With a nice smile!

How much does Francois earn?

Y.N. from Tokyo SEARCH

I earn more than enough for my labor.

The market rate for a supercompetent butler like Francois is around tens of millions of yen per year!

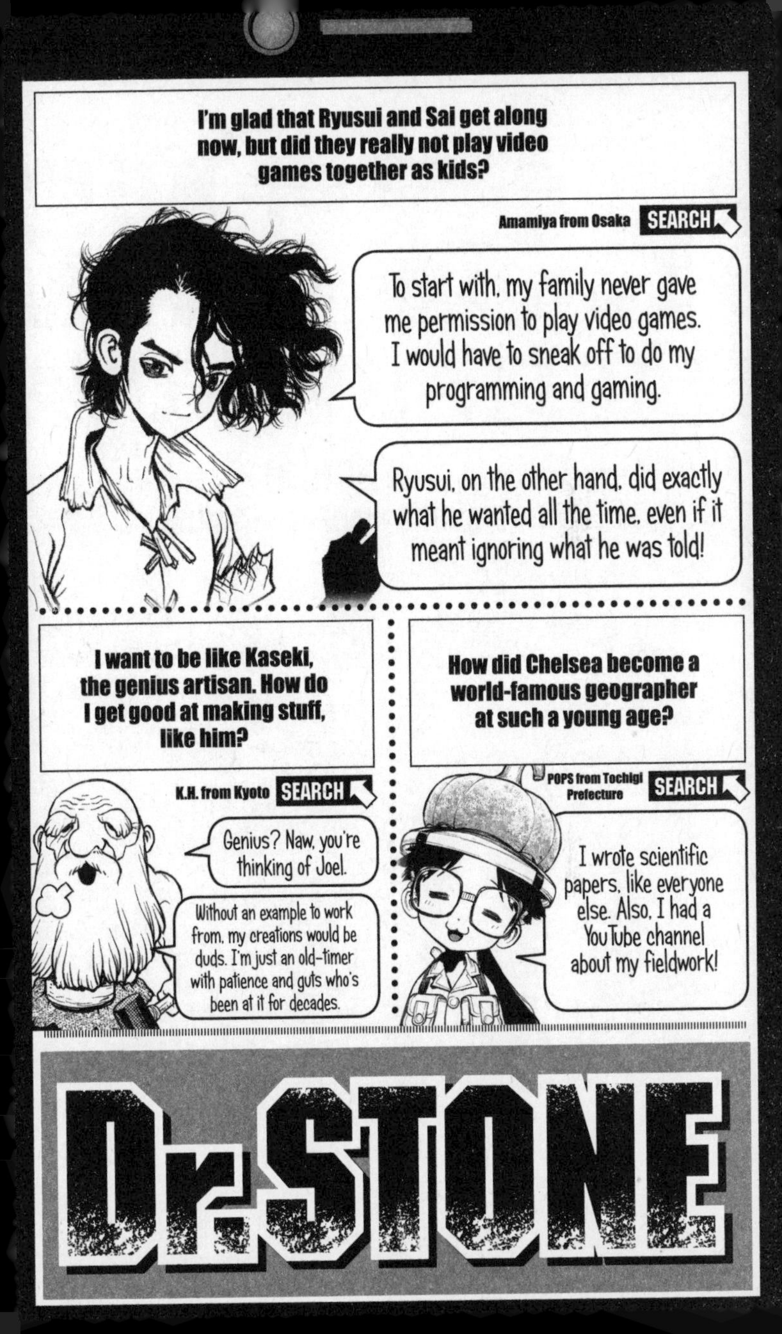

I'm glad that Ryusui and Sai get along now, but did they really not play video games together as kids?
Amamiya from Osaka
SEARCH
To start with, my family never gave me permission to play video games. I would have to sneak off to do my programming and gaming.
Ryusui, on the other hand, did exactly what he wanted all the time, even if it meant ignoring what he was told!
How did Chelsea become a world-famous geographer at such a young age?
POPS from Tochigi Prefecture
SEARCH
I wrote scientific papers, like everyone else. Also, I had a YouTube channel about my fieldwork!
I want to be like Kaseki, the genius artisan. How do I get good at making stuff, like him?
K.H. from Kyoto
SEARCH
Genius? Naw, you're thinking of Joel.
Without an example to work from, my creations would be duds. I'm just an old-timer with patience and guts who's been at it for decades.
Dr.STONE

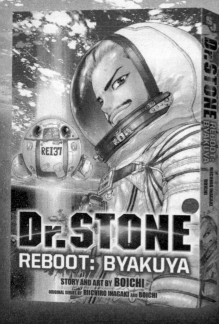

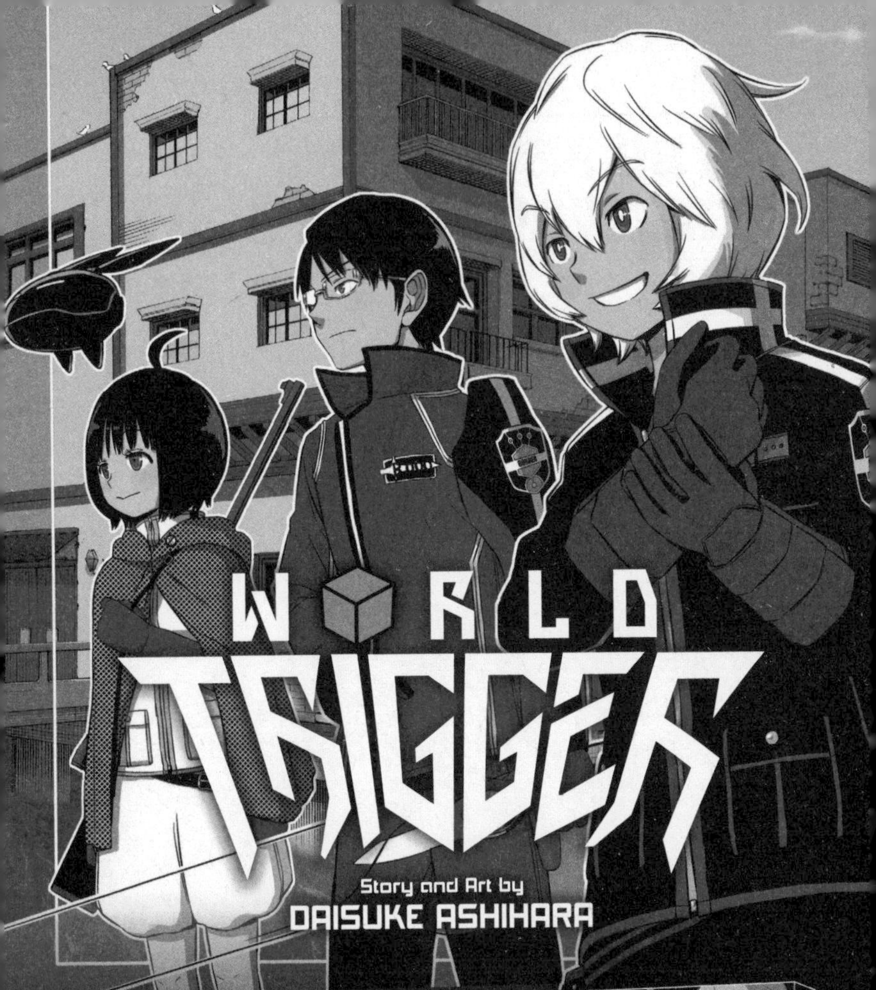

WORLD TRIGGER

Story and Art by
DAISUKE ASHIHARA

DESTROY THY NEIGHBOR!

A gate to another dimension has burst open, and invincible monsters called Neighbors invade Earth. Osamu Mikumo may not be the best among the elite warriors who co-opt other-dimensional technology to fight back, but along with his Neighbor friend Yuma, he'll do whatever it takes to defend life on Earth as we know it

YOU'RE READING THE WRONG WAY

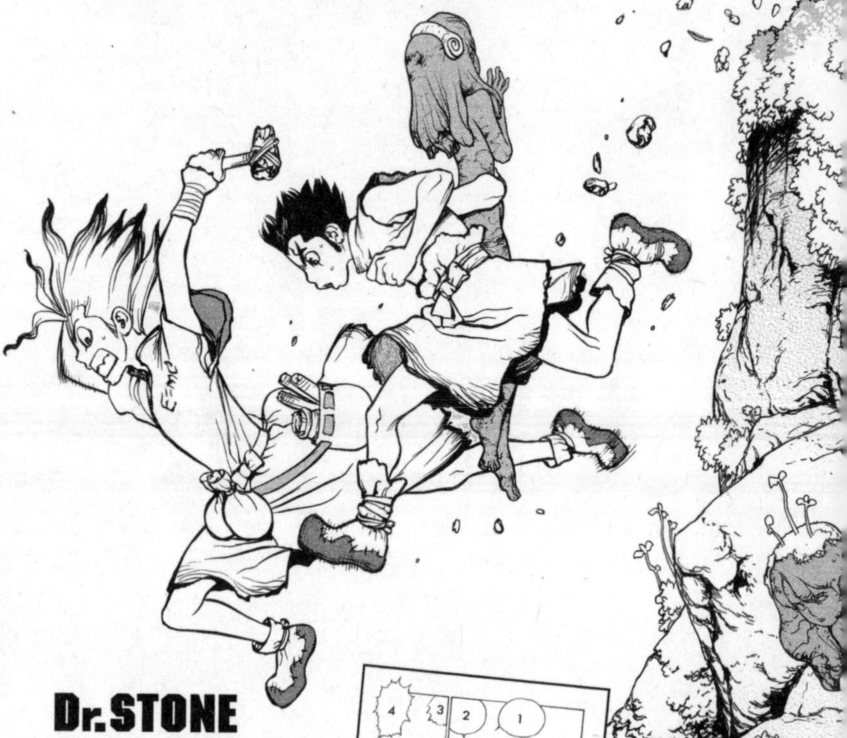

Dr.STONE

reads from right to left, starting in the upper-right corner. Japanese is read from right to left, meaning that action, sound effects, and word-balloon order are completely reversed from English order.

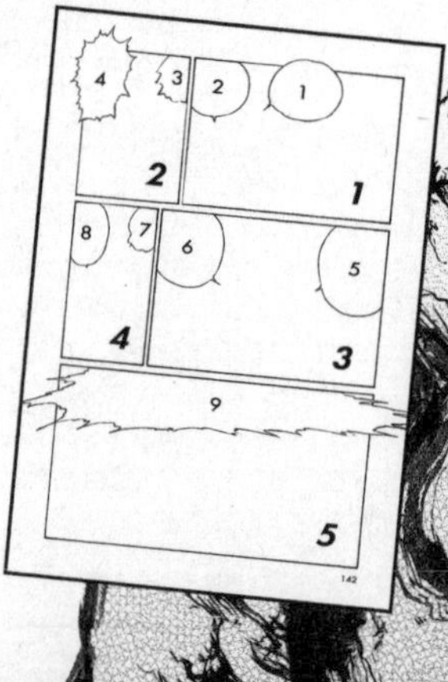

1
2
3
4
1
2
5
6
7
8
3
4
9
5
142